This is a timely and much needed effort. Leaders in both Europe, North America, Africa and elsewhere, need to learn from the experience of Latin America regarding the negative consequences of insufficiently regulated financialization. The editors of this volume are making a significant contribution to debates about these issues by making this work available to the English speaking public.

Fernando Leiva, Department of Latin American and Latino Studies, University of California Santa Cruz, USA

Financialisation in Latin America

Financial capital continues to dominate Western economic organisations, despite major financial and economic crises. While these have not affected Latin American countries in the same way, other economic problems emerged after the reversion of loose monetary policies that debilitated the export-led growth model. This book discusses the issue of the financialised globalisation model in Latin America, looking at the region's relationship with the international market.

This edited collection is divided into three main sections. The first section discusses regional trends highlighting issues of trade and payments in financialised economies, the impact on deindustrialisation, its effect on inequality, external capital movements and monetary policies. The second section analyses the failure of comparative advantages of the export-led model in Colombia, Argentina and Mexico. Finally, the last section deals with the growth of financial balance sheets in small and developing economies such as Chile; how growth, investment and big corporation evolution were affected in Brazil and Mexico; and the effects of foreign exchange activity in Mexico. Through these discussions, this book aims to deepen the understanding of the crisis of financialisation and the export-led model, raising the question of whether it is possible for this model to continue or if it requires major readjustments to unfold economic growth.

This book provides a distinctive analysis of the financialisation mechanisms in developing countries in order to emphasise affinities and differences between the countries of the region in productive and financial terms. It will be of great interest to economic and social science scholars and students, to journalists specialising on economic and development issues, and, more importantly, to policy makers.

Noemi Levy is a full-time Professor at the Economic Faculty of the National Autonomous University of Mexico (UNAM). Her research is concentrated in finance, monetary theory and policy, and financial institutions in developing economies.

Jorge Bustamante is a full-time Associate Professor at the Postgraduate School of Economics at the UNAM. His lines of interest are effects of financialisation on big corporations, profit strategies and financial structure of firms, development models and industrial policy.

Routledge Critical Studies in Finance and Stability

Edited by Jan Toporowski

School of Oriental and African Studies, University of London, UK

The 2007–8 Banking Crash has induced a major and wide-ranging discussion on the subject of financial (in)stability and a need to revaluate theory and policy. The response of policy-makers to the crisis has been to refocus fiscal and monetary policy on financial stabilisation and reconstruction. However, this has been done with only vague ideas of bank recapitalisation and 'Keynesian' reflation aroused by the exigencies of the crisis, rather than the application of any systematic theory or theories of financial instability.

Routledge Critical Studies in Finance and Stability covers a range of issues in the area of finance including instability, systemic failure, financial macroeconomics in the vein of Hyman P. Minsky, Ben Bernanke and Mark Gertler, central bank operations, financial regulation, developing countries and financial crises, new portfolio theory and New International Monetary and Financial Architecture.

12 **Financial Regulation in the European Union After the Crisis**
A Minskian Approach
Domenica Tropeano

13 **Labour, Finance and Inequality**
The Insecurity Cycle in British Public Policy
Suzanne J. Konzelmann, Simon Deakin, Marc Fovargue-Davies and Frank Wilkinson

14 **Financial Stability, Systems and Regulation**
Jan Kregel
Edited by Felipe C. Rezende

15 **Financialisation in Latin America**
Challenges of the Export-Led Growth Model
Edited by Noemi Levy and Jorge Bustamante

For more information about this series, please visit www.routledge.com/series/RCSFS

Financialisation in Latin America

Challenges of the Export-Led Growth Model

Edited by Noemi Levy and Jorge Bustamante

Routledge
Taylor & Francis Group
LONDON AND NEW YORK

First published 2019
by Routledge

2 Park Square, Milton Park, Abingdon, Oxfordshire OX14 4RN
52 Vanderbilt Avenue, New York, NY 10017

Routledge is an imprint of the Taylor & Francis Group, an informa business

First issued in paperback 2020

British Library Cataloguing-in-Publication Data
A catalogue record for this book is available from the British Library

Library of Congress Cataloging-in-Publication Data
Names: Levy, Noemi, editor. | Bustamante, Jorge, 1978– editor.
Title: Financialisation in Latin America: challenges of the export-led growth model / edited by Noemi Levy and Jorge Bustamante.
Description: Abingdon, Oxon; New York, NY: Routledge, 2019. |
Series: Routledge critical studies in finance and stability |
Includes bibliographical references and index.
Identifiers: LCCN 2018036533 (print) | LCCN 2018039683 (ebook) |
ISBN 9780429464034 (Ebook) | ISBN 9781138614536 (hardback: alk. paper)
Subjects: LCSH: Investments, Foreign—Latin America. |
Finance—Latin America. | Economic development—Latin America.
Classification: LCC HG5160.5.A3 (ebook) |
LCC HG5160.5.A3.F56 2019 (print) | DDC 332.098—dc23
LC record available at https://lccn.loc.gov/2018036533

ISBN: 978-1-138-61453-6 (hbk)
ISBN: 978-0-367-66400-8 (pbk)

Typeset in Sabon
by codeMantra

Contents

Figures

Tables

Contributors

Cecilia Allami is a PhD candidate in Social Sciences at the University of Buenos Aires, and Researcher and Professor of Political Economy at the Universidad Nacional de General Sarmiento in Buenos Aires.

Nora Ampudia Márquez is a Professor-Researcher of the School of Economic and Entrepreneurial Sciences, Universidad Panamericana, Guadalajara.

Jorge Bustamante is an Associate Professor at the Postgraduate School of Economics, Universidad Nacional Autónoma de México, Mexico City.

Sergio Cámara is a Senior Professor in the Department of Economics, Universidad Autónoma Metropolitana – Azcapotzalco, Mexico City.

Santiago Capraro is an Associate Professor at the Economic Faculty of Universidad Nacional Autónoma de México, Mexico City.

Alan Cibils is a Professor and Chair of the Political Economy Department at the Universidad Nacional de General Sarmiento in Buenos Aires, Argentina.

Gonzalo Cómbita is a Professor at the Universidad de la Salle and PhD candidate in economic science at Universidad Nacional de Colombia, Bogota.

Nicole Favreau Negront is a Consultant of the Economic Commission for Latin America and the Caribbean (ECLAC) Review, Santiago.

Luiz Fernando de Paula is a Senior Professor of Economics at the University of the State of Rio de Janeiro (UERJ) and Brazilian National Research and Development Council (CNPq).

Thomas Goda is a Professor of Economics and module leader of International Economics at the School of Economics and Finance, Universidad Escuela de Administración y Finanzas, Inginiería y Tecnología (EAFIT), Medellin, Colombia.

Gabriel Gómez Ochoa is a Senior Professor in the Economics Department, Facultad de Estudios Superiores-Acatlán, Universidad Nacional Autónoma de México, Mexico City.

Camilo Guevara is a PhD candidate in economic science, Universidad Nacional de Colombia, Bogota.

Diego Guevara is a Professor at the Universidad Nacional de Colombia, Bogota.

Guadalupe Huerta Moreno is a Senior Professor-Researcher at the Faculty of Administration, Universidad Autónoma Metropolitana – Azcapotzalco, Mexico City.

Luis Kato is a Senior Professor-Researcher at the Administration Faculty of Universidad Autónoma Metropolitana – Azcapotzalco, Mexico City.

Noemi Levy is a Senior Professor at the Economic Faculty of Universidad Nacional Autónoma de México, Mexico City.

Photis Lysandrou is a Research Fellow at the Political Economy Research Centre, City University, and Associate Professor of Economics, School of Oriental and African Studies (SOAS).

Abelardo Mariña is a Senior Professor in the Department of Economics, Universidad Autónoma Metropolitana – Azcapotzalco, Mexico City.

Tiago R. Meyer is a doctorate candidate in the Post-graduation Program in Economics at the UERJ.

Esteban Pérez Caldentey is Chief of the Financing for Development, Economic Development Division of the ECLAC, Santiago.

Katya Pérez Guzmán is a Researcher at the International Institute for Applied Systems Analysis, Laxenburg.

Alicia Puyana Mutis is a Professor-Researcher at the Facultad Latinoamericana de Ciencias Sociales, Mexico City.

Luis Raúl Rodríguez Reyes is a Professor-Researcher in the Department of Economics, Management and Marketing, Instituto Tecnológico y de Estudios Superiores de Occidente, Guadalajara.

Hanna Szymborska is a Lecturer in economics at the Open University, London.

Jan Toporowski is a Professor of Economics and Finance at the SOAS, University of London, London.

Acknowledgements

This book emerged from wide discussions held by members of the Economic Faculty, the research project *The limits of financialisation of developing economies and export-led economies challenges: Latin America present and future* (IN 305217) supported by the Dirección General de Personal de Asuntos del Personal Académico – Universidad Nacional Autónoma de México (DGAPA-UNAM) , the Master and PhD Program of Economic Science of the Metropolitan Autonomous University, and affiliates of the Economic Department of the SOAS, University of London, UK, that visited Mexico in May 2017.

We would like to thank these institutions and the contributors to the research project, in particular, professors Roberto Escorcia at the (Universidad Autónoma Metropolitana (UAM)) and José Antonio Romero at the Colegio de Mexico, and the Programa de Apoyo a Proyectos de Investigación e Innovación Tecnológica (PAPIIT) project assistants who supported the discussions and ordered the texts. We would also like to thank Dr Jan Toporowski for helpful advice in placing this book in the Routledge Critical Studies in Finance and Stability.

Introduction

The challenges facing the export-led model in Latin America beginning in the second half of the current decade must be understood in the context of the systemic crisis of the neo-liberal-financialised production model of the first decade of the twenty-first century that have yet to be resolved.

A decade after the Global Financial Crisis (GFC), analysts have not reached any consensus about a new way of organising production that would promote robust economic growth. Specifically, no clarity exists about the mechanisms needed to deploy financing, production and the distribution of income and wealth globally to renew economic growth. This explains why the economies of the developed and developing capitalist countries, among the latter those in Latin America, are subject to spurts and stops and have not been able to achieve a pathway to firm, stable economic growth.

The signs of recovery in the US economy and its 2014 attempt to normalise its monetary policy coincided with a profound social and economic crisis in Latin America, which has been complicated by the 2017 change in the US administration. Beginning in 2014, the main Southern Cone economies with "progressive" governments – outstanding among them Brazil, Argentina, Chile and Ecuador – suffered considerable economic setbacks and cancelled redistributive policies. This has been complicated by the fact that the USA is attempting to limit international trade by levying tariffs; also, Europe has not been able to overcome the 2010 crisis, and the euro zone is coming under severe fire due to Greece's profound crisis and Brexit, with Great Britain leaving the European Union, among other factors.

The origins of the financialised globalisation model can be traced to the recessions of the 1970s in industrialised countries (the USA and Great Britain), which were overcome via mergers and acquisitions that empowered financial capital *vis-à-vis* productive capital, changed the organisation of production and the international division of labour, and prompted a huge concentration of income. The financialised globalisation model's central characteristics are the disappearance of borders within the trade, financial and productive system, led by capital's great mobility in the form of foreign investment. This is accompanied by structural imbalances in external accounts, limited domestic markets and great concentration of income. All these were preceded by deregulation, withdrawing the state from direct economic decision-making, and imposing price stability as the only aim of economic policy.

The characteristic of the financialised globalisation model is the growing flow of highly liquid capital and the profound imbalances among nations and regions, sparked by disloyal, beggar-thy-neighbour mercantile practices (Parguez 2009) that strengthen economies' export sectors. In this context, supply decoupled from demand and the international division of labour changed. In addition, the demonetisation of gold created a world money market that made money endogenous internationally, private debt became predominant, and central banks lost control over money supply. In addition, although the international currency unit continued to be the US dollar, it circulated via promises of payment (bank deposits). Access to the means of international payment, the US dollar, for the countries that were part of the global financial system changed, imposing the convertibility of private promises of payment from the countries participating in the international financial market. The structure of banking and non-banking financial institutions changed, spearheaded by highly liquid capital flows. Credits became internationalised and financing was divorced from savings, thus broadening international liquidity.

Specifically, the international banks became multinational corporations that transcended borders, moving into the financially open emerging countries, such as those in Latin America. In this region, foreign banks came to dominate the national banking system structure, particularly in Mexico. Institutional investors come on the scene with the privatisation of public services (pensions, healthcare and education) and also developed the insurance sector. Particularly prominent in the development of these countries' financial systems are pension funds, insurance companies and investment banks that strengthen the market-based financial system and weaken the bank-based financial system, with an uneven impact for developed and emerging countries. The world's big financial centres (the City of London and New York's Wall Street) became stronger and unevenly distributed financing, favouring the big multinationals, with the resulting uneven development in the emerging countries. Although the market-based system developed in Latin America, the financial system did not become deeper or broader (Stallings and Studart 2006).

The deepening of the financial system went through different stages. It began in the developed countries, headed by institutional investors in a context of overcapitalisation of companies (Toporowski 2000). A second moment was led by financial innovations that changed balance sheets, particularly of the banks (for example, the securitisation of debt). A third moment was the huge issue of government securities that strengthened the shadow bank (Lysandrou and Nesvetailova 2014) and preceded the GFC. A fourth moment was the financial innovations based on commodities and currencies, followed by the expansion of the bond market (Bonizzi 2016), which generated great influxes (refluxes) of capital towards the emerging financial markets.

In Latin America, the main manifestation of the opening took place through capital accounts, which reached their peaks after the 2008 GFC as a result of excess liquidity derived from the USA quantitative easing policies. This was accompanied by positive differentials in interest rates and stable or overvalued exchange rates to attract foreign capital.

The weakness of financial globalisation has been the instability of capital flows; this created expansionary cycles led by rising prices for financial securities, followed by an economic slowdown and the fall in the prices of financial securities linked to a contraction of the economy, which could become a recession if pending financial commitments were not met. Thus, economic growth combined with financial inflation and growing debt, the expansion of the financial balance sheets of all agents, followed by a process of instability, which, in turn, sowed the seeds of recessive cycles, lower prices for financial securities and insolvency. Thus, "the deeper cause of business cycles in an economy with the financial institutions is the instability of portfolios and financial interrelations" (Minsky 1975, 57).

The determining factors for the exchange rate in the neo-liberal-financialised model uncouple from the movement of goods (exports and imports) and become a function of the movement of capital; outstanding in this is foreign direct investment (FDI) and portfolio investment and currency market transactions. This series of financial flows becomes independent of savings and investment, and is relatively independent of the imbalances in the current account (Borio and Disyatat 2015). This leads to a rejection of the traditional view based on the *ex ante* equality of the current account and the capital account, and the capital account is divorced from financing investment.

The emerging countries with structural deficits in their current accounts – outstanding among them, the Latin American nations – are increasingly dependent on the external sector since they must offer a higher interest rate than the developed countries and accept the demands of transnational capital to continue to be a favourite destination for foreign capital flows. This implies, first of all, a greater cost of credit in national currency, to the detriment of medium- and small-sized national firms without access to the international market. Second, price stability depends to a great extent on the exchange rate, which is generally overvalued in order to avoid negatively impacting the size of the foreign debt. Third, the countries that receive large capital flows must maintain large amounts of their international reserves inactive as a guarantee for meeting pending obligations. Fourth, rising interest rates impede the deepening and broadening of emerging countries' financial markets. This implies that in these economies, the financial system cannot take off at the same rate or in the same way as those of the developed economies or carry out the same functions. Specifically, consumption and real estate dealings financed by financial innovations do not become the driving force behind these economies' growth.

The financialised globalisation model also changed how production is organised. Large corporations come on the scene organised in global chains that divide the production process, spreading it to different regions and countries, guided by the reduction in production costs, access to large markets and government support, among other factors. "Downsize and distribute" productive organisation displaced the "retain and reinvest" mode (Lazonick and O'Sullivan 2000; Milberg 2008). Demand decoupled from supply, and based on this, the export-led economic models emerged. One of the most noteworthy results of this form of organisation was the huge concentration of income, particularly in developed countries.

The USA, as the hegemon of the capitalist system, and Great Britain must be analysed separately from the other economies. These countries became net importers, and their economic activity was driven by consumption and the real estate sector; credit and financial innovations became the main sources of financing that seek to maximise financial capital and maintain the value of wealth and debt. The balance sheets of the big corporations were defined in the context of strategies to maximise corporate share value, which reduced investment spending in the countries with robust financial markets. The USA and Great Britain began to grow their service sector divorced from the maturation of industrialisation, that is, this transition took place based on lower average wages compared with previous processes (Rodrik 2016). These nations saw a combination of unemployment (or badly paid jobs) and stagnant production and low wages, which they attempted to counter by making large amounts of financing available to neutralise the fall in demand. In this context, the balance sheets of families, financial and non-financial corporations, and governments expanded.

The impact of the development of the large corporations was different in the rest of the economies. Although the leadership of global chains remained in the developed countries that controlled technological innovation and know-how, corporations also developed in Asia and Latin America. One of the characteristics of the *translatinas* (big Latin American corporations that expanded to the rest of the world, to both developed and developing countries, through FDI) was that when they globalised, they operated independently of their geographical location and on a par with the big multinationals, delisting on their home countries' stock markets. The big corporations developed through mergers and acquisitions, generating a process of overcapitalisation, which implied acquiring significant volumes of financial securities based on the predictions of greater price hikes for financial securities, which should have produced financial profits without developing the financial markets of the emerging countries.

The transnationalisation of productive chains triggered structural imbalances that weakened the financialised globalisation model because net importing countries depressed their productive activity and wage earners' incomes; in developed countries, this was accompanied by increasing indebtedness based on the expectations of financial inflation. Meanwhile, in the net exporting countries, productive activity depended on the demand from the net importing – particularly developed – countries. This made it possible for the latter to operate with low costs, especially wages. Latin America was the exception in this rearrangement because it established itself as a region with an export-led growth model, without achieving structural surpluses in its current account, forcing it to totally open up, thus creating a high degree of dependency on foreign capital flows with strong disadvantages in the formation of fixed capital.

To summarise, the developed and emerging countries that went down the path of export-led economic growth and were successful in achieving a surplus in their current accounts occupied different positions in the productive chains. Central Europe, led by Germany, which controlled technological innovations and know-hows, specialised in capital goods exports, amidst profound processes of pauperisation and precarisation of the work force. Asia also achieved considerable external surpluses, particularly China, with strong government intervention that forced the big multinationals to transfer phases of production with growing technological development, backed by considerable state-directed investment in production. Until the GFC, this process unfolded based on low wages, while production itself was carried out outside their geographical borders.

There is no doubt that China was one of the economies that came out of this process the winner, while the central economies (the USA) were the big losers, because they weakened their production and increased their debt in the context of a strong deindustrialisation process. This model's big limitation is that USA demand had become the driving force behind growth, and when it weakens, global production falls, making the growth of the Asian countries difficult. These countries initially attempted to diversify their exports towards Latin America. This was successful until 2014, when the region's economies weakened due to the fall in commodities prices as a result, as pointed out above, of the attempts to normalise US monetary policy combined with a reflux of capital towards the financial centres.

There can be no doubt that in Latin America, this process is reaching its limits. Just like in the rest of the economies, the export sector was invigorated on the basis of raw materials, following the rules of comparative advantages. In this context, minerals, basic grains and oil became the sectors with the highest growth, accompanied by manufactures in Central America (Mexico and Costa Rica, among others). The region did not achieve current accounts with surpluses; therefore, it had to undertake rapid, profound economic openings, offering better profitability conditions to transnational capital (low wages and high interest rates). The domestic market stagnated without modernising or deepening the financial sector. One big disadvantage in this process is that the global chains created in the region did not transfer technology, leading the fixed-capital-goods producing sector to stagnate and creating productive processes with low value added (the maquiladora sector).

The low investment spending in Latin America was not due to a lack of savings, but to primary activities directed by transnationals and the economies' insertion in the simplest phases of the global production chains. On that basis, we can say that the region's big competitive advantage was not its natural resources (food, minerals and oil), but cheap labour and growing profits in the financial sector. Weak investment in capital goods, a legacy of the import-substitution industrialisation model, deepened in the neo-liberal-financialised model. Based on this, Latin America also went through a process of deindustrialisation in the financialised globalisation period, with very low wages and without a developed financial sector.

One could conclude that Latin America's emerging countries went through a *sui-generis* process, explained on the basis of their subordinate insertion into production with low levels of accumulation, thin, narrow financial markets, high interest rates, overvalued exchange rates, and US-dollar-denominated debt. Financialisation happened by opening to capital without developing the financial system. We can say that the international market offered viability to a subordinate productive model by inserting Latin America into the international market, while the international flows offered these economies financial viability and conditioned their productive evolution. This explains why, once the financialised globalisation model unfolded in the last half of the 1990s, the region did not go into financial crisis, but rather experienced economic paralysis, even in the context of the GFC of 2008.

Based on all of this, the limits of the financialised globalisation process and the challenges of Latin America's export-led model must be discussed in terms of the dominant economic model and the region's insertion into the international market. The paralysis of external demand and the reversal of capital flows to the central countries make the economic model unviable. Despite their common characteristics, the response of each Latin American country will be different: it will depend on their different specialisations, political relationship of forces and even geographical particularities.

This book discusses the issue of the financialised globalisation model and its specificities in Latin America in 15 chapters divided into three sections. The first Part "Regional trends", includes six chapters. Chapter 1 entitled "Multilateralism and regional trade and payments" is penned by Jan Toporowski. The author analyses the problems of multilateral payment systems based on Keynes's and White's historical considerations. He then explains Schumacher's, Kalecki's and Balogh's critiques, facilitating an analysis that is more consistent with the theory of the optimum currency area in vogue today. He concludes that international trade and the system of payments are globally integrated, and that foreign currency market instruments, particularly currency swaps, are more functional than the flexible exchange-rate structure.

Chapter 2 entitled "Capital inflows, current account deficits, and deindustrialisation in Latin America commodity-producing economies" is written by Thomas Goda and Photis Lysandrou. They argue that despite the increase in FDI flows towards Latin America in the past two decades as a result of the hike in commodities prices, the current account balance in countries receiving that capital inflow has not improved due to the repatriation of profits by transnational companies and the deindustrialisation due to their specialisation in the export of primary goods.

Chapter 3, "Limits and perspectives of the export-led growth model and foreign direct investment in Latin America and Mexico" by Guadalupe Huerta Moreno and Luis Kato, analyses the dynamics of FDI in Latin America and Mexico. This chapter shows that the FDI flows have replaced public and private domestic capital investment without fostering a restructuring of local industry or creating an export platform for global trade based on technological development and knowledge.

Jorge Bustamante contributes Chapter 4 entitled "Internationalisation, big corporations and accumulation in the Latin American experience". He analyses the dynamics of the internationalisation of the large corporations based in Latin America and Mexico, showing that the expansion of *trans-latinas* centred on a strategy of mergers and acquisitions based on issuing bonds and shares in international credit markets. This has led to a concentration of industries with a negative impact on growth levels and capital accumulation in the region.

Chapter 5, "Financialisation and economic inequality in Latin America" by Hanna Szymborska, analyses the relationship between financialisation and inequality in Latin America. She argues that growing household debt, spurred further by financial liberalisation and inclusion, generates an unequal distribution of risk and increases the fragility both of families and economic activity.

In the last chapter in this section, "The effect of inflation target regimes in commodities-based, financialised economies on income growth and distribution in Latin America", Santiago Capraro shows that inflation-target-regime models do not take into account the structural characteristics of the Latin American economies. This has undesired economic consequences such as stagnation and regressive income distribution because price stability and inflation-target regimes destabilise economic growth and make wages a smaller portion of overall income.

The second Part, "The failure of comparative advantages", has four chapters. The first of these (Chapter 7 in this book) is "Structural change in Colombia: from import substitution to export-led growth illusion", in which authors Diego Guevara, Gonzalo Cómbita, and Camilo Guevara demonstrate that in the context of its export-led growth model, the Colombian economy has introduced a series of institutional and structural changes that have created a weak, fragmented productive structure. This has become more visible over the last decade due to the fall in raw material prices, which shows up the model's limitations in the context of the Colombian economy's financialisation.

In Chapter 8 entitled "Financialisation of commodities, reserve accumulation and debt in Argentina", authors Alan Cibils and Cecilia Allami analyse the relationship between financialisation of the commodities market in the developed countries, taking into account the accumulation of reserves, and cycles of public indebtedness in the developing countries. They study the transmission mechanism of financialisation from the central countries to the periphery for the case of the Argentinean economy, with special emphasis on its external accounts.

The following chapter is "A sectoral analysis of Mexico's external economic opening", by Abelardo Mariña and Sergio Cámara. They analyse the evolution of the structure of the Mexican economy's most important sectors with regard to their links to the world market in the neo-liberal period. Their main argument centres on Mexico's subordination to the world market through the relocation of transnational corporations in Mexico to take advantage of low labour costs and the proximity of the US market.

In this section's final chapter, "The natural resource curse and financial development of Mexico", authors Alicia Puyana Mutis and Katya Pérez Guzmán analyse the effects of the productive specialisation of Mexico's export-led development model on financial development. The chapter's hypothesis is that the countries that concentrate on exporting natural resources have low growth rates and limited financial development; this is the case of the Mexican economy, despite not having specialised in the export of primary products.

This book's final Part, "The growth of financial balance sheets", contains five chapters. Chapter 11, written by Esteban Pérez Caldentey and Nicole Favreau Negront, is "Financialisation in a small, open developing economy: the case of Chile". The authors argue that the implementation of the neo-liberal agenda has contributed to the process of financialisation in Chile, clearly shown by the pattern of productive specialisation in primary goods (metal ore), in which the financial sector has become one of the country's most important economic activities in terms of growth, participation in the GDP, wages and profits. This has been accompanied by growing indebtedness by non-financial corporations and marked financial fragility.

Chapter 12 is titled "Financialisation, growth and investment in Brazil", written by Luiz Fernando de Paula and Tiago R. Meyer. The object of analysis of these authors is the relationship between financialisation and investment in Brazil during the implementation of the Real Plan (1995–2017). Their aim is to discuss the determining factors for investment in Brazil as well as the relationship between financialisation and the distribution of profits and dividends. They also ask themselves if a crowding-out process is underway, in which financial profits compete with productive income.

Gabriel Gómez Ochoa contributes Chapter 13, "Financial structure and big corporations in scenarios of increasing indebtedness in Mexico". He argues that Mexican firms have dramatically increased their foreign-currency-denominated debt since 2005, and particularly since 2009, and that this is not reflected in the gross formation of fixed capital or the economy's overall output. Therefore, the disproportional risk of indebtedness for some firms creates the risk of bankruptcy, with destabilising effects on the economy and public finances.

In Chapter 14, Noemi Levy presents "Financial capital flows and FOREX activities in Mexico: finance or speculation?" She seeks to explain why Mexico's currency achieved a privileged place in world exchange-rate market rankings and how that affected the stability of financial and productive systems. Her central hypothesis is that Mexico's entry into the international market was profound and generalised due to the merger of productive and financial structures with those of the USA. This has created the basis for the internationalisation of the currency, without the ability to stabilise Mexico's financial system because the volume of its foreign transactions is much higher than the value of production, thus making the central bank incapable of controlling the financial variables.

The final chapter is titled "Exchange rate policy restrictions on a high-volatility environment: the Mexican currency", written by Nora Ampudia Márquez and Luis Raúl Rodríguez Reyes. The authors show the growing ineffectiveness of Mexico's exchange-rate policy with a global, financialised currency. This is the context for an export-led accumulation model heavily affected by exchange-rate volatility due to excessive liquidity, globalisation and financial liberalisation in international financial markets that have created conditions for growing instability.

References

Bonizzi, B. (2016) 'Institutional investors and capital flows to emerging markets', *PhD Thesis*. SOAS. University of London, from http://eprints.soas.ac.uk/id/eprint/23797

Borio, C. & Disyatat, P. (2015) 'Capital flows and the current account: Taking financing (more) seriously', *BIS Working Papers*, No. 525, October.

Lazonick, W. & O'Sullivan, M. (2000) 'Maximizing shareholder value. A new ideology of corporate governance', *Economy and Society*, 29(1), 13–35.

Lysandrou, P. & Nesvetailova, A. (2014) 'The role of shadow banking entities in the financial crisis: a disaggregated view', *Review of International Political Economy*. doi:10.1080/09692290.2014.896269

Milberg, W. (2008) 'Shifting sources and uses of profits: sustaining US financialization with global value chains', *Economy and Society*, 37(3), 420–451.

Minsky, H. (1975) *John Maynard Keynes*, Columbia University Press, USA.|

Parguez, A. (2009) 'The tragic and hidden history of the European Monetary Union', *unpublished paper*, Université Franche Comptée, Besançon, November.

Rodrik, R. (2016) 'Premature deindustrialization', *Journal of Economic Growth*, 21(1–33), doi:10.1007/s10887-015-9122-3

Stallings, B. with Studart, R. (2006) *Finance for development, Latin America and comparative perspective*, Brookings Institution Press, Washington.

Toporowski, J. (2000) *The end of finance, capital market inflation, financial derivatives and pension fund capitalism*, Routledge Frontiers of Political Economy, London, UK.

Part I

Regional trends

1 Multilateralism and regional trade and payments[1]

Jan Toporowski

The question of multilateralism emerged in the 1930s as a result of the breakdown of the gold standard. Faced with insufficient gold reserves to maintain payments on cross-border debt obligations, most notably in the case of the German reparations, the issuers of the major trading currencies suspended the convertibility of their currencies into gold, and sought to create international currency areas in which the currency of the central bank at the monetary centre of the currency area could be used as a means of payment (Kindleberger, 1973, Chapter 11). For residents in those areas, this in effect introduced a two-tier trading system in which trade, income and capital payments to countries within the currency area could be made freely, while such payments to counterparts outside the currency area were subject to exchange rate risk and bureaucratic impediments, such as blocked accounts or obligations to transfer at expensive official exchange rates. Formally, or informally, such currency areas were ways of economising on international reserves or, to put it another way, preventing the circulation of reserves between currency areas.

In this situation, multilateralism represented an ideal international payment system, in which revenue from trade with one country could be used to pay for trade with any other country at a stable and convenient rate of exchange between the currencies. This ideal was originally represented by the gold standard, under which gold obtained from exports to any country on the gold standard could be used to pay for imports from any other country on the gold standard. But gold had the disadvantage of being inelastic in supply and, by the end of the Second World War, of being concentrated in the USA. The solution made famous in the Keynes Plan was to substitute gold for a bookkeeping currency (Keynes's "bancor"), whose supply would be more elastic than that of gold. The first departure from multilateralism following Bretton Woods was a gold and dollar standard, whose presence in the reserves of governments committed to the new fixed exchange rates was insufficient to support international trade. In a situation of widespread capital controls, this reserve insufficiency appeared as problems in balancing foreign trade. This was the beginning of a reduction of the *monetary* question of multilateralism to a *real* issue of foreign trade that came to be soluble by the autonomous monetary policy of a given country's government by means of official interest or exchange rates. In academic discussions, the problems of balancing foreign trade were a prelude to a reconstruction of currency area theory in *real* terms, in which a currency area represents an "optimal" solution when the labour market is flexible, as opposed to the way in which currency areas appeared in the 1930s, and more recently, in response to a shortage of foreign currency reserves.

This chapter argues that currency areas are a means of economising on foreign currency reserves, and they arise in order to overcome a scarcity of such reserves that inhibits international payments. The essence of a currency area is a sharing of such reserves. Hence, a currency board is not necessarily a currency area: Argentina, during its ill-fated currency board with the US dollar, clearly was not in a currency area with that currency. (The question of whether the US Federal Reserve's swap agreements with its counterparts in the European Monetary Union, Canada, the UK, Japan and Switzerland constitute a "currency area" is not for this paper.)

The section that follows examines the historical discussion preceding the Bretton Woods conference, and the emergence of multilateralism as an essential monetary counterpart to free trade. This is followed by a summary of the criticism, presented by "Fritz" Schumacher, Michał Kalecki and Thomas Balogh, which addressed the official proposals at Bretton Woods and assessed them against the standard of multilateralism. The final section examines how the Bretton Woods arrangements gave way to a re-emergence of currency areas, a re-emergence that is not explained by optimal currency, or floating exchange rates, but by the shortage of international reserves built into the international monetary system.

The Bretton Woods discussions

In 1933, a World Economic and Monetary Conference was held in London to consider measures to reverse international economic deflation and rescue free trade from protectionist pressures. The failure of the conference gave way to tariffs and bilateral payment agreements between governments. Interwar financial and economic diplomacy was succeeded in wartime by autarky. At the start of the Second World War, regulations were introduced in Britain to give the government control over foreign assets and payments. This in effect reduced international payments to bilateral clearing between the British government and the governments of its allies and neutral states, while freezing payments to "hostile powers". Already in 1941, partly in response to German plans for a payments union in Europe, economists employed in the British War Cabinet were working on the question of how bilateral payments could be replaced after the War by multilateral payments, that is, payments directly between traders in different countries and in currencies that were directly convertible against each other. While there was general agreement that free trade was desirable, the British Treasury's advisor on the question of international payments, John Maynard Keynes and his US counterpart, Harry Dexter White, wanted to establish a system of multilateral payments in which exchange rates were fixed but adjustable, although they were famously to differ on how this was to be achieved. In April 1943, Keynes's proposals were published in London as a Government White Paper, simultaneously with the publication in Washington of White's proposals (White Papers proposals, 1943, 1944). The key difference between them was that Keynes wanted a Clearing Union with a currency, provisionally called "bancor", issued by an International Clearing Bank that would serve as the benchmark against which exchange rates would be fixed. Trade surpluses would be automatically deposited in an investment fund for on-lending to deficit countries, and interest payments, deducted from surpluses above a certain quota necessary for trade, were supposed to discourage excessive surpluses. Governments in deficit would have automatic borrowing rights, subject to similarly modest interest payments. The White's proposal recommended an exchange rate stabilisation fund, into which member countries would pay gold, foreign currency and government bonds, in exchange for overdraft facilities with a right to automatic borrowing against a quota set by the deposits of the government in the fund. Above quota borrowing would require the agreement of a majority of depositors in the fund (weighted by their deposits).[2] In May 1943, the US government started meetings, with representatives of Allies and governments associated with them, to discuss and agree financial and monetary arrangements for the post-War peace, with a clear view to avoiding the financial difficulties that had exacerbated economic instability in the 1920s and 1930s.[3]

Despite the high level of these discussions, the key issues surrounding multilateralism were outlined outside the official exchanges in a paper that Schumacher published in 1943, but whose foundations date back to 1941 (Schumacher, 1943a; Keynes, 1980, CW, Vol XXV:21). Keynes paper (ibid.), entitled "Multilateral Clearing", laid out the advantages of multilateralism and the disadvantages of bilateralism. Under multilateralism, anyone in any country could buy goods anywhere else in the world using their income irrespective of whether it had been accrued in the home market, in the domestic currency of the purchaser or in any other market in a foreign currency. By contrast, bilateralism restricts trade to bilateral balance with all trading partners:

> Under a regime of bilateral clearing each country has, one might say, free access to the trade and raw materials, not of the world as a whole, but only of those other countries which are its customers. Under pool (multilateral) clearing access to trade is universally free.[4]

In this way, Schumacher underlined the dependence of free trade on the international payments system. This was a radical break with the conventional theory of international trade and payments: in Schumacher's time, and in ours, the arguments around free trade, such as the theory of absolute or comparative advantage, or the more recent "new" trade theory, are conducted in real terms, usually using stylised bilateral trade analysis, whose conclusions are then supposed to apply also to multilateral trade. Similarly, exchange rate theory is presented in a bilateral way, with the currency unit of the home market, or its interest rate, compared to that of the "rest of the world". This real or bilateral thinking applies as much to the recent "optimal currency area" analysis that is used to frame the discussion on currency areas, as it did during the Bretton Woods discussions. As a result, the actual rationale for currency areas, in the shortage of international reserves to the needs of international trade and payments, is largely ignored, or reduced to its symptom, such as the "dollar shortage" in international trade in the middle of the last century.

In the summer of 1943, a special supplement of the Oxford Institute's *Bulletin*, on international payments, was prepared by economists at Oxford University. The editor of the Supplement explained the rationale for it as follows:

> The subject matter of international trade and finance is of a highly technical nature and discussions of these problems tend, therefore, to be confined to 'experts', city circles and business men. It is, of course, appropriate that the efforts to come to a satisfactory plan should be left to the experts of the Allied Nations whenever technical details are concerned. It is important, however, that a wider circle than the mere experts should understand the general issues involved and help to shape the line along which agreement should be sought by the experts. For, although questions of social security and full employment would appear to affect the life of the average citizen more immediately and fundamentally, there can be no doubt that his welfare and standard of living will be greatly influenced by the sort of international order or disorder in the economic relations between States which will emerge after the war, see Lessons of the Past.
>
> (1943)

Apart from the editorial, approximately two-thirds of the Supplement consisted of a long article by Schumacher summarising the key mechanisms of the Plans proposed by Keynes and White. Given that one of the other two papers in the Supplement was co-authored with Kalecki, it could be said that the Supplement owed more to Schumacher than to anyone else at the Institute. Schumacher's summary endorsed the view in both plans that free trade alone could not secure full employment. Left to themselves, market forces would not make trade balances converge on equilibrium, and the absence of equilibrium would deflate demand in trade deficit countries, reinforcing a tendency towards deflation in the global economy as a whole. However, he considered that both plans were inadequate to provide the liquidity necessary to maintain multilateralism, and this brought with it the danger that individual governments would revert to rationing foreign exchange or bilateralism, that is, settlements between central banks on a net basis. The net basis (transferring only the foreign currency or gold equivalent to the *balance* between imports and exports during the settlement period) would inevitably encourage the direction of exports towards countries from which excess imports were being purchased, or else limitations on those imports. In this way, bilateralism undermines free trade.

According to Schumacher, although the Keynes Plan offered a higher level of international reserves to support free trade, it suffered from a lack of clarity about the concept of equilibrium. "Under the British Plan 'equilibrium' is defined as the absence of bancor credits and debits". However, this supposes that the flow of bancor credits and debits is determined by trade flows. In fact, the balance of payments consists of three parts: the balance of trade and income payments (the current account), the balance of long-term capital flows and the balance of short-term bank transactions. These last, in the Keynes proposal, would be the bancor credits and debits. The flaw in the Keynes Plan was its presumption that long-term capital flows are balanced or non-existent, so that the balance of trade and income payments is equal to the net flow of bancor credits and debits. But if there are long-term capital flows, then their balance can seriously disrupt the flows of short-term bancor credits and debits (Schumacher, 1943b). Keynes did indeed advocate capital controls to eliminate such disruption (Skidelsky, 2001:231). But then he could not also claim, as the White Paper stated, that foreign exchange transactions can be "carried on as freely as in the best days of the gold standard", that is, as Schumacher noted, without even having to notify the monetary authorities of the transaction.

The Kalecki/Schumacher plan

The third paper in the Supplement was jointly written by Schumacher and Kalecki. Like Schumacher's summary paper on the White and Keynes Plan, the paper co-authored with Kalecki found the Keynes Plan to be preferable to the White Plan. But the Keynes Plan would not be effective unless modified and extended. Kalecki and Schumacher started with a fundamental critique of the whole idea that the aim of international trade policy should be balanced trade:

> Both the British and the American Currency Plans are based upon the idea of "equilibrium" ... they aim at creating rules and machinery through which, after a start has been made (after the war), each country would be "kept in balance" with the rest of the world. Neither of them succeeds in giving more than a purely formal definition of "equilibrium", a definition which ... is not necessarily relevant. It may be questioned whether the very concept of equilibrium is sufficiently precise

> and significant to be introduced at this level at all. There is no merit in a general policy aiming at *Current account equilibrium* for all countries, because different countries are at different stages of economic development, and a regular flow of investment from the more highly developed to the more backward regions of the world may redound to benefit of all. This is implicitly recognised in both schemes, since they are both to be supplemented by proposals for an International Investment Board.[5]

Kalecki and Schumacher did not think that charging governments for surpluses deposited in the international clearing bank would provide an adequate incentive to expand domestic demand in their countries. They concluded that the long-term goal of current account equilibrium should be abandoned, to allow governments to pursue whatever levels of aggregate demand they may wish to have. However, this, in the view of Kalecki and Schumacher, suffers from the disadvantage that governments may in those circumstances resort to overvaluing their currencies in the foreign exchange markets in order to hold down import costs. The authors argued that therefore, currency support arrangements should be differentiated, according to whether a country has a trade deficit, because it is in the process of industrialisation, or because there are other reasons for the deficit. They suggested an extension of the powers of the International Investment Board at the International Clearing Union. The proceeds of the trade surpluses of the surplus countries would be deposited with the Investment Board. The Board would direct the surpluses to industrialising countries that had used up a quarter of their quotas as loans. However, industrialising countries that went on to use up half of their quotas would be required to devalue their currency.

The direction of loans to developing countries was supposed to allow for the additional imports required for industrialisation. A further twist to the scheme was recommended by Kalecki and Schumacher to reinforce equilibrating mechanisms in industrialised countries. The International Investment Board, they suggested, should be given the power to direct that loans to *industrialising* countries had to be spent in *industrialised* countries that were in trade deficit. In this way, the weak equilibrating mechanism in the Keynes Plan, of charging interest to deficit *and* surplus countries, would be assisted by recycling the surpluses of industrialised countries through orders for industrial equipment for developing countries from industrialised countries in deficit. Kalecki and Schumacher defended this proposed breach in "the free play of market forces" by pointing out that the White Plan had a similar suggestion to ration the exports of surplus countries. The difference between the two proposals was that the White Plan "is neither expansionist nor multi-lateral", while the scheme proposed in Oxford provided liquidity to assist current account equilibrium in industrialised countries, simultaneously facilitating the "unbalanced equilibrium" required in developing countries (Kalecki and Schumacher, 1943).

Unlike the Keynes Plan, which sought to eliminate private capital flows, but then declared that this elimination was "not essential" to the international clearing scheme,[6] the Kalecki/Schumacher scheme did not altogether ban private sector capital flows. Its authors argued that *net* foreign short-term lending in the private sector would need to be eliminated, presumably leaving scope for short-term lending balanced on the balance sheet of the central bank. But long-term private sector or intergovernmental lending would be allowed, providing that the lender country had exhausted half of its bancor quota. In this way, surplus governments would only be able to engage in international lending after they had committed half of their quota to trade. However, the function of the International Investment Board would be to support current account equilibrium in countries that needed, for development purposes, to run current account deficits and which did not wish to become indebted to other governments and private finance. To be able to do this efficiently, Kalecki and Schumacher argued that the International Investment Board and the International Clearing Union needed to be combined in one institution, rather than separating international investment from the clearing of trade payments. In effect, this would ensure that international investment targeted at deficit countries would rise with growing trade imbalances. In contrast, the Keynes Plan offered limited resources to international investment, and the White Plan even more modest finance.

Two other aspects of their proposal deserve note. This is the authors' dissent from the classical doctrine that the purpose of international monetary arrangements was to assure convergence on equilibrium in the current account of the balance of payments. Kalecki and Schumacher's argument, that countries in the process of industrialisation require financing to be able to run trade deficits, was to become a feature of the development economics that emerged after the War, as well as Kalecki's later approach to the economics of the developing countries (United Nations, 1950). The other aspect of their proposal that is perhaps even more radical, and links Kalecki's pre-War ideas on full employment with his later work on multilateralism, is the idea that trade imbalances were the inevitable outcome of attempts to reach full employment by aggregate demand management. The reason for this was that capital equipment for industrial production was not distributed among countries in such a way as to secure potential full employment with trade balance. The condition for full employment with trade balance was investment in productive capacity in the developing countries. The neoclassical view that prices, including exchange rates, could adjust the demand of the full-employed and their families to the resources available through balanced trade was placing demands on market mechanisms that it could not deliver (Samuelson, 1964).

The final paper in the supplement was by the Hungarian economist Thomas Balogh who was, at that time, a lecturer at Balliol College. Balogh had been one of the earliest critics of the Keynes Plan (Skidelsky, 2001:334–335). He reiterated their common view that market forces would tend to work in deflationary ways in the international economy. They would be overcome by the Schumacher/Kalecki scheme for generating and financing exports of capital equipment to the developing countries. One problem that he foresaw was that a requirement to use development loans to buy from mature economies in trade deficit may end up with the developing countries buying at a higher cost than they may be able to buy from surplus countries. Balogh's answer to this was to argue for subsidies to make the cost of industrial equipment exported by deficit countries equal to that of surplus countries. He dismissed the idea that currency devaluation could do the job better, since exchange rate devaluation was a *general* subsidy from the domestic market to export markets, while targeted subsidies were likely to be less costly. Among the counterarguments to this, the possibility of retaliation was less likely if all economies are enjoying high employment. The charge that subsidies might constitute "dumping" could just as easily be levelled against currency devaluation, or policies of wage reductions. In any case, subsidies would be superior to bilateral clearing agreements, which often resulted in the exchange of goods for which there was not much of a market in either country.

Finally, Balogh considered whether the scheme put forward by Kalecki and Schumacher would work equally well if adopted by a smaller group of countries instead of the whole world. In his view, such a partial scheme would work less well, because its member governments would need to take measures to counteract the effects of business cycles in countries outside the scheme and this may involve quotas for trade with countries outside the bloc. The effect of such a reduced area of the scheme would therefore depend on the degree of self-sufficiency of the bloc: in a large, self-sufficient bloc like the sterling area, the loss of labour productivity due to the reduced, in relation to the world economy, scope for the international division of labour would likely be small (Balogh, 1943).

The International Monetary Fund emerges

In April 1944, the British government published a White Paper, presenting the outcome of the earlier negotiations between Keynes and White on the proposed International Monetary Fund (IMF). The British government still had strong reservations about the proposed fund. Chief among them was the reduction in the resources of the fund, in relation to the Keynes Plan proposal, and the realisation of the international investment facility as an International Bank for Reconstruction and Development, which was clearly not going to direct its resources to Great Britain, whose reconstruction and development needs were modest in comparison with the colonies, developing countries, and countries on the mainland of Europe. The British negotiators had therefore agreed to a reduction in the loan capacity of the Fund (White Paper, 1944; Skidelsky, 2001:338–340). Schumacher and Balogh wrote an extended comment on the White Paper for the Oxford Institute's *Bulletin*. They objected to the inadequate resources of the IMF, and the requirements imposed on its members. Among those requirements were the obligations to maintain free trade in accordance with criteria laid down by the Fund, rather than their development needs, and to seek balanced trade which, in Schumacher and Balogh's view, could only be deflationary. They commended the Kalecki/Schumacher Plan as a more effective way of avoiding deflation and offering a more discriminating way of securing trade equilibrium (Schumacher and Balogh, 1944).

Conclusions

The discussions around the Bretton Woods conference included contributions that raised important issues lost in the focus that was given in those discussions, and post-War controversies, on the difficulties of maintaining fixed exchange rates and the consequences of capital controls. Among those issues was the need to provide adequate reserves not only for trade, but also for the industrialisation of developing countries. Reserve inadequacy then became the crucial factor precipitating the emergence of currency areas: the sterling area, as a mechanism for conserving and sharing the gold and foreign currency reserves of its member countries, in particular Great Britain, and later the European Monetary System and its successor the European Monetary Union. In the view of the authors of the Oxford critique of Bretton Woods, currency areas are a departure from the monetary efficiency of multilateralism, which is the ultimate "optimal" currency area because it is a global currency area. Currency areas may limit free trade by guiding it towards other members of a given currency area. But such areas remain preferable to bilateralism, restricting trade to other countries that buy from a given country, and to the trade equilibrium ideal that underpinned the British and the American proposals, which set the agenda for the Bretton Woods conference.

The efficiency of sharing reserves of international liquidity was acknowledged by Robert Mundell in his later, less well-known, "Uncommon Arguments for Common Currencies".[7] But not before his "optimal currency area" theory had made international payments into a labour market issue, rather than the matter of monetary analysis.

Notes

1 The chapter draws on and extends materials in the second volume of Toporowski (2018). I am grateful to Noemi Levy-Orlik and Julio Lopez Gallardo for their helpful discussions in the course of the research for this chapter. I retain responsibility for the remaining errors.
2 In effect, it was the US Treasury's proposals that won out at the United National Monetary and Financial Conference at Bretton Woods in July 1944.
3 These talks, and Keynes's part in them, are detailed in Skidelsky (2001), Vol 3, Chapters 9–11 and Keynes (1980), CW, Vol XXV.
4 Schumacher op. cit.

5 Kalecki and Schumacher, "International Clearing and Long-Term Lending", 1943. The International Investment Board proposal was realised at Bretton Woods in the form of the International Bank for Reconstruction and Development, or the World Bank.
6 White Paper, *Proposals for an International Clearing Union*, London, 1943, par 32 and 33.
7 Mundell, "Uncommon Arguments for Common Currencies", 1973.

References

Balogh, T. (1943) 'The Foreign Balance and Full Employment', *Bulletin of the Oxford Institute of Statistics*, 5(5), 33–39.

Kalecki, M. & Schumacher, E.F. (1943) 'International Clearing and Long-Term Lending', *Bulletin of the Institute of Statistics Oxford Supplement*, 5(5), 29–33.

Keynes, J.M. (1980) *The Collected Writings of John Maynard Keynes Volume XXV Activities 1940–1944, Shaping the Post-War World The Clearing Union*, edited by D.E. Moggridge, Cambridge University Press, London.

Kindleberger, C.P. (1973) *The World in Depression 1929–1939*, Allen Lane, London.

'Lessons of the Past' (1943) *Bulletin of the Institute of Statistics Oxford Supplement*, 5(5), 3–8.

Mundell, R.A. (1961) 'A Theory of Optimum Currency Areas', *American Economic Review*, 51/4, September, 657–665.

Mundell, R.A. (1973) 'Uncommon Arguments for Common Currencies', in Johnson, H.G. & Swoboda, A.K., *The Economics of Common Currencies*, George Allen and Unwin, London.

Preliminary Draft Outline of a Proposal for an International Stabilisation Fund of the United and Associated Nations Made Public by the Secretary of the Treasury on April 17, 1943, US Treasury, Washington DC.

Samuelson, P.A. (1964) 'Theoretical Notes on Trade Problems', *Review of Economics and Statistics*, 46(2), 145–154.

Schumacher, E.F. (1943a) 'Multilateral Clearing', *Economica New Series*, 10(38), 150–165.

Schumacher, E.F. (1943b) 'The New Currency Plans', *Bulletin of the Institute of Statistics Oxford Supplement*, 5(5), 8–29.

Schumacher, E.F. & Balogh, T. (1944) 'An International Monetary Fund', *Bulletin of the Institute of Statistics Oxford*, 6(6), 81–93.

Skidelsky, R. (2001) *John Maynard Keynes Volume Three Fighting for Freedom 1937–1946*, Viking, New York.

Toporowski, J. (2018) *Michał Kalecki An Intellectual Biography Volume II By Intellect Alone 1939–1970*, Palgrave, Basingstoke.

United Nations (1950) 'Growth, Disequilibrium and Disparities: Interpretation of the Process of Economic Development', in *Economic Survey of Latin America 1949*, United Nations, New York.

White Paper (1943) *Proposals for an International Clearing Union*, HM Stationery Office Cmd 6437, London.

White Paper (1944) *Joint Statement by Experts on the Establishment of an International Monetary Fund*, HM Stationery Office Cmd 6519, London.

2 Capital inflows, current account deficits and deindustrialisation in Latin American commodity-producing economies

Thomas Goda and Photis Lysandrou

During the global commodity price boom of 2003–2013, foreign capital flows became an important source of finance for commodity-producing developing economies. This was especially true for foreign direct investment (FDI) inflows, which helped these countries to increase the exploitation of their natural resources and to achieve growth rates well above their long-term ones (IMF 2011; UNCTAD 2015). Latin America was one of the regions that benefited most from the boom, but it was also the region that suffered most when it came to an end, experiencing growth contractions, large current account and fiscal deficits, and weak domestic demand (IMF 2015, 2017b).

The recent experience of Latin America appears to be in line with the findings of some economists that show that natural resource abundance and growth have an inverse relationship in the long-run, the so-called "natural resource curse" (Auty 1993; Sachs & Warner 1995, 2001; Arezki & van der Ploeg 2011). However, these findings are debatable, given that countries like Australia, Canada, the Netherlands and Norway show that natural resource abundance per se is not necessarily a curse and can even be a blessing (Davis 1995; Lederman & Maloney 2007, 2008; Brunnschweiler 2008).

The most prominent economic explanation as to why some countries experience an inverse relationship between natural resource production and long-term growth is that provided by the Dutch Disease theory. This theory holds that resource boom induced relocation and spending processes can lead to an increase in the prices of non-tradable goods and thus to an appreciation of the real effective exchange rate (REER) that can, in turn, lead to a crowding-out of other tradable sectors (Corden & Neary 1982). These adjustments are not necessarily harmful for an economy on the assumption that a simple reversal of the sectoral recomposition can take place once a commodity price boom ends. However, in the particular case of emerging market economies experiencing a commodity boom, the disappearance of some industries might be irreversible (Krugman 1987) as might also be the widening technological gaps with other economies (Cherif 2013), with both developments resulting in a sharp and lasting decline of economic growth rates following the end of that boom.

Dutch Disease effects can be triggered by improvements in extraction technologies, by the discovery of new natural resource deposits, by a rise in global commodity prices and by boom-related foreign capital inflows (Corden & Neary 1982; Corden 1984). The latter two factors appeared to be most at play in the recent commodity boom in Latin America. In contrast to the 1990s when foreign portfolio investment (FPI) inflows fostered REER appreciations in the region (Calvo et al. 1993; Corbo & Hernández 1996; Athukorala & Rajapatirana 2003), this chapter argues that in the more recent period, it was FDI inflows – and especially commodity-related FDI inflows – that led to an appreciation of REER across the region, the result being further deindustrialisation with the decline in the tradable-to-non-tradable output ratio.

Moreover, we provide evidence that indicates that the FDI inflows also led to current account deficits due to the repatriation of profits from the multinational corporations (MNCs) that invested in these countries. Policymakers and scholars typically assume that the impact of natural resource-seeking FDI on the current account is beneficial, given its positive impact on commodity exports (Brouthers et al. 1996; UNCTAD 1999). However, in the case of the Latin American commodity-producing countries, the negative effects of MNC profit and dividend payment repatriation on their net primary income (NPI)[1] far outweighed the positive effects on their trade balance stemming from the boom in natural resource exports.

This chapter is structured as follows. The second section following this introduction outlines the effects of the commodity boom and bust in Latin America during the period 2003–2014. The third section discusses the impact of commodity-related FDI inflows on the current account balance of Latin American commodity producers during the boom period. The fourth section discusses how the commodity-related FDI inflows led to Dutch Disease symptoms in the region that have persisted since the end of the boom. Finally, the fifth section summarises the main findings and gives some conclusions.

The commodity boom and bust in Latin America and capital flows to the regions commodity-producing countries

It is well documented that between 2003 and 2013, the world experienced a commodity price boom[2] and that several countries in Latin America benefited substantially from this boom. According to Hailu and Kipgen (2017) and Dobbs et al. (2013), eight Latin American economies can be regarded as commodity producers; they are Bolivia, Brazil, Chile, Colombia, Ecuador, Mexico, Peru and Venezuela. All of them experienced a strong increase in commodity exports as a percentage of merchandise exports during the boom period. To be more precise, energy and mining exports rose by 35% in Bolivia, 33% in Colombia, 20% in Peru, 18% in Ecuador, 16% in Chile, 12% in Brazil, 11% in Venezuela and 7% in Mexico. Furthermore, the commodity boom also led to a 64% increase in the countries' terms of trade index between 2003 and 2013 (Figure 2.1).

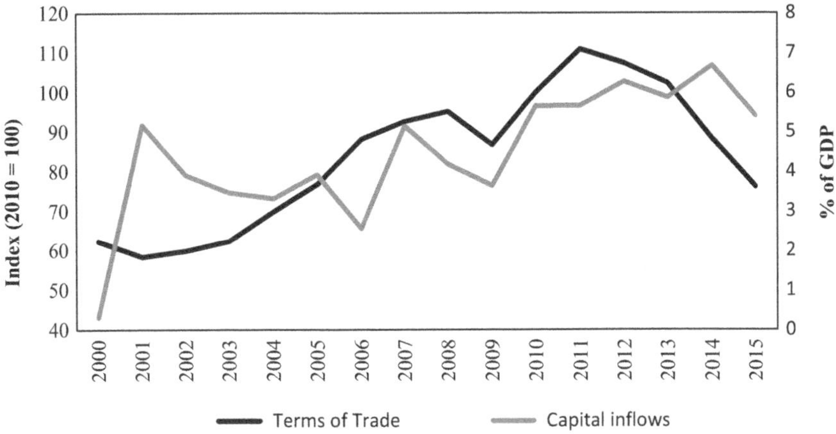

Figure 2.1 Terms of trade and capital flows to Latin American commodity-producing countries.

Source: WDI (2017).

Note: The figure presents unweighted averages for the countries Bolivia, Brazil, Chile, Colombia, Ecuador, Mexico, Peru and Venezuela.

As an outcome of these favourable developments, these eight countries also experienced a substantial increase in their growth rates. While their average growth rate was 3.0% between 1992 and 2002, it rose to 4.5% between 2003 and 2013 (WDI 2017). In addition to the positive effect on growth, the commodity boom also led to a substantial increase in capital inflows. While FDI and FPI inflows to these countries were on average only 0.1% of GDP in 2000, they rose to 6.5% of GDP in 2014 (Figure 2.1). In contrast to the 1990s, when Latin American countries mainly received FPI inflows (Calvo et al. 1993; Corbo & Hernández 1996; Athukorala & Rajapatirana 2003), FDI inflows were those that especially increased during the boom years:

> FDI inflows grew from less than US$ 50 billion in 2003 to a peak of US$ 189.951 billion in 2013 (in nominal terms) on the back of high commodity prices, which boosted FDI in natural resources, and steady GDP growth across most of the region, which increased FDI in services and manufacturing for the domestic market.
>
> (ECLAC 2015a:19)

Hence, it is widely accepted that Latin America (together with Africa) was the region that benefited most from the commodity boom. However, when the boom ended abruptly in mid-2014,[3] the commodity-producing countries of the region were affected severely. To be more precise, their capital inflows, terms of trade index and growth rates declined substantially, with

Brazil and Venezuela being especially hit hard and subsequently experiencing a deeper prolonged recession.

In addition to the above, the region's commodity exporters suffered from a significant reduction in fiscal revenues and from a severe deterioration in their trade balances that made sharp import compressions necessary (IMF 2015). As the reduction in imports was driven not only by decreasing domestic consumption demand, but also by a reduction in the imports of capital and intermediate goods (ECLAC 2015b), the consequent impact on the region's long-term growth prospects is likely to be negative. This is because many of these types of goods, which are most crucial for rising industrial productivity, are not produced domestically.

In sum, the post-boom developments in Latin America cast doubt on the sustainability of the resource-based, export-led growth model as a model of economic growth for the region. The remainder of this chapter will argue that a major reason why Latin American commodity-producing countries were hit so hard by the end of the commodity boom was the fact that much of the increased production for export was financed by foreign capital inflows that ultimately led to persistent current account imbalances and to growing Dutch Disease effects.

Capital inflows and their effect on the current account of Latin American countries

Capital inflows in the form of FDI, FPI and bank credits affect a recipient country's balance of payments through its financial account and its current account.[4]

$$Financial\ Account = FDI + FPI + Bank\ \ Credits \tag{1}$$

$$Current\ Account = Trade\ \ Balance + NPI \tag{2}$$

The financial account covers the claims and liabilities that a country has with other countries, and FDI and FPI flows into this account are typically considered to be beneficial for a country, especially if it is a developing country. Domestic savings in developing countries tend to be relatively low, which, in turn, explains their relatively low levels of investment and low capital stocks. According to the Solow growth model, the inflow of foreign savings in the form of FDI and FPI is thus vital for developing countries to be able to accumulate sufficient capital to achieve high growth rates in the long run (see, e.g., Bosworth et al. 1999).

The current account reports the trade balance and net income flows. The potential effects of capital inflows for this part of the balance of payments are ambiguous. This is especially true in regard to FDI inflows because, while these can carry a mixture of positive and negative effects for the trade balance side of a country's current account, they invariably carry negative effects for the net income side. Consider the trade balance side. In the case of efficiency-seeking FDI, where MNCs situate parts of their global value chain in developing economies to reduce costs and improve the profitability of their operations, the effects of that type of FDI on a recipient country tend to be seen as positive. Inclusion in global value chains tends to increase the diversification and amount of developing economies' exports, while the diffusion of technological and managerial know-how from foreign to domestic firms might also boost these economies' long-run trade balances by boosting the industrial competitiveness and hence the export capacities of domestic firms (Orr 1991; UNCTAD 2013; Cieslik & Hagemejer 2014; Mijiyawa 2016).

The effects of market-seeking FDI, motivated by MNCs' aim of locating production in recipient countries to be nearer to local customers, tend to be more nuanced because these effects are mainly channelled through the impact on imports. On the one hand, MNCs might replace imported final goods or intermediate inputs, hence reducing a recipient country's imports and benefiting its trade balance; on the other hand, however, there could result what is termed "vertical crowding-out" as imports also rise if MNCs substitute imported capital or resource inputs for local inputs (Brouthers et al. 1996; UNCTAD 1999; Pacheco 2005; Aparecida Fernandes & Carvalho Campos 2008). As regards the effects of natural resource-seeking FDI on a developing country's trade balance, these are generally held to be positive, in that although this type of FDI entails the import of capital goods and specialised intermediate inputs, the aggregate values of these imports are usually lower than those of the subsequent commodity export volumes (Brouthers et al. 1996; UNCTAD 1999, 2007, 2013).

The impact of capital inflows on the NPI, on the contrary, is unambiguously negative. Rational and reasonably well-informed investors can be expected to direct their investments towards profitable projects, that is, those whose expected returns exceed the initial investments. As the majority of the investors or shareholders in the investing companies typically reside in developed economies, it follows that the majority of the profits that are extracted from the foreign investments will be repatriated back to their economies. This means that NPI outflows are bound to rise in tandem with capital inflows and, what is more, are likely at some point to even exceed capital inflows.

In sum, three potential current account net effects can be identified with commodity-producing countries that receive substantial capital inflows during a boom: a current account surplus when the positive trade balance effect exceeds the negative NPI effect; a current account in equilibrium when the negative NPI effect equals the positive trade balance effect; and, finally, a current account deficit when the negative NPI effect exceeds the positive trade balance effect.

Surprisingly, the potential adverse impact of capital inflows on the current account of developing countries' balance of payments has received comparatively little attention in the empiric academic literature. Notable exceptions in this regard are Jansen (1995), Mencinger (2007) and Rios Ballesteros and Goda (2017), which all find that capital inflows have a negative impact on the current account. Jansen (1995) finds that during 1970–1991, FDI flows to Thailand generated profit outflows that exceeded the increase in exports, and that the widening current account deficit during these years was greater than the subsequent increase in FDI inflows. Mencinger (2007) obtains similar results when addressing the impact of FDI inflows on the current accounts for eight European Union New Member States during 1999–2006. More precisely, he concludes that FDI inflows erode the current account by increasing deficits in the NPI account that are not offset by reductions in trade balance deficits.

The study from Rios Ballesteros and Goda (2017) is the most interesting for our purpose. This is because it estimates the net effect of natural resource-seeking FDI on the current account of 31 commodity-producing countries from Africa, Asia, Latin America and the Mideast during 1995–2013. The main finding of the authors is that "the average net effect of a 1% increase in natural resource-seeking FDI was a 0.23% decline in the current account (measured as percentage of GDP)" (ibid.:1). In line with the other two studies, the explanation for this finding is that the amount of profit repatriation exceeds the positive trade balance effect of commodity-related FDI.

The data provided in Figure 2.2 show that the same applies for the eight Latin American commodity-producing countries. Despite these countries' sharp rise in net exports after the start of the commodity price boom, their current account balances were invariably negative from 2007 onwards because of the substantial NPI payments that had to be made during the boom (approximately 4% of GDP on average). In other words, while the increase in capital inflows during the boom years was beneficial for these countries' trade balances, the negative impact on NPI payments was still stronger during most of this period (one reason for this being that the boom-related income increases led to an increase in the demand for imported goods that then lowered the trade surplus after 2006). Thus, contrary to the conventional view that natural resource-seeking FDI usually enhances the current account, the net effect of capital inflows on the current accounts of Latin American commodity producers was negative during most of the recent commodity boom. Indeed, the unfavourable current account situation continued to be aggravated even after the end of the boom in 2014, for, although NPI payments declined due to a lowering of the profits on foreign investments, the negative effect of the commodity price decline, in turn, had a stronger counter impact on these countries' trade balances, as can be seen in Figure 2.2.

The upshot of the above is that their current account problems carry serious implications for the long-run growth prospects of the Latin American commodity-producing countries. On the one hand, these countries need to attract

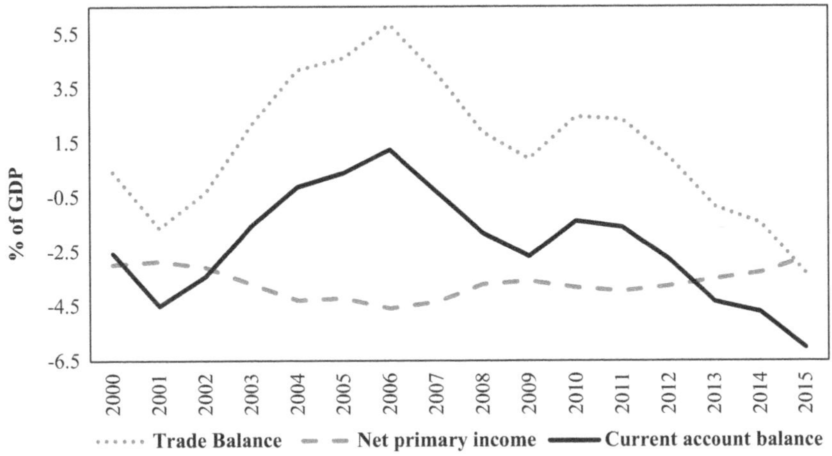

Figure 2.2 Current account balances of Latin American commodity-producing countries.

Source: WDI (2017).

Note: This figure shows the unweighted average trade balance, NPI balance and their sum for the countries Bolivia, Brazil, Chile, Colombia, Ecuador, Mexico, Peru and Venezuela.

continuous foreign capital inflows to finance their current account deficits that then entail an accumulation of foreign liabilities; on the other hand, the need to service these ever-growing volumes of foreign liabilities makes it harder and harder for these countries to improve their current account balance in the future. These deficit countries must therefore at some point reduce their imports to equilibrate their current accounts, which typically implies unfavourable income adjustments and investment contractions that then negatively impact their productivity growth prospects (as discussed in the second section). As if this is not all, it should be noted that an ongoing accumulation of external financial liabilities can ultimately provoke a balance of payments crisis when a commodity-producing country is no longer in a position to meet its mounting financial obligations. At the time of writing, Venezuela seems to be on a verge of such a balance of payment crisis, given that it has started to partially default on the payment of its foreign liabilities (El Tiempo 2017).

The link between the capital inflows and the Dutch Disease in Latin America

The interrelation among natural resource booms, industrialisation and long-term economic growth has been the subject of economic analysis for some time. One of the first studies that developed a theory related to the "natural resource curse" was that by Prebisch (1950). His theory stated that the long-term costs of concentrating on the production and export of raw materials and food are higher than the resultant benefits because over the longer term there is likely to be a deterioration in the terms of trade for primary products, thus making the import of industrial goods increasingly expensive and thus, in turn, making sustained high growth rates increasingly unlikely. The policy conclusion, which inevitably comes out of Prebisch's theory, is that it would be far preferable for a developing country to increase its industrial production and decrease its dependence on primary exports when it aspires to become a high-income country.

To a certain extent, this policy recommendation has been backed by the empirical findings of Sachs and Warner (1995, 2001) and Arezki and van der Ploeg (2011), who similarly report a negative relationship between resource abundance and economic growth. The dependence on natural resources can lead to lower productivity growth when it causes disincentives for human capital formation and less investment in state-of-the-art technologies (Gylfason 2001; Lederman & Maloney 2007). The volatility of natural resource prices has also been identified as an additional important explanatory factor (Blattman et al. 2007; Lederman & Maloney 2008; van der Ploeg & Poelhekke 2009) inasmuch as abrupt changes in natural resource prices are likely to cause fiscal and macroeconomic disequilibria (Gelb 1988), and to negatively impact the transparency and accountability of institutions, all of which can, in turn, foster corruption and rent-seeking (Williams 2011).[5]

The most widely discussed mechanism that can explain the poor long-run growth performance of many resource-rich countries is, however, the so-called "Dutch Disease" effect. This effect was first formalised by Corden and Neary (1982) and Corden (1984), who show that a boom in the natural resource sector tends to have a negative impact on the production of other tradable sectors (mainly the industrial sector) and a positive impact on the non-tradable sector. To be more precise, their model predicts that natural resource booms induce "spending" and "resource movement" effects. The latter effect is the movement of labour out of the lagging tradable sectors into the booming and non-tradable sector, a movement which typically lowers the production of the lagging sectors. The "spending" effect refers to an increase in demand for non-tradables, on the assumption that the extra income from the booming sector is mainly spent on non-tradable goods, an increase that then leads to an increase in non-tradable goods prices. Given that the tradable goods prices are not affected by these changes inasmuch as they depend on global prices, these two effects taken in conjunction lead to an appreciation of the REER and to a decline of the tradable-to-non-tradable output ratio.

The REER may be affected not only by these traditional "spending" and "relocation" effects, but also by massive inflows of external capital that are used to finance the exploitation of raw materials (Bresser Pereira 2009; Goda & Torres García 2013; Botta et al. 2016; Botta 2017). This is because the inflow of foreign capital fosters a nominal appreciation and enhances the expansion in aggregate demand for non-tradable goods and thus their prices (spending effect). The appreciation and the change in demand, in turn, also contribute to a shift of productive resources out of the tradable into the non-tradable goods sector (resource movement effect), leading to a decline in the tradable-to-non-tradable output ratio and to a decline in the manufacturing sector.[6]

Figure 2.3 suggests that such a scenario was at play in Latin American commodity-producing countries during the boom years. When the boom started and capital inflows to these countries increased, the REER of these countries also increased considerably from 88 index points in 2004 to 107 index points in 2013. During the same period, the tradable-to-non-tradable output ratio decreased from 44% to 36%, and the manufacturing value added decreased from 16.6% to 13.8% of GDP, with the result that manufacturing exports also decreased from 6.3% to 5.0% of GDP.

The more pronounced decline in the tradable-to-non-tradable output ratio compared to the decline in manufacturing value added and manufacturing exports can be explained by the fact that the participation of the manufacturing sector and manufacturing exports was already low prior to the boom. When one considers instead the decline in growth figures, the situation reverses: between 2003 and 2013, the tradable-to-non-tradable output ratio declined by 14%, whereas the manufacturing value added declined by 17% and manufacturing exports by an even larger percentage, 19%. In other words, the figures presented show that the recent commodity boom lead to the appearance of Dutch Disease effects in Latin America's commodity-producing economies, which further diminished an already weak manufacturing sector.[7]

Figure 2.3 (a) REER appreciation and the decline of the tradable-to-non-tradable output ratio and the manufacturing sector in Latin American commodity-producing countries. REER index (2010=100). (b) Tradable-to-non-tradable output ratio and manufacturing value added and exports (dotted line = Manf. value added; dashed line = Manf. exports).

Source: WDI (2017); CEPAL (2017).

Note: The figures present unweighted averages for the countries Bolivia, Brazil, Chile, Colombia, Ecuador, Mexico, Peru and Venezuela.

Our observation that capital inflows are partly responsible for the ongoing deindustrialisation in Latin American commodity-producing countries by virtue of being partly responsible for the REER appreciation and the decline of the tradable-to-non-tradable output ratio in these countries is in line with two recent country studies from Ibarra (2011) and Goda and Torres García (2015). Ibarra (2011) studied the impact of capital inflows on the REER of Mexico for the period from 1988 to 2008 and found that capital inflows in general, and FDI inflows in particular, helped to cause the strong appreciation of the Mexican Peso during this period, which, in turn, contributed to a slowdown in Mexico's industrial production growth. By contrast, Goda and Torres García (2015) studied the impact of capital inflows on the REER, the tradable-to-non-tradable output ratio and the manufacturing share as a percentage of GDP of Colombia's economy during the period from 2000 to 2012. They also find that capital inflows had an appreciating effect on Columbia's REER and a negative impact on its tradable and manufacturing sectors over this period. Most importantly, they found that FDI inflows into Colombia's mining and energy sector had an especially strong deindustrialisation effect.

It is important to note that such a commodity- and capital inflow-induced macroeconomic adjustment process is not per se harmful to long-run growth. Indeed, it can be the case that following the end of the boom, a sectoral recomposition takes place such that it can leave a country in a position similar to the one prior to the boom. In such a scenario, a commodity boom can be on balance beneficial, so that there "is no apparent economic reason to interfere with that adjustment process, except to smooth it over time" (Corbo & Hernández 1996:63). However, this case is generally not typical for developing countries, in that the lagging sectors in these countries do not usually recover from a decline (Krugman 1987), with the result that pre-existing technological gaps tend to widen and the long-term growth prospects of the affected countries tend to decline (Cherif 2013).

It seems that the latter general case applies as much to the Latin American economies as to the developing economies in the other regions of the world, given that the latest commodity boom contributed to a state of affairs in which, as an ECLAC report put it,

> [Latin America's] situation with production and exports, locked into an undiversified structure concentrated in natural resources and low-technology goods and with limited participation in international value chains, contrasts with its far more diversified import structure, in which higher-technology goods are strongly represented, especially intermediate inputs and capital goods essential to the functioning of the production and investment apparatus. External trade crises thus necessarily translate into slow growth and lower gross capital formation [and] its heavy dependence on raw material exports is an impediment to the structural shift towards more technology- and knowledge-intensive goods and services that is needed.
>
> (ECLAC 2015b:41)

Conclusions

This chapter has provided evidence showing that commodity boom-related capital inflows contributed to the appearance of the Dutch Disease effects in eight Latin American commodity-producing countries. Moreover, it has been shown that these capital inflows have led to substantial profit repatriations with the result that despite the increase in natural resource exports, the current accounts of Latin American commodity-producing countries have been negative for most of the boom years.

The negative impact of the capital inflows on the current accounts and manufacturing bases of these countries has shown that a resource-based export-led growth model was not in their case a viable and sustainable model. It might have otherwise had the boom-related foreign capital inflows triggered technology spillovers, fostered human capital formation or directly spurred employment levels. However, none of these things happened. As a result, once the boom came to an end, the Latin American commodity-producing countries experienced sharp contractions in their exports, income growth rates and fiscal incomes, all of which, in turn, forced them to engage in destabilising balance-of-payments adjustments. In the longer term, their continuing current account deficits and the decreasing diversification of their economies will make them very vulnerable to external demand and price shocks.

The cardinal lesson is that a strong manufacturing sector is more likely to achieve sustainable long-term growth because of its positive spillover effects, higher value added and innovation, as shown by the fact that nearly all developing countries that have managed to catch up with advanced industrialised countries are manufacturing exporters (Chang 2002; Rodrik 2007). Thus, it is vital for the long-term development of the Latin American region that its countries improve their innovative capacities and the productivity of their manufacturing sectors so as to compete more successfully in those world markets that are not related to the commodity sector.

Notes

1 NPI is net dividend and profit payments on foreign direct and portfolio investment (and compensations paid to non-resident workers, and receipts on reserve assets).
2 The boom is reflected by a 250% increase in commodity prices between 2003 and 2013 (IMF 2017a).
3 Between June 2014 and December 2015, commodity prices declined by more than 50% (IMF 2017a).
4 For simplicity reasons, we omit net unilateral transfers from our analysis.
5 Boschini et al. (2007:594) find that the "effect of resources is not determined by resource endowments alone, but rather by the interaction between the type of resources that a country possesses, and the quality of its institutions".
6 Similar effects can occur when a country receives large aid (see, e.g., Rajan & Subramanian 2011; Fielding & Gibson 2013), remittances (see, e.g., Bourdet & Falck 2006; Bayangos & Jansen 2011; Lartey et al. 2012) or non-boom-related capital inflows (see, e.g., Corbo & Hernández 1996; Cardarelli 2010; Benigno & Fornaro, 2014; Benigno et al. 2015).

7 The reason for the initial weakness of the manufacturing sector in these Latin American countries is that they are concentrating on the commodity sector since various decades (in line with the recommendation of the comparative advantage theory).

References

Aparecida Fernandes, E. & Carvalho Campos, A. (2008) 'Foreign Direct Investment and the Performance of Brazilian Exports', *Revista de Economia Politica*, 28(3), 490–509.

Arezki, R. & van der Ploeg, F. (2011) 'Do Natural Resources Depress Income per Capita?', *Review of Development Economics*, 15(3), 504–521.

Athukorala, P.-C. & Rajapatirana, S. (2003) 'Capital Inflows and the Real Exchange Rate: A Comparative Study of Asia and Latin America', *The World Economy*, 26(4), 613–637.

Auty, R.M. (1993) *Sustaining Development in Mineral Economies: The Resource Curse Thesis*, Routledge, London.

Bayangos, V.B. & Jansen, K. (2011) 'Remittances and Competitiveness: The Case of the Philippines', *World Development*, 39(10), 1834–1846.

Benigno, G. & Fornaro, L. (2014) 'The Financial Resource Curse', *Scandinavian Journal of Economics*, 116(1), 58–86.

Benigno, G., Converse, N., & Fornaro, L. (2015) 'Large Capital Inflows, Sectoral Allocation, and Economic Performance', *Journal of International Money and Finance*, 55, 60–87.

Blattman, C., Hwang, C., & Williamson, J.G. (2007) 'Winners and Losers in the Commodity Lottery: The Impact of Terms of Trade Growth and Volatility in the Periphery 1870–1939', *Journal of Development Economics*, 82(1), 156–179.

Boschini, A.D., Pettersson, J., & Roine, J. (2007) 'Resource Curse or Not: A Question of Appropriability', *Scandinavian Journal of Economics*, 109(3), 593–617.

Bosworth, B.P., Collins, S.M., & Reinhart, C.M. (1999) 'Capital FLOWS to Developing Economies: Implications for Saving and Investment', *Brookings Papers on Economic Activity*, 30(1), 143–180.

Botta, A. (2017) 'Dutch Disease-Cum-Financialization Booms and External Balance Cycles in Developing Countries', *Brazilian Journal of Political Economy*, 37(3), 459–477.

Botta, A., Godin, A., & Missaglia, M. (2016) 'Finance, Foreign (Direct) Investment and Dutch Disease: the Case of Colombia', *Economía Política*, 33(2), 265–289.

Bourdet, Y. & Falck, H. (2006) 'Emigrants' Remittances and Dutch Disease in Cape Verde', *International Economic Journal*, 20(3), 267–284.

Bresser Pereira, L.C. (2009) 'The Tendency of the Exchange Rate toward Overvaluation', in Bresser Pereira, L.C. (ed.), *Globalization and Competition*, Cambridge University Press, Cambridge, 125–147.

Brouthers, L.E., Werner, S., & Wilkinson, T.J. (1996) 'The Aggregate Impact of Firms' FDI Strategies on the Trade Balances of Host Countries', *Journal of International Business Studies*, 27(2), 359–373.

Brunnschweiler, C.N. (2008) 'Cursing the Blessings? Natural Resource Abundance, Institutions, and Economic Growth', *World Development*, 36(3), 399–419.

Calvo, G.A., Leiderman, L., & Reinhart, C.M. (1993) 'Capital Inflows and Real Exchange Rate Appreciation in Latin America: The Role of External Factors', *IMF Staff Papers*, 40(1), 108–151.

Cardarelli, R., Elekdag, S., & Kose, M.A. (2010) 'Capital Inflows: Macroeconomic Implications and Policy Responses', *Economic Systems*, 34(4), 333–356.

Chang, H.-J. (2002) *Kicking Away the Ladder: Development Strategy in Historical Perspective*, Anthem Press, London.

Cherif, R. (2013) 'The Dutch Disease and the Technological Gap', *Journal of Development Economics*, 101, 248–255.

Cieslik, A. & Hagemejer, J. (2014) 'Multinational Enterprises, Absorptive Capacity and Export Spillovers: Evidence from Polish Firm-level Data', *Review of Development Economics*, 18(4), 709–726.

Corbo, V. & Hernández, L. (1996) 'Macroeconomic Adjustment to Capital Inflows: Lessons from Recent Latin American and East Asian Experience', *World Bank Research Observer*, 11(1), 61–85.

Corden, W.M. (1984) 'Booming Sector and Dutch Disease Economics: Survey and Consolidation', *Oxford Economic Papers*, 36(3), 359–380.

Corden, W.M. & Neary, P. (1982) 'Booming Sector and De-Industrialisation in a Small Open Economy', *The Economic Journal*, 92(368), 825–848.

Davis, G.A. (1995) 'Learning to Love the Dutch Disease: Evidence from the Mineral Economies', *World Development*, 23(10), 1765–1779.

Dobbs, R., Oppenheim, J., Kendall, A., Thompson, F., Bratt, M., & van der Marel, F. (2013) *Reverse the Curse: Maximizing the Potential of Resource-driven Economies*, New York: McKinsey Global Institute.

ECLAC (2015a) *Foreign Direct Investment in Latin America and the Caribbean, 2015*, Economic Commission for Latin America and the Caribbean, Santiago de Chile.

ECLAC (2015b) *Latin America and the Caribbean in the World Economy. The Regional Trade Crisis: Assessment and Outlook*, Economic Commission for Latin America and the Caribbean, Santiago de Chile.

El Tiempo (2017) 'Venezuela entra en default parcial de su deuda', viewed 14 November 2017, from www.eltiempo.com/mundo/venezuela/agencia-de-standard-poors-declaro-a-venezuela-en-default-parcial-150996.

Fielding, D. & Gibson, F. (2013) 'Aid and Dutch Disease in Sub-Saharan Africa', *Journal of African Economies*, 22(1), 1–21.

Gelb, A. (1988) *Oil Windfalls: Blessing or Curse?* Oxford University Press, New York.

Goda, T. & Torres García, A. (2013) 'Overvaluation of the Real Exchange Rate and the Dutch Disease: The Colombian Case', CIEF Working Paper, 13–28.

Goda, T. & Torres García, A. (2015) 'Flujos de Capital, Recursos Naturales y Enfermedad Holandesa: el Caso Colombiano', *Ensayos sobre Política Económica*, 33(78), 197–206.

Gylfason, T. (2001) 'Natural Resources, Education and Economic Development', *European Economic Review*, 45(4/6), 847–859.

Hailu, D. & Kipgen, C. (2017) 'The Extractives Dependence Index (EDI)', *Resources Policy*, 51, 251–264.

Ibarra, C.A. (2011) 'Capital Flows and Real Exchange Rate Appreciation in Mexico', *World Development*, 39(12), 2080–2090.

IMF (2011) 'Recent Experiences in Managing Capital Inflows-Cross-Cutting Themes and Possible Policy Framework', International Monetary Fund, Washington.

IMF (2015) *Regional Economic Outlook. Western Hemisphere: Northern Spring, Southern Chills*, International Monetary Fund, Washington.

IMF (2017a) 'Primary Commodity Price Index', viewed 15 November 2017, from www.imf.org/external/np/res/commod/External_Data.xls.

IMF (2017b) *Regional Economic Outlook. Western Hemisphere Region: Tale of Two Adjustments*, International Monetary Fund, Washington.

Jansen, K. (1995) 'The Macroeconomic Effects of Direct Foreign Investment: The case of Thailand', *World Development*, 23(2), 193–210.

Krugman, P. (1987) 'The Narrow Moving Band, the Dutch Disease, and the Competitive Consequences of Mrs. Thatcher: Notes on Trade in the Presence of Dynamic Scale Economies', *Journal of Development Economics*, 27(1/2), 41–55.

Lartey, E., Mandelman, F., & Acosta, P. (2012) 'Remittances, Exchange Rate Regimes and the Dutch Disease: A Panel Data Analysis', *Review of International Economics*, 20(2), 377–395.

Lederman, D. & Maloney, W.F. (2007) *Natural Resources: Neither Curse Nor Destiny*, World Bank and Stanford University Press, Washington.

Lederman, D. & Maloney, W.F. (2008) 'In Search of the Missing Resource Curse', *Economía*, 9(1), 1–39.

Mencinger, J. (2007) 'Addiction to FDI and Current Account Balance', in Becker, J. & Weissenbacker, R. (eds.), *Dollarization, Euroization and Financial Instability*, Metropolis, Marburg, 109–126.

Mijiyawa, A.G. (2016) 'Does Foreign Direct Investment Promote Exports? Evidence from African Countries', *The World Economy*, early online view, doi:10.1111/twec.12465.

Orr, J. (1991) 'The Trade Balance Effects of Foreign Direct Investment in US Manufacturing', *Quarterly Review (Federal Reserve Bank of New York)*, 16(2), 63–76.

Pacheco, P. (2005) 'Foreign Direct Investment, Exports and Imports in Mexico', *The World Economy*, 28(8), 1157–1172.

Prebisch, R. (1950) 'The Economic Development of Latin America and its Principal Problems', *Economic Bulletin for Latin America*, 7(1), 1–22.

Rajan, R.G. & Subramanian, A. (2011) 'Aid, Dutch Disease, and Manufacturing Growth', *Journal of Development Economics*, 94(1), 106–118.

Rios Ballesteros, N. & Goda, T. (2017) 'Natural resource-seeking FDI Inflows and Current Account Deficits in Commodity-producing Developing Economies', CIEF Working Paper, No. 17-02.

Rodrik, D. (2007) 'How to Save Globalization from its Cheerleaders', *The Journal of International Trade and Diplomacy*, 1(2), 1–33.

Sachs, J.D. & Warner, A. (1995) 'Natural Resource Abundance and Economic Growth', NBER Working Paper No. 5398.

Sachs, J.D. & Warner, A. (2001) 'The Curse of Natural Resources', *European Economic Review*, 45(4–6), 827–38.

UNCTAD (1999) *World Investment Report: Foreign Direct Investment and the Challenge of Development*, United Nations, New York and Geneva.

UNCTAD (2007) *World Investment Report: Transnational Corporations, Extractive Industries and Development*, United Nations, New York and Geneva.

UNCTAD (2013) *World Investment Report: Global Value Chains: Investment and Trade for Development*, United Nations, New York and Geneva.

UNCTAD (2015) *World Investment Report: Reforming International Investment Governance*, United Nations, Geneva.

Van der Ploeg, F. & Poelhekke, S. (2009) 'Volatility and the Natural Resource Curse', *Oxford Economic Papers*, 61(4), 727–760.

WDI (2017) World Development Indicators Databank, retrieved at 15 November 2017 from http://databank.worldbank.org/data/reports.aspx?source=world-development-indicators.

Williams, A. (2011) 'Shining a Light on the Resource Curse: An Empirical Analysis of the Relationship between Natural Resources, Transparency, and Economic Growth', *World Development*, 39(4), 490–505.

3 Limits and perspectives of export-led growth model and foreign direct investment in Latin America and Mexico

Guadalupe Huerta Moreno and Luis Kato

In clear opposition to the economic strategies of the import substitution industrialisation (ISI) model, structural reforms implemented in Latin American countries since the last quarter of the twentieth century have sought to redefine the spaces in which the state and market operate, in order to lay the foundations for an economic liberalisation to be consolidated through an export-led growth model. These changes were made so that exports could lead the way in linking the Latin American region to international markets and the global economy.

In parallel, financialisation triggered a process of imbalanced economic integration with the global market, shifting away from productive investments in favour of financial ones. This process was accompanied by a series of economic reforms resting on two pillars: first, eliminating trade protection and opening up the market to force domestic companies to improve their productivity and thus increase their share of the export chains of higher value-added manufactured products; and second, attracting inflows of foreign capital in the form of foreign direct investment (FDI) to help overcome limited internal resources for the financing of investment and trade deficits in the balance of payments' current account.

While Asian states showed economic leadership and imposed strict financial regulation[1] with the emergence of economic liberalisation and the adoption of a development model, thus strengthening and diversifying exports that benefitted the linking of private local capital with FDI, in Latin America the structural reforms have taken a different route. Initially, in the 1980s, macroeconomic reforms focussed on ensuring balanced public finances, and, on a microeconomic level, steps were taken to address the distortions in specific sectors and in manufacturing that created internal and external imbalances. In that sense, privatisations and economic deregulation sought to reduce the state's direct involvement in economic issues. Trade liberalisation and financial reforms have subsequently deepened.

After the turn of the new millennium, with the third round of reforms, specific institutional frameworks were set up to ensure property rights, as a means of improving foreign capital's business opportunities. Labour costs were also reduced[2] as a means of increasing business competitiveness throughout the region, leading to the flexibilisation of the labour market. Finally, the structural reforms implemented after the 2008 crisis were focussed on promoting private investments in sectors related to the provision of basic public services and infrastructure development. Hence, the main driver for attracting FDI inflows originated in the reforms implemented by Latin American governments, many of which followed the recommendations made by multilateral financial organisations to the countries in this region. This guidance was designed to promote external financing, given the lack of internal financial resources, in order to boost the restructuring of the region's economy (IMF 2006, OECD 2007).

As a result, the waves of FDI to Latin America are linked to the rhythms of accumulation of the neoliberal strategy that drove trade liberalisation, financial deregulation and the export-led development model applied in the region. In that sense, the entry of capital reinforced the policy of fiscal discipline and limited the state's interference in economic activities. This situation increased the opportunities for external capital to enter traditional cross-border investment niches such as the manufacturing industry, as well as infrastructure developments, mass transport and basic services. Therefore, the strategy across virtually the entire region unequivocally promoted FDI inflows to Latin America for imposing a development based on economic openness and exports – an export-led growth model.

However, the market liberalisation reforms over the past 35 years, accompanied by policies applied to create an FDI-backed export base and the government's reduced role in regulation and economic activities, have increased the vulnerability of Latin American countries – not only to external financial or trade shocks, but also since financing has a limited capacity to support the building of industrial and trade structures more closely linked to the internal development of Latin American nations.

This has resulted in a number of questions being asked about the economic liberalisation model which, following the inflow of capital in the form of external financing, has led to the development of an export sector that is incapable of efficient coordination with internal productive structures, thus deepening the already-existing lack of articulation among industries in the region. This makes it essential to analyse the characteristics (the composition and destination) of FDI inflows to Latin America as being central to the economic debate, in order to understand why they have not significantly boosted productive capabilities, innovation and technological development, as required in highly competitive external markets.

Within this context, this chapter aims to show that the changes and amounts of the waves of FDI produced in Latin America and Mexico since the 1990s are more closely related to the substitution of domestic public and private capital for foreign financing than to the restructuring of local industry and the creation of an export platform that might allow the region as a whole to respond to the demands of dynamic, technology and knowledge-based global trade. While not seeking to downplay the international situation, this substitution of domestic capital for foreign capital derives from the particular characteristics of the liberalised, export-led economic model that has been imposed in Latin America, which is protected by the state's reduced involvement in regulatory and economic activities and the implementation of a series of structural reforms designed to attract FDI. Based on the above-mentioned considerations, the proposed scope of analysis allows us to gain an understanding of FDI's real contribution to supporting Latin American trade, which should reveal the structural diversification of the region's exports.

This chapter is divided into four sections. Following this introduction, the second section sets out the particular features of the various rounds of structural reforms linked to the liberal economic model applied in Latin America and Mexico, to show its impact on the export-led growth strategy and the growing acceptance of FDI in the region. In the third section, we analyse the composition and changes to FDI in Latin America and Mexico since 2000. This makes it possible to describe its limitations as a driver of growth, which, to serve a useful purpose, must be based on reindustrialisation – non-existent in Latin America's export model strategy – and the expansion of internal markets, which would place it in a stronger position to handle different external shocks, and to ensure sustained and long-term growth. In the final section, we detail the chapter's main conclusions.

Structural reforms and adjustments in Latin America and Mexico

In the early 1990s, the economic conditions of the Latin American region underwent far-reaching changes as a result of the previous decade's structural reforms, which obliged governments to reduce their involvement in economic activities, giving way to private capital and leading to economic liberalisation (Rodrik 1999, CEPAL 2000a, OECD 2005). During this period, the strategy for macroeconomic stability was maintained by implementing new structural reforms focussed on modernising economies. Efforts to control the public deficit intensified and government bodies were successfully restructured, with further rounds of privatisations and cuts to public programmes and investments. At the same time, efforts were constantly being made to expand financial liberalisation and deregulation for the purpose of improving access to different options of external financing, either in the form of credits, official development aid, or additional inflows of FDI. The reforms and improved business environment were essential to attract the necessary external funding to help develop the export platforms required by multinational corporations (MNCs) (Palley 2011). FDI is the most stable source of external resources, as opposed to portfolio investments that are highly volatile due to their lower entry and exit costs, a similar pattern to bank financing and share placements (see Figure 3.1).

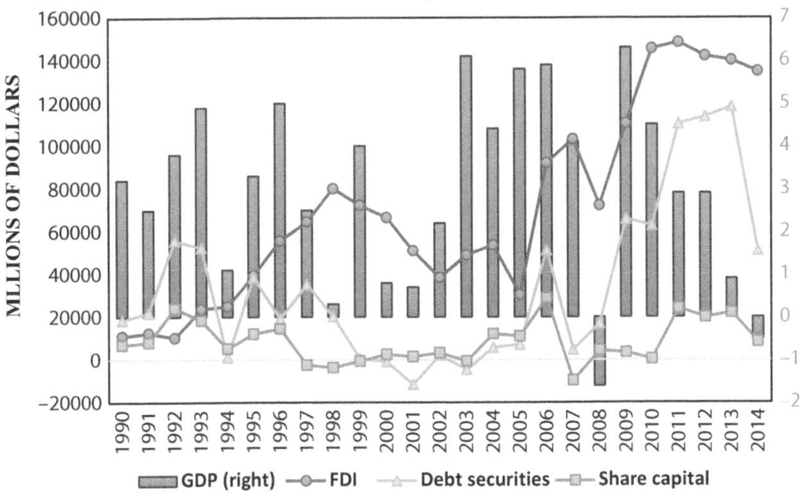

Figure 3.1 Capital inflows to Latin America and the Caribbean.
Source: Authors' calculations based on data from CEPALSTAT.

We should highlight that during this period, two related trajectories emerged in connection to the growth of the Latin American region's share in international trade. The first, as in the case of Mexico, was noted for being a debt-led growth model, where stabilisation and liberalisation policies opened the door for a large inflow of debt capital that supported private consumption. The second refers to a weak export-led growth model, as observed in Argentina and Brazil, where external imbalances did not create substantial changes in the traditional export structure (Hein & Mundt 2012, Lavoie & Stockhammer 2012). As a result, stark contrasts exist between Latin American countries in terms of their production and the type of assets with which they participate in international trade.

In Mexico, during the first five years of the new millennium, the percentage weighting of high-tech manufacturing exports increased (25.1%), as well as the mid-tech sectors (36.5%), and primary products (17.0%). In Mercosur,[3] the highest export percentages were found in primary goods (35.5%), mid-tech manufacturing (25%) and manufacturing based on the use of natural resources (23%). In the Andean Community,[4] exports were focussed mainly on primary products (71.3%), manufacturing based on the use of natural resources (12.1%) and mid-tech manufacturing (6.6%) (Sánchez 2009).

Therefore, as a result of the structural reforms and their emphasis on economic liberalisation and attracting FDI, in the face of the progress of an export-led model centred on higher value-added exports that require significant technological progress, the exports of raw materials and manufactured products containing a high content of raw materials continued to be predominant.[5] Therefore, given changes in demand and their international prices, the terms of exchange tend to be less favourable for the region. In that context, Latin America's trade with the international market only led to increased revenues through the sale of traditional export products such as raw or manufactured materials that use primary products as their main component. And although, in Mexico's case, high-tech manufactured products already represented 25% of total exports by type of good, this did not improve the country's trade deficit.

Under these conditions, the structural reforms at the start of the new century were focussed first on increasing the efficiency of economies in the face of external shocks, second on protecting the property rights of private investors and third on implementing labour reforms for extreme flexibilisation for the benefit of capital. This is because the region's export bias made countries more vulnerable to the import performance of developed countries, especially in economies whose foreign trade is concentrated on manufacturing, assembly, foodstuffs, minerals and metals. But also, because maintaining foreign capital inflows entailed offering greater reductions in labour costs and creating legal frameworks that ensured investors' property rights in the case of possible disputes (expropriations, rulings, mediations, etc.) that might arise with FDI recipient countries. This resulted in Bilateral Investment Promotion and Protection Agreements (BIPAs), legal agreements negotiated between the FDI recipient countries and investors (Granato & Nahuel 2007). These agreements are designed to afford legal protection to foreign investors in the manufacturing sector, and include issues related to intellectual property, most-favoured nation treatment, compensations due to expropriations and advantageous labour conditions for big capital.

The export orientation of the dominant economic model has produced a differentiated trading structure between, on the one hand, the north-centre (Mexico and Central America) of the Latin American region, which is more closely interconnected to the US economy with exports mainly of intermediate and assembled goods, and on the other, the South American block whose export platform shows a combination of mid-tech manufactured goods, goods based on the use of natural resources and natural resources, with diversification towards Europe and the Asian region. Hence, the value of the region's export basket changes depending on variations in international prices and sales volumes in connection to the demand of developed countries (the US and European Union countries) and emerging economies (China and India). This fact deepened the transmission channel of foreign trade in Latin America.

Furthermore, the lack of domestic savings means that the coverage of regional trade imbalances meant that between 2007 and 2014, this increased from US$8.6 to US$188.8 billion, and this requires permanent inflows of

FDI. Therefore, countries' margin for manoeuvre to finance their trade deficit, affected by the outflow of capital and/or temporary drop in foreign investments, weakened regional growth forecasts. Therefore, capital outflow in the region since 2009 caused currency devaluations in several Latin American countries, alongside reduced exports and problems of financing the external deficit, which contributed to a relatively low annual average GDP growth (1.7% between 2009 and 2016). This regional growth was lower than that seen between 2003 and 2007, when prices of raw materials and foodstuffs increased in international markets (CEPAL 2000b, CEPAL 2009, CEPAL 2016a).

In the face of weak growth compounded by financial restrictions, the wave of structural reforms promoted to attract FDI after the 2008 crisis sought to diversify investments in sectors providing basic public services, social infrastructure[6] and financial markets. This period was notable for the search for investments in traditional FDI sectors in Latin America that was complemented by the promotion of projects linked to the environment (Penfold & Curbelo 2013). The premise was that these investments would help raise competitiveness, productivity and growth in the region – despite the fact that the evolution of regional GDP, the reliance on external finance and the concentration of exports into low and medium value-added manufactured goods, raw materials and minerals show that the export-led and externally financed development model has produced scant benefits for Latin American countries.

Although some changes have taken place in sectors receiving FDI, these inflows have neither been aimed towards developing an export base with solid backward integration, nor focussed on the development of high-tech activities, an essential aspect to overcome the current pattern of external trade in the region. In a context of financialised accumulation, this mainly benefits large private capital that operates in oligopolistic industrial and financial structures. Therefore, under the current liberalisation regime, FDI has been focussed on making the most of business opportunities created through economic restructuring and structural reforms applied in the region over the past three and a half decades.

FDI in Latin America and Mexico

Since the end of the twentieth century, the accelerated increase in commodity prices attracted large FDI inflows to Latin America, deepening the export-led growth model. Although the 2008 crisis temporarily reduced these amounts, they rose again until 2014, when the USA reverted its crisis policies and launched a new economic strategy to restructure global trade flows, which led to an increase in its target interest rate and the promotion of repatriating the flow of its investments.

In that context, and in the framework of the export-led, open economy development model that revolves around FDI, economic growth in Latin

America and Mexico presented two contrasting trends: one between the years 2000 and 2007, a time of strong economic growth in most countries; and the other, a period which began in 2008 and continues until the time of writing (2017), which has seen weaker growth. The growth during the first period can be explained by two factors that include the arrival of capital associated with exceptional conditions of external liquidity, the sharp rise in the global cost of raw materials and foodstuffs, and the high levels of remittances being sent by Latin American migrants back to their countries of origin (an important factor for economies in close geographical proximity to the USA).

A new development during this period was the ability to generate rapid growth at the same time as creating a current account surplus and, consequently, a net outflow of resources. This combination, characteristic of East Asia's tiger economies, has no precedent in the region's history, particularly in the case of South America (Ocampo 2007). This set of economic phenomena increased the revenues of countries specialising in the agro-industrial and manufacturing sectors, as in the cases of Brazil and Argentina, or in countries focussed on the export of metals such as Chile and Colombia. Mexico's growth during this period can be accounted for by the significant increase in automobile manufacturing and the consolidation of productive chains, linking the Mexican and US economies via import-export processes of manufactured products.

The growth seen between 2000 and 2008 in Latin America and the Caribbean strengthened further with the large and increasing FDI inflows, but there were wide variations in the destination structure and amounts directed towards the different countries in the region depending on the predominant value chain in the recipient country. In terms of trade, between 2003 and 2007, the average annual growth rate in the volume of exports of the region's goods and services was 6.7%, far higher than the amount recorded in the previous five-year period, when it only reached 3.2%. This period was notable for FDI in the automotive industry and in manufacturing in general, sectors which not only bolstered the growth of assembly plants, but also made it possible to attract investments to local industries partially connected to global production chains. At the same time, there was a notable increase in FDI towards the natural resources sector, reaching 17% of total FDI inflows to Latin America.

However, since 2009, FDI inflows began to decrease sharply. Between 2008 and 2009, they saw an absolute fall of US$30.8 billion, from US$103 billion to US$72.2 billion. This indicates that despite economic restructuring focussed on stabilising economies and improving the business climate, the permanence of capital in the region is determined by the international situation, a fact that prevents the development of long-term investments in the industrial sector, with which significant progress can be made in high value-added activities. Towards the end of 2015, CEPAL (Comisión Económica para América Latina y el Caribe) reported a decrease in FDI stocks in the region and an even greater fall in the profitability of investments. As a result, earnings as a percentage of FDI stocks peaked in 2011 before decreasing to 5% in 2015, the lowest level in 13 years (CEPAL 2016b).

Since 2008, the combination of decreasing trade as a result of recession in developed countries and the drop-off in demand from the fastest growing emerging economies such as China and India lowered the value of Latin America's exports. Therefore, the fall in prices and the lower volumes of exports reduced revenue in the region and dented growth prospects. The following year, in 2009, FDI to the region fell by 29%, before later bouncing back to grow by 53% in 2010 and 39% in 2011. However, between 2013 and 2016, FDI has been falling in Latin America by approximately –3.4%. This trend reflects the decreasing importance of some natural resource-intensive activities (mining) as an FDI destination and highlights the growing importance of external investments in spaces that had hitherto been the preserve of the state, as in the case of economic and social infrastructure. This explains the increasing FDI in the service sectors, particularly basic infrastructure, telecommunications, renewable energies and retail trade.

Hence, the composition of FDI in Latin America is partly a result of business opportunities created in the 1990s with privatisations, the opening of the financial, telecommunications and public services sectors (electricity and water). Once the raw materials price increase levelled out in 2009, there was a slowdown in the flow of capital towards natural-resource extraction in Latin America and the Caribbean regions, and the FDI's sectorial composition was modified. Therefore, after 2010, the proportion of FDI in the natural resources sector began to decrease, falling from an 18% share to a 13% share of the total between the years 2010 and 2015. By contrast, in 2016, its contribution to manufactured goods and services represented 40% and 47% of the total, respectively. On this issue, CEPAL warned:

> In countries where extractive industries have traditionally attracted foreign capital, there was a greater change in structure by sector. In Colombia, for example, FDI in natural resources fell from 48% to just 17% of the total between 2010–2015. The share of natural resources in Brazil reached its maximum level of 31% in 2010 and then decreased constantly, until bottoming out at 16% in 2016. In Mexico, natural resources represented just 5% in 2016, at the same time as the importance of manufacturing increased, attracting 61% of FDI. The long-term growth of FDI in manufacturing, mainly concentrated in Mexico and Brazil, is linked to the development of the automotive industry and disruptive technological changes in the sector. Meanwhile, in Colombia as well as Central America and the Dominican Republic, services have become the main recipients of FDI, which represented a share of 69% and 65%, respectively.
>
> (2016b:39)

It is worth mentioning that the FDI in the services sector accounted for 49.9% of the total in Brazil in 2015, compared to 47% and 64% for Mexico and Central America, respectively.

Despite the economic reforms and imposition of an export-led development model that needed to include a new phase of reindustrialisation supported by FDI, in Latin America the industry's share of GDP in 2016 was 11.68% on average, a value that varied, depending on the size of the economies and how each country was positioned in industry global value chains (services and natural resources).

In the past decade, we should note that FDI has entered Latin American countries through mergers and acquisitions between national and multinational companies, which explains why the reinvestment of profits and loans between companies has formed two of the main channels for FDI resources in Latin America. This has not produced enough investment to support long-term gains in productivity in Latin American economies, since the FDI amounts are not converted into new developments or investments in technology, but instead come to depend on the revenue streams obtained in recipient countries and the purchase of highly profitable local companies using foreign capital through mergers and acquisitions.

Despite the fact that between 1990 and 2016 in Latin America, FDI inward stocks by region and economy[7] saw continuous growth, this was subject to global economic cycles, increasing during booms and contracting at times of crisis (see Figure 3.2). Therefore, although the economic stagnation experienced in the region after the 2008 crisis can be traced back to various root causes, the accumulation of FDI stocks is associated with the

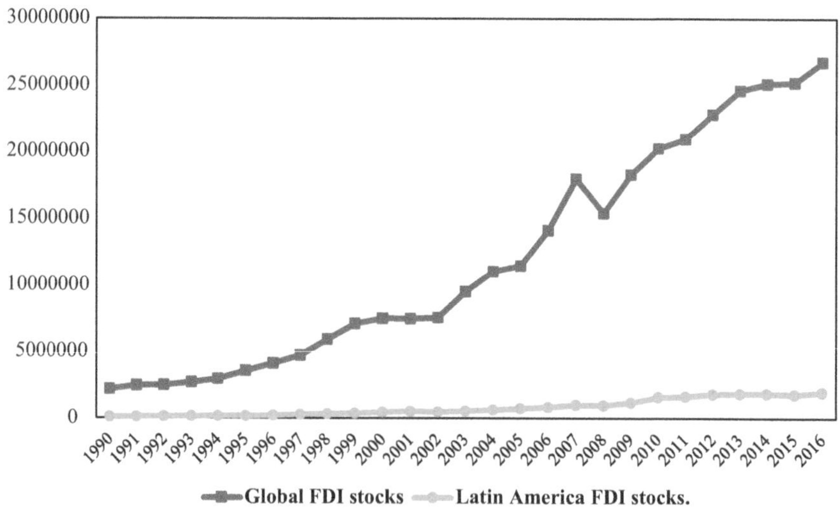

Figure 3.2 FDI stocks (millions of dollars).
Source: Authors' calculations based on data from UNCTAD (2017).

conclusion of the stage of externalising products and services processes to global production value chains that came about when the large corporations began to suffer large losses. Hence, there has been no significant change in the share of the total FDI stocks in Latin America, which could indicate that the continent is undergoing an extraordinary accumulation process.

Therefore, the region's share as a recipient of FDI flows compared to the global total has remained relatively stable and it is also insignificant in relation to the total international volume. In other words, FDI inflows to Latin America are oriented towards economic sectors that enjoy significant competitive advantages and/or are linked to large, transnational value chains. In this sense, the decline in raw materials prices and the falling global trade volumes were the main channel for transmitting the crisis to countries in the Latin American region. This situation explains the strong increase in the trade deficit in the years 2008 and 2009, while, after 2010, the decline in the flow of FDI was mainly due to the particularly low investment amounts linked to cross-border mergers and acquisitions in the region, though also to the falling reinvestment of earnings. In fact, the slowing economic growth in various Latin American countries directly affected companies' earnings.

This context explains why the three most important Latin American economies in terms of their size (Brazil, Mexico and Argentina), which have a clearly defined manufacturing and trade specialisation by sector (automotive industry, intermediate goods and agricultural products), concentrate 60.5% of the region's total FDI. Brazil and Mexico have 56% of the total FDI stocks, although the significance of this percentage is relative, if compared to what it represents in terms of the global FDI stocks (with values barely reaching 2.3% and 2.2%, respectively); both countries receive just 4.5% of total FDI stocks.

Furthermore, approximately 90% of FDI flows are created by large MNCs that hold power over broad swathes of the global marketplace, with enormous financial resources at their disposal and an extraordinary level of expenditure on research and development, giving them competitive advantages that local companies find hard to match. (UNCTAD 2017). This process was strengthened with structural reforms that stimulated a business climate, deregulation processes, property rights protection and labour reforms, which together influenced the integration of Latin American countries into global production chains, led by a multinational, divided among countries and economies of differing strengths.

In that sense, investment decisions in FDI recipient countries can be explained on the basis of the demands of capital and multinationals that are looking for low-cost factors in emerging or less developed economies, producing an unequal integration that exposes the origin of the intra-industrial flows and intra-firm trade linked to the imports of parts and intermediate supplies from subsidiaries to their parent companies or other, more autonomous and developed subsidiaries. This behavioural trend among MNCs has been observed since the first decade of the new millennium, when these companies' subsidiaries became a complementary part of their production and distribution networks. These were not only integrated regionally and globally, but also modified their activities based on the situation of the economies in which they were located (UNCTAD 2000, Mogrovejo 2005).

Therefore, the nominal amount of FDI inflows to the Latin American region in 2016 was comparable to 2010 figures, while various countries experienced strong reductions. In other words, the behaviour of FDI is highly procyclical in relation to international trade, which decelerated since early 2011, after the fast recovery made following the crisis at the end of the last decade. In this way, the effects of the crisis were deep because of the connection with the region's export performance.

However, if we consider, on the one hand, that economic restructuring has had a limited impact on producing sustained and long-term growth in Latin America, due to its emphasis on market liberalisation and macroeconomic stability to ensure the valorisation of capital invested in the financial markets, and, on the other, that the region's weak economic recovery affects transnational earnings, it becomes difficult to achieve increased FDI inflows to sectors that strengthen internal markets. Furthermore, the lowering profitability of investments in key sectors such as telecommunications can reduce the interest of foreign investors. In brief, the reduced profitability of FDI can mean that MNCs' investments can become insufficient in areas that are vitally important for reducing poverty, such as basic infrastructure.

In that sense, despite its importance as a source of financing, FDI can have only a meagre impact on innovation and developing technical knowledge at a local level; this prevents Latin American economies from making progress in terms of productivity and competitiveness in relation to other countries (CEPAL 2016b). This can be largely explained by the lack of linkages between MNCs and local companies, because FDI inflows to Latin America are essentially export oriented, with very weak production chains to integrate local industry. Governments in Latin America can therefore be said to have failed to develop integral policies of industrial development that could help stimulate technology transfer through FDI, or that demand a broader inclusion of local content through licenses, technical cooperation and joint ventures with FDI. Due to these shortcomings, none of the positive effects ascribed to FDI have been fully realised, especially since mergers and acquisitions do not introduce new technological capabilities, but instead tend to concentrate market power. For example, FDI in capital-intensive mining activities has very limited linkage or employment effects (Kwame & Chowdhury 2017).

Another important example are South American countries that specialise in the production of primary products, such as oils and minerals (Bolivia, Ecuador, Venezuela), and which have close trade relationships with China.

These have been seriously affected by the sluggish growth of the global economy. In this case, FDI inflows to South America fell sharply (14% in 2016, rising to just 101 billion dollars), with a concomitant decrease in GDP which, in 2016, was –2.4, compared to –1.3 in 2015. Furthermore, in those economies, in mid-2016, Gross Fixed Capital Formation (GFCF) and private consumption began to contract, with a knock-on effect on aggregate demand in the subregion. In that context, the average annual fall of 16% in the price of crude oil and the 5% decrease in minerals and metals prices caused a major shock in the terms of exchange which undermined regional GDP and, in turn, the outlook for consumption and investment (UNCTAD 2017).

Although the share of total accumulated FDI stocks has remained at the same level compared to global levels, important changes can be seen in regard to the impact of the total stocks in regard to the GDP of the region and of each individual country. For Latin America as a whole, in 1994 the share of total stocks of FDI as a percentage of GDP was 9.1% and in 2016 it rose to 39.3%. In South America, during the same period, these coefficients amounted to 9.0% and by 36.3%, respectively. In Mexico, these values were 7.5% and 45.3%, respectively. In 2016, however, the countries with the highest share of FDI to GDP were Chile (96.6%) and Colombia (58.2%), and in Brazil and Mexico, this ratio amounted to 35% and 45.3%, respectively (UNCTAD 2017). These data reveal that in view of falling public investment and a contraction of internal markets (due to economic restructuring in favour of private capital), FDI has filled in the gaps left by the state following the implementation of policies and reforms to modify the accumulation model. This marked the shift away from the productive capacity-led development model, and the strengthening of internal markets, towards the model that favoured global production chains and commercialisation of the open economy's financialised model.

In that transition, the performance of the region's economy shows that foreign participation in investments failed to trigger an accumulation that could support sustained growth; instead, it replaced FDI-recipient sectors without creating significant increases in productive jobs that could help reduce unemployment levels, the number of jobs in the informal sector, concentration of income and, therefore, the inequality that is rife throughout Latin America.

In terms of FDI's role in productive investment, it is noted that annual variations are significant and related to the levels of prevailing economic activity in the region, highlighting significant differences between countries (see Figure 3.3). Chile has the largest FDI share in the average GFCF, as well as in the FDI/GDP coefficient; and Bolivia has a low share in this latter indicator, but a high FDI/GFCF share. This means that FDI in countries with a high FDI/GFCF indicator and a low FDI/GDP share is focussed on priority sectors for their economic growth and that have not been able to expand accumulation sectors for FDI.

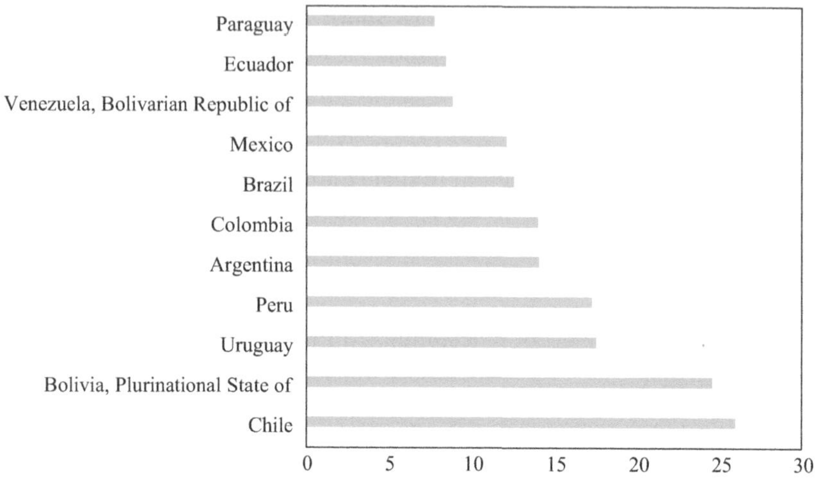

Figure 3.3 Average FDI in terms of GFCF, by country.
Source: Authors' calculations using data from UNCTAD (2017).

Meanwhile, in Mexico and the other Latin American countries, the share of FDI in GFCF is very low, indicating that it has not stimulated economic growth. Since 2010, this phenomenon has gained strength since cross-border mergers and acquisitions were the main sources of FDI for Latin America. From 1990 to 2010, Mexico and Brazil have been the countries with the largest number of mergers and acquisitions, followed by Chile, Argentina, Colombia and Peru. The raw materials sector was the most active acquirer of such investment strategies, and between 2012 and 2016, it accounted for almost 40% of total inbound mergers and acquisitions, with 839 deals worth a total of 43 billion dollars. In terms of deal values, the energy and power sector led the field with US$60.9 billion (see Baker & Mackenzie 2016).

Of the total FDI inflows to Mexico between 2000 and April 2017 (US$473 billion), 47.1% were new investments and 52.9% reinvested earnings, and inter-company accounts with foreign participation (Banxico 2017). For Brazil in 2016, 56.9% were new investments and 43.1% related to reinvested earnings and inter-company accounts with foreign participation. That same year, the figures for Colombia and Chile were 45.8% and 54.2% for new investments, and 48.6% and 51.4% for reinvested earnings and inter-company accounts with foreign participation, respectively. The advantage for private capital is that the acquisition of pre-existing assets allows it to expand companies' operations, without needing to inject additional capital and technology, or to expand existing production plants. Hence, they only make a very limited immediate contribution to economic growth, employment and consumption. This supports the idea that the base of FDI growth is earnings made in recipient countries and, therefore, the behaviour of FDI accumulation is highly cyclical. In times of crisis, FDI can help exacerbate economic downturns because, in the face of exchange-rate risks, MNCs' earnings can slump, leading to a massive repatriation of their profits, causing a crash in the volume of foreign currency and therefore in exchange rates.

This indicates, first, that most FDI is concentrated in sectors linked to the export of natural resources and/or service-based commodities. Second, that FDI targeted at developing productive structures in Latin American countries, and consequently transforming export platforms in nontraditional sectors, remains scarce. Third, that the recent dynamic of FDI is closely connected to the opportunities created by changes in government policies and reforms designed to offer concessions or to support private-public partnership investment projects for infrastructure and services, as well as in capital-intensive sectors such as oil, gas and mining. And, fourth, that the exhaustion of accumulation factors that lead to a recomposition of FDI inflow characteristics (privatisations, global production chains, freely convertible currencies and exchange-rate stability) further cemented its connection to the dominant cyclical process, which is currently intensifying crises and damaging growth prospects in Latin American countries.

Conclusions

The structural reforms applied in Latin America have had different objectives, from economic stabilisation and the redefinition of spheres of accumulation benefitting private capital, to the structural modernisation of economies and the imposition of an open economic model tied to the creation of a broad export base. This is all framed by the domination of external sources of financing, mainly FDI. However, until now, the results of this strategy have been disappointing when compared to the initial expectations for economic growth.

As part of the economic liberalisation and the export-led growth model, FDI continues to be the main source of financing of the current account deficit with investments concentrated in the most profitable sectors, mostly those areas in which the state no longer participates directly or has deregulated in order to create opportunities for private business. This largely explains the process of cross-border mergers and acquisitions in Latin America, which, apart from helping to increase the existing economic concentration in Latin America, further strengthens the rentier approach of investments, which are not targeted at increasing production capacity that improves the connectedness of local companies as a whole.

The situation described above has been detrimental to the performance of Latin American economies because they are more exposed to financial and trade transmission channels. On the one hand, by failing to tackle the weakening of internal demand, driven by lower private consumption and the shrinking of the internal market, there will be an even stronger effect on investment in the production of national content, as well as in the services sector. Compounded by a more drastic fall in prices for the region's main basic export products, this situation will probably delay investment projects in the mining industry and slow down the reinvestment of earnings. On the other hand, in a crisis – when profits and interests are repatriated – economies become more fragile and widespread capital flight poses a risk to the financial stability of the countries in the region.

To summarise, the main evidence about the recent behaviour of FDI in Latin America is not only that it is concentrated geographically and by sectors, but also that it is not as stable as supposed by the prevailing orthodoxy. FDI tends to be procyclical, amplifying the fluctuations of economic cycles, while also bringing with it financial filtrations resulting from the repatriation of earnings. In that sense, the search for greater benefits based on reforms designed to attract greater FDI inflows could lead to insufficient investments in crucial areas for the sustainable development of industry or infrastructure improvements. Therefore, despite its importance as a source of financing, FDI may have a meagre effect on innovation and increasing the knowledge economy locally, thus continuing to prevent progress in productivity, regional industrial transformation and long-term growth.

Notes

1 By maintaining control over investments and associations with foreign capital, the state could first make a direct impact on creating vertical production chains, and then horizontal ones to expand and diversify their export platforms.
2 Some of the labour reforms implemented in Latin America include pension system reforms, new types of individual contracts as opposed to collective contracts in both the private and public sectors, changes to retirement and redundancy schemes.
3 Member countries of Mercosur are Argentina, Brazil, Paraguay, Uruguay and Bolivia; associate members are Chile, Colombia, Ecuador, Guyana, Peru and Surinam.
4 The Andean Community member countries are Bolivia, Colombia, Ecuador and Peru.
5 Mexico is the exception, as it mainly exports manufactured goods (machinery and equipment).
6 Particularly important in this regard is infrastructure related to drinking water, water treatment and drainage systems, as well as the promotion of foreign investments in education. These activities have a high social impact, and the consequences could potentially be explosive if they are promoted under a free market approach.
7 FDI inward stocks by region and economy compiled by UNCTAD (2017) are presented at book cost or historical cost to reflect prices at the time the investment was made. For many economies, FDI stocks are estimated by either accumulating FDI flows over a period of time or adding flows to an FDI stock that has been obtained for a particular year from national official sources or the International Monetary Fund data series on assets and liabilities of direct investment.

References

Banxico (2017) *Sistema de Información Económica*. Available at www.banxico.org.mx/SieInternet/consultarDirectorioInternetAction.do?accion=consultarCuadro&idCuadro=CE131&sector=1&locale=es. Accessed 26 November 2017.

Baker & Mackenzie (2016) *Mergers and Acquisitions in Europe and Latin America 2016*. Available at www.bakermckenzie.com/-/media/files/insight/publications/2017/02/2016-europe-latam-ma/bk_eur_mergersacquisitionreport_2016.pdf?la=en.

CEPAL (2000a) *Crecer con estabilidad. El financiamiento del desarrollo en el nuevo contexto internacional*, Comisión Económica para América Latina, Santiago de Chile.

CEPAL (2000b) *Balance preliminar de las economías de América Latina y el Caribe*, Comisión Económica para América Latina, Santiago de Chile.

CEPAL (2009) *Balance preliminar de las economías de América Latina y el Caribe*, Comisión Económica para América Latina, Santiago de Chile.

CEPAL (2016a) *Balance preliminar de las economías de América Latina y el Caribe*, Comisión Económica para América Latina, Santiago de Chile.

CEPAL (2016b) *La Inversión Extranjera Directa en América Latina y el Caribe*, Comisión Económica para América Latina, Santiago de Chile.

Granato, L. & Nahuel, C. (2007) 'La Protección Internacional del Inversor Extranjero a través de los Acuerdos Bilaterales de Inversión', *TENDENCIAS, Revista de la facultad de Ciencias Económicas y Administrativas*, Universidad de Nariño, 8(2), 43–66.

Hein, E. & Mundt, M. (2012) *Financialisation and the Requirements and Potentials for Wage-led Recovery. A Review Focussing on the G20*, Project 'New perspectives on wages and economic growth: the potentials of wage-led growth', Conditions of Work and Employment Series, 37, ILO, Geneva.

IMF (2006) *Growth and Reforms in Latin America: A Survey of Facts and Arguments*, IMF Working Paper, WP/06/210.

Kwame, J. & Chowdhury, A. (2017) *Coping with Foreign Direct Investment*, viewed 3 October 2017, from www.networkideas.org/news-analysis/2017/11/coping-with-foreign-direct-investment.

Lavoie, M. & Stockhammer, E. (2012) *Wage-led Growth: Concept, Theories and Policies*, International Labour Office, Geneva.

McKenzie, B. (2016) *Mergers and Acquisitions in Europe and Latin America 2016*, viewed 25 October 2017, from www.bakermckenzie.com/-/media/files/insight/publications/2017/02/2016-europe-latam-ma/bk_eur_mergersacquisitionreport_2016.pdf?la=en.

Mogrovejo, J.A. (2005) 'Factores Determinantes de la Inversión extranjera Directa en algunos países de Latinoamérica', *Estudios Económicos de Desarrollo Internacional*, AEEADE, 5(2), 63–90.

Ocampo, J.A. (2007) 'La Macroeconomía de la Bonanza Económica Latinoamericana', *Revista de la CEPAL*, 93, 7–29.

OECD (2005) *Handbook on Economics Globalisation Indicator*, OCDE, Paris.

OECD (2007) *Export Processing Zones: Past and Future Role in Trade and Development*, Trade Policy Working Paper No. 53.

Palley, T. (2011) 'The Rise and Fall of Export-led Growth', *Levy Economics Institute*, Working Paper No. 675, Annandale-on-Hudson, NY.

Penfold, M. & Curbelo, J.L. (2013) *Hacia una nueva agenda en inversión extranjera directa. Tendencias y realidades en américa latina*, Banco de Desarrollo de América Latina. Serie Políticas Públicas y Transformación Productiva no. 10, CAF, Caracas, viewed 3 December 2017, from http://scioteca.caf.com/handle/123456789/381.

Rodrik, D. (1999) *The New Global Economy and Developing Countries: Making Openness Work*, Overseas Development Council Policy Essay, 24, John Hopkins University Press, New York.

Sánchez, D. (2009) 'El Modelo Económico en América Latina desde los Años Noventa hasta la Gran Crisis. ¿Un modelo razonable o un fracaso liberal?' *Revista CIDOB d'Afers Internacionals*, No. 85–86),133–155.

UNCTAD (2000) *Cross-border Mergers and Acquisitions and Development, United Nations*, Geneva, viewed 13 October 2017, from http://unctad.org/en/Docs/wir2000_en.pdf.

UNCTAD (2017) *World Investment Report. Investment and the Digital Economy*, United Nations, Geneva, viewed 28 September 2017, from http://unctad.org/en/PublicationsLibrary/wir2017_en.pdf.

4 Internationalisation, big corporations and capital accumulation in the Latin American experience

Jorge Bustamante

The 1960s' crisis in industrial profitability generated profound transformations in the productive sector; this, together with the financial sector's activation that offered an alternative for valorisation, boosted processes of the internationalisation of capital. Since then, the productive sector has been characterised by a series of cost-reduction strategies to deal with tough international competition, mainly from Europe and Japan, in an environment increasingly dominated by short-term financial profit-taking.

The large non-financial corporations (LNFCs) have had to restructure their activities and cut costs, particularly labour costs, effected mainly by relocating productive processes and gradually re-specialising production.[1] This is the characteristic of the fourth wave of mergers and acquisitions from 1978 to 1989 called industrial deconglomeration; its distinguishing feature is the hostile takeover based on leverage buyouts (Davis, G. & Stout, S. 1992).[2]

In this context, the deregulation that favoured centralisation of capital and promoted the takeovers and flows of foreign direct investment (FDI) made it possible for the large companies to increase their profits. They did this either through cutting labour costs or by accessing new markets and other sources of profits. This has led to a concentration of industry in a small number of companies worldwide.

At the same time, the financial activities boom led to a series of innovations that initially made it possible to stabilise profits for the LNFC through accessing different forms of financing, short-term investments and acquisitions of other companies (Toporowski 1993, 2008), or directly, through the creation of financial subsidiaries (Sinapi et al. 2016).[3] Although this process allows the LNFC to access short-term earnings in the sphere of circulation, it has negative effects on accumulation and technological innovation since a large part of the profits are distributed among shareholders through dividends and capital earnings (Tori 2016, Orhangazi 2008).

Based on this, theoretical analyses point out that the dynamic of production in developed countries lines up with the financial logic through mergers and acquisitions (Guttmann 2008). This is due to the fact that investment community pressure to achieve profits and the resulting influence on the companies' valuation in financial markets lead to investments channelling into safer projects or to corporations divesting themselves of productive processes in which they are not specialists, unrelated to their core activities. This is because a bad market valuation and the threat of a takeover penalise growth in productive investment and favour market concentration. This opens up a period of centralisation of capital due to the easy access to liquid resources, which fosters the growth of international financial markets where issuing debt is one of corporations' preferred mechanisms for accessing resources (Palley 2007).

As part of this dynamic, developing countries have become receivers of FDI, attracted by the privatisation of public companies, low wages and high yields from the exploitation of natural resources. The transnational LNFCs have become leaders in Latin American export models, which, despite their success at promoting exports, have not increased productive link-ups, technology transfer or value added in the region.

Neither Latin America nor Mexico has eliminated dependency on the outside economy. On the contrary, the export model led by the transnational LNFC deepened the developing economies' industrial heterogeneity and weakened the already scanty productive link-ups. This has caused these economies to gradually deindustrialise and return to dependency on primary sector production; this process has been accompanied by a huge dependence on short-term financial capital, growing reserves in foreign currency, overvalued currencies and strong imbalances in current accounts.

One of the effects of the hegemony of finance in developing countries is the movements of short-term capital to take advantage of growing financial yields (the interest-rate differential) in receiving countries. Another important phenomenon in Latin America that began with the export model dominated by finance is the outflow of FDI in the form of investments abroad by the large Latin American companies.

What have been called "translatinas", originating with the privatisation of public companies, have taken on outward-oriented growth strategies because domestic markets have stagnated. This is itself a product of neo-liberal policies that have decreased government involvement in economic activities and sought fiscal balance that could guarantee payment to international financial capital.

Thus, the "translatinas" joined the process of internationalisation to expand their markets abroad, not mainly to lower costs. These corporations have used the tactic of mergers and acquisitions boosted by access to financing in international credit markets and issuing debt in international financial markets, in a context in which the pressure of foreign stock markets favours their strategy of acquiring companies in international markets, turning them into corporate raiders.

The extraordinary access to liquidity began to be limited by the 2014 shift in US monetary policy to normalise interest rates. Beginning then, this growth tactic increased translatina's fragility because their expected earnings had become dependent on the availability of large volumes of liquidity made possible in a context in which world demand became sluggish after the 2008 crisis. Thus, continuing this strategy depends on the availability of liquidity in international markets, although financial costs and exchange-rate risks increase, thus creating high volatility.

This chapter studies the growth dynamic of Latin America's and Mexico's LNFCs in light of FDI flows and mergers and acquisitions from 1990 to 2016. I argue that the translatinas are expanding abroad maintained by the access to international credit markets, guided by the boom in foreign-currency-based bond issues.

The chapter is divided into five sections. After this introduction, the second section briefly reviews the internationalisation strategy through FDI movements from a theoretical point of view to determine its implications for accumulation. The third section presents a discussion of the characteristics of FDI movement in Latin America and their influence in the region's export model. The fourth section analyses the outward-oriented growth strategy in Latin America and Mexico, underlining goals and mechanisms. And finally, the fifth section presents my conclusions.

FDI and mergers and acquisitions: a growth strategy under financial hegemony

Starting with the profitability crisis in the mid-1960s, the LNFCs carried out a profound productive restructuring in order to cut costs. Outstanding among their strategies was relocating productive processes on a local and world level. Locally, they sought to relocate production in places with weak unions.[4] Worldwide, global value chains were created that tended to maximise LNFC competitiveness to face down international competition, take advantage of wage differentials and expand their spheres of influence by seeking to exploit natural resources and penetrate new markets. In this context, developed countries' FDI in developing countries played a crucial role.

Other related restructuring mechanisms were the re-specialisation of activities, spin-offs[5] and outsourcing. This was complemented by the deregulation of the 1980s, which made it possible to create corporate control through stock markets; this, in turn, aligned companies' behaviour with the interests of the financial market. The investment community's valuation of companies is the crucial mechanism whereby the latter can maximise share value. Company managers implement a series of productive and financial strategies to achieve greater cash flows in order to satisfy the investment community's short-term earnings expectations. One of the most prominent strategies for maximising share value is mergers and acquisitions to increase company growth (Toporowski 1993) in a context of a financial market dominated by institutional agents and investors with a short-term vision pressing for the distribution of dividends and capital earnings in stock markets.

The dominance of agency theory on public policymakers' agendas in the 1980s made the takeover the main way to decrease the problem of agency (Garfield 1989).[6,7] It would also discipline managers, aligning them with shareholders' aims by creating a mechanism for corporate control whereby managers could be implicitly threatened with replacement by more efficient outsiders (Manne 1965, Franks and Mayer 1995). This would lead many conglomerates to have a low rating in financial markets (Hal and Goudzwaard 1976), mainly because unrelated businesses would perform less well than market expectations, leading to a lower overall rating of the conglomerate as a whole, forcing it to sell off its unrelated companies to centre on its core activities. This partially explains the great wave of mergers and acquisitions in the 1980s, which generated a process of concentration and re-specialisation of industrial activity.

However, the boom in mergers and acquisitions is linked with productive re-specialisation to increase efficiency and a series of financial manoeuvres in accordance with the inflation of stock prices (Toporowsky 1993). The latter increases LNFC financial wealth and short-term liquidity.

This mechanism can be understood based on the earning expectations it generates in the financial market insofar as,

i industrial concentration produces positive expectations of profitability among investors,[8] since greater monopolisation of activities and markets decreases uncertainty about future earnings;
ii in the short term, the demand for and the prices of shares in companies that grow due to mergers and acquisitions (Gugler et al. 2012) tend to increase. Their access to liquidity also grows since inflated share prices increase their collateral and ability to take on debt[9];
iii it makes it possible to finance the acquisition by paying the owners of the company to be acquired with shares, given the appreciation of the shares themselves and the growth in financial wealth expected after the purchase. This is a strong incentive for accepting shares in the purchasing company as payment.

Putting a priority on this growth strategy tends to lower accumulation because it does not expand productive capacity, but only changes who controls already existing capacity and redistributes earnings among shareholders and financial sector investors (Jarrell et al. 1988). That is, financial market investors' pressure for higher yields reduces the resources available for accumulation and innovation by lowering the retention ratio (Stockhammer 2005, Özgür 2007, Dallery 2009, Sen 2015, Tori & Onaran 2016).

Today, the LNFC must concentrate on safer investments and take into account the effect that their expansion policy has on the mood of the financial market. This is because announcements about their investment policies and dividends have consequences for portfolio decisions of investors who have prioritised short-term earnings, which means that any corporate investment decision investors consider risky will lead to the sale of that company's shares. In line with this, the theory of overcapitalisation argues that in a situation dominated by financial short-termism, companies put the priority on horizontal mergers and acquisitions as a growth strategy, based on their handling of liquidity and debt structure since it fosters share price inflation.

Along these same lines, FDI flows from developed to developing countries follow the same path since the idea is purchasing already existing companies or exchanging debt for assets in debt-equity swaps. This boosts capital centralisation because it only makes for changes in ownership without increasing productive capacity.

LNFCs from developing countries, where the translatinas are located, have benefitted from the expansion of international financial markets by obtaining resources to develop a growth strategy similar to that of developed country corporations, freeing themselves from the financial restrictions of their thin local markets. Their concentrated ownership corporate structure also favours them (Watkins 2013, Clarke 2016), allowing them to develop their growth and indebtedness strategies without exposing the control of their companies in financial markets, since they have been cautious about how they have issued stock to finance themselves.[10]

Thus, we can say that globally, LNFCs in both developing and developed countries are committed to growth strategies that deepen capital centralisation worldwide. This is reflected in the mediocre economic growth and investment stagnation that has deepened until today (see Table 4.1).

FDI performance and characteristics in developing countries and in Latin America's export model

During the fourth wave of mergers and acquisitions, industry – particularly US industry – concentrated horizontally in the developed countries. What distinguished the industrial dynamics in the 1990s was the internationalisation of capital reflected in FDI flows. Some authors have called this the fifth wave of transborder international mergers and acquisitions (Black 2000).[11] This does not mean that developed countries' LNFCs did not make FDIs in the 1960s, 1970s and 1980s; rather, they became much larger in the 1990s globally. For example, world FDI grew an average of 20% annually during the entire period, skyrocketing from US$196.31 billion in 1990 to US$1.4 trillion in 2000.[12] This FDI boom, explained by overseas mergers and acquisitions, had its origin in the neo-liberal trade openings and financial deregulation policies that have continued until today.

The 1990s were characterised by a deepening of the LNFC internationalisation strategy worldwide. This meant that more dynamic companies, mainly from Europe and North America, established themselves in developing countries, and represented 77.9% of FDI outflow in the 1990s. Another part of this dynamic that stands out is the growth of FDI into developing countries (Table 4.2).

Table 4.1 Average annual growth rate of GDP and GFCF, selected countries (1960–2016)

Gross domestic product (average annual growth rate, 1960–2016)							
Period	*World*	*USA*	*European Union*	*Latin America and Caribbean*	*Germany*	*China*	*Mexico*
1960–1970	4.9	4.1	4.6	5.0	ND	3.5	6.1
1970–1980	3.5	2.9	2.9	5.5	2.6	5.6	6.1
1980–1990	2.8	3.0	2.3	1.3	2.1	8.4	1.6
1990–2000	2.6	3.1	2.0	2.8	1.8	9.4	3.3
2000–2016	2.6	1.7	1.3	2.5	1.1	8.9	2.0
Gross fixed capital formation (average annual growth rate, 1960–2016)							
Period	*World*	*USA*	*European Union*	*Latin America and Caribbean*	*Germany*	*China*	*México*
1960–1970	ND	6.0	ND	ND	ND	ND	11.7
1970–1980	3.1	3.0	1.7	7.1	1.5	ND	7.7
1980–1990	3.0	3.2	2.5	-2.0	1.8	ND	-1.1
1990–2000	2.4	4.9	2.1	4.3	1.8	23.5	4.5
2000–2016	3.3	1.0	0.9	3.0	0.7	12.7	2.5

Source: Author's own elaboration based on World Bank Database.

However, beginning in 2000, a countertrend in FDI develops, manifested in increased outflows from developing countries, that is, the LNFC based in developing countries have become serious competitors of those from developed countries as part of the internationalisation process. Outgoing FDI from developing countries' LNFCs went from 5.4% of world outflows in 1990 to 26% in 2016. Amidst this dynamic of internationalisation of developing countries, the corporations that have benefitted the most have been Asian, but mainly those from China, which represented 11% of all FDI outflows in 2016 (see Table 4.2).[13]

It should be underlined that while this worldwide capital internationalisation strategy increased FDI flow growth, at least until 2007 when they reached their peak, the main mechanism for entry has been transborder mergers and acquisitions. Green field projects – new investment – and the reinvestment of profits account for the change to a lesser degree. Thus, this FDI has had little impact on the rate of investment by region, which can be seen in the continual drop in the annual average rate of growth in the gross formation of fixed capital (see Table 4.1). That is, both its growth and its proportion of GDP have dropped, except in the case of Asia and China, whose investment as a percentage of GDP represented 42% in 2016 according to the World Bank.

Table 4.2 Outward and inward FDI flows as a percentage of the world total (Selected Economies, 1990–2016)

	FDI inflows as a percentage of the world total											
Period	*1990*	*1994*	*1996*	*1998*	*2002*	*2004*	*2006*	*2008*	*2010*	*2012*	*2014*	*2016*
Developed economies	83.1	59.1	60.8	73.6	69.4	57.5	66.6	52.6	49.0	53.8	42.6	59.1
Developing economies	16.9	40.2	37.8	25.3	28.9	38.3	29.2	39.5	46.4	42.1	53.2	37.0
North America	27.3	20.9	24.2	28.6	16.2	19.4	21.1	24.5	16.4	15.2	17.4	24.3
European Union	46.6	32.3	32.0	41.4	47.5	29.9	38.7	20.4	26.2	30.9	19.4	32.4
Asia	11.2	26.8	25.0	13.5	16.1	25.5	20.8	25.3	29.7	25.2	34.8	25.3
Latin America and Caribbean	4.2	10.9	11.2	10.3	9.5	9.8	5.2	9.3	12.2	11.9	12.8	8.1
	FDI outflows as a percentage of the world total											
Period	*1990*	*1994*	*1996*	*1998*	*2002*	*2004*	*2006*	*2008*	*2010*	*2012*	*2014*	*2016*
Developed economies	94.6	83.9	84.4	93.7	90.3	85.5	82.4	79.7	69.4	70.2	56.5	71.9
Developing economies	5.4	16.0	15.4	6.1	8.9	13.0	15.4	16.8	27.0	27.5	37.7	26.4
North America	23.7	32.1	26.2	27.0	31.7	35.0	15.5	16.7	22.1	24.9	24.5	19.9
European Union	50.0	42.1	46.3	59.7	50.5	45.0	61.5	59.1	38.1	36.6	22.7	40.7
China	0.3	0.6	0.5	0.6	1.0	0.7	1.1	2.2	3.3	3.7	7.5	11.4
Latin America and Caribbean	0.5	1.2	0.8	1.2	0.6	1.3	1.9	1.4	2.6	1.7	2.9	1.5

Source: Author's own elaboration based on World Bank and World Investment Report Database.

In Latin America, FDI inflows have had two particular objectives: (i) controlling natural resources via the purchase of public and private companies and (ii) cutting costs through the establishment of maquiladora plants for export.

This multinational corporation strategy has contributed to developing the region's export model in three ways:

- i re-asserting the centrality of raw materials in the region's economies by deepening the model of raw material exports;
- ii consolidating a heterogeneous productive structure in which the transnational and national LNFCs concentrate on markets, the exploitation of natural resources, public concessions, technology and access to both internal and external financial resources. Alongside this, a large number of small- and medium-sized companies exist with financial restrictions and low technological development;
- iii establishing a manufacturing maquiladora export model with little or no development of local suppliers or technology transfer, thus increasing the import of intermediary inputs.

All of this prevents changing the region's external account imbalance and deepens its dependence on external, short-term capital. Meanwhile, short-term capital entry is required to finance the current account and control domestic prices through the accumulation of reserves and overvaluing the currency (Rodrick 2008, Bresser Pereira 2009, Huerta 2016), at the cost of a highly attractive interest rate differential for short-term capital.

Transnational corporation activities in Latin America have developed in the following ways: first, decreased costs and global efficiency, mainly in agribusiness and the auto and electronics sectors (Mexico, Caribbean Basin, and Brazil). Second, the quest for raw materials: oil and gas (Venezuela, Colombia, Argentina, Bolivia, Brazil and, recently, Mexico), and minerals (Chile, Argentina and Peru). Third, access to the financial market (Brazil, Mexico, Chile, Argentina, Venezuela, Colombia and Peru), telecommunications (Brazil, Mexico, Argentina, Chile and Peru), electricity (Colombia, Brazil and Argentina), the distribution of natural gas (Argentina, Brazil, Chile and Colombia) and the retail trade (Brazil, Argentina and Mexico).

Multinational corporations have also become a larger proportion of the region's large companies. In 1992, of the 500 largest firms, 149 were foreign-owned; 267, domestically owned; and 87, government-owned. By 2000, 196 were foreign; 194, national; and 110, public companies. Of the 100 largest manufacturing companies in 1992, 48 were foreign-owned; 48, nationally owned; and 4, state-owned. By 2000, 59 were foreign; 40, national; and 1, government-owned, according to the ECLAC report *La inversión extranjera en América Latina y el Caribe* (Foreign Investment in Latin America and the Caribbean) (2000, 2005).

Brazil and Mexico were the Latin American economies that received the most FDI in the whole region, rising from 42% in 1990 to 60% in 2016. In addition, they concentrate the largest stock of FDI, since in 2016, they represented 56% of what had been received in the whole region.

Transnational corporations have been the biggest beneficiaries of FDI, since results have been less than expected in terms of investment and growth. The data show stagnant gross capital formation for the periods 1990–2000 and 2000–2010, with a 4.3% average investment growth rate for both periods, and an actual drop from 2010 to 2017 to 0.6% annually (see Table 4.1).

All of this is in line with the fall in the annual average GDP growth, since for 1990–2000 and 2000–2016, the rate was 2.8% and 2.5%, respectively (see Table 4.1). In addition, FDI flows have lost dynamism within the region, particularly in recent years in the aftermath of the 2008 crisis. This has been accompanied by the resulting fall in commodities prices in 2013 and 2014 due to the worldwide slowdown, which has led to lower foreign investment being attracted to the region because profitability has dropped (ECLAC 2016).

Thus, the results of the FDI-led export model have been disappointing in terms of growth and investment, leading to a concentration of economic activities, control of natural resources by transnational corporations and no long-term benefits for the region.

In the case of the Mexican economy, while FDI has been one of the most dynamic sectors of export-oriented manufacturing (automobiles and electronics), the impact on the country's development has been mediocre. It has not promoted deep productive linkages that would make technology transfer possible; also, transnational corporations' strategy is to cut costs through the wage differential and tax breaks, plus lax environmental protection enforcement.

This has led the country to be profoundly dependent on the exterior for importing intermediate inputs, which represent approximately 60% of the total intermediate demand, in turn, deepening the imbalance in the current account and putting a priority on exchange-rate overvaluation. In overall terms, this limits the development of national industry because it blocks the integration of small- and medium-sized companies into the global value chain of transnational companies, plus the loss of competitiveness due to exchange-rate appreciation.

For this reason, it is necessary to ensure the entry of short-term capital to finance the trade imbalance, accumulate reserves and appreciate the exchange rate, which favours importing inputs and final consumer goods and influences price stability via exchange rate pass-through.

In just this same way, low wages imply a continual limitation for developing the domestic market. This has meant that large national companies implement a growth strategy in foreign markets to overcome the regressive income distribution and to gain access to better financing conditions. In turn, this has implied slower rhythms of internal accumulation and stagnant economic growth, a distinctive trait of Mexico and Latin America's economy as long as this export model exists.

The outward-oriented growth model in Latin America: growing instability

The internationalisation of developing nations' companies has been something new in the 2000s. The growing trend of outward FDI flows in which the emerging countries are immersed, among them Latin America's and Asia's LNFCs, has made for a wave of mergers and acquisitions led by large companies in developing countries internationally.[14] However, this developing country LNFC strategy has been backed by a growing trend in debt placement for all the companies in this group.

We must remember that the large companies in Latin America were the main beneficiaries of the neo-liberal era economic reforms. They came into existence due to the privatisation of public companies and were favoured by the availability of financing in international financial markets through different mechanisms. The main ones are the following:

1 issuing shares on international markets. For example, American depositary receipts (ADRs) had a dual objective[15]: on the one hand, they provided access to liquid resources in external stock markets. On the other hand, they are a way of establishing confidence in international financial markets for accessing other financing mechanisms. This forced the LNFC to implement a series of corporate principles posited by international agencies to promote accountability, transparency and growing protection of minority shareholders' interests[16];
2 issuing foreign-currency-denominated bonds. This seems to be one of the preferred strategies among the region's companies, since, given the interest rate differential, it is less costly to finance yourself in external markets through foreign-currency-denominated debt. And, although this strategy involves tanking on risk with regard to the exchange rate, in contrast with issuing shares, it does not compromise assets and/or put control over the corporation in foreign hands.[17]

These two financing strategies are the main reason these companies have been able to deepen their internationalisation process, but not all of them have achieved the status of global companies. Given the heavy competition worldwide, only a small group of companies from Mexico and Brazil are among the highest international rankings. For example, in 2017, outstanding among the United Nations Conference on Trade and Development (UNCTAD) 100 top companies from developing countries were Mexican (CEMEX, América Móvil, Fomento Económico, Bimbo, Alfa, Grupo México and Mexichem) and Brazilian (Vale, JBS, Gerdau, Petróleo Brasileiro,

Embrear and BRF). In terms of the world ranking of the 100 most important corporations overall, only Brazil's Vale and Mexico's América Móvil are included.[18]

In Latin America, this outward-oriented expansion strategy intensified after the 2000 and 2008 crises due to the expansionary monetary policy of the USA. In addition, the volatility of stock-market indices and the financial straits some corporations from the developed countries found themselves in added to the chances of success for the Latin American corporations in seeking to acquire companies in those countries.

However, the dynamic of transborder mergers and acquisitions by Latin American LNFCs has declined recently, shrinking from US$16.724 billion in 2010 to US$686 million in 2016, according to data from the UNCTAD's World Investment Report. This change in the trend can be explained by three factors: (1) the normalisation of US monetary policy, which limited its indebtedness abroad; (2) the falling demand worldwide, which makes companies more cautious about their expansion strategies; and (3) the consolidation of international oligopolistic structures in different markets and sectors, which makes entry through mergers and acquisitions more difficult.

The large Mexican companies' performance has been among the most dynamic, together with that of the Brazilians, in this process of internationalisation of capital. In 2016, seven Mexican companies were among the top 100 transnational corporations in the developing countries measured by foreign assets (in the same ranking, China and Hong Kong had 32 companies, and Brazil, 6).

While merger and acquisition activities have slowed down since 2007, the stock of FDI from Mexican corporations abroad continues to grow and is more pronounced than for the rest of the companies in Latin America (see Table 4.3). However, one of the important issues that makes analysts doubt that this growth strategy will continue is the progressive indebtedness in foreign currency (Hattori and Takáts 2015) in an economic context of deceleration of world demand and exchange-rate volatility. This is reflected in the increase in the stock of debt issues in foreign currency by all the Latin American LNFCs in recent years (see Table 4.3).

In the case of the Mexican corporations, share issues have increasingly complemented debt placement in international markets, as has investment in FDI abroad. This dynamic is fostered by the big corporations' merger and acquisition growth strategy globally. It makes it possible to acquire target firms through issuing shares and floating a debt. However, the Mexican and regional LNFCs face three drawbacks in continuing with this strategy.

The first involves the relationship between the concentration of industrial activity and the global rate of profit. It is true that industrial concentration and market clout generate an increase in the absolute amount of profits, since the flows of cash from a specific industry concentrate in few companies. However, this is not necessarily reflected in profit indicators, since, as recent analyses of these indicators for large Mexican companies have

Table 4.3 Latin America and Mexico, selected indicators as a per cent of GDP (1990–2016)

Period	*1990*	*1994*	*1996*	*1998*	*2000*	*2004*	*2007*	*2009*	*2010*	*2012*	*2014*	*2016*
Latin America FDI outward stock	4.5	3.7	3.6	4.1	4.9	8.0	8.2	8.6	8.2	9.2	9.2	11.4
Mexico FDI outward stock	0.9	0.8	1.1	1.2	1.2	6.6	8.2	9.9	11.5	12.6	11.3	14.2
Latin America not financial sector international debt issue	0.3	1.4	1.7	2.3	2.4	1.8	1.6	1.8	1.9	2.8	3.8	5.4
Mexico not financial sector international debt issue	1.2	2.8	3.2	3.8	3.0	1.9	2.1	3.0	3.6	6.1	9.0	13.8
México stocks	7.1	10.8	10.9	5.6	6.5	5.7	11.3	8.7	10.6	10.1	9.9	10.7
Latin America mergers and acquisitions	0.1	0.1	0.1	0.2	0.2	0.5	0.7	0.2	0.3	0.5	0.1	0.0
Mexico mergers and acquisitions	0.1	0.2	0.2	0.1	0.6	0.2	1.7	0.4	0.3	0.5	0.4	0.4

Source: Author's own elaboration based on World Bank Database and World Investment Report.

shown, the return on equity ratio (ROE) and the return on capital employed (ROCE) have dropped overall for the large companies traded on the stock market. In other words, the absolute mass of profits rises due to concentration, but the overall profit rate drops.

The second drawback involves the volatility of financial markets due to the 2008 crisis, the European crisis, Brexit and the threat of a trade war. Together with the normalisation of US monetary policy, all this makes this strategy more fragile, maintained on the basis of floating foreign-currency-denominated bonds and issuing shares, due to the increase in financial costs and exchange-rate risk. As Table 4.3 shows, the growth of Mexican companies' FDI stock abroad has been accompanied by an increased stock of debt and shares. However, by 2016, we can see that the stock of debt surpassed that of shares as a percentage of GDP (in 2016 it came to 13.8%). This generates growing risk for all the companies since it increases debt with a dropping rate of profit and shrinking collateral (Kalecki 1937).

Finally, the third drawback is the effect of decreasing FDI in Latin America and the outward growth strategy of the translatinas with regard to investment and economic growth in the region. On the one hand, incoming FDI worldwide has become less dynamic: the average annual growth rate was 2.7% between 2000 and 2016. In Latin America, the situation is no different: the average annual growth rate for FDI was 0.8% between 2010 and 2016, explained by the drop in the FDI profit rate in the region (ECLAC 2017). On the other hand, Mexican and Latin American LNFC investment has concentrated abroad and decreased in the domestic market; in global terms, this is expressed in Latin America in a continual drop in investment rates (see Table 4.1).[19]

All of this seems to trace the limits of the expansion strategy through mergers and acquisitions and other mechanisms that deepen capital centralisation.[20] This is due to financial instability and the changes in access to liquidity worldwide, which is a sign of crisis of the global financial hegemony model of accumulation. This makes the translatinas' outward-oriented growth strategy more fragile and unviable in the long run because of economic stagnation, the concentration of income and the growing financial fragility this generates in Latin America.

Conclusions

The crisis of profitability in the late 1960s sparked an industrial restructuring to stabilise the profit rate, underscoring the specialisation of activities and increased relocation of capital regionally and worldwide. The aim was to increase productive efficiency by cutting costs and creating a global value chain.

The main mechanisms in this restructuring process have been FDI movements through a growth strategy based on global mergers and acquisitions. This has been facilitated mainly by deregulation in the neo-liberal era and financial hegemony worldwide, which has implied international growth in liquidity and the availability of resources for big companies in their internationalisation processes.

In addition, the financial markets give priority to the growth strategy based on mergers and acquisitions through the financial inflation that benefits shareholders in these markets. However, this has had a negative impact on accumulation levels globally, since the world economy is seeing a centralisation of capital, the concentration of earnings and the resulting stagnation.

The dynamic of FDI from developed countries has determined the course of Latin America's export model, following the lead of the big transnational corporations in their quest for profits through control over natural resources, low wages and the creation of global value chains to deal with tough international competition.

A new trend that began in the 1990s but deepened in the 2000s is the growth of outward-directed FDI from the developing countries. This has been led mainly by the Asian countries, but also includes the Latin-America-based LNFCs.

However, this strategy has been based on a continual indebtedness in international credit markets, mainly by issuing foreign-currency-denominated bonds. This practice grew extraordinarily after 2008 and has been fundamental in financing the large companies stock of FDI abroad.

These two trends include the large Mexican firms, which have benefitted the most from all the reforms passed during the neo-liberal era. However, in 2016, the strategy seemed to have arrived at its limit due to financial markets' growing volatility and the changes in liquidity conditions worldwide, making it rather unviable in the medium and long terms due to the financial fragility it implies.

In addition, this LNFC dynamic has been based on a continual monopolisation of industry, creating a huge concentration of income. This is reflected in stagnant investment and world economic growth with the resulting regressive impact for the vast majority of the population in terms of growth, employment and income.

Notes

1 Productive re-specialisation aimed at gradually dismantling large companies that had made inroads into unrelated businesses (a conglomerate) from 1960 to 1973 and ensuring its specialisation in its core activity.

2 Analysts have identified four waves of mergers from the late nineteenth century and during the course of the twentieth century: from 1895 to 1903, mergers and acquisitions that consolidated the great monopolies characterised by the big cartels and trusts; from 1920 to 1929, the consolidation of oligopolistic industry; from 1960 to 1973, mergers and acquisitions that tended to create conglomerates of unrelated businesses; and the wave from 1978 to 1989, characterised by the re-specialisation of production or deconglomeration of industry.

3 This is the case of the large auto companies, whose earnings from their financial subsidiaries rival their operational earnings.

4 One example of this is Eaton Corporation in the 1960s. This was a company linked to the US auto industry dynamic production model for car transmissions and suspension systems set up in Cleveland, near Detroit. In 1960, the company began restructuring its US activities, closing plants in Cleveland to move them to Kentucky. The aim was to cut labour costs by relocating to areas where unions were weaker (Phelps 2002). Today, the company is an industrial conglomerate operating worldwide, in both the automobile and the aerospace sectors.
5 Spin-offs are a corporate strategy to uncouple productive processes, so they can be carried out by a subsidiary or even by selling the subsidiary to completely outsource the process.
6 Agency theory points out the conflict of interests between management and shareholders. It sees the former as opportunistic agents in the contractual relationship, arguing that they take advantage of shareholders by giving themselves perks based on their power inside the corporation's controlling group, mainly due to a problem of information generated in the agency relationship, characteristic of companies with shareholders.
7 The 1982 *Edgar v. Mite Corp.* US Supreme Court decision rescinded the ban on takeovers included in the Williams Act of 1968 in the USA.
8 Datta el al. (1992) and Jarrell (1988) agree in pointing out that, on average, mergers of related companies produce better results than mergers of unrelated companies.
9 In the developed, deregulated market, this strategy can be applied using different sources of financing (such as issuing debt in financial markets), and it will be profitable as long as it is accompanied by an increase in stock prices in the company performing the takeover.
10 They have built a series of relationships abroad, acquiring companies or partnering with others to get financing. Some of them have issued shares on international markets (like ADRs), allowing them to grow their reputations and be well thought of there. This has positively affected their stock-market value and boosted their capacity for being subjects of credit internationally whether through access to credit, issuing debt, or issuing stocks.
11 Examples of this international concentration trend are Daimler-Chrysler and Vodafone's takeover of Mannesmann in Germany (Jackson & Hopner 2001).
12 The average yearly growth in the 1980s was 12.9%.
13 For example, in 2016, the Midea Group became the biggest shareholder in Germany's KUKA Robotics; in that same year, Haier acquired the applications division of General Electric for US$5.4 billion.
14 One characteristic example of this dynamic is the Chinese corporation Zhejiang Geely Holding Group's purchase of Volvo from Ford in 2010 for €1.3846 billion.
15 In July 1990, Compañía de Teléfonos de Chile was the first company to float an ADR on the New York Stock Exchange, with an offering of US1.126 billion, the equivalent of 23% of its entire assets. In May 1991, TELMEX placed an offering of US$2 billion. It should be pointed out that Mexican companies are the ones that have used this mechanism the most; by 1992, this included Televisa (with US$1.1 billion), Grupo Carso (US$442 million), Cemex (US$312 million) and Vitro (US$228 million).
16 These guidelines were developed in the document "Principios de la OCDE para el Gobierno de las Sociedades" in 1999. Its main objective is to protect shareholders and ensure appropriate practices by managers to create certainty among financial market investors.
17 It should be underlined that the first Latin American company that issued bonds on the international market was CEMEX in 1989, for US$150 million.
18 Among the main translatinas are (1) Argentina: Arcor, Techint, Impsa and Bagó; (2) Brazil: Petrobras, CVRD, Gerdau, Usiminas, Embraer, CSN, Varig, Camargo

Correa, Norberto Odebrecht, Votorantim Cimentos, TAM, Andrade Gutierrez, Klabin, Weg and Sabó; (3) Chile: ENAP, Falabella, Lan Airlines, Arauco, CMPC, CGE, ENTEL, Molymet and Madeco; and (4) Mexico: América Móvil, Grupo Femsa, CEMEX, Grupo Alfa, Bimbo, Grupo México, Grupo IMSA, Grupo Vitro, Gruma, Grupo Xignux, Grupo ICA and Grupo Posadas.

19 The average annual growth rate in gross capital formation has been 4.5% from 1990 to 2000; 2.2% from 2000 to 2010; and 2.6% from 2010 to 2017.

20 Such as investment in intangible assets, brands, patents, franchises, etc.

References

Bresser-Pereira, L. (2009) 'La Tendencia a la Sobrevaluación del Tipo de Cambio', *Economía UNAM*, 6(8), 75–88.

ECLAC (2017) *Foreign Direct Investment in Latin America and the Caribbean 2017*, Economic Commission for Latin America and the Caribbean, Santiago de Chile.

ECLAC (2016) *Foreign Direct Investment in Latin America and the Caribbean 2016*, Economic Commission for Latin America and the Caribbean, Santiago de Chile.

ECLAC (2005) *Foreign Direct Investment in Latin America and the Caribbean* 2005, Economic Commission for Latin America and the Caribbean, Santiago de Chile.

ECLAC (2000) *Foreign Direct Investment in Latin America and the Caribbean*, Economic Commission for Latin America and the Caribbean, Santiago de Chile.

Clarke, T. (2016) 'The Continuing Diversity of Corporate Governance: Theories of Convergence and Variety', *Ephemera Journal*, 16(1), 19–52.

Dallery, T. (2009) 'Post Keynesian Theories of the Firm under Financialization', *Review of Radical Political Economics*, 41(4), 492–515.

Davis, G. & Stout, S. (1992) 'Organization Theory and the Market for Corporate', *Administrative Science Quarterly*, 37, 605–633.

Datta, D., Pinches, G., & Narayanan, V.K. (1992) 'Factors Influencing Wealth Creation from Mergers and Acquisitions: A Meta-analysis', *Strategic Management Journal*, 13(1), 67–84.

Franks, J. & Mayer, C. (1995) 'Hostile Takeovers in the UK and the Correction of Managerial', *London Business School, Institute of Finance and Accounting*, Working Paper 156.

Garfield, A. (1989) 'State Competence to Regulate Corporate Take Overs: Lessons from State Takeover Statutes', *Hofsfra Law Review*, 17(3), 535–598.

Gugler, K., Mueller, Dennis C., & Yurtoglu, B. (2012) 'The Determinants of Merger Waves', *International Journal of Industrial Organization*, 30(1), 1–15.

Guttmann, R. (2008) 'A Primer on Finance Led Capitalism and Its Crisis', *Revue de la Regulation*, No. 3/4, viewed 8 May 2018, from http://journals.openedition.org/regulation/5843; DOI: 10.4000/regulation.5843.

Hal, M. & Goudzwaard, M. (1976) 'Performance of Conglomerate Firms: A Portfolio Approach', *Journal of Finance*, 31(1), 39–48.

Hattori, M. & Takas, E. (2015) 'The Role of Debt Securities Markets', *Bank for International Settlements*, BIS Papers No 83.

Huerta, A. (2016) *El ocaso de la globalización*, Facultad de Economía- UNAM, México.

Jackson, G. & Hopner, M. (2001) 'An Emerging Market for Corporate Control? The Mannesmann Takeover and German Corporate Governance', *Max-Planck-Institute for the Study of Societies*, Discussion Paper No. 01/4, viewed 3 April 2018, from SSRN: https://ssrn.com/abstract=285232 or http://dx.doi.org/10.2139/ssrn.285232.

Jarrell, G., Brickley, J., & Netter, J. (1988) 'The Market for Corporate Control: The Empirical Evidence Since 1980', *Journal of Economic Perspectives*, 2(1), 49–68.

Kalecki, M. (1937) 'The Principle of Increasing Risk', *Economica*, 4(16), 440–447.

Manne, H. (1965) 'Mergers and the Market for Corporate Control', *Journal of Political Economy* 73(2), 110–120.

Özgür, O. (2007) 'Financialization and Capital Accumulation in the Non-financial Corporate Sector: A Theoretical and Empirical Investigation of the U.S. Economy: 1973–2003', *Political Economy Research Institute*, Working paper 149.

Palley, T. (2007) 'Financialization: What It is and Why It Matters?', *Levy Economics Institute*, Working paper 525.

Phelps, N. (2002) 'When Was Post-Fordism? The Uneven Institution of New Work Practices in a Multinational', *Antipode*, 34(2), 205–226.

Rodrick, D. (2008, Fall) 'The Real Exchange Rate and Economic Growth', Brookings Papers on Economic Activity.

Sen, S. & DasGupta, Z. (2015) 'Financialization and Corporate Investments: The Indian Case', *Levy Economics Institute of Bard College*, Working Paper 828.

Sinapi, C. (2016) 'Financialization of Non-financial Companies: An Insight in the Automotive Sector', *LIMES*, 13(1), 35–60.

Stockhammer, E. (2005) 'Shareholder Value Orientation and the Investment-profit Puzzle', *Journal of Post Keynesian Economics*, 28(2).

Toporowski, J. (1993) *The Economics of Financial Markets and the 1987 Crash*, Aldershot: Edward Elgar.

Toporowski, J. (2008) 'Excess Capital and Liquidity Management', *Levy Economics Institute*, Working paper 549.

Tori, D. & Onaran, Ö. (2016) 'The Effects of Financialization on Investment: Evidence from Firm-level Data for the UK', *Post Keynesian Economics Study Group*, Working Paper 1601.

Watkins, K. (2013) 'Efecto de la Ley Corporativa y la Concentración de la Propiedad en el Desempeño Empresarial en Chile y México', *Ensayos Revista de Economía*, 32(2), 1–22.

5 Financialisation and economic inequality in Latin America

Hanna Szymborska

The aim of this chapter is to analyse the forces behind economic inequality in Latin America and their connection to the processes of financialisation. The key motivation is that Latin America is one of the most unequal regions of the world. Simultaneously, Latin American economies have undergone substantial changes in the course of financialisation (Correa & Vidal 2012:542), which have compromised the performance of the productive sector (Levy-Orlik 2013:110).

The analysis of the link between the experiences of financialisation and high levels of inequality in Latin America is important because it highlights the structural forces behind the unequal distribution of wealth and income in the region. This is instrumental in understanding how institutional structures and policy shape distributional outcomes vis-à-vis individual characteristics related to marginal contribution to the production process and human capital accumulation, which are common explanations of inequality in the literature (Stiglitz 2012:37; Galbraith 2016:74). Together with the consideration of social justice, identification of the systemic drivers of inequality has significant implications for economic performance as unequal distribution hinders growth and contributes to its volatility (Stockhammer 2015).

From a Kaleckian perspective, this is because resources are taken away from those who are more likely to spend them to those who are more likely to hoard them (Kalecki 1954). The negative impact of income concentration and uneven wealth accumulation possibilities on growth has been highlighted as one of the key contributory factors to the Great Recession (Kumhof & Ranciere 2010; Rajan 2010; Mian & Sufi 2013; Goda et al. 2016; see Van Treeck & Sturn 2012 for a review).

Consequently, examining the channels of inequality is vital for economic prosperity in Latin America. The main hypothesis of this chapter is that forces of financialisation associated with the liberalisation of trade and finance, together with the push for financial inclusion, have influenced income and wealth inequality by hampering wage growth and increasing financial instability of Latin American households.

This chapter is structured in six sections. Following the introduction, the second section reviews the different dimensions of financialisation observed around the world and in Latin America. The third section analyses their distributional consequences taking the example of the USA, focussing on the functional distribution of income between labour and capital as well as household wealth inequality. In the fourth section, we discuss the recorded patterns of income and wealth inequality in Latin America and their explanations proposed in the literature. Drawing lessons from the US experience, the fifth section argues that financialisation poses a challenge to economic prosperity in Latin America in so far as wealth and income inequality can be exacerbated by an increase in financial obligations of households resulting from the financialisation processes. The sixth section concludes.

Dimensions of financialisation

Financialisation is defined as the increased dominance of financial institutions over the real economy (Epstein 2005) and the transformation in the role of financial intermediaries from traditional intermediation between creditors and debtors to the originate-and-distribute model based on financial deregulation and innovation (Palley 2007; Dymski et al. 2013; Pollin & Heintz 2013). It was facilitated by the right-wing governments of Ronald Reagan in the United States of America (USA) and Margaret Thatcher in the United Kingdom (UK) in the 1970s, leading to some of the highest levels of financial deepening in the world economy in these countries.

The processes of financialisation have also been observed in Europe, albeit to a varying extent and at different points in time in various countries. This has been manifested primarily in the development of common currency and deregulation of financial activity within the European Union, which generated imbalances between the core Eurozone countries, sustaining export-led growth in Germany, and debt-led expansions in peripheral countries, notably Ireland and Spain (Rossi 2013). In post-soviet countries, financialisation has been characterised by bank restructuring and dominance of foreign-owned commercial banks focussed on short-term lending to government (Gabor 2012), which not only hampered industrial profitability, but also opened the doors to less regulated non-bank intermediaries and payday lenders.

Furthermore, in emerging economies, financialisation processes have been manifested through increased financial inflows (particularly in East Asian economies), financial deregulation (in South Africa and emerging Europe), as well as expansion of stock markets, private debt levels and increased asset price volatility (Karwowski & Stockhammer 2017).

In Latin America, financialisation processes have taken the form of rising inflows of portfolio and direct investments throughout the 1990s to serve financial sector expansion and privatisation (Correa & Vidal 2012). Moreover, since the 2000s, large international banks have dominated local financial markets in Latin America, generating substantial outflows of repatriated earnings and financial income (ibid.). This was enabled by the privatisation of banking sectors and dismantling of large public banks, which was particularly notable in Mexico, Colombia and Peru. Furthermore, institutional reforms committed to restrictive fiscal and monetary policy, exchange rate flexibility, deregulation of lending practices and foreign reserve accumulation were instrumental in maintaining the viability of foreign banks and institutional investors in Latin American economies.

The ascendency of foreign financial institutions in Latin America increased demand for foreign currency, induced stock market expansion and spurred financial innovation (ibid.) Reliance on financial capital inflows replaced fixed investment as the engine of growth in favour of exports (Levy-Orlik 2013). However, this export-led growth strategy has not been sustainable due to persistent current account deficits leading to dependence on further capital inflows to sustain the economic expansion. Together with dollarisation of the Latin American economies due to high foreign currency demand, banking sectors and the economies as a whole in the region have become more fragile. Subsequent policy responses in Latin American countries became focussed on austerity, which sustained the earlier financialisation processes, simultaneously constraining the ability of internal markets to revive domestic growth.

Distributive impact of financialisation – the US experience

The impact of financialisation on inequality is particularly vivid in the USA. One of the key consequences of financialisation was more rapid growth of financial income and profits over wages and other non-financial income. Given the concentration of financial income among households at the top of the distribution, financialisation has been directly linked to rising inequality levels in advanced economies (Galbraith 2012). Income concentration has been further exacerbated by growing wage inequality, with financial sector executives earning the highest and most rapidly growing wage income compared to the rest of the workforce (Philippon & Reshef 2012). Importantly, this financial wage premium has been shown to be unequally distributed among gender and race, which highlights the role of financialisation in reinforcing these intersectional disparities (Arestis et al. 2013).

An important feature of the financialisation experience in the USA with a direct impact on inequality has been the shift of the focus of financial intermediaries from corporate lending to household debt. Since the late 1980s in the USA, total private credit to households and non-profit institutions serving households (NPISHs) relative to GDP surpassed the corresponding contribution of total private credit to corporations (Federal Reserve of St. Louis Economic Database). Household debt rose substantially from 49% in the second quarter of 1980 to its peak of 98% of GDP in the first quarter of 2008. In the second quarter of 2016, the size of household debt relative to GDP of 79.4% still outweighed the share of 72.8% accruing to corporate debt.

Rising household indebtedness in the USA has been directly linked to financialisation. Financial deregulation permitting joint commercial and investment banking activities sparked innovation of financial instruments derived from pooling loans to households. This process of securitisation of household credit was perceived to minimise systemic risk associated with lending to low-income borrowers by diversifying loan portfolios, which formed the basis of asset-backed securities. Securitised assets were then divided into tranches and sold depending on the risk-return preferences of investors (Marcantoni 2014). Given their apparent safety and potential for high returns, securitised instruments became highly demanded by financial investors (Goda & Lysandrou 2011).

To keep up with this demand, financial intermediaries in the USA had incentives to increase lending to households, whose demand for credit was additionally raised by stagnant wage growth and rising costs of privatised services. Increasing credit supply and demand were validated by the housing bubble in the 2000s. Rising house prices prior to 2007 generated the possibility of home equity withdrawal through mortgage refinancing, which turned unviable when the house price bubble burst in mid-2006. This had consequences for financial fragility of individual borrowers and the USA economy as a whole, culminating in the Great Recession (Mian & Sufi 2013).

Financial innovation based on securitisation had a direct impact on economic inequality in the USA. This is not due to rising household debt as such, but rather because of disparities in leverage owing to differences in the types of assets and debt accumulated by different households (Szymborska 2017). On the one hand, although household towards the top of the distribution have has accumulated the highest levels of debt in terms of its value and ownership rates, their leverage has been kept low and stable because of high and rising wage income and diverse asset holdings. Together with high wage incomes, diversity of asset portfolios has enhanced stability of wealth accumulation at the top of the income distribution. Moreover, it has enabled access to secured credit characterised by favourable terms and low repayment rates, as well as to more profitable forms of wealth, which require large initial down payments and are often restricted to highly exclusive (and expensive) wealth management funds (Atkinson 2015). Consequently, not only did USA households at the top of the distribution earn higher returns on their wealth, but their balance sheets suffered less in the aftermath of the Great Recession compared to low-income households (Wolff 2014).

On the other hand, lax financial regulation allowed for the development of opaque and predatory lending practices, pushing low-income households into unsustainable financial positions. These sub-prime borrowers, who had been previously deemed not creditworthy enough to access formal credit, became an object of racial and gender profiling (Dymski et al. 2013). In result, wealth accumulation of female, minority and other low-income or young households became dominated by housing and was thus highly volatile to house price movements. This translated into lower returns to wealth and rising leverage among households towards the middle and the bottom of the distribution, so that wealth gains among these groups prior to the Great Recession became largely wiped out during the crisis (cf. Wolff 2014).

It should be noticed that even though sub-prime mortgage expansion has diminished substantially after the Great Recession, similar patterns of sub-prime lending are now taking place in other parts of the credit market, primarily for unsecured auto loans. Coupled with sluggish wage growth and lack of sustainable wealth accumulation possibilities, increased reliance on unsecured debt among low-income households perpetuates their low position in the income distribution due to higher penalties and interest rates on this form of credit compared to secured debt.

In sum, while the US experience of financialisation is unique in many aspects, it highlights the potential consequences of increasing financial obligations of households for inequality. Focus on household balance sheet dynamics alongside functional income distribution provides a more complete picture of economic inequality in times of financialisation (Piketty & Zucman 2014). Wealth inequality has been documented to be persistently higher than income inequality in advanced economies. Moreover, wealth inequality has been characterised by different dynamics than income. While both income and wealth inequality increased since the 1980s in the USA, wealth inequality continued to rise throughout the Great Recession (from 0.82 in 2007 to 0.86 in 2010, estimates based on the USA Survey of Consumer Finances), while income inequality declined (from 0.57 to 0.54 between 2007 and 2010, ibid.). This occurs because returns to wealth have become dependent on the absolute size of wealth holdings, which is illustrated by the different trajectories of wealth accumulation and balance sheet composition across the distribution. Consequently, there are systemic determinants of inequality arising from the financialisation processes, which define wealth accumulation opportunities across households.

Inequality in Latin America

The motivation to examine the distributive consequences of financialisation in the Latin American context arises from the fact that Latin America has had one of the highest levels of income inequality in the world. Inequality is an important economic issue in itself as it undermines social justice and carries a range of negative consequences for public health, social cohesion and democracy (Pressman 2016). Moreover, it has been shown to have a negative impact on growth in advanced economies (Alesina & Rodrick 1994; Persson & Tabellini 1994; Li et al. 1998; Ostry et al. 2014). Consequently, high levels of inequality pose a challenge to future inclusive economic growth in Latin America.

Table 5.1 shows comparable data on the Gini index of income in selected Latin American countries between 1960 and 2016, contrasting them with patterns of inequality observed in advanced financialised economies of USA and UK, as well as other countries pursuing an export-led growth strategy, namely China and Germany. In contrast to the high-income economies and China, income inequality in Latin America has been declining since the beginning of the twenty-first century. Among large Latin American economies, the highest

Table 5.1 Gini coefficient for disposable income, 1978–2014

	1978	*1984*	*1990*	*1996*	*2002*	*2008*	*2014*
Argentina	36.4	39.4	42.3	44.1	47.5	42.3	38.5
Brazil	51.6	51.1	52.9	52.2	50.9	47.3	44.9
Chile	47.3	49.7	51.1	50.8	50	48	45
Colombia	50.3	50.7	51.1	52.2	52.6	51.6	49.1
Mexico	48.3	45.2	46.1	47.5	46.7	46.9	45.9
Peru	54.4	54.3	54	53.7	52.6	49.2	45.6
Venezuela	41.3	40.9	39.9	42.7	42.9	38.5	36.2
USA	31.4	33.4	34.7	35.8	36.1	37.3	37.8
UK	26.9	30.2	33.7	34.2	34	33.9	33
China	32.8	32.7	36.8	41.4	49.9	51.6	51.5
Germany	26.2	26.1	25.9	26.5	27.3	28.7	29

Source: SWIID (The Standardized World Income Inequality Database) version 6.1, October 2017.

Note: Gini index multiplied by 100. The years 1978 and 2014 are the earliest and latest points, respectively, for which information on the harmonised Gini coefficients is available for all analysed countries.

inequality levels have been observed in Colombia, Peru, Chile, Brazil and Mexico, while Argentina and Venezuela have been comparatively less unequal.

Following general declines in income inequality in the 1960s and 1970s across the majority of large Latin American economies (except for Brazil and Venezuela), income distribution became increasingly unequal with the onset of trade liberalisation in the 1980s, continuing to rise throughout the financial liberalisation period in the 1990s (with the exception of Brazil, Colombia and Peru). Conventional explanations point to disparities in human capital accumulation (IDB 1999), as well as skill-biased technological change and global competition with foreign labour markets associated with trade liberalisation (Goldberg & Pavcnik 2007).

However, systemic forces of financialisation have been instrumental in widening the observed income disparities in the 1980s and 1990s. This can be explained by the downward pressure on wages and worsening functional distribution of income needed to maintain low production costs, high financial rents and overvalued currencies for the export-led growth strategy to be viable (Székely 2003; Levy-Orlik 2013).

There are several reasons behind the decline in income inequality in Latin America since the 2000s, which have been put forward in the literature. One of the explanations indicates new political regimes focussed on explicit redistributive policies and increased welfare state, particularly in South American economies (Gasparini et al. 2011:170). Nevertheless, the equalising impact of conditional cash transfer policies implemented in a number of Latin American countries (most notably Mexico, Brazil and Colombia) cannot fully account for the drops in income inequality in the 2000s due to low coverage of these programmes and relatively small amounts of associated transfers (ibid.). Rather, favourable terms of trade owing to rising global commodity prices are a likely factor contributing to the decline in income inequality by generating substantial growth in employment. However, this explanation too cannot fully account for the trajectory of income inequality in Latin America as in recent years global commodity prices have been on the decline (World Bank 2017), while income inequality continued to decrease. Furthermore, Gasparini et al. (2011) argue that falling income inequality since the 2000s may not constitute a structural shift but can rather be a consequence of recovery from crises (particularly in Argentina and Venezuela). Nevertheless, given the variety of explanations, not enough research has analysed the comparative contribution of the proposed factors to the decline in income inequality in Latin America since the 2000s.

One of the key challenges to understanding inequality in Latin America is insufficient availability of reliable and comparable data on incomes and wealth at the individual or household level. In advanced economies, earnings data have been the traditional source of information on income, but they do not take into account social transfers and taxes. Recent efforts have been focussed on using tax revenue data to infer the size of disposable income and wealth among the population (World Inequality Report 2018). However, in emerging economies, income tax data are less useful due to low tax revenues, ranging typically between 10% and 20% of GDP, compared to over 40% in high-income countries (Besley & Persson 2014). Consequently, household surveys are a more typical source of data on income in Latin America.[1] However, the richest households are known to be less likely to participate in survey data collection, particularly when sensitive topics such as income and personal finances are discussed (Korinek et al. 2006; Fessler & Schürtz 2013). Consequently, the degree of income inequality is likely to be underestimated, and it can exclude the contribution on financial income, which is concentrated at the top of the distribution.

Moreover, there is virtually no comprehensive information on household wealth in Latin America, which inhibits accurate estimation of the degree of wealth inequality. This is further exacerbated by the fact that income and wealth are often conflated in the inequality literature. However, flows of income and stocks of wealth are characterised by fundamentally different dynamics. Specifically, compounding of the returns to wealth over time has resulted in historically higher growth of aggregate wealth than income (estimated at an average of 5% versus 1% by Piketty 2014). Thus, given the heterogeneity of wealth holdings across the distribution and the positive relationship between returns to wealth and its absolute size highlighted in the previous section, we expect wealth inequality in Latin America to be even higher than income inequality.

Table 5.2 presents preliminary data on the inequality of net worth[2] in Latin America (measured by the Gini coefficient in individual countries and the top 1% share of wealth in the region as a whole) compiled from the Credit Suisse Global Wealth Reports between 2011 and 2017. As expected, levels of wealth inequality across countries are higher than income inequality. Overall, the share of wealth accruing to the top 1% in Latin America increased

Table 5.2 Wealth inequality indicators, 2011–2017

	2011	*2012*	*2013*	*2014*	*2015*	*2016*	*2017*
Argentina	76.8	78.2	79.6	80.9	81.8	78.7	72.3
Brazil	79.5	81.2	82.1	82.3	83	82.9	83.2
Chile	78.2	77.4	81.4	78.9	79.5	80.5	78.6
Colombia	79.2	78.8	79.7	76.8	76.9	76.2	74.2
Mexico	77.4	78	78	75.9	75.9	77.9	73.2
Peru	72.5	77.4	70.8	81.7	80.3	80.7	77.8
Venezuela	80.6	79.6	82.5	81.8	81.8	83.7	94.2
USA	82.4	85.2	85.1	84.6	85	86.2	85.9
UK	67	67.5	67.7	68.2	67.8	73.2	73.5
China	74.4	68.9	69.5	71.9	73.3	81.9	78.9
Germany	75	77.7	77.1	77.1	77.5	78.9	79.1
Share of Top 1% (Latin America & Caribbean)	33.9	36.5	38.1	40.5	42.7	42	36.8

Source: Credit Suisse Global Wealth Databook 2011–2017.

Note: Gini coefficient times 100. Wealth share of Top 1% in per cent.

from 33.9% in 2011 to 36.8% in 2017, with a peak of 42.7% in 2015. This is higher than the recorded top 1% share of wealth in Europe (30.4% in 2011 rising to 31.8% in 2017) and slightly lower than the measure in North America (an increase from 35.6% to 37.8% between 2011 and 2017). Moreover, wealth inequality in Latin America has been on the rise since the data series was first recorded in 2011, with a slight decline in the most recent year. Nevertheless, the precise trajectory of wealth inequality has been varied across countries, and the interpretability of the particular movements of the series is impeded by the short period for which data are available.

While we are able to observe some degree of increasing wealth inequality in Latin America in the 2010s, little can be said about the precise determinants of wealth inequality over time. This is due to the lack of detailed data on household finances and tax revenues. To gauge the potential role of financialisation in rising wealth inequality, in the next section we draw lessons from the US experience described earlier in this chapter to flag potential challenges for Latin American development arising from increasing financial obligations of households associated with the push for financial inclusion.

Financial inclusion and wealth inequality in Latin America

In the previous section, we documented high levels of income and wealth inequality in Latin America, describing the link between trade and financial liberalisation and rising income inequality throughout the 1980s and 1990s. Several factors including redistributive policies and sustained export demand due to favourable terms of trade have been put forward as explanations for the decline in income inequality since the 2000s. However, while we observed a rise in wealth inequality in the 2010s, lack of more detailed data prevented us from analysing its precise determinants.

Drawing from the distributive consequences of financialisation in the USA outlined above, we propose that one potential factor contributing to rising wealth inequality in Latin America is increased financial commitments of households associated with financialisation. In the Latin American context, this has been linked to increasing financial inclusion efforts. A substantial part of daily financial activities of families in Latin America is conducted through informal financial institutions. The unbanked population in Latin America (defined as those without a bank account) was estimated at 210 million in 2014, which constituted roughly a third of the region's population that year (Global Findex 2014). This has been related to high costs of formal financial services, sparse spatial coverage of formal financial institutions and insufficient enforcement of contracts between creditors and debtors (Demirguc-Kunt et al. 2015). Since 2010, efforts of Latin American governments and international organisations (primarily International Monetary Fund (IMF) and the World Bank) have been focussed on increasing the proportion of financial services to households provided by the formal *private* financial sector. These have been led by programmes such as the Financial Inclusion Initiative for Latin America and the Caribbean (FILAC) and the Consultative Group to Assist the Poor (CGAP), which work with local governments to increase the formality of household financial activities in the region.

Financial inclusion programmes in Latin America have been motivated by arguments that greater access to formal financial services among low-income households is conducive to development. This is because it has been seen to increase the allocative efficiency between creditors and debtors, facilitate consumption smoothing over the life cycle and help the poor lift themselves out of poverty by nurturing a more long-term, responsible and productive financial behaviour (Rojas-Suárez 2016).

However, this narrative neglects the instrumental role of financial inclusion policies in generating high asset returns to support financial liberalisation and innovation, and it has been based on contestable empirical evidence of its benefits (Kvangraven & Dos Santos 2016).

In the aftermath of these financial inclusion strategies, the proportion of adults with an account at a formal financial institution rose from 39% in 2011 to 51% in 2014 (Global Findex 2014). Moreover, household indebtedness has increased. Figure 5.1 shows that while the size of private debt to households relative to GDP in Latin America has been low compared to advanced economies, its relative size has been on the rise since the 1990s, increasing most rapidly in Chile, Colombia and Brazil.

In addition to the large degree of informality of household financial activities, an important reason for such low levels of private debt to households is related to less formalised housing markets compared to advanced economies. Rather than through mortgage lending by the private banking sector, housing is often obtained through financial assistance from the governmental

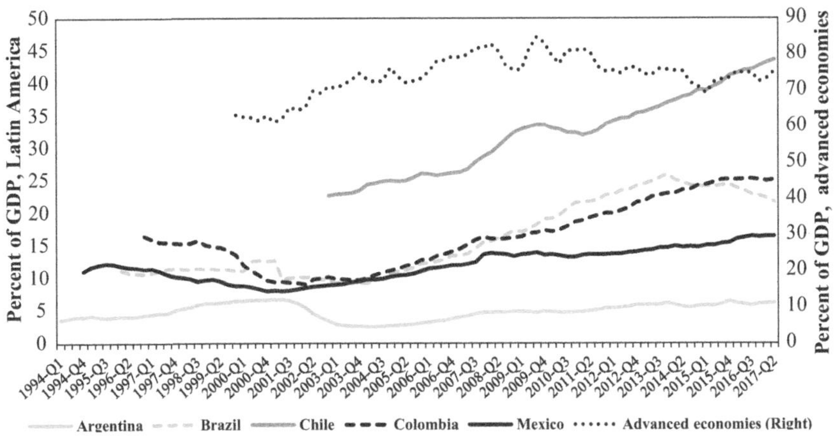

Figure 5.1 Total credit to household and non-profit institutions serving households, 1994q1–2017q2.

Source: BIS (Bank of International Settlements).

Note: Aggregate for advanced economies based on conversion to US dollars at market exchange rates. Advanced economies include Australia, Canada, Denmark, the euro area, Japan, New Zealand, Norway, Sweden, Switzerland, the UK and the USA.

housing funds (such as Infonavit in Mexico), legalised squatter settlements or illegal housing developments (Gilbert 2001; Ortega-Alcazar 2006; Herbert et al. 2012). Moreover, the stock of existing houses which are affordable to low-income household remains insufficient and of low quality (Gilbert 2001). Consequently, the value of housing remains low for many households, which further exacerbates asset and wealth inequality. This is because without asset building opportunities increased household indebtedness is bound to worsen financial fragility and leverage of low-income households. Indeed, rising household debt-to-income ratios have been observed in Brazil, Chile and Colombia (Mazer & Navajas 2012). Moreover, lack of detailed data on household finances in Latin America obscures the true scale of this adverse impact of financial inclusion on inequality.

The push to formal finance based on increasing household indebtedness can have particularly detrimental consequences for inequality in the context of the export-led growth strategy pursued by many Latin American countries. This is because the need to maintain competitiveness to sustain export viability has kept wages low (Levy-Orlik 2013). Simultaneously, financial returns accruing to the richest households and foreign investors have experienced above-average growth (ibid.). This further exacerbates leverage problems across households towards the middle and bottom of the income distribution, and perpetuates the disparities in asset accumulation. A further pitfall of the financial inclusion narrative based on private financial sectors is the shift of responsibility for personal financial fragility towards the individual and the focus on micro-level policy strategies. This neglects the systemic determinants of poverty and inequality in Latin America and the role of macroeconomic policy in decreasing inequality.

Given low wages, rising household indebtedness, uneven returns to wealth and disparate asset accumulation possibilities, wealth inequality in Latin America is likely to increase in the future. First, this is because low incomes and asset ownership may lead to a rise in leverage and financial fragility of households towards the middle and the bottom of the distribution given the ongoing credit expansion in the course of financial inclusion. Second, heterogeneity of the returns to wealth induced by the dominance of foreign financial institutions is likely to perpetuate wealth concentration due to the compounding of the returns to wealth over time (Piketty 2014). It is vital that more efforts are directed to understanding the distributional consequences of financial inclusion policies and the export-led growth strategy in order to level out the opportunities for sustainable wealth accumulation among low-income households through access to savings and higher incomes.

Conclusion

This chapter analysed the link between financialisation and economic inequality in Latin America. It highlighted increasing financial commitments of households as a fundamental challenge to reigning in high levels of income and wealth inequality in the region. This has been induced by the narrative of financial inclusion strategies portraying private financial institutions as indispensable in promoting growth in Latin America. Drawing from the analysis of the distributive impact of financialisation in the USA, we argued that rising financial inclusion, manifested in increasing provision of formal private credit to households, may exacerbate disparities in household balance sheet stability. This is because low wages and pressures to increase financial rents induced by financial liberalisation in Latin America since the 1990s have generated uneven asset accumulation possibilities and disparate returns to wealth. This has contributed to increasing financial fragility of Latin American households, which may explain rising wealth inequality levels in the recent years. In order to reduce the persistent gaps in income and wealth in the region, it is crucial that the pitfalls of financial inclusion are recognised and Latin American governments take an active role in improving asset distribution and raising wages at the macroeconomic level.

Notes

1 Examples include the Socioeconomic Database for Latin America and the Caribbean (SEDLAC), Encuesta Permanente de Hogares (EPH) in Argentina, Encuesta de Caracterización Socioeconómica Nacional (CASEN) in Chile, Encuesta Nacional de Hogares-Fuerza de Trabajo (ENH-FT) in Colombia, Encuesta Nacional de Ingresos y Gastos de los Hogares (ENIGH) in Mexico, Encuesta Nacional de Hogares Sobre Medición de Niveles de Vida (ENNIV) in Peru and

Encuesta de Hogares por Muestreo (EHM) in Venezuela. Based on these surveys, inequality measures are provided by the World Bank, ECLAC (Economic Commission for Latin America and the Caribbean) and the Inter-American Development Bank (cf. Gasparini 2003).

2 Net worth is defined as assets less liabilities.

References

Alesina, A. & Rodrik, D. (1994) 'Distribution Politics and Economic Growth', *The Quarterly Journal of Economics*, 109(2), 465–490.

Arestis, P., Charles, A., & Fontana, G. (2013) 'Financialization, the Great Recession, and the Stratification of the US Labor Market', *Feminist Economics*, 19(3), 152–180.

Atkinson, A.B. (2015) *Inequality. What Can Be Done?* Harvard University Press, London.

Bank for International Settlements Data (2017) Viewed 15 January 2018, from www.bis.org/statistics/.

Besley, T. & Persson, T. (2014) 'Why Do Developing Countries Tax So Little?', *Journal of Economic Perspectives*, 28(4), 99–120.

Credit Suisse Global Wealth Report and Databook, 2011 to 2017. Viewed 15 January 2018, from www.credit-suisse.com/corporate/en/research/research-institute/global-wealth-report.html.

Correa, E. & Vidal, G. (2012) 'Financialization and Global Financial Crisis in Latin American Countries', *Journal of Economic Issues*, 46(2), 541–548.

Demirguc-Kunt, A., Klapper, L., Singer, D., & Van Oudheusden, P. (2015) 'The Global Findex Database 2014. Measuring Financial Inclusion around the World', *World Bank Policy Research*, Working Paper No. 7255.

Dymski, G.A., Hernandez, J., & Mohanty, L. (2013) 'Race, Gender, Power, and the US Subprime Mortgage and Foreclosure Crisis: A Meso Analysis', *Feminist Economics*, 19(3), 124–151.

Epstein, G.A. (ed.) (2005) *Financialization and the world economy*. Edward Elgar, Cheltenham.

Federal Reserve Economic Database, Federal Reserve Bank of St. Louis. Viewed 1 June 2017, from https://fred.stlouisfed.org.

Fessler, P. & Schürtz, M. (2013) 'Cross-country comparability of the Eurosystem Household Finance and Consumption Survey', Monetary Policy and the Economy Q2/13, Oesterreichische Nationalbank.

Gabor, D.V. (2012) 'The Road to Financialization in Central and Eastern Europe: The Early Policies and Politics of Stabilizing Transition', *Review of Political Economy*, 24(2), 227–249.

Galbraith, J.K. (2012) *Inequality and Instability. A Study of the World Economy Just before the Great Crisis*, Oxford University Press, Oxford.

Galbraith, J.K. (2016) *Inequality. What Everyone Needs to Know*, Oxford University Press, Oxford.

Gasparini, L. (2003) 'Income Inequality in Latin America and the Caribbean: Evidence from Household Surveys', *CEDLAS*, Working Paper No. 2.

Gasparini, L., Cruces, G., & Tornarolli, L. (2011) 'Recent Trends in Income Inequality in Latin America', *Economía*, 11(2), 147–190.

Gilbert, A. (2001) 'Housing in Latin America', *INDES – European Union Joint Program*, Working Paper I-7UE.

Global Findex (2014) World Bank. Viewed 15 January 2018, from www.worldbank.org/en/programs/globalfindex
Goda, T. & Lysandrou, P. (2011) 'The Contribution of Wealth Concentration to the Subprime Crisis: A Quantitative Estimation', CIBS Working Paper No. 22.
Goda, T., Onaran, Ö., & Stockhammer, E. (2016) 'Income Inequality and Wealth Concentration in the Recent Crisis', *Development and Change*, 48(1), 3–27.
Goldberg, P.K. & Pavcnik, N. (2007) 'Distributional Effects of Globalization in Developing Countries', *Journal of Economic Literature*, 45(1), 39–82.
Henry, B., Reese, J., & Torres, A. (2013) *Wasted Wealth. How the Wall Street Crash Continues to Stall Economic Recovery and Deepen Racial Inequity in America*, Alliance for a Just Society.
Herbert, C.E., Belsky, E.S., & DuBroff, N. (2012) 'The State of Mexico's Housing – Recent Progress and Continued Challenges', *Joint Center for Housing Studies of Harvard University*, Working Paper W12-8.
Inter-American Development Bank (IDB) (1999) 'Facing up to Inequality in Latin America', Report on Economic and Social Progress in Latin America, Washington.
Kalecki, M. (1954) *Theory of Economic Dynamics: An Essay on Cyclical and Long-run Changes in Capitalist Economy*, Allen and Unwin, London.
Karwowski, E. & Stockhammer, E. (2017) 'Financialisation in Emerging Economies: A Systematic Overview and Comparison with Anglo-Saxon Economies', *Journal of Economic and Political Studies*, 5(1), 60–86.
Korinek, A., Mistiaen, J.A., & Ravallion, M. (2006) 'Survey Nonresponse and the Distribution of Income', *Journal of Economic Inequality*, 4, 33–55.
Kumhof, M. & Ranciere, R. (2010) 'Inequality, Leverage and Crises', IMF Working Paper WP/10/268.
Kvangraven, I.H. & Dos Santos, P.L. (2016) 'Financial Inclusion and Its Discontents', Private Debt Project. Viewed 15 January 2018, from http://privatedebtproject.org/view-articles.php?Financial-Inclusion-and-Its-Discontents-16.
Levy-Orlik, N. (2013) 'Financialization and Economic Growth in Developing Countries', *International Journal of Political Economy*, 42(4), 108–127.
Li, H., Squire, L., & Zou, H. (1998, January) 'Explaining International and Intertemporal Variations in Income Inequality', *Economic Journal*, 108, 26–43.
Marcantoni, E. (2014) *Collateralized Debt Obligations*, Springer, Gabler.
Mazer, R. & Navajas, S. (2012) 'Consumer Lending and Overindebtedness in Latin America', CGAP Blog, 24/9/2012. Viewed 15 January 2018, from www.cgap.org/blog/consumer-lending-and-overindebtedness-latin-america.
Mian, A. & Sufi, A. (2013) *House of Debt*, University of Chicago Press, Chicago.
Ortega-Alcazar, I. (2006) 'Mexico City: Housing and Neighbourhoods', in Burdett, R. (ed.) *Mexico City: Growth at the Limit?* LSE Cities Project.
Ostry, J.D., Berg, A., & Tsangarides, C.G. (2014) 'Redistribution, Inequality, and Growth', IMF Staff Discussion Note SDN/14/02.
Palley, T.I. (2007) 'Financialization: What It Is and Why It Matters', *The Levy Economics Institute*, Working Paper No. 525.
Persson, T. & Tabellini, G. (1994) 'Is Inequality Harmful for Growth?', *American Economic Review*, 105(5), 48–53.
Philippon, T. & Reshef, A. (2012) 'Wages and Human Capital in the U.S. Finance Industry: 1909–2006', *The Quarterly Journal of Economics*, 127(4), 1551–1609.

Piketty, T. (2014) *Capital in the Twenty First Century*, Harvard University Press, Harvard USA.

Piketty, T. & Zucman, G. (2014) 'Capital is Back: Wealth-income Ratios in Rich Countries 1700–2010', *The Quarterly Journal of Economics*, 29(3), 1255–1310.

Pollin, R. & Heintz, J. (2013) 'Study of U.S. Financial System', FESSUD Studies in Financial Systems No. 10.

Pressman, S. (2016) *Understanding Piketty's Capital in the Twenty First Century*, Routledge, Abingdon.

Rajan, R.G. (2010) *Fault Lines How Hidden Fractures Still Threaten the World Economy*, Princeton University Press, Princeton.

Rojas-Suárez, L. (2016) 'Financial Inclusion in Latin America: Facts, Obstacles and Central Banks' Policy Issues', Inter-American Development Bank Discussion Paper No. IDB-DP-464.

Rossi, S. (2013) 'Financialisation and Monetary Union in Europe: The Monetary–Structural Causes of the Euro-area Crisis', *Cambridge Journal of Regions, Economy and Society*, 6(3), 381–400.

Standardized World Income Inequality Database (SWIID), version 6.1, October 2017.

Stiglitz, J. (2012) *The Price of Inequality*, Penguin Books Ltd, London.

Stockhammer, E. (2015) 'Rising Inequality as a Cause of the Present Crisis', *Cambridge Journal of Economics*, 39, 935–958.

Székely, M. (2003) 'The 1990s in Latin America: Another Decade of Persistent Inequality, But with Somewhat Lower Poverty', *Journal of Applied Economics*, 6(2), 317–339.

Szymborska, H.K. (2017) *Financial Sector and Household Balance Sheet Dynamics: Rethinking the Determinants of Income and Wealth Inequality in the USA since the 1980s*. Unpublished PhD thesis. University of Leeds.

U.S. Survey of Consumer Finances (1989–2013) Federal Reserve. Viewed 1 August 2017, from www.federalreserve.gov/econres/scfindex.htm.

Van Treeck, T. & Sturn, S. (2012) 'Income Inequality as a Cause of the Great Recession? A Survey of Current Debates', Conditions of Work and Employment Series No.39, International Labour Office, Geneva.

Wolff, E.N. (2014) 'Household Wealth Trends in the United States, 1983–2010', *Oxford Review of Economic Policy*, 30(1), 21–43.

World Bank (2017) *Commodity Markets Outlook October 2017*. A World Bank Report. Viewed 15 January 2018, from http://pubdocs.worldbank.org/en/743431507927822505/CMO-October-2017-Full-Report.pdf.

World Inequality Report (2018) Viewed 1 January 2018, from http://wir2018.wid.world (Accessed 1 January 2018).

Young, B. (2010) 'The Gendered Dimension of Money, Finance and the Subprime Crisis', in Bauhardt, C. & Caglar, G. (eds.), *Gender and Economics*, Feministische Kritik der politischen Oekonomie, VS Verlag für Sozialwissenschaften, Wiesbaden.

6 The effect of inflation target regimes in commodities-based, financialised economies on income growth and distribution in Latin America

Santiago Capraro

The last 30 years have produced an institutional convergence in monetary policy in Latin America. Since the early 1990s, the number of countries implementing inflation target regimes (ITRs) as their monetary policy has increased, with Argentina as the most recent addition in 2016. In this institutional set-up, monetary and not fiscal policy is the centre of economic policy; this makes the head of the central bank the country's most important policymaker (Bhaduri, 2011; Epstein, 2015).

The adoption of inflation target policies in Latin America has been governed by the pillars of the Washington Consensus (Williamson, 2003), which moved from import substitution industrialisation and state involvement in economic activity towards a model of globalisation and financialisation, increasing financial sector leadership, and an export-driven growth strategy. As a whole, this model involved a process of trade opening and liberalisation of the capital account.

This chapter seeks to show that ITR-policy-based macroeconomic models do not take into account important structural characteristics of the Latin American economies. This means that they generate undesired economic consequences such as stagnation and a regressive redistribution of income. That is to say, although they may create inflationary stability (maintaining inflation within the expected limits), ITRs destabilise economic growth and lower wage participation in overall income.

This chapter is structured in four sections, including this introduction. The second section develops a theoretical critique of the inflation target models applied in Latin America based on the region's economic structural characteristics. The third section discusses the main stylised facts in the Latin American countries that apply inflation targets, emphasising the evolution of growth, inflation, the terms of trade (TT) and income distribution. Finally, the fourth section presents the chapter's most important conclusions.

ITRs in small, open economies with export-driven models

In ITRs, central banks' priority objective is to fulfil an inflation target, for which they have been given autonomy (Capraro & Panico, 2018). Their independence means that they cannot be obligated to finance the public sector by printing money (Panico & Rizza, 2003). According to the literature on dynamic inconsistency, greater independence for central banks is accompanied by a communications policy aimed at the public regarding monetary policy that aims to make their operations more transparent. ITR proponents argue that inflation targets are reached by moving the short-term interest rate (Blanchard, 2011; Blanchard & Summers, 2017).

ITRs are the subject of various polemics; their most controversial aspect is the role of the nominal exchange rate (NER) in monetary policy. According to the simplest versions, the NER is freely determined in the market and responds to the fundamentals of the economy, among others, the interest rate, the public sector deficit and the current account (CA) (Ball, 2000; Taylor, 2001). However, in practice, central bankers see the NER as an intermediate target (Bordo, 2016).

The mechanisms whereby they attempt to control the NER if it reaches inconsistent levels with the inflation rate include, first, the central bank seeking to reverse undesired NER fluctuations by varying the interest rate, and therefore, the interest rate rises (drops) to counter a depreciation (appreciation) of the NER. Second, it makes sterilised interventions in the foreign exchange market (Capraro & Perrotini, 2012) to avoid undesired depreciations (appreciations), which leads it to sell (purchase) international reserves.

These mechanisms are not contradictory; rather, they complement each other. The economic literature has identified two of their particularities. The first underlines the fact that central banks behave asymmetrically, which implies that they increase the interest rate to avert an undesired depreciation; however, the interest rate does not drop to neutralise an NER. The systematic application of this bias makes the real exchange rate (RER) tend to appreciate, which can negatively affect economic growth.[1]

The second particularity is that modifying the interest rate does not work when liquidity is the source of the problem in the foreign exchange market. This implies that fluctuations in the interest rate are not effective and, therefore, the central bank must intervene, selling or buying international reserves. The literature indicates that just like in the case of the first mechanism, central banks are more active when they seek to control an undesired NER depreciation than an appreciation. Therefore, the two mechanisms tend to appreciate the RER.

Céspedes et al. (2014) state that the NER could be a final target for some central bankers in developing countries since they want to stabilise the NER in situations of greater volatility, which increases uncertainty and destabilises both the nominal and real variables in the economy.

Under circumstances in which monetary policy focusses on ITRs, fiscal policy is not used to achieve full employment, and the central objective becomes stabilising public sector debt. This can be achieved by legal reforms, particularly a law to establish fiscal responsibility to control the fulfilment of primary surpluses and public spending (Combes et al., 2017). It should be noted that the main Latin American economies stand on two pillars. The first is central bank monetary and exchange rate policies that aim for low, stable inflation in order to eliminate volatility in the economic system. Second, fiscal policy is subordinate to monetary policy and, as a result, the management of aggregate demand centres on stabilising the economy, disregarding growth or full employment goals.

This institutional configuration of the Latin American economies divorces economic growth from industrialisation, focussing attention on private economic activity and putting private investment and exports at centre stage. This implies that economic policies are used to stabilise the economic cycle. Meanwhile, growth is driven by exports and private investment. Therefore, growth is subject to the lottery of each country's endowments and world market swings in the demand for and prices of the goods it exports.

ITRs in the period before and after the 2008–2010 global financial crisis

During the periods of the great economic moderation (1985–2008) and the global financial crisis (2008–2010), a consensus was reached about how ITRs worked. In the theoretical model for inflation targeting, the price variation rate is controlled through movements in the interest rate, which changes aggregate demand through different transmission mechanisms. Next, Phillips curve mechanisms make inflation converge on its target. I should underline that the model predicts that this result can be achieved at the same time that the economy approaches full employment. During the process of controlling inflation, phases can exist in which the economy does not exhibit full employment, although the tendency is to the optimum use of productive resources (Woodford, 2003).

In light of the great financial crisis in the USA and Europe, the model's adjustment mechanisms were harshly criticised. International Monetary Fund (IMF) representative Blanchard (2011) says:

> Before the crisis, mainstream economists and policymakers had converged on a beautiful construction for monetary policy. . . . We had convinced ourselves that there was one target, inflation. There was one instrument, the policy rate. And that was basically enough to get things done. If there is one lesson to be drawn from this crisis, it is that this construction wasn't right, that beauty is unfortunately not always synonymous with truth. The fact is that there are many targets and there are many instruments.
>
> (Blanchard, 2011, p. 1)

Lavoie (2016) explains from a post-Keynesian perspective that the financial crisis revealed a series of weaknesses of ITRs in developed countries, underlining the processes of financialisation unleashed during the great moderation from 1985 to 2007 despite having achieved price stability. However, the same author emphasises that the developed countries were able to abandon the ITR libretto to adopt a nontraditional monetary policy. Finally, he underlines that central banks recognise the principle of endogenously creating money (2016) (see McLeay et al., 2014 for the case of the Bank of England).

Based on this, we can infer that developed countries' central banks dealt with the world economic crisis using pragmatic monetary policies to stabilise financial markets and expand economic activity by restoring liquidity and lowering the short-term interest rate and using non-conventional policies to lower the long-term interest rate (Epstein, 2015). Therefore, within the legal limits set by their mandates – and with mixed results – the developed countries' central banks attempted to temper the effects of the financial and economic crisis.

By contrast, in Latin America, the central banks continued to apply the inflation targeting model,[2] despite the fact that it does not appropriately reflect those economies' important structural characteristics. In this context, the ITR must be critiqued in terms of central bank functioning and the macroeconomic model underlying it. This general critique goes beyond the scope of this chapter; therefore, I will concentrate solely on analysing the role of the exchange rate and the potential output of an inflation targeting regime. In particular, I will analyse the mechanisms whereby these variables affect inflation, economic growth and income distribution in the inflation targeting regime.

Critical analysis of the ITR based on Thirlwall's law and structural inflation

In macroeconomic ITR models, the fundamental origin of inflation is linked to excess demand, while a central aspect for calculating it and constructing the Phillips curve is potential output. Svensson (2001, p. 3) states that potential output is the level of output that would result if prices and wages were flexible, which is the same as saying that it operates at full employment levels. Empirically, as Taylor suggested (1993), the tendency or simple moving average of real output can be used to estimate potential output. However, the tendency of output does not necessarily provide information about the degree of employment in the economy due to the high level of informal labour. Therefore, when output surpasses its tendency, it does not spark inflation since the model's transmission mechanisms do not begin to operate. To analyse this problem, we can look at two fundamental equations of this model:

$$\pi_t = \pi_{t-1} + \theta_0\left(y_t - y^p\right) + \theta_1 e_t + \theta_2 p_t^* \text{ con } \theta_0 > 0,\ \theta_1 > 0,\ \theta_2 > 0 \tag{1}$$

$$r_t = \alpha_0 + \alpha_1\left(y_t - y^p\right) + \alpha_2\left(\pi_t - \pi^T\right) \ con\ \alpha_1 > 0,\ \alpha_2 > 0 \tag{2}$$

Equation (1) is a Phillips curve applied to an open economy with adaptive expectations, which indicates that inflation (π) depends on the inflation of the previous period; the gap in output $\left(y_t - y^p\right)$ – which, in turn, depends on the level of output in the current period $\left(y_t\right)$ and potential output $\left(y^p\right)$; and, finally, on the devaluation of the exchange rate $\left(e_t\right)$ and the evolution of international prices (p_t^*).

Equation (2) is the central bank's reaction function, through which it determines the real interest rate (r_t), which depends on an intercept (α_0), the output gap and the differential between inflation and the inflation target $\left(\pi^T\right)$. Factors α_1 and α_2 are determined in accordance with the central bank's commitment to reaching the inflation target and its interest in maintaining a certain employment level. In an open economy, the coefficient α_0 can be related to the natural interest rate and the real international reference rate.

Equation (1) indicates that when output surpasses (or is less than) its tendency, inflation increases (or decreases). Two transmission mechanisms produce this effect. First, when full employment is surpassed, workers can demand a wage increase. And, second, when, as Svensson (2010) underlines, once full employment is surpassed, an increase in output would raise production costs.

The thesis is false if the tendency of output gives no information about the economy's level of full employment, although the tendency can be a useful indicator. In most developing countries, the tendency of output is equal to the level of gross domestic product (GDP) consistent with equilibrium in the balance of payments (EBPGDPs); and this changes the nature of the inflation target model. This is because the EBPGDP is often lower than full-employment GDP (Thirlwall, 1973).[3]

If the tendency of output is the same as EBPGDP, we can infer that inflation will be determined by the evolution of the exchange rate (see equation [1]) and costs (following the ECLAC (Economic Commission for Latin America and the Caribbean) theory of structural inflation) (Bielschowsky, 2009). In addition, the central bank would change its monetary policy to not fall into a balance-of-payments crisis, which happens when output consistently exceeds its tendency, that is, when it is over the level of activity consistent with EBPGDPs (Moreno-Brid, 1998).

If this alternative is correct and the interest rate's transmission mechanisms to aggregate demand are effective, the central bank would maintain an inflation target and a level of economic activity consistent with EBPGDPs. In this way, the level of economic activity would be constrained by the structural characteristic of exports, imports and the other components of the balance of payments and would not achieve full employment as orthodox inflation targeting models suppose. In addition, due to the fact that inflation stops depending on demand, the central bank will tend to adjust the interest rate to determine the NER in accordance with the inflation target. Any policy pegged to the NER tends to appreciate the RER.

In this regard, the economic stabilisation model contradicts the growth model. On the one hand, the main driver of growth is exports, and increasing the RER makes domestic production less competitive and fosters imports. While this process has a negative effect on production levels, in the last analysis, it affects the economy's growth rate in accordance with equilibrium of the balance of payments, cutting off possibilities for the Latin American countries to develop.

Therefore, we can infer that the macroeconomic model underlying ITRs is not appropriate for the economies of Latin America, indicating that analysing the situation in Latin America using this tool may lead us to mistaken conclusions.[4] Observers say that the ITRs implemented in Latin America are structured to control the economic cycle with the central aim of making effective inflation converge on the inflation target. This has negative consequences for the level and rate of growth of economic activity. In addition, if the aim is to compensate for the loss of competitiveness sparked by the appreciation of the RER by cutting wages, this could generate a redistribution of income to the detriment of workers.

This section analysed the consequences of controlling the economic cycle in a small, open economy that sets inflation targets without studying the factors that determine long-term growth. This implies examining investment determinants in the framework of an open, export-driven economy, whose level of activity is constrained by the balance of payments.

Economic growth in an inflation targeting regime: investment determinants

Investment has at least three determinants. The first is public investment, which is autonomous *vis-à-vis* the level of activity.[5] The second is the differential between the expected profit rate for real investment and the market interest rate, which can represent the opportunity cost of investment or the cost of borrowing. And third, investment depends on the use of existing capacity, whose operationalisation presupposes incorporating the differential between effective use of productive capacity and a desired level of use of existing capacity, a concept that is similar to that of the output differential expressed in equation (1).

At least since the 1980s debt crisis, the economic literature has taken as a stylised fact that in Latin America the first public expenditure adjusted when it is necessary to decrease the fiscal deficit is investment. This therefore implies that public investment becomes intermittent and uncertain, making it impossible to carry out long-term projects. This procyclical behaviour makes the evolution of activity levels more unstable. Therefore, in the sphere of an ITR in which fiscal policy tends to be adjusted in accordance with the needs of monetary policy, public investment cannot become the key for escaping economic stagnation.

ITRs affect the expected profit differential in different ways. Two of them tend to decrease it and therefore lower investment: first, since inflation must be controlled by a real interest rate determined by the central bank, it must be kept high *vis-à-vis* the international rate and its historic level when the ITR is launched in order to gain credibility, and then it must be kept high in order to control inflation. The second way is by appreciating the RER because this negatively affects the profit rate (Dutt, 2017).

ITRs can have a positive effect on the profit differential if, once inflation is controlled, the supply shocks pass through decreases. Therefore, in the face of international price hikes or exchange rate devaluations, the profit rate rises. The price that determines that this happens is wages; therefore, if wages are not adjusted to supply shocks, the participation of wages in output drops, and this is what drives the profit rate up. The negative effect is that changes in income distribution will be to the detriment of workers.

With regard to the differential in output, I explained above that it is never narrow in developing countries because, in these economies, the constraints on activities come from the level of activity consistent with EBPGDPs. This level of activity is usually less than full employment; therefore, capitalists see no incentive to invest. And this generates recessive processes and lower long-term growth.

In accordance with the logic of the ITR model, there are two ways to escape from this bleak prospect for investment and, therefore, for prospects for growth in developing countries. First, as established above, ITRs stabilise the economy, hoping for growth through exports. In this way, a shock from increased demand for exports would be one solution to the problem of stagnation. This exogenous shock generates increased exports and a higher profit rate for the sectors involved, which, in turn, could generate increased investment.

Second, I explained above that ITR monetary policy tends to raise the RER, creating a contradiction with export-driven growth. One way of overcoming this tension is by modifying exchange rate policy, for example, by generating a stable, competitive RER that sparks the potential of exports. However, the proponents of ITRs, like Taylor (2001) and Svensson (2010), maintain that this kind of exchange rate policy would risk not being able to reach the inflation target, which is the central bank's main objective. Therefore, one guideline for untying this Gordian knot is by reducing workers' negotiating power in labour relations, recovering lost competitiveness by appreciating the currency by lowering nominal wages. In this way, the external sector can deal with growth without endangering the inflation target.

However, this kind of policy implies a transfer of income from workers to capitalists, mainly because business persons can benefit from advances in productivity and supply shocks to the detriment of workers. It would seem that the Latin American countries with ITRs chose to apply this solution. This kind of redistributive policies can have a negative effect on economic growth if the economy is wage-led. Therefore, one of the possible scenarios that emerges from applying these policies is an economy in which exports grow and effective inflation tends to converge on the inflation target, but with low economic growth. The drop in workers' participation in national income is what generates economic stagnation. In the next section, I will present a series of stylised facts that demonstrate this scenario for a group of Latin American countries.

Stylised facts of inflation, growth and income distribution in periods of financialised globalisation in Latin American countries

Arestis and Sawyer (2003, 2013) show that a correlation exists between the application of an ITR and lower inflation. However, they also demonstrate that no causality exists between applying inflation targets and the drop in price variations. In the Latin American countries analysed (Brazil, Chile, Colombia, Guatemala, Mexico and Peru), inflation decreased after they implemented the ITR.

In these countries, the correlation between the ITR and economic growth is less clear than for price control; this makes for a complex situation. Among the six countries, two, Chile and Mexico, grew less after implementing the ITR; Guatemala grew slightly with and without the ITR and, finally, three countries, Brazil, Peru and Colombia, grew significantly in the framework of the ITR.[6]

The analysis above does not cover the same period. To better understand the evolution of growth in the selected countries, we must study the period from 2002 to 2016. A fundamental indicator for understanding growth in Latin American countries is the evolution of the TT. These improved due to the rise in the prices of raw materials between 2002 and 2011, a trend which reversed between 2012 and 2016. Figure 6.1 shows the relationship between the exponential growth rate of the TT and GDP in the periods mentioned. Clearly, between 2002 and 2011, the countries that grew the most were those that experienced the greatest growth in TT (Peru, Colombia, Chile and Brazil), which grew more rapidly than Mexico and Guatemala, whose TT varied less; in Guatemala, the TT even decreased.

In the years between 2012 and 2016, the countries whose TT deteriorated the most also showed marked drops in their growth rate, notably Chile, Colombia and Peru. By contrast, the countries with smaller declines in their TT accelerated their growth, albeit slightly (Guatemala and Mexico). The Brazilian economy is special because, in this period, it implemented a strong public sector adjustment, although the drop in its TT explains part of the reduction in the growth rate (see Serrano & Summa, 2015). From all of this, we can infer that a positive correlation exists between the evolution of the TT and economic growth. Therefore, given the volatility and historic tendency of the TT in Latin America, it does not seem optimum for the long-term growth strategy to depend on exceptionally high TT.

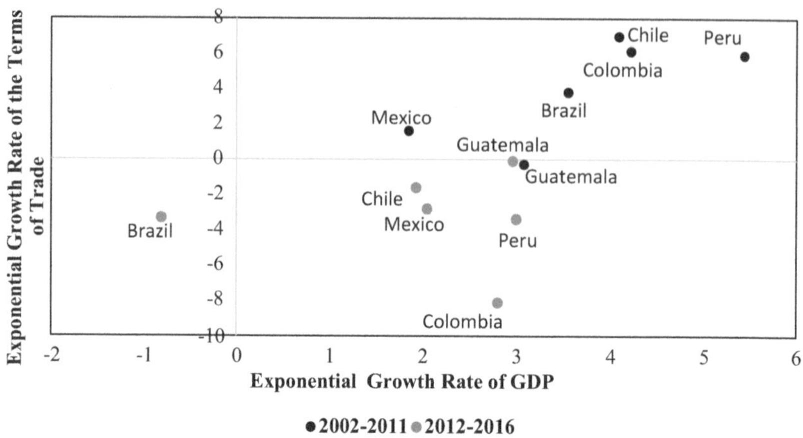

Figure 6.1 Growth and evolution of the TT in Latin American countries applying an ITR before and after the raw materials price boom.

Source: Developed by the author using data from World Development Indicators and ECLAC.

Key: black: economic growth data and evolution of the TT, 2002–2011; grey: economic growth data and evolution of the TT, 2012–2016.

The mechanisms whereby the TT increased an economy's growth rate are multiple. Among the main ones are, first, the increase in demand leads to short-term hikes in production; second, improved TT increases the profit rate in export sectors, and, according to the determinants of investment analysed in the previous section, this implies increased investment in these sectors. In the countries studied, this was the case particularly in agriculture and mining.

Reversed growth in the sectors benefitted by better TT in the last 40 years (see ECLAC, 2014) puts pressure on national prices (mainly in food-producing countries that export consumer goods, like Brazil), which generates an appreciation of the RER. Following the economic literature, this unleashes the so-called "Dutch disease" (Wong & Petreski, 2014), which produced a return to raw-material exports in the years from 2002 to 2011 in Latin America, particularly in Brazil (ECLAC, 2014).

Statistics from the Bank for International Settlements show the appreciation of the RER in Brazil, Colombia and Chile in the period of improved TT between 2002 and 2011. This did not happen in Mexico, which maintained a stable exchange rate in that period, which coincides with the last part of the period of great moderation. Peru is a special case: its exchange rate remained steady despite important improvements in the TT. This is due mainly to the fact that its ITR is *sui generis* because its economy is widely dollarised and its central bank is particularly interested in stabilising the NER by establishing quantitative targets on monetary aggregates in dollars, administered through legal reserve requirements (Armas & Gripa, 2005).

According to what the previous section pointed out, ITRs seem effective in stabilising inflation, although they are responsible for destabilising economic growth and employment. They do not include an institution obligated to explain why economies do not grow because growth depends on international market conditions.

However, the RER could be used to achieve a growth objective, but this is not operational because the imposed inflation targets could not be reached. Thus, the alternative is wage deflation through which international competitiveness lost in the processes of RER appreciation is recovered. Figure 6.2 captures this process by looking at the participation of wages in GDP (PWGDP). For the two countries specialised in the export of assembled/manufactured goods, Mexico and Guatemala, the PWGDP clearly drops throughout the period under study, accompanied by a process of wage deflation and lower PWGDP. Also, these two countries experienced the lowest growth, which would confirm that growth through exports made competitive by cheap labour is not the best strategy.

The evolution of this variable in the economies of Chile, Colombia and Peru is more complex. They display anti-cyclical performance; in the period when raw material prices rose, they showed economic growth with lower PWGDP, but when the growth rate drops due to the deterioration of the TT (2012–2016), the PWGDP rises, although the Colombian and Chilean economies did not recover their initial PWGDP. The economic literature points to PWGDP as the growth at different speeds of price and wage adjustments, with lower volatility in employment levels *vis-à-vis* levels of economic activity (Charpe, 2011). However, in the context of ITRs, this evolution can be said to respond to the fact that wages, in the last analysis, are the nominal anchor of the economy. In periods of rising raw material prices, workers

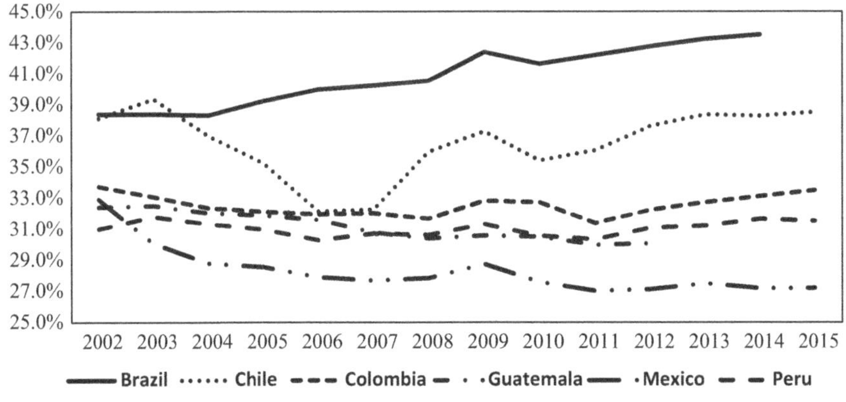

Figure 6.2 The share of wages in GDP (current values in national currency) 2002–2016.

Source: Developed by the author with data from ECLAC and UNSTAT (United Nations Statistics).

maintained constant wages without receiving benefits from these economies' growth, that is, the commodities boom only benefitted capital.

The Brazilian economy's performance is specific and interesting because it shows that the wage policies of the early 2000s had a positive impact on functional distribution of income. This made it possible to accelerate economic growth during the raw material boom without endangering economic stability since the CA had a surplus. From 2012 to 2016, these policies were reversed, explained in part by the reversion of the distribution of income; and, in addition to the adjustments in public spending, this created stagnation and a contraction of the Brazilian economy (Serrano & Summa, 2015).

The RER, the TT and the trajectory of economic growth determined the evolution of the CA of the balance of payments. Figure 6.3 demonstrates that during the years the TT improved, the CAs showed exceptional surpluses in most of the sample countries, and, as the raw material boom dissipated, CAs again began to show a deficit. This process reflects the growing financial fragility of the region's countries, while the scant economic growth from 2012 to 2016 could only be maintained due to extraordinary conditions of liquidity created by the developed countries' unconventional monetary policies (Calvo, 2016). This result clearly shows that the GDP growth rate consistent with EBPGDPs has decreased. Therefore, following the theoretical argument, the effective level of growth is also affected, adding another element to state that ITRs in Latin America stabilise inflation and destabilise economic growth.

The trajectory of CAs shows the failure of the growth-via-foreign-trade project, while profits from foreign trade would only come from a better assignation of resources and not via increased demand.

One thing that is not thoroughly analysed in the economic literature on increased raw material prices is that the hike caused public spending to

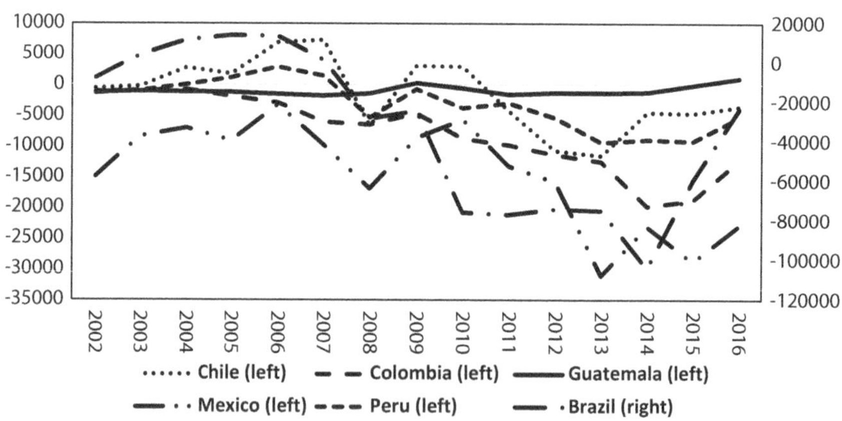

Figure 6.3 Current account balance (millions of dollars) 2002–2016.
Source: ECLAC.

rise, reflected in increased public investment.[7] However, as explained in the previous section, public investment is the government expenditure that undergoes the most adjustments when economic growth conditions face a reverse. This was a clear beginning in 2008, when the public investment growth rate plummeted, reaching negative levels in 2012 and 2015. This confirms that public investment is procyclical; therefore, it has not been used as an instrument for development, since it is the expense most quickly adjusted. This does not imply that there were no attempts at implementing expansive fiscal policies during the 2008–2010 international financial crisis, but they were very weak and did not avert a sizeable adjustment in the economies. The events between 2012 and 2016 caused the emergence of twin deficits in the public, external sector (CA).

The theoretical part of this chapter showed that the macroeconomic model that ITRs are based on has conceptual fallacies because they do not take into account fundamental characteristics of the Latin American economies. Specifically, this model does not incorporate the main limitation on growth, which is external, reflecting the supply conditions of these economies. I pointed out that despite being able to control inflation by anchoring the exchange rate and maintaining stable – and even further worsening – the distribution of income, growth, which depends exclusively on the evolution of external markets, is destabilised.

This section contributes elements that ratify this chapter's central idea that Latin American ITRs stabilise inflation at the expense of economic growth. Underlying this is the appreciation of the RER and the pauperisation of workers through regressive income distribution. At the same time, the fact that governments do not take into account the structural conditions that determine the external restriction is reflected in financial fragility as the CA deficit increases for each GDP level. This has not unleashed a balance of payments crisis due to the high liquidity over the entire period analysed. Finally, adding the lack of coordination between monetary and fiscal policies to the procyclical nature of public investment, the ITRs endanger long-term economic growth (Panico, 2014; Capraro & Panico, 2018).

Conclusion

This chapter has shown that the structural reforms stemming from the Washington Consensus and reinforced by ITR-based monetary policies have not been capable of developing a socially inclusive economic growth strategy in Latin America.[8] Inflation was stabilised at the cost of a regressive redistribution of income. Based on this, what is needed is to put forward changes in economic policies. And, although the current institutional arrangements can continue (for example, independent central banks), their objectives must change, so they can deploy new policies.

In this sense, based on what has been explained here, the Latin American economies' growth must be stabilised; therefore, the first objective of economic policy must not be to control inflation, but rather to achieve growth-rate goals. The second objective must be the functional distribution of income and improving workers' incomes. A key variable in this sense is public investment, which must play a central role in public policy.

Can these policies be implemented in a financialised global economy? Argentina's recent experience indicates that it is by no means easy to put these policies into practice, and they cannot always be implemented successfully (Amico, 2017). More research is needed about what makes it possible to deploy these policies in a context of financialised globalisation such as capital control and regional integration. We must always keep in mind Epstein's maxim, "To answer these questions, more case studies are required since, in the end, though general lessons are helpful, the true solutions are to be found in specific national settings" (2015, p. 12).

Finally, this chapter poses several theoretical and empirical challenges for future research. The first is the need to create new macroeconomic models for middle-income economies like Latin America's economy that can explain the determinants of inflation, because, today, the ITR model does not represent these economies' structural characteristics.[9] Second, among the empirical aspects we need to continue researching is how public investment can coordinate with private investment to diminish the external restriction to growth by increasing domestic production's international competitiveness, thus making it possible for the Latin American economies to grow with social inclusion.

Notes

1 Consensus currently exists that achieving competitive RERs is a precondition – although not sufficient – for growth (Frenkel & Ros, 2006; Rodrik, 2008; Frenkel & Rapetti, 2010; Bresser-Pereyra, 2016).

2 Taking into account that each central bank implements its ITR with certain specificities (Calvo & Reinhart 2002).

3 In empirical terms, if y^p provides no information about potential output, the inflation targeting model's regular mechanisms of transmission pointed out above do not engage. Since full employment is never reached, growth stops before reaching that level of activity.

4 In this sense, Serrano and Summa (2015) state that, for the case of Brazil, "Most analyses of Brazilian inflation during this period (even that of economists that consider themselves heterodox or critical) tend to confuse the institutional framework of inflation targeting, which actually exists, with the so-called new consensus model (or sometimes even with its more complex and unrealistic DSGE (Dynamic stochastic general equilibrium) or new neoclassical synthesis version) that is often used rhetorically to justify and explain the inflation targeting system. But that model (in any of their versions) has no basis in Brazilian reality and seems to exist only in the minds of some economists" (p. 1).

5 At every moment in time, public investment is a given since public budgets are set a year in advance.

6 This information about growth is from World Development Indicators, accessed February 14, 2018.

7 For more information, see the IMF's Capital Stock Dataset, www.imf.org/external/np/fad/publicinvestment/, accessed February 14, 2018.
8 Levy (2014) came to similar conclusions for the Mexican economy.
9 Trajtenberg et al. (2015) show empirical results that contradict the inflation target model with regard to the determinants of inflation, but do not propose new theoretical models.

References

Amico, F. (2017) 'Inflation Targeting, External Constraint and Distributive Conflict in Argentina', Working Paper, PPGE-IE-UFRJ.

Arestis, P. & Sawyer, M. (2003) 'Inflation Targeting: A Critical Appraisal', *The Levy Economic Institute of Bard College*, Working Paper No. 388.

Arestis, P. & Sawyer, M. (2013) 'Moving from Inflation Targeting to Prices and Incomes Policy', *Panoeconomicus, Savez ekonomista Vojvodine, Novi Sad, Serbia*, 60(1), 1–17.

Armas, A. & Grippa, F. (2005) 'Targeting Inflation in a Dollarized Economy: The Peruvian Experience', *Inter-American Development Bank, Research Department*, RES Working Paper No. 4423.

Ball, L. (2000) 'Policy Rules and External Shocks', *Central Bank of Chile*, Working Paper No. 82.

Bhaduri, A. (2011). '*Essays in the Reconstruction of Political Economy*', Aakar Books, Dehli, India, ISBN: 9789350020586, 9350020580

Bielschowsky, R. (2009) 'Sesenta años de la CEPAL: estructuralismo y neoestructuralismo', *Revista CEPAL*', 97, 173–186.

Blanchard, O. (2011) 'Monetary Policy in the Wake of the Crisis', *International Monetary Found*, Macro Conference, viewed 17 February 2018, from https://goo.gl/JcmA5W.

Blanchard, O. & Summers, L. (2017, October). 'Rethinking Stabilization Policy. Back to the Future', *Peterson Institute for International Economics,* Working Paper.

Bordo, M.D. (2016) 'History of Monetary Policy', in Palgrave Macmillan (ed.), *The New Palgrave Dictionary of Economics*, doi:10.1057/978-1-349-95121-5_2743-1, 1–9.

Bresser-Pereira, L.C. (2016) 'Reflecting on New Developmentalism and Classical Developmentalism', *Review of Keynesian Economics*, 4(3), 331–352.

Calvo, G. (2016) *Macroeconomics in Times of Liquidity Crisis*, MIT Press, Cambridge, MA, and London.

Calvo, G.A. & Reinhart, C.M. (2002) 'Fear of Floating', *Quarterly Journal of Economics*, 117(2), 379–408.

Capraro, S. & Panico, C. (2018) 'Organización institucional de la política monetaria, política cambiaria y crecimiento en México', Revista Mexicana de Economía, 2018, No 3.

Capraro, S. & Perrotini, I. (2012) 'Intervenciones cambiarias esterilizadas, teoría y evidencia: el caso de México', *Revista de Contaduría y Administración*, 2(57), 11–44.

Céspedes, L.F., Chang R., & Velasco, A. (2014) 'Is Inflation Targeting Still on Target? The Recent Experience of Latin America', *International Finance*, 17 (2), 185–208.

Charpe, M. (2011) 'The Labour Share of Income: Determinants and Potential Contribution to Exiting the Financial Crisis', *World of Work Report*, (1), Vol. 2011 (1), 55–74.

Combes, J-L., Debrun, X., Minea, A., & Tapsoba, R. (2017) 'Inflation Targeting, Fiscal Rules, and the Policy Mix: Cross-Effects and Interactions', *The Economic Journal*, doi:10.1111/ecoj.12538.

Dutt, A. (2017) 'Income Inequality, the Wage Share, and Economic Growth', *Review of Keynesian Economics*, 5(2), 170–195.

ECLAC (2014) 'Challenges to Sustainable Growth in a New External Context', *Economic Survey of Latin America and the Caribbean*, NU. CEPAL, 214, viewed 17 February 2018, from https://goo.gl/j8RXsH.

Epstein, G. (2015) 'Development Central Banking: A Review of Issues and Experiences', *ILO*, Employment Working Paper No. 182.

Frenkel, R. & Rapetti, M. (2010) A Concise History of Exchange Rate Regimes in Latin America, UMass/WP.

Frenkel, R. & Ros, J. (2006) 'Unemployment and the Real Exchange Rate in Latin America', *World Development*, 34(4), 631–646.

Lavoie, M. (2016) 'Rethinking Monetary Theory in Light of Keynes and the Crisis', *Brazilian Keynesian Review*, 2(2).

Levy, N. (2014) 'Financialization and Economic Growth in Developing Countries: The Case of the Mexican Economy', *International Journal of Political Economy*, 42, 108–127.

McLeay, M., Radia, A., & Thomas, R. (2014) 'Money Creation in the Modern Economy', *Bank of England*, Quarterly Bulletin, 2014, Q1.

Moreno-Brid, J.C. (1998) 'On Capital Flows and the Balance-of-Payments-Constrained Growth Model', *Journal of Post Keynesian Economics*, 21(2), 283–298.

Panico, C. (2014) 'Política monetaria y derechos humanos: un enfoque metodológico y su aplicación a Costa Rica, Guatemala y México', *ECLAC*, LC/MEX/L.1162.

Panico, C. & Rizza, M.O. (2003) 'CBI and Democracy: A Historical Perspective', in Arena R. & Salvadori N. (eds.), *Money, Credit and the Role of the State: Essays in Honour of Augusto Graziani*, Ashegate, Aldershot, 445–465.

Rodrik, D. (2008) 'The Real Exchange Rate and Economic Growth', *Brookings Papers on Economic Activity, Fall*, 2, 365–412.

Serrano, F. & Summa, R. (2015, August) 'Aggregate Demand and the Slowdown of Brazilian Economic Growth from 2011–2014', *CEPR*.

Svensson, L. (2001). 'Independent Review of the Operation of Monetary Policy in New Zealand: Report to the Minister of Finance', *Reserve Bank of New Zealand Bulletin*, vol. 64,

Svensson, L., (2010). 'Inflation Targeting'. Handbook of Monetary Economics, in: Benjamin M. Friedman & Michael Woodford (ed.), Handbook of Monetary Economics, edition 1, volume 3, chapter 22, 1237–1302, Elsevier.

Taylor, J.B. (2001) 'The Role of the Exchange Rate in Monetary Policy Rules', *American Economic Review*, Papers and Proceedings, 91(2), 263–267.

Taylor, J.B. (1993) 'Discretion versus Rules in Practice', *Carnegie-Rochester Conference Series on Public Policy*, 39, 195–214.

Thirlwall, A. (1973). 'The Balance of Payments Constraint as an Explanation of International Growth Rate Differences', *BNL Quarterly Review*, 1979, 32(128), 45–53.

Trajtenberg, L., Valdecantos, S., & Vega, D. (2015) 'Los determinantes de la inflación en América Latina: un estudio empírico del período 1990–2013', in Bárcena, A., Prado, A., & Abeles, M. (eds.), *Estructura productiva y política macroeconómica. Enfoques heterodoxos desde América Latina*, CEPAL-UN, Santiago de Chile.

Williamson, J. (2003) 'The Strange History of the Washington Consensus', *Journal of Post Keynesian Economics*, 27(2), 195–206.

Wong, S. & Petreski, M. (2014) 'Dutch Disease in Latin American countries: De-industrialization, How it Happens, Crisis, and the Role of China', *MPRA*, Paper No. 57056, posted 3. July 2014 05:13 UTC.

Woodford, M. (2003) *Interest and Prices: Foundations of a Theory of Monetary Policy*, Princeton University Press, Princeton.

Part II

The failure of comparative advantages

7 Structural change in Colombia

From import substitution to export-led growth illusion

Diego Guevara, Gonzalo Cómbita, and Camilo Guevara

In recent years, the low dynamism of the global economy and fall in commodity prices has led to fragility throughout the Latin American region, and Colombia has been no exception. However, conventional analyses argue that the fragility occurred due to policy errors, such as failing to save sufficiently from the increased oil revenues of the commodity price boom (2003–2014), which would have helped the country to deal with "rainy days" later on (Kalmanovitz 2014). This chapter takes a different position, aiming to demystify the Colombian export-led growth model, and exploring a different hypothesis put forward by the financialisation literature, under which it is argued that the economic arrangements need to be changed.

The chapter is divided into five sections. In the second section, after this introduction, changes to the dominant development model are outlined to shift the discussion to a long-term perspective (Braudel 1970). Thus, the institutional arrangements undergone in that period are analysed, such as the elimination of public banking and effects of the multi-banking structure that financialised the economy. In the following section, capital flow effects on the structural changes to the Colombian economy are discussed, for which purpose an econometric model is put forward. In addition, through a Kaleckian framework, it is explored how changes in domestic aggregate demand, along with the new structure of accumulation, resulted from the 1990s reforms, which created new scenarios for accumulation, and impacted stock market prices and the prices of real assets, such as housing.

In the penultimate section, the consequences of the export-led growth model are discussed, along with the need to introduce new institutional arrangements, within growth policies guided by domestic demand, and the need to transcend net exports led by the energy and mining sector. The final section puts forward the main conclusions of the discussion.

From the failed industrialisation model to the illusion of the export-led growth model

It is widely known that during the 1990s, a rupture took place in Latin America regarding the orientation of the productive and financial model, although the first signs of liberalisation had occurred during the 1970s. In Colombia specifically, a first financial reform was carried out in 1974, which lifted the restrictions on the interest rate and discouraged forced loans. The most notable change in this reform was an increase in the profitability of savings rates, which went from 8.5% in 1974 to 18% in 1976, and whose dynamics generated a significant increase in deposits.

Clearly, these types of reforms were inspired by the neoclassical vision of a deregulated financial system, where savings determine investment and the financial market serves as a lubricant that efficiently allocates surplus resources to the economy.

According to Azuero (1980), these were the evidence of the willingness to abandon the interventionist and protectionist model taking into account Chicago School recommendations. Under this new scenario, by the end of the 1970s, Latin American countries also began to receive credit flows, through the recycling of financial surpluses from the eastern petrodollars.

From the mid-1970s to the beginning of the 1980s, the level of foreign investment was close to 19% of GDP. However, under the Latin American external debt crisis scenario, by 1982 a net transfer of resources of –3.2% of GDP had been generated (CEPAL, 2002).

This first stage of this model did not bring the great benefits that were offered by policymakers, who had insisted that the liberalisation of interest rates would lead to capital being attracted to the most efficient activities. Finally, it ended up favouring speculation and the dominant position of the great economic conglomerates of the country, with monopolistic advantages consolidated.

Despite these initial changes introducing some elements of liberalisation, the real transformation began in the 1990s with the policies of the Washington Consensus, which radically transformed the productive structures of Colombia and Latin America.

All these policies deepened the aforementioned initial advances of the previous decades and were justified as the great solution to the crisis of the lost decade. Many Latin American economists trained in the "new paradigm" at US universities that embraced the Washington Consensus.

Bianchi et al. (1987) insisted that in order to overcome the debt crisis, it was essential to establish a growth model based on high productivity and savings, while others, such as Fajnzylber (1990), insisted that the region needed pro-market reforms, with a certain degree of focus on the population below the poverty line.

Thus, in the 1990s, the benefits of financial and commercial globalisation were promoted, without no emphasis of the volatility and instability risks that took place in the first part of that decade, and were accentuated by the crisis of the end of the century in various emerging and developing economies. In the Colombian case, reform packages focussed on the liberalisation of the capital account, and commercial opening became a reality in the first years of the 1990s. At this time, a strong wave of privatisations of public banking[1] and friendly privatisations with transnational capital also took place. More than 800 public companies were sold between 1988 and 1997, accompanied by the abolition of many other restrictions on foreign direct investment (FDI)[2] (Guevara 2016). These changes, among others, allow us to raise the idea of a second moment that can be termed "complete financialization", which will be analysed in more detail later.

In Colombia, in line with the new world view of development, during the first year of Gaviria's government (1990–1994), a series of reforms were consolidated in different areas, such as financial (Law 45 of 1990), commercial (Law 7 of 1991), labour (Law 50 of 1990) and taxes (Law 49 of 1990), among others. This first group has been named by Estrada (2006) as the first generation of structural reforms.

Along with these reforms, the country adopted a new political constitution (1991), which gave rise to the consolidation of a technocracy, akin to the Washington Consensus and which has been in charge of the formulation and execution of the country's economic policies ever since.

This was accompanied by the granting of independence to the central bank and the setting as its supreme objective of the consolidation of the inflation target, strongly rooted in the world views of the current mainstream, and whose consequences will be shown later.

Another key moment took place after the reforms of 1990 and 1991, with the deepening of deregulation and promotion of the creation of new markets (see Law 143, promoted in 1994, which transformed the electricity sector and gave a greater chance to private actors and foreigners in transmission services and energy marketing).

Law 100 of 1993, which transformed health and social security, also gave a determining role to the private sector and financial actors in the provision of health services and pensions, generating a high concentration of financial activity in the country.[3]

On the other hand, Law 35 of 1993 favoured the growth of the financial sector. This law established the norms and criteria (more flexible than before) to be used by the Colombian government for the regulation of finances, the stock market, insurance and activities associated with the management of public money in general. Within the framework of this phase, it is also important to mention Law 226 of 1995, known as the "Privatization Law", that allowed the government to sell important mining-energy assets in the coal, gas and electricity sectors, in addition to the privatisation of financial entities and public banks.

Another important element is the behaviour of capital flows after the financial liberalisation. In Colombia, four stages are recognised in terms of the behaviour of the capital flows. The first stage is associated with the period between 1990 and 1997, which derived from the aforementioned reforms. This period shows increasing inflows in the capital account, especially in

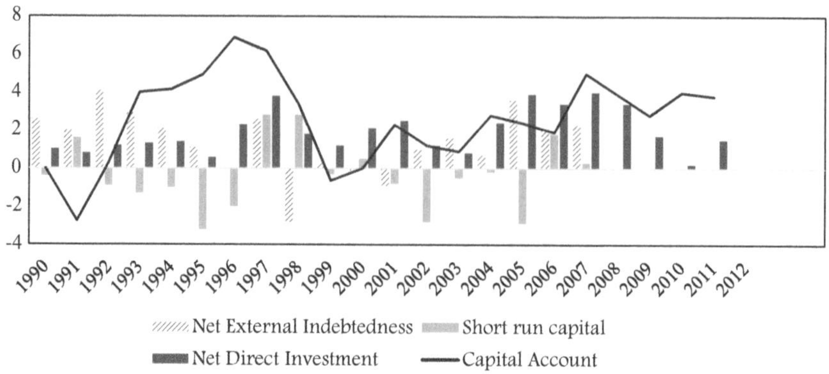

Figure 7.1 Capital account, net direct investment, net external indebtedness and GDP gap: 1990–2011.

1993 (foreign portfolio investment) and 1996 and 1997 (FDI and external indebtedness) (see Figure 7.1). It is worth noting that an important part of these capital inflows was the result of the privatisation processes of this era, in sectors such as banking, energy and telecommunications.

The second stage is associated with capital outflows (1998–2002). This occurred in light of the Asian and Russian crises (1997) and the political crisis of the Colombian government (1998). The conditions led to the 1999 crisis, the worst financial crisis that Colombia has faced in its history.

The third stage covers 2002 and 2014, which was characterised by capital inflows, motivated by the orientation of Uribe's government (2002–2010) to protect investors and allow private investment in the energy (oil and gas) and mining sector. Finally, making up the fourth stage, there have been significant capital outflows since 2014, which are associated with the fall in the oil price and the profitability of the energy and mining sector.

The reforms that took place in Colombia, in that period, had a structural character that generated profound change in the Colombian economy. Thus, the 1990 reforms mark the beginning of the Colombian structural change, which accelerated dramatically in the 2000s. In fact, the financial sector has been the dominant force behind economic growth in the last 15 years, with its rise going hand in hand with a substantial increase in the contribution of the energy and mining sector, accompanied by lower contributions to growth from industry and agriculture.[4]

The economic cycle, valuation of assets and economic structure in Colombia: an econometric estimation

The data that support the previous section arguments, regarding the structural change in the Colombian economy, and the institutional arrangements and economic policies introduced since 1990, are presented in Table 7.1.

Table 7.1 Accumulation and asset valuation throughout the Colombian productive cycle: evaluation of the use of installed capacity with respect to other relevant macroeconomic variables

Independent variable	*1990-I to 2017-II*	*1990-I to 2003-III*	*2003-IV to 2017-II*
Investment/GDP	ß = 0.6953***	ß = 0.963***	ß = −0.13
	R^2 = 0.194	R^2 = 0.639	R^2 = 0.01
FDI/GDP	ß = 0.2781***	ß = 0.1915***	ß = 0.2352
	R^2 = 0.172	R^2 = 0.162	R^2 = 0.084
Index price log of existing	ß = 1.1537*	ß = 2.363***	ß = −1.5
housing	R^2 = 0.03	R^2 = 0.358	R^2 = 0.026
Index log stock market value	ßv= −2.1936	ß = −6.197***	ß = −1.18
	R^2 = 0.002	R^2 = 0.1953	R^2 = 0.003
Net exports/GDP	ß = 0.098*	ß = 0.093	ß = −0.1567
	R^2 = 0.02	R^2 = 0.046	R^2 = 0.010
Index log real exchange rate	ß = 1.222***	ß = 1.08**	ß = 1.65***
	R^2 = 0.06	R^2 = 0.071	R^2 = 0.086
Industry/GDP	ß = 0.1632***	ß = 0.21***	ß = 0.09*
	R^2 = 0.149	R^2 = 0.507	R^2 = 0.037

Source: Authors' calculations.

Note: *** Significant to 1%, ** Significant to 5%,* Significant to 10%.

The table is organised into three columns, which represent the different periods of analysis: first, the entire period from the first quarter of 1990 to the second quarter of 2017, then two subperiods, from the first quarter of 1990 to the third quarter of 2003, and from the fourth quarter of 2003 to 2017.[5]

The reason for splitting the period was that the preliminary results for each subperiod showed different patterns in the reactions of the variables, as well as the statistical significance. At the same time, it was evident that the point of fracture of the series was at the end of the prolonged recession of 1999, which was then reversed by the rise in the prices of commodities in 2003.

Keen (2014), Leon (2002) and Winkler (2009) highlight that in the analysis of time series, when subperiods are studied, specific characteristics appear. They emerge in the changes imposed by social dynamics, through the imposition of forms and paths that result from struggles, relationships of resistance, imposition and competition between social classes.

Table 7.1 shows estimates of linear regressions and dispersion diagrams of simple functions,[6] where installed capacity (ECI) acts as an independent variable[7] with respect to a series of dependent variables such as investment in proportion to GDP (IPIB), foreign investment in proportion to GDP, the real price index for used housing (IPVUR), the real stock price index on the Colombian Stock Exchange (IGBCP), the real exchange rate index (ITCR), exports on GDP (XNPPIB) and the participation of industry in the GDP (INDPIB).[8] The regression coefficient, R^2, is also presented, together with the level of significance estimated using robust least squares by the Huber-White covariance method.

The variables were used to analyse the relationship of the productive cycle of the Colombian economy with the appreciation/depreciation of financial assets and with changes in the productive structure. The variable that represents the production cycle is the use of installed capacity that, during the crisis of 1999, reached a value of 60%. However, even in times of the boom period (2007), the economy only achieves 77% of its utilisation capacity.

Petri (2003) shows that not reaching full employment is a normal condition of capitalist economies, given that the flexibility of the use of installed capacity during the cycle allows for the expansion of the supply stimulated by the demand. This implies that companies maintain a use of capacity below 100% to be able to capture new demand, and then increase their supply of goods with the aim of always maintaining this possibility that stimulates productive capacity via effective demand. This would imply that studying the behaviour of firms and the economy as a whole under conditions of full employment would be an error, since growth always occurs in conditions of underutilisation and demand-led scenarios.

The revision of the data indicates that investment, responsible for the productive capacity expansion through capital accumulation, showed a positive relationship with the Colombian cycle, corroborating the Kaleckian thesis on the use of installed capacity as a determinant of investment (Felipe 2009, Gallardo & Assous 2010, Kalecki 1939, Setterfield 2005). Since the variables involved are percentages, the regression coefficient can be regarded as an elasticity. Thus, the elasticity of domestic investment (or gross fixed capital formation) with respect to the use of installed capacity is 0.6 for the entire period. However, in the subperiods, the value changes, observing a high elasticity close to unity during the 1990s, which becomes negative and is no longer significant in the second subperiod. The foregoing is an indication of how structural change destroyed the link between domestic aggregate demand and investment incentives, which would constitute a boost to speculative activities, leaving aside the sustained expansion derived from the domestic market.

On the other hand, the behaviour of the FDI, anchored to the use of the installed capacity, turned out to be more intense in the last period of analysis, as seen in the increasing elasticity, the highest R^2 and a stable degree of statistical significance for the two subperiods. This shows the greater structural dependence of the Colombian economy on external financing, clarifying that according to the estimates, net capital flows did not play the same role as FDI in an isolated manner. The greater external dependency brought about a greater financial fragility in the balance of payments, which lead to a speculative growth strategy (Kregel 2004).

In addition to the investment, net exports show a weak relation with the use of the installed capacity during the first period of analysis. Then, in the second period, that connection, measured by the elasticity, is diluted and even becomes negative, given the value of the coefficient and the estimated R^2. This verifies the hypothesis of authors such as Sarmiento (2015), who explains that the Colombian economy, since its opening up, has become dependent on imports, so that growth itself shows the beginning of the next crisis through the growing deficit in the current account. The above arguments highlight that the fundamental link between the Colombian economy and the balance of payments is not reflected in a connection between net exports and the use of installed capacity, but between them and the financial component, particularly FDI.

One of the most important indications is the fall in the elasticity between the participation of industrial production and the use of installed capacity. During the period 1990–2003, an increase of 1% in industry participation in GDP created a 21% increase in the use of installed capacity, while in 2003–2017, a 1% increase in industry participation boosted capacity utilisation by 9%. This is also reflected in the goodness of fit and in the significance of the regression coefficient. The regressive structural change suffered by the Colombian economy for more than two decades is reflected in the systematic loss of industry participation in the total activity (as will be seen in the next section), in the concentration of more than half of all exports in five goods and in the fall of domestic demand observed in the coefficients presented in Table 7.1. Sarmiento (2002, 2014) confirms these patterns, showing how Colombian industry, after the 1990 reforms, destroyed its links with other sectors and increased the dependence on imported supplies by substituting the national demand for them.

In short, the change in elasticity from 22% to 9% is reflected in the reduced power of the industry to push the rest of the economy, evidence of a weakening of the industry as a growth engine, in the best style of Kaldor's First Law.

In addition to the structural changes discussed above, we review the impact of domestic demand and economic activity on the price of assets such as used housing and shares.[9] The variables that were used to estimate the valuation of the assets were the existing housing price index[10] and the Colombian Stock Exchange index.

The results indicate that changes in the use of installed capacity positively affected the price of existing housing only during the first period of analysis, when the goodness of fit is acceptable and the regression coefficient is positive and statistically significant. On the other hand, during the second period, the housing price, and, during the entire valuation period, the assets in the stock market are totally disconnected from the real activity of the economy. This can be seen in the fall of the R^2, in the value of the coefficient of regression that becomes negative, and in its level of significance that indicates that the results are statistically irrelevant.

An inspection analysis of the series in level terms shows that in the case of housing and the General Index of the Colombian Stock Exchange (IGBC), the price recovers from the crisis of the end of the century, together with the use of installed capacity. After 2003, the trajectory of the series can be explained independently of the cyclical changes in the economy. Therefore, it is presumed that the dynamics of the price of housing follow the logic of a speculative asset with the same lag as its fundamental variable of explanation (Mandelbrot & Hudson 2010, Shiller 2015). The IGBC, meanwhile, far from having the adjustment that housing prices had during the crisis of the 1990s, continued to grow, especially at the beginning of the period analysed and from the first quarter of 2001 to the first quarter of 2006. To sum up, the inverse, non-adjusted and non-significant relationship between the regression coefficients of asset valuation indexes such as housing and shares shows the deepening of the financialisation of the Colombian economy. Following these arguments, Yasuhara (2013) mentions that the greater capital accumulation may not correspond to the greater use of installed capacity as a symptom of the presence of speculative and Ponzi regimes.

Developing countries must ensure the use of productive capacity, while expanding production. However, the results obtained in the econometric model presented above show that the use of the installed capacity of the Colombian economy has been separating from the processes of capital accumulation, and endogenous reinforcement via the size of the domestic market. In the same vein, the valuation of assets, especially housing, has been separated from the real sector and added to the speculative behaviour of the stock market. All this seems to be a reflection of a process of regressive structural change that disconnected the internal market from the processes of business accumulation.

Therefore, the process of structural change has been regressive, as a result of the in-depth adoption of a development model, whose first tentacles appeared in the 1970s – but which deepened in the 1990s, and not of an isolated outcome, a product of contingencies or a particular policy wrongly adopted. That is why we consider it pertinent to globally question the Washington Consensus and one of its tentacles, the export-led growth model.[11]

Why are the Washington Consensus and export-led growth model exhausted in Colombia and how can we go beyond them?

The Washington Consensus, together with the export-led growth model, based on trade liberalisation and export development, and directed in accordance with the comparative advantages of a country (Palley 2002), has ended up leading Colombia to focus on the comparative advantages of the oil and mining sector (Cardenas 2013). It was believed that it did not matter what type of sector the country specialised in, and the economic growth of 2006 and 2007, of 6.8% and 7.5%, respectively (Banco Mundial, 2017), seemed to support the argument that the country had chosen the right model. It was thought that Colombia was part of a set of new countries (CIVETS[12]) with the greatest potential for growth. However, the results three decades after the 1990s rupture are not very encouraging.

Colombia has gone through a process of deindustrialisation, understood as a fall in the participation of industrial production in GDP, from 20.9% of GDP in 1991 to 12.6% of GDP in 2016 (World Bank 2017). There are several arguments dissociating this deindustrialisation from lower industrial production, such as the argument of higher productivity or the fracturing of value chains (outsourcing) (Chang 2012). However, in Colombia, deindustrialisation is definitely linked to a decline in industrial production that can be observed in the closure of plants and factories[13] and that is associated not only with the mining and energy boom, via the revaluation of the exchange rate, as some argue (Clavijo et al. 2012), but also with the whole model adopted in the 1990s, which led fundamentally to the *mantra* that "the best industrial policy is not to have an industrial policy". This orientation can be better evidenced after 2002, when the ministries of Industry, Foreign Trade and Tourism were merged. This decision was taken with the aim of subsuming productive development under foreign trade policy and foreign investment. Since this period, more than ten free trade agreements have been signed and implemented, but there is no clear orientation towards facing international competition. For example, for several years, the Productive Transformation Programme (PTP) of the Ministry of Commerce, Industry and Tourism has prioritised some sectors and regions, adopting ever more the perspective of "correcting market failures", but without major results when it comes to "reindustrializing" the country. There is a lack of desire to discuss the orientation of the model or the macroeconomic conditions that support it, since the benefits of the supposed "macroeconomic stability" are accepted as a sacralised idea.

Parallel to the deindustrialisation process, agriculture has also lost its share of the national GDP. The reduction of the agriculture share in GDP has taken place since the 1960s, was accentuated in 1991, and this share has since then fallen from 17.4% of GDP to 7.1% in 2016 (World Bank 2017). However, it should be clarified that in recent years, the agriculture share in GDP increased, and in the first half of 2017, the growth in agricultural production was 6%, as a result of the protection, given via subsidies to this sector (Sarmiento 2017), granted as a result of farmers' strikes and strong mobilisations. However, there is no clear promotion of an industrialised agriculture.

This structural change (deindustrialisation and agriculture reduction) generated an increase in the participation of the mining and energy sector, so as the financial sector in the GDP, which makes the country dependent on capital flows, attracted on the basis of low taxation and legal stability contracts. This scenario, along with the high prices of commodities, created the possibility to accrue short-term high returns. The pattern of *stop and go* growth, characterised by external dependence, high volatility in the event of external shocks, returned to the Colombian economy. This is what happened with the fall in the price of commodities that has profoundly destabilised the economy.

It needs to be emphasised that the growth of the financial sector has not been neutral, in fact the opposite, as the size of the sectors and the weight in the productive structure have had profound effects on the share of wages in national income (Panico & Pico 2015).

Thus, the model introduced in the 1990s with the purpose of increasing the participation of institutions and relationships, and for financial reasons, was also the beginning of a process of increasing inequality in the functional distribution of income. This process began with the inflation reduction process initiated in the 1990s (first through a process of open economy and second by adopting an inflation-targeting regime in 2001). This reduced inflation by 32.4% in 1990 (World Bank 2017), towards the 2–4% range set by the target inflation regime, a range above which it has gravitated in recent years (inflation of 5.75% in 2016). The inflation reduction has not been a *free lunch,* as is usually thought of under the theoretical perspective of the new macroeconomic consensus that maintains the monetary dichotomy and the long-term neutrality of money. On the contrary, it has affected the functional distribution of income,[14] seeing the share of wages in the national income going from 49% in 2001 (when the inflation target was adopted) to 41% in 2008 (Moreno 2014). In turn, the model has maintained almost constant inequality in the personal distribution of income.

In Colombia, in 2010, the richest 1% had a 20.4% share of the national income, the same level as when measurements were taken back in 1993 (Londoño & Alvaredo 2014). This places Colombia among the countries with the highest income inequality in the world.

However, in the face of these structural problems, subsidy policies targeting demand, such as the *Conditional Cash Transfers*, among others, have managed to contain and even reduce poverty. Some observers have even called the period from 2002 to 2011 "the won decade", because in this period, "the real per capita income of households grew 36%, the middle class as a share of the total population went from 16% to 27% and poverty decreased from 50% to 34%" (Angulo et al. 2014: 154).

Nonetheless, these advances have not improved the personal distribution or the functional distribution of income, nor have they generated a change in the productive structure of the economy. At the same time, working conditions have been getting worse. The last major labour reforms (Law 50 of 1990 and Law 789 of 2002) deepened labour flexibility by lengthening the day shift, reducing the cost of overtime and reducing the cost of compensation, among other things.

In conclusion, these problems are part of a highly polarised political environment made up of those who agree with the way the end of the armed conflict was negotiated with the oldest guerrilla group in the world, the FARC (Revolutionary Armed Forces of Colombia), and believe that there was impunity in that process. This issue has fundamentally defined the political agenda in recent years, and continues to postpone, at a popular level, any shift from discussion of the armed conflict to the distributive conflict (Moreno 2016). In this context, there are relevant questions: what type of model is required? which institutions and policies could lead us to high rates of sustained economic growth with an increase in formal employment and reduction of income and wealth inequality? Which is the path for a sustainable real exit to the armed conflict?

As a first approximation, the export-led growth model is increasingly limited in its ability to achieve sustained growth and income redistribution, because global economic conditions have changed, and this affects both the developed and emerging economies. The end of the high price cycle for commodities has put countries such as Colombia, which are highly dependent on the export of oil and coal, in serious trouble. This has generated a great economic slowdown in the country that is getting worse, because the solutions have ended up being worse than the disease.[15]

At a global level, the model has generated a race between countries to determine which can generate the best competitive environment, which includes lower taxes and the degradation of nature and social conditions, including those at work. This is reinforced by the fact that China has adopted the export-led growth model (Palley 2011), which generates a problem for many national industries due to the low labour costs in China. In Colombia, for example, Chinese footwear threatens the national industry, with a pair of shoes arriving in the country costing less than a dollar (Manga 2016), making it impossible to compete. What, then, are possible ways forward for Colombia?

Towards a demand-led growth domestic model

The challenge then is to understand the fatigue of the export-led growth model and start to change the emphasis. Of course, without stopping exportation, there is a need to put a greater emphasis on the development of the domestic market. Also, a change in the accumulation regime is needed, in the way in which the GDP is distributed between wages and benefits. This means strengthening the domestic market and aggregate demand.

The fundamental axes are the following: (I) macroeconomic policies that go beyond the conceptual framework outlined by the dominant macroeconomic consensus, renouncing the idea that monetary policy can adjust the economy through the interest rate (Rochon 2017). Thus, fiscal activism need to be recovered to reach full employment, with demand policies that, in turn, boost the accumulation and expansion of productive capacity, ensuring stability in the balance of payments and greater sophistication of the productive apparatus. (II) To change the focus of employment policies, from employability policies to employment programmes that should be guaranteed by the state, in activities that can be coordinated by local communities. (III) That the monetary policy on interest rates does not have a bias towards an inequitable functional distribution of income. This is achieved when the interest rate is equal to the growth rate of labour productivity (Rochon 2017) and not greater than it, as has been the case in Colombia over the last decades (Moreno 2014). (IV) Policies aimed at improving the conditions of workers (starting with the repeal of labour flexibilisation), as well as showing progress in the improvement of social security for both formal and informal workers (who make up close to 61% of the population and are often unprotected) (World Bank 2017). (V) To improve wages to generate greater growth, since, in Colombia, growth is led by wages (wage-led growth).[16] In turn, we must tie the growth of wages to the growth of labour productivity. Finally, (VI) the financial sector power must be limited, resuming public banking policies aimed at the development of both formal and informal sectors and empowering the public pension scheme, that some want to let wither, among others the National Association of Financial Institutions (ANIF).

These are some of the axes that could represent a turning point, would generate great resistance, but should be considered by all interested in the construction of a truly democratic society, a less unequal one that builds the foundations of sustainable peace, in which social conflicts are recognised and in which a democratic approach is attempted to be taken.

Conclusions

The main purpose of this chapter has been to analyse the fragility of the Colombian economy from a long-term perspective, relating it to the growth model led by exportation and the Washington Consensus. First, we explore the hypothesis of different financialisation moments or stages in the Colombian economy, in which major institutional changes are introduced, paving the way for structural change towards the export of raw materials, mainly oil and coal. Unlike other processes of financialisation, especially in developed countries where the increase in the number of agents and transactions in the stock market is crucial, in Colombia this process is fundamentally linked to the introduction of institutional arrangements and economic policies, such as the independence of the Banco de la República, the inflation targeting scheme, the issuance of debt securities of Títulos de Tesoreria, TES by the Ministry of Finance and Public Credit and the concentration of the banking sector on multi-banking. Later, in the first decade of the 2000s, among others, a legal framework for investor confidence is introduced, the free trade policy is deepened with more than 10 treaties of Free Trade Agreement, FTA signed and the orientation of the development model is not clear.

Second, with an econometric model, the use of installed capacity, which represents the economic cycle, and a series of selected variables (such as FDI, national investment, industry size, net exports and financial assets) are evaluated. It can be concluded that the correlations support the formulated analysis of a regressive structural change that destroyed the link between domestic aggregate demand and incentives to invest, turning economic activity into speculative activities. This shows the greater structural dependence the Colombian economy now has on external financing. In turn, in relation to financial assets, the inverse, unadjusted and non-significant relationship between the economy and the regression coefficients of asset valuation indexes such as housing and shares shows the deepening of the financialisation of the Colombian economy. This seems to be the reflection of a process of regressive structural change that has disconnected the internal market from the processes of business accumulation.

Finally, we conclude that in order to promote a progressive structural change, it will be necessary to come out of the export-led growth model that has been exhausted by both internal and external conditions, and instead go further towards a domestic demand-led growth model.

Notes

1 In the 1960s, half of the banks were public and sectorised to encourage development. Today, less than 1% are public (Ocampo 2015).
2 For example, the abolition of restrictions on bank ownership, in which commercial banks – before the opening up of the 1990s – could not have more than 49% foreign ownership.
3 As of Law 100 of 1993, private pension funds are given free rein to compete with the average pay as you go public system. The two largest AFPs (*Administradora de Fondos de Pensión*) are Porvenir and Protección. The first is part of the AVAL group, owned by billionaire Luis Carlos Sarmiento Angulo, and the most important local financial group in the country (when adding up all the assets of its banks). The second AFP belongs to the SURA group, which owns Bancolombia and GEA, the largest bank in the country, with the largest number of assets.
4 Own calculations with information from the Departamento Nacional de Estadística, DANE.
5 Not all variables have the same length as not all the data are available from the first quarter. FDI starts in 1996, the IGBC in 1991, the volume of investment in 1994 and exports in 1995.
6 The estimates were made using ordinary least squares regression. First, the dispersion diagrams were made, and then the estimation was used to corroborate the degree of adjustment with the R^2, the value of the relevant coefficient with the theoretical analysis and its degree of statistical individual significance.
7 Except for net exports where the suggested causality is reversed for theoretical reasons.
8 The data were taken from the National Department of Statistics, DANE, Banco de la República, Economática, Fedesarrollo and the Financial Superintendency.
9 The bond market was not used because access to information on the interest rate and price is available only from 2006.
10 As mentioned (Shiller 2015), the financial analysis of the housing market and its speculative behaviour should be reviewed with respect to the price of used housing, as it is not anchored to production costs, as is the case with the new housing price index.
11 The relationship between the Washington Consensus and the export-led growth model has been pointed out by Palley (2011).
12 Acronym for Colombia, Indonesia, Vietnam, Egypt, Turkey and South Africa.

13 Some of the plants that have closed in the last seven years are Kraft Foods Colombia, Chiclets Adams, Icollantas-Michellin, Bayern, the Colombian Automobile Company, etc.
14 The theoretical perspective that sustains the relationship between interest rate and functional income distribution, see Rochon (2017) and Moreno (Monetary policy and functional income distribution, 2014).
15 The recent tax reform of 2016 is an example. One of its pillars was to increase VATs (Value-Added Taxes) by 3 percentage points. It has helped to decrease people's disposable income.
16 "This is, distributive changes in favour of wages that increase aggregate demand and the growth rate of the economy" (Moreno 2016).

References

Angulo, R., Gaviria, A., and Morales, L. (2014) 'La década ganada: Evolución de la clase media, la pobreza y a vulnerabilidad en Colombia 2002–2011', *Coyuntura Económica* XLIV(1), 173–209.

Azuero, F. (1980) 'El Liberalismo Financiero. Balance de una Experiencia', *Cuadernos de Economía* 1(2), 29–52.

Base de Datos del Banco Mundial, accessed November 4, 2017, https://datos.bancomundial.org/indicator/NV.IND.MANF.ZS?locations=CO

Bianchi, A., Devlin, R., and Ramos, J. (1987) 'The adjustment process in Latin America: 1981–1986', *International Monetary Fund and World Bank Symposium on Growth-Oriented Adjustment Programs*, Washington, DC.

Braudel, F. (1970) *La historia y las ciencias sociales*, Alianza Editorial, Madrid.

Cardenas, M. (2013) *Introducción a la economía Colombiana*, Alfa-omega, Bogotá.

CEPAL (2002) *La inversión extranjera en América Latina y el Caribe*, Ediciones CEPAl, Santiago de Chile.

Chang, H-J. (2012) *23 cosas que no te cuentan sobre el capitalismo*, Debate, Madrid.

Clavijo, S., Fandiño, A., and Vera, A. (2012) *La desindustrialización en Colombia: análisis cuantitativo de sus determinantes*, Anif, Bogotá.

Estrada, J. (2006) 'Las reformas estructurales y la construcción del orden neoliberal en Colombia', in C. G. CLACSO, ed., *Los desafíos de las emancipaciones en un contexto militarizado*, pp. 247–284, CLACSO Libros, Buenos Aires.

Fajnzylber, F. (1990) *Unavoidable industrial restructuring in Latin America*, Duke University Press, Durham, NC.

Felipe, J. (2009) *Inclusive growth, full employment and structural change: implications and policies for developing Asia*, Anthem Press, Cambridge.

Gallardo, J., and Assous, M. (2010) *Michal Kalecki*, Palgrave Macmillan, New York, NY.

Gómez, J., Silva, L., and Restrepo, S. (2012) 'Flujos de Capital y Fragilidad Financiera', *Reportes del Emisor*, 160.

Guevara, D. (2016) 'Auge de las finanzas y desigualdad en la distribución del ingreso', www.bdigital.unal.edu.co/50985/

Kalecki, M. (1939) *Collected work*, Oxford University Press, Oxford.

Kalmanovitz, S. (2014) 'Se Acabo la Fiesta', *El espectador*, accessed September 28, 2017, www.elespectador.com/opinion/se-acaba-la-fiesta-columna-519451.

Keen, S. (2014) *Desenmascarando la economía*, LAES, México.

Kregel, J. (2004) 'External Financing for Development and International Financial Instability', *Discussion Papers* No. 32.

Leon, P. (2002) 'La Industrializacion Colombiana: Una Vision Heterodoxa', *Revista Innovar* 20, 3–100.

Londoño, J., and Alvaredo, F. (2014) 'Altos Ingresos e Impuesto de Renta en Colombia, 1993–2010', *Revista de Economía Institucional* 16(31), 157–194.

Mandelbrot, B., and Hudson, R. (2010) *Fractales y finanzas: una aproximación matemática a los mercados arriesgar perder y ganar*, Tusquets, Barcelona.

Manga, G. (2016) 'El Cuento de los Zapatos Chinos en Colombia', accessed July 28, 2017, www.semana.com/opinion/articulo/german-manga-el-cuento-de-los-zapatos-chinos-en-colombia/483654.

Moreno, A. (2014) 'Política Monetaria y Distribución Funcional del Ingreso', *Documento Escuela de Economía* 50, 1–39.

Moreno, A. (2016) 'Desigualdad y Macroeconomía', *Documentos FCE* No. 84, 1–27.

Ocampo, J. A. (2015) *Una historia del sistema financiero colombiano*, Asobancaria/Portafolio, Bogotá.

Palley, T. (2002) 'Domestic demand-led growth: a new paradigm', in Weaver, J., Jacobs, D., and Baker, J., eds., *After neoliberalism: economic policies that work for the poor*, pp. 36–48, New Rules for Global Finance Coalition, Washington, DC.

Palley, T. (2011) 'The rise and fall of the export-led growth model', *Levy Economics Institute*, Working Paper No 675, 1–24.

Panico, C., and Pico, A. (2015) 'Income distribution and the size of the financial sector', *Centro Sraffa*, Working Papers No. 15, 1–22.

Petri, F. (2003) 'Should the theory of endogenous growth be based on Say's Law and full employment of resources?', in Salvadori, N., ed., *The theory of economic growth: a classical perspective*, pp. 139–160, Edward Elgar, Northampton.

Rochon, L.-P. (2017) 'Rethinking monetary policy', in Rochon, L. P., and Rossi, S., eds., *A modern guide for rethinking economics*, pp. 120–130, Edward Elgar, London.

Sarmiento, E. (2002) *El Modelo Propio*, Escuela Colombiana de Ingenieros Julio Garavito, Bogotá.

Sarmiento, E. (2014) *Crecimiento con distribución es posible*, Escuela Colombiana de Ingenieros Julio Garavito, Bogotá.

Sarmiento, E. (2015) 'Déficit en cuenta corriente y devaluación', Revista Colombiano de Ingeniería 100(1), 12–25.

Sarmiento, E. (2017) 'Regreso a la protección agrícola', *El Espectador*, September 2.

Setterfield, M. (2005) *Crecimiento Dirigido por la Demanda*, Akal, Madrid.

Shiller, R. (2015) *Exuberancia irracional*, Deusto, Barcelona.

Winkler, O. (2009) *Interpreting economic and social data: a foundation of descriptive statistics*, Springer, New York.

Yasuhara, T. (2013) 'Inestabilidad Financiera en América Latina desde la Perspectiva Kaleckiana y Minskiana', *Problemas Del Desarrollo* 4(172), 9–27.

8 Financialisation of commodities, reserve accumulation and debt in Argentina

Alan Cibils and Cecilia Allami

The end of the Bretton Woods international monetary system in the early 1970s resulted in a series of profound economic transformations at the national and global level. Domestic and international financial regulation and capital controls were progressively dismantled to give way to financial liberalisation policies. This resulted in a process of ever-increasing trade and finance integration and, with it, a massive increase in international capital flows, increased volatility and economic instability.

One result of this process of global deregulation is what critical social scientists have labelled "financialisation". However, despite the increasing use of the term, there is no single generally agreed upon that definition. Rather, there is a set of what one could consider broadly complementary definitions. As Dore (2008: 1097) astutely observes, "[f]inancialisation' is a bit like 'globalisation' a convenient word for a bundle of more or less discrete structural changes in the economies of the industrialized world".

Dore's observation points to an additional issue with financialisation: most of the original writings on the subject focussed almost exclusively on the industrialised world. Increasingly, however, research has focussed on the impacts of financialisation on periphery countries, the multiple forms it takes and the channels through which it is propagated from the centre. General definitions of financialisation in the periphery are not available or even desirable, since different levels of development of productive and financial structures impose specificities, which make generalisations difficult.

This chapter has two objectives: first, to provide a survey of the range of views on financialisation in both centre and periphery countries and, second, to analyse the Argentine case from the perspective of the relationship between commodity market financialisation in centre countries and international reserve accumulation and public debt cycles in the periphery. In other words, our objective is to explore the transmission of financialisation from centre to periphery countries, with special emphasis on Argentina's external accounts.

The chapter is structured in five sections, with this introduction as the first section. In the second section, we present a brief survey of definitions of financialisation used in centre countries.[1] This is followed by a third section that contains a survey of the literature on financialisation in the periphery. Following the literature surveys, in the fourth section, we analyse financialisation in Argentina, focussing specifically on three aspects: (a) the financialisation of commodity markets, Argentina's main exports; (b) the accumulation of international reserves by central banks since the 1990s; and (c) the cycles of growing public indebtedness and crises. In the last section, we conclude with a brief summary of our findings on the impact of financialisation on Argentina.

Financialisation: early definitions and issues

The term "financialisation" was first used in 1993, according to Foster (2007). Since then, it has become widely used in heterodox economics and the critical social sciences more generally. In general terms, it is used to denote the growing ascendance of finance capital over industrial capital, or the financial over the "real" economy since the end of the Bretton Woods system. Perhaps the most widely cited definition is Epstein's (2005: 3): "Financialization is the increasing role of financial motives, financial markets, financial actors and financial institutions in the operation of the domestic and international economies".

Epstein (2015) classifies the growing body of research on financialisation into three categories. The first focusses on clarifying the definition of financialisation with the purpose of determining whether it is a new phase of capitalist development or a new accumulation regime. The second focusses on the effects of financialisation, with a view to determining, through theoretical models and empirical analyses, the impact of financialisation on productive investment, wages, distribution and crises. The third research category is more policy oriented, seeking to determine what policies are needed to curb the effects of financialisation and to increase policy space for progressive macroeconomic policies.

Van der Zwan (2014) adopts a different classification of the literature, identifying three broad approaches to financialisation. The first he identifies as the French regulationist approach, which sees financialisation as a new regime of accumulation. This group includes not only regulationist, but also some post-Keynesian and radical political economists. They view the emergence of the finance-led or finance-dominated regime of accumulation as a response to the fall in productivity of the late 1960s (Boyer 2000). The second approach identifies financialisation with the emergence of shareholder value as the main guiding principle for corporate behaviour. In other words, they posit that the main objective of the financialised corporation is to generate quarterly profits for its shareholders, producing substantial changes in corporate behaviour and investment horizons (Aglietta 2000; Crotty 2002). The third approach focusses on the financialisation of everyday life (Erturk et al. 2007; Martin 2002). This approach questions policies that seek to include every segment of society, especially low- and middle-income segments, into the financial sphere.

Krippner (2005: 181) takes a different approach, arguing that financialisation definitions generally focus on aggregate or sectoral economic activity, which makes it more difficult to identify a financialisation process. Krippner defines financialisation as a "particular pattern of accumulation in which profit-making occurs increasingly through financial channels, rather than through trade and commodity production". In other words, it is necessary to study the evolution of sectoral profits and changes in their composition over time to be able to fully grasp the process of financialisation.

Lapavitsas (2013: 70–71) combines elements of the different definitions, defining financialisation as "a systemic transformation of capitalist economies" that changes the relation between the corporate and banking sectors, with the former turning more to self-financing and the latter turning more to financial investments as a source of profits.

Most empirical research on financialisation can broadly be classified under two headings: microeconomic and macroeconomic. Microeconomic research includes studies that focus on the activities of large industrial corporations, using firm-level data to identify the ways in which investment and growth are impacted by firms investing in financial assets rather than productive capacity. Examples of this are Orhangazi's (2007) research on financialisation in the US economy, Demir's (2007) research on a sample of several peripheral countries, Plihon and Miotti's (2001) study of the relationship between financialisation and bank crises, and Stockhammer's (2004, 2006, 2008) studies of the impact of firm-level financialisation on accumulation.

Macroeconomic-focussed research uses aggregate sectoral, financial and macroeconomic data to explore mechanisms of financialisation, integrating strategies of a broad number of economic actors. We can broadly classify them according to the economic school of thought authors subscribe to into regulationist (Boyer 2000), post-Keynesian (Palley 2007) and radical (Epstein 2002, 2005; Krippner 2005; Lapavitsas 2009a, 2009b).

What then has been the impact of financialisation? In general, the research, as discussed above, concludes that financial liberalisation and financialisation have transformed the functioning of economic systems at both the macro and micro levels. Its principal impacts have been to (1) elevate the significance of the financial sector relative to the real sector, (2) transfer income from the real sector to the financial sector, and (3) increase income inequality and contribute to wage stagnation (Palley 2007: 2).

Despite the volume of literature on financialisation, there are key questions that do not have single, clear-cut answers (Epstein 2015). For example, when did the process of financialisation begin? Is financialisation the result of financial market liberalisation starting in the 1980s, or is it a consequence of reduced profitability and stagnation in the real economy in centre countries since the 1960s? Finally, the overarching question is: what is the relationship between financialisation, globalisation and neo-liberalism? In the literature, financialisation is frequently presented as almost a second stage of financial liberalisation. According to Epstein (2015: 5), this topic ultimately cannot be resolved since these phenomena have all arisen more or less together since the 1980s.

Financialisation in periphery countries

How does financialisation in the centre affect the periphery? What are the transmission channels from financialised centre countries to the periphery? Does financialisation manifest itself in the same way in the periphery as it does in the centre? Is there a variety of periphery financialisations? In the following section, we discuss some of the ways financialisation manifests itself in periphery countries. According to Bonizzi, financialisation is "not a linear process and assumes different forms in developing countries vis-à-vis advanced economies, as well as country specific forms" (2014: 85). Bonizzi identifies different manifestations of financialisation in peripheral countries, of which the first is non-financial corporation investment behaviour, which increasingly favours investment in financial assets over production. This has resulted in decreased productive investment and also a decrease in its share of gross domestic product (GDP). High-return assets are often the result of inflation-targeting monetary policy or public debt policies, strongly promoted by international financial institutions.

Financialisation in the periphery also operates through transformations of banking systems and the financial sector more generally. According to a study of large transnational banks by dos Santos (2009), bank profits are increasingly generated from consumer credit to individuals, from financial investments and from services, including investment banking. Thus, bank profits are increasingly generated in the sphere of circulation and, to a lesser extent, in the sphere of production. Since the early 1990s, periphery banking systems have either been taken over by foreign banks, or have adopted international bank behaviour in order to compete.[2] This has had a profound impact on periphery banking and on household financial behaviour and indebtedness (Bonizzi 2014; Cibils & Allami 2013). A particularly innovative – and perverse – aspect of financialisation has been the incorporation of even the poorest households and individuals into the financialised banking system through policies of "financial inclusion" and microfinance (see Aitken 2013; Bond 2013; Mader 2013, 2014; Soderberg 2013).

Since the end of Bretton Woods, and especially since the 1990s, deregulation of domestic and international capital markets has resulted in massive increases in capital flows worldwide, greatly contributing to the volatility and instability of the world economy and especially the economies of developing countries. Low-risk markets, typically in the USA or Europe, are generally not as profitable as riskier periphery country or "emerging" markets, where high real interests compete to attract foreign capital. When flows are attracted, they are usually short term, and capital flight is easily triggered by domestic or foreign events, often with devastating effects. According to Lapavitsas (2009b), the links between domestic financialisation in developed countries and international financialisation affecting developing countries derive in large part from these capital flows.

Becker et al. (2010: 228) identify two forms of financialisation: "financialization based on the take-off of a second circuit of 'fictitious capital'... i.e. securities, and financialisation based on interest-bearing capital and thus, on high interest rates". This second form of financialisation is related to a key characteristic of periphery countries, namely the foreign exchange constraint, resulting in a dependence on foreign exchange and, therefore, capital inflows. Policies geared towards attracting foreign flows can include overvalued exchange rates coupled with high interest rates, which often allow banks to appropriate a considerable share of the surplus while promoting financial speculation over productive investment.

Levy-Orlik (2013b: 206), analysing the effects of post-Bretton Woods financial and productive globalisation, characterises financialisation as having three central aspects: a new organisation of production, a new way of profit appropriation and a change in the behaviour of economic agents. The transnationalisation of production and the consequent decoupling of demand and supply has led to the growth of imbalances within, and between, countries and regions. Centre countries have the role of liquidity providers and demanders of goods and services, resulting in structural current account deficits and capital account surpluses. Periphery countries have adopted export promotion policies, but do not always manage to achieve a current account surplus and face difficulties attracting capital flows to balance their external sector. They are therefore forced to offer increasingly higher financial returns and repress real wages[3] in order to compete (Levy-Orlik 2013a: 109–110). This structural characteristic of the globalisation era has led to increasing financialisation in the periphery, especially in Latin America.[4]

A little explored aspect of financialisation in periphery countries, especially those that like Argentina depend heavily on exports of primary commodities, is the link between the financialisation of commodity markets in centre countries and the historic problem of developing countries, that is, the foreign exchange constraint (Cibils & Allami 2017). ECLAC (Economic Commission on Latin America and the Caribbean) dedicated considerable thought and research to this issue and its impact on Latin American development in the mid-twentieth century. Their policy proposal was import substitution industrialisation (ISI) as a way to industrialise and, eventually, lessen the constraint.

In the case of Argentina, for example, decades of ISI did not result in an easing of the foreign exchange constraint and economic liberalisation policies implemented since the mid-1970s have had several additional impacts. First, commercial liberalisation has resulted in a sustained deindustrialisation process and a return to dependence on primary production and exports (re-primarisation).[5] Second, financial liberalisation has allowed for a temporary alleviation of the foreign exchange constraint through the capital account (capital inflows and debt). This process has been unstable with cyclical crises and it has changed the nature of the foreign exchange constraint problem. Finally, these problems have been compounded due to commodity market financialisation in the centre and the resulting increased instability of primary commodity prices.

The case of Argentina: commodities, reserve accumulation and debt

In the following sections, we look into the impact of commodity market financialisation and its impact on reserve accumulation and public debt cycles, focussing specifically on the case of Argentina.

The financialisation of commodities

As a result of the spread of financial deregulation since the end of Bretton Woods, many periphery countries have experienced a process of deindustrialisation and increased dependence on primary sector (commodity) exports. This is certainly the case of Argentina, where primary exports (including primary-based manufactures) accounted for almost 70% of the total exports in 2016, according to the national statistics agency (Instituto Nacional de Estadísticas y Censo, INDEC).

In recent years, a relatively new phenomenon has emerged, the financialisation of commodities, due to which a financial logic has increasingly permeated commodity markets and prices. This has meant that prices have become increasingly influenced by financial phenomena and less so by the physical conditions of production, leading to much greater commodity world price volatility.

The links between commodities and finance go back a few centuries, to the early stages of agricultural product futures markets when credit, and other financing instruments, were issued by banks. Futures agricultural markets[6] were eventually used to hedge against weather and price variations, thus protecting producers from risks in physical markets. In this way, futures markets served as market, price and profit stabilisers, aiding forward budgetary planning (Gras 2013: 31–32, Murphy et al. 2012: 29).

In recent decades, significant changes have occurred in the relationship between commodities and finance due to financialisation. Since the commodity price boom that began in 2000, investors have begun to take financial positions in commodity futures markets as a way to increase returns, diversify portfolios and reduce risks. This process was aided by the deregulation of Chicago's futures markets and the creation of new financial instruments, such as derivatives. Furthermore, since the 1990s, new commodity markets have emerged in which hedge funds and investment banks can transact future contracts with no limitations or controls (Gras 2013).

In this way, more recent financial deregulation has resulted in more intense and intricate links between commodity and financial markets. In some cases, derivatives have combined agriculture-based assets with assets based on other primary products linking commodity markets for all types of primary production (agriculture, livestock, mining, etc.). In addition, the volumes of exchange traded on commodity futures markets have increased exponentially. According to Bichetti and Maystre (2012: 3–4), the volumes of exchange-traded derivatives on commodity markets are now 20–30 times greater than physical production. Furthermore, in the 1990s, financial investors accounted for less than 25% of all market participants; today, financial investors represent more than 85% of all commodity futures market participants (Bichetti & Maystre 2012: 3–4).

These new trends mean that primary product prices are increasingly influenced by factors not related to physical availability. Whether financial speculation in commodity markets is one of these factors has been the subject of considerable debate in recent years. However, there is a degree of unanimity on the fact that such financial speculation has, at the very least, a short-run impact on the price of food.

Other factors found to have an impact on the determination of commodity prices are the aggregate risk appetite for financial assets and the investment behaviour of diversified commodity index investors. According to Tang and Xiong (2010: 4), the presence of these investors can lead to a more efficient sharing of commodity price risk, but portfolio rebalancing can introduce spillover of price volatility from outside into commodities markets and also across different commodities. Belke et al. (2013) found that financialisation of commodities has led to a large flow of investment into commodity markets, especially into index investments. The growing volumes of financial investments in commodity derivatives markets have led to a synchronised boom and bust of seemingly unrelated commodity prices, thus driving commodity prices away from levels justified by commodity market fundamentals. Similarly, the United Nations Conference on Trade and Development (UNCTAD 2011) found that increased speculation has probably accelerated and amplified price fluctuations. Tang and Xiong (2010) also point out that concurrent with the rapid growing index investment in commodities markets since the early 2000s, futures prices of different commodities in the USA became increasingly correlated with each other.[7]

The main effect of commodity financialisation is uncertainty and potential destabilisation of commodity markets. Consequently, those who suffer most from commodity market financialisation are commodity-producing periphery countries that depend on primary exports for foreign exchange. Those periphery countries most dependent on commodity production and exports are the most exposed to external destabilising factors, such as inflation, trade deficits and currency devaluations (Bichetti & Maystre 2012: 28).

According to the Food and Agriculture Organization of the United Nations (FAO) (2011: 7), food-price uncertainty and volatility affect the poor most intensely – especially the urban poor – who can spend up to 75% of their income on food. High food prices reduce the quantity and quality of the food they can consume, threatening food security and generating malnutrition. According to the FAO, the 2007–2008 food price increase resulted in an increase in world poverty. Robles et al. (2008) estimated that the 2006–2008 price increases generated 21 million new poor in Latin American middle-income countries.

In Argentina, commodity financialisation has impacted primarily through the fluctuation of prices of its main exports: soybean, soybean oil, wheat and maize. The increase in price volatility can be estimated through the standard deviation, on a yearly basis, of monthly price variations. Figure 8.1 shows an increase in price volatility starting in the mid-1970s and a considerable increase in fluctuation frequency starting in the 1990s. We have also included the price of soybean (right axis) for comparative purposes. In the case of soybean, Argentina's main export during the last decade, the commodity price bubble of the first part of this century resulted in windfall export earnings, fuelling a significant international reserve build-up as we shall see in the following section. It was this reserve build-up that allowed the successive Kirchner administrations to substantially reduce the public debt load. When the commodity bubble burst, Argentina's foreign reserve stock declined sharply and the foreign exchange constraint emerged once again.

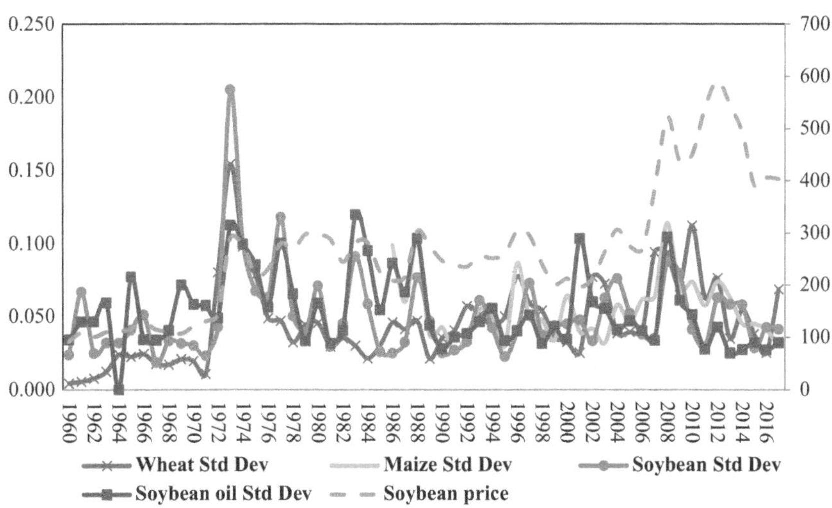

Figure 8.1 Standard deviation of monthly price variations and soybean price (per ton).
Source: Authors' calculations based on UNCTAD data.

The accumulation of international reserves

A new phenomenon of the past few decades has been the significant increase in the stock of foreign reserves held by periphery-country central banks. Since the late 1990s, following a series of substantial financial crises in periphery countries,[8] international reserve accumulation has become even more marked (Mendoza 2004). According to the literature, there are three reasons for this development. First, countries have needed to increase international reserves due to the increase in trade (as a percentage of GDP) (Baker & Walentin 2001). Second, the international monetary system has become more unstable since the 1980s, making reserve accumulation by periphery countries a necessity to protect themselves from sudden capital flow reversals. And third, reserves are accumulated for exchange rate stability (Painceira 2009). The last two reasons for international reserve accumulation are directly linked to the growth of financial globalisation and financialisation in the global capitalist economy.

Reserve accumulation requires net flows of capital from developing to developed countries. This resource transfer carries significant costs for periphery countries: rather than putting received funds to productive use, they sit idle as prevention for a potential future crisis. The precise composition of international reserves is not known, but according to Lapavitsas (2009b: 119–120), there is little doubt that the bulk – about two-thirds – are US dollars. The policy of reserve accumulation thus amounts to developing countries storing dollars and other hard currencies, usually in the form of official financial assets. Their accumulation is nothing short of a very substantial low-cost loan to the issuing countries.[9]

Figure 8.2 shows international reserves to GDP ratio in current dollars for the period 1962–2016 for two periphery countries, namely Argentina and Brazil. The figure shows that both countries exhibit a clear upward trend for the ratio during the period. It is important to highlight that, for centre countries, the trend has a downward slope during the same period.[10] If we look at the period 2000–2016, we find that Brazil held an average stock of international reserves equivalent to 13% of its GDP, while for Argentina the average was 9% during the same period. These averages are substantially higher than those corresponding to the second half of the twentieth century.

If we look specifically at Argentina, we find that 2002–2010 is a period of intense international reserve accumulation, due primarily to the increase in soybean exports and to record high international prices. Even when international prices dropped after 2010, Argentina's international reserve ratio was still considerably higher than those observed for countries in the centre.

What are the costs of reserve accumulation? Although reserves provide some return, the cost of holding reserves is the difference between the opportunity cost and the real return on reserves. The portion of reserves held as interest-bearing deposits, or as the short-term government debt of the

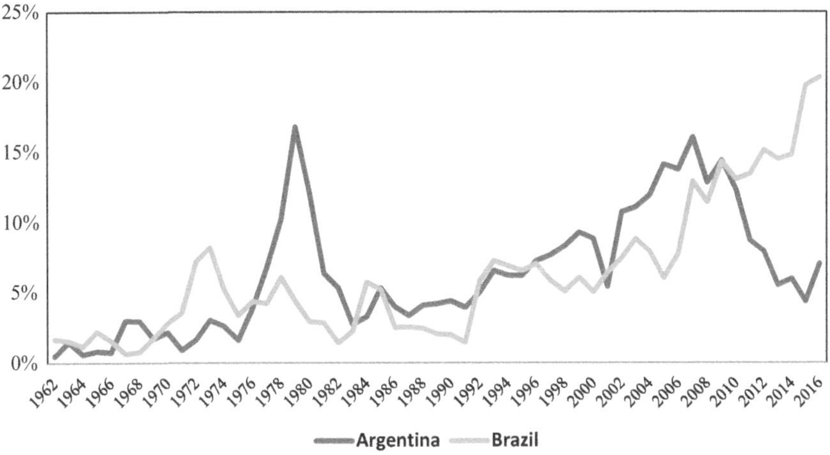

Figure 8.2 International reserves/GDP (current dollars, percentage).
Source: Authors' calculations based on World Bank data.

USA, will typically earn a small positive real rate of interest (1%–2%), whereas reserves held as gold, currency, or in non-interest bearing accounts will provide no real return. Given the mix of assets held as reserves, the average return is approximately 1% (Baker & Walentin 2001). On the other hand, periphery countries issue short-term debt from abroad at substantially higher commercial rates of interest, increasing the cost of international reserve holdings. In the case of Argentina, the composition of reserves in October of 2017 was 50% hard currency, 45% hard-currency denominated assets and 5% gold (Argentine Central Bank).

There are various estimates of the costs to periphery countries of holding international reserves. Rodrik (2006) estimates the social cost of this policy at 1% of developing country GDP; Baker and Walentin (2001) estimate the cost to be 1%–2% of GDP for most periphery countries, while Akyüz (2008) estimates the annual cost to be $100 billion (also Mendoza 2004: 73). If we applied Rodrik's calculations to Argentina, the cost of holding international reserves during 2016 was 5400 million dollars.

Parallel to reserve accumulation, there has been a very substantial growth of periphery country public debt mostly due to monetary sterilisation needed to offset the inflationary impact of foreign capital inflows.[11] As we shall see in the following section, Argentina is not exempt from this trend. Domestic bond markets have grown strongly in periphery countries since the mid-1990s. The liabilities issued by central banks in these countries typically have significantly higher rates of return than the official rates on the foreign public assets also acquired by central banks. This rate of return differential adds to the periphery's costs (Lapavitsas 2009b).

In other words, the periphery's accumulation of reserves as protection, due largely to the increase in financialisation, has generated direct costs resulting from the difference in the interest rate on reserves and what must be paid for public debt. It has also generated indirect costs, as accumulated reserves sit idle and cannot be put to productive use for development.[12]

Financialisation – which has already resulted in an increase in volatility, short-term orientation and financial fragility in periphery economies – has forced these countries to accumulate reserves with substantial costs. Meanwhile, there are substantial stocks of foreign reserves being kept as "crisis insurance" that could be put to work for more socially beneficial development purposes.

Public debt

One of the most salient characteristics of the Argentine economy in the post-Bretton Woods period has been the occurrence of recurrent financial and debt crises. The causes of these crises have changed over the years, however, as international financial liberalisation and financialisation deepened and spread from the centre to the periphery.

The initial theoretical underpinning of financial liberalisation policies can be found in the 1973 writings of McKinnon and Shaw (Allami & Cibils 2010). A decade later, building on the work of these authors, Cooper and Sachs (1984) lay down the orthodox theoretical foundations to support foreign indebtedness in a global context of liberalised capital flows. According to Cooper and Sachs, foreign indebtedness had two main benefits. First, developing countries can finance their development processes with foreign savings.[13] Thus, foreign savings would make up for insufficient local saving and at potentially lower costs. In this context, the current account would be the indicator of foreign debt sustainability. The second advantage is that the supply of foreign savings would allow for a smoothing of consumption during periods of lower economic activity, following the intertemporal approach to the current account according to which the balance of payments is determined by agents' forward looking investment and saving decisions.

Cooper and Sachs' theory implies that if a periphery country borrows externally, it is either financing its development of smoothing consumption. Either way, there should be no need for concern. However, the multiple and recurrent debt crises that have occurred since financial deregulation began in the mid-1970s, and at best erratic behaviour of investment, have resulted in strong criticisms of Cooper and Sachs' views. Furthermore, it makes little sense to take the current account as an indicator of debt sustainability when the capital account has been the main locus of imbalances in recent decades (Bonizzi et al. 2015).

According to Salama (2006), debt crises in the 1980s can be explained mainly due to the weight of foreign debt service and the need to pay it with trade surplus proceeds. However, since the 1990s crises originated mainly because of financial deregulation and the large magnitude and volatility of capital flows that resulted from liberalisation. The State was a key player in both scenarios, even if growth regimes were substantially different.

According to Salama, the State-finance relationship changed substantially after financial liberalisation policies became the norm. First, it no longer gave priority to industrial capital, privileging financial capital and financialisation instead. Second, the high interest rates that resulted from inflation targeting monetary policies, the need to attract foreign capital and foreign indebtedness result in a higher cost of credit, making financial investment more profitable than productive investment. Salama concludes that financialisation is the threshold beyond which the financial sector becomes more lucrative than productive sectors and develops at their expense. Financial liberalisation policies have produced the impression that the financial sector is autonomous from productive sectors, and thus becoming toxic to productive investment.

Financialisation has also had an impact on the ability of periphery countries to issue debt on international markets. According to Hardie (2011: 141–142), investors "reward or punish governments for policy decisions directly through the cost and availability of financing. The more a government can borrow, the greater its immediate ability to carry out its chosen policies".[14] Defining financialisation as the "ability to trade risk", Hardie asks how the deepening of financialisation has aided or hurt periphery governments' ability to issue debt. The author concludes that "the more (less) financialised an emerging government bond market, the lower (higher) the capacity of governments to borrow on a sustainable basis. In emerging markets, financialised markets are debt intolerant markets" (Hardie 2011: 142–143).

Given this general framework for emerging country foreign debt under financialisation, we turn briefly to the case of Argentina. Financial liberalisation and financialisation have meant that countries like Argentina have additional channels – issuing debt – through which to temporarily address the historic foreign exchange constraint. The financialisation of commodity markets has added volatility and unpredictability for foreign exchange revenues in primarised economies of periphery countries like Argentina. This context has added new dynamics to Argentina's foreign debt accumulation.

Figure 8.3 shows Argentina's public debt/GDP ratio for the period 1960–2016. There are several interesting clearly visible phenomena in the figure. First, the pre-financial liberalisation or ISI period (up to the mid-1970s) shows relatively stable and low debt/GDP ratios. Second, the two cycles of unsustainable build-up and crises in 1982 and 2001–2002 are clearly visible. Third, the post 2001–2002 crisis shows a sharp decline lasting till 2011. Finally, the trend has changed after 2011, which could be indicating the beginning of a new debt cycle. In other words, public debt was not a policy problem during the ISI years of "financial repression", but it became a problem when financial liberalisation became the dominant policy setting.

The remarkable post 2001–2002 crisis drop in debt/GDP can be explained by three main factors. First, Argentina's December 2001 sovereign

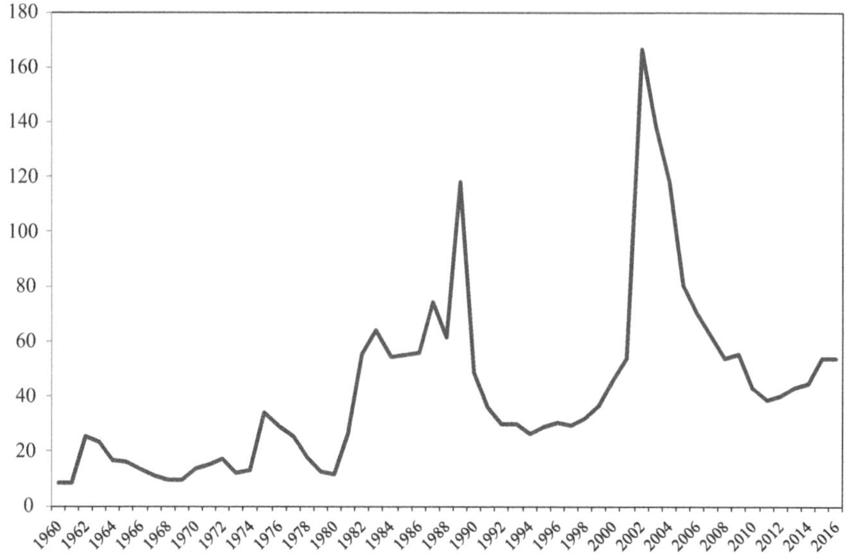

Figure 8.3 Argentina's public debt to GDP ratio 1960–2016.

Source: Authors' calculations based on Ferreres (2005) (for the period 1960–1993) and Comisión Económica para América Latina y el Caribe, CEPAL (for the period 1994–2016).

default and debt restructuring (in 2005 and 2010) substantially reduced Argentina's public debt stock. Second, the commodity price speculative bubble resulted in windfall export earnings and foreign reserve accumulation during the period 2003–2011. The successive Kirchner administrations made it an explicit policy to avoid new foreign currency debt issues. Third, very high growth rates between 2003 and 2009 also contributed to a drop in the ratio. With the change of government in 2015, a new cycle of foreign debt growth appears to have begun. This implies that, as in the 1990s, Argentina's economic growth prospects will become increasingly linked to centre's financial and economic cycles that result from financialisation.

A note of caution is due regarding Argentina's debt dynamics. One should not attribute debt accumulation exclusively to foreign exchange constraint dynamics. While it is true that commodity price fluctuations play an important role, other historic factors such as capital flight and accumulation of foreign assets by local residents have also played an important part in Argentina's debt build-up.[15]

Conclusions

As we have seen in preceding sections, centre financialisation has a substantial and varied impact on periphery countries. In this chapter, we explored the links between the financialisation of commodity markets in centre countries and its impact on countries like Argentina that operate under an almost permanent foreign exchange constraint. Specifically, we focussed on the impacts of commodity market financialisation and Argentina's response through the accumulation of international reserves, and/or the accumulation of public debt.

For Argentina, commodity market financialisation in the centre has resulted in increased price volatility of its main exports: soybean, soybean oil, maize and wheat. In the case of soybean, Argentina's main export, we observe a strong price increase as of 2007, which allowed for a substantial foreign reserve accumulation by Argentina's Central Bank and easing of the foreign exchange constraint during the following years. This also facilitated Argentina's debt-reduction strategy of the Kirchner administrations. When the commodity bubble burst, Argentina's foreign reserve stock declined sharply and the foreign exchange constraint emerged once again.

The accumulation of international reserves emerged, when international market conditions allowed, and served as a protection against increased volatility and financialisation, also allowing greater exchange rate policy space. Reserve accumulation generates direct costs due to interest rate differentials between reserve yields and foreign debt issues. It also generates indirect costs, as accumulated reserves sit idle instead of contributing to the development process. In the case of Argentina, as with other periphery countries, we observe a clear upward trend in the stock of international reserve to GDP ratio between 1962 and 2010. Between 2002 and 2010, intense foreign reserve accumulation was the product of large trade surpluses resulting primarily from the international commodity price boom. Following that, reserves declined sharply and the fragility of Argentina's external accounts emerged once again.

Financialisation has also had an impact on the evolution of Argentina's public debt through two different channels. First, the interaction between commodity market volatility and the foreign exchange constraint, in the absence of significant reserves, results in the accumulation of foreign debt as a means to alleviate the constraint. Second, financialisation in centre financial markets imposes conditions on debt issuers that are often unsustainable. When coupled with monetary and interest rate policies aimed exclusively at controlling inflation and attracting foreign capital flows, centre financialisation has additional channels through which to affect periphery countries. In the case of Argentina, starting in the mid-1970s, there is a strong increase in the debt-to-GDP ratio, with two clearly marked cycles of unsustainable debt growth and the inevitable ensuing crises. It is important to highlight that the very substantial drop in the ratio between 2003 and 2011 was due in great measure to an explicit government policy of paying off dollar-denominated debt, enabled by the international reserve accumulation that resulted from the commodity price bubble. However, when the bubble burst and foreign reserves began to dwindle, the debt-reduction trend was reduced. The change of government in 2015 also marked a radical change in foreign-currency debt issues, putting Argentina once again in a situation of increasing financial fragility, with the next crisis awaiting a reversal in financial market conditions.

In sum, financialisation's multiple effects, together with the globalisation of production and finance, impose strong restrictions on the periphery's development possibilities. In the case of Argentina, policies implemented since the mid-1970s have resulted in deindustrialisation and renewed dependence on primary exports, thus giving a renewed life to the historic foreign exchange constraint problem. Financialisation deepens the problems, as it makes foreign exchange income more volatile, resulting in countries resorting to inefficient and costly foreign reserve accumulation or costly and potentially explosive debt accumulation. In this way, the periphery becomes inextricably linked to the centre's financial cycles, speculative bubbles and crises.

Notes

1 The second and third sections draw from more detailed presentations in Cibils and Allami (2013, 2017) and Allami and Cibils (2017).
2 See Tonveronachi (2006) for a case study of the Argentine banking system in the 1990s.
3 Becker et al. (2010) point out that real wage repression often results in growing household debt, adding to the financialisation process.
4 See also Cibils and Pinazo (2016) for a complementary account of productive transformation in the periphery in the era of globalisation.
5 Indeed, since the dismantling of the system of trade barriers that began with the 1976 dictatorship and taken to an extreme in the 1990s, much of Argentina's manufacturing and manufactured exports have all but disappeared. As a result, the weight of agriculture and agriculture-based manufactures has taken a dominant role as foreign exchange producers, see Cibils (2011), Bolinaga and Slipak (2015), Giarraca and Teubal (2013), and Grigera (2011), among many others.
6 These markets, of which the Chicago Mercantile Exchange founded in 1898 is the oldest, allow those who want to reduce risks to transfer them to others who are willing to take them on. In this way, contracts are drawn up between those who wish to buy or sell at some future time for an agreed-to price. These markets were typically used by wholesalers and food industry producers to hedge against risks (Gras 2013: 31–32).
7 According to the FAO, the transfer of financial market price increases to domestic food markets varies by country. For most developing countries, international commodity price increases in 2007/2008 resulted in domestic food price increases, although in some cases with considerable lags. Furthermore, the subsequent drop in international prices was only partially transmitted to domestic food markets (FAO 2011:10–11).
8 There were crises in Mexico (1994), Southeast Asia (1997), Russia (1999), Brazil (1999), Turkey (2001) and Argentina (2001–2002).
9 Periphery country costs have a counterpart in gains for the US economy, since the dollar is the main reserve currency. According to Lapavitsas (2009b: 121),

> ... the international arrangements of capital flows and world money have created an unprecedented source of gain for the US economy. Developing countries have been implicitly subsidizing the hegemonic power in the world economy purely because it issues the dominant form of (valueless) quasi-world-money.

10 For example, the UK and Australia show downward sloping trends for the period according to World Bank data.
11 "Sterilization is the practice of issuing public debt by the Treasury or the central bank with the aim of absorbing increases in domestic liquidity (the money supply) due to surpluses of foreign exchange" (Painceira 2009: 13).
12 Cruz (2006) evaluates these costs for the Mexican case, and Singh (2006) for India.
13 Cooper and Sachs make the same conceptual mistake as McKinnon and Shaw, namely that productive investment is financed by saving. As many heterodox economists have pointed out, productive investment is financed with credit, not saving. This means that the State's financial and credit policies are of key importance when it comes to financing investment and development.
14 Massó (2016) uses a similar analytical framework to that of Hardie to analyse the case of Spain.
15 Basualdo (2017) provides a comprehensive historical review of this issue.

References

Aglietta, M. (2000) 'Shareholder and Corporate Governance: Some Tricky Questions', *Economy and Society*, 29 (1), 146–159.

Aitken, R. (2013) 'The Financialization of Micro-Credit', *Development and Change*, 44 (3), 473–499.

Akyüz, Y. (2008) 'Managing Financial Instability in Emerging Markets: A Keynesian Perspective', *Turkish Economic Association Discussion*, Paper No. 4. Ankara: Turkish Economic Association.

Allami, C. & Cibils, A. (2010) 'Crisis financieras y regulación: Propuestas heterodoxas', *Política y Cultura*, 34, 57–85.

Allami, C. & Cibils, A. (2017) 'Financialization and Development', in Munck, Ronaldo & Fagan, Honor, eds., *Handbook of Development and Social Change*, Edward Elgar, Cheltenham, UK.

Baker, D. & Walentin, K. (2001) 'Money for Nothing: The Increasing Cost of Foreign Reserve Holdings to Developing Nations', *Center for Economic Policy and Research Briefing Paper*, Washington, DC.

Basualdo, E. (ed.) (2017) *Endeudar y fugar*, Siglo XXI Editores, Buenos Aires.

Becker, J., Johannes, J., Leubolt, B. & Weissenbacher, R. (2010) 'Peripheral Financialization and Vulnerability to Crisis: A Regulationist Perspective', *Competition and Change*, 14 (3–4), 225–247.

Belke, A., Bordon, I. & Volz, U. (2013) 'Effects of Global Liquidity on Commodity and Food Prices', *World Development*, 44, 31–43.

Bichetti, D. & Maystre, N. (2012) 'The Synchronized and Long-Lasting Structural Change on Commodity Markets: Evidence from High Frequency Data', Munich Personal RePEc Archive Paper No. 37486.

Bolinaga, L. & Slipak, A. (2015) 'El Consenso de Beijing y la Reprimarización Productiva de América Latina: El Caso Argentino', *Problemas del Desarrollo*, 46 (183), 33–58.

Bond, P. (2013) 'Debt, Uneven Development and Capitalist Crisis in South Africa: From Moody's Macroeconomic Monitoring to Marikana Microfinance *Mahonisas*', *Third World Quarterly*, 34 (4), 569–592.

Bonizzi, B. (2014) 'Financialization in Developing and Emerging Countries: A Survey', *International Journal of Political Economy*, 42 (4), 83–107.

Bonizzi, B., Laskaridis, C. & Toporowski, J. (2015) 'Developing Countries' External Debt and International Financial Integration', *FESSUD*, Working Paper No. 121.

Boyer, R. (2000) 'Is a Finance-Led Growth Regime a Viable Alternative to Fordism? A Preliminary Analysis', *Economy and Society*, 29 (1), 111–145.

Cibils, A. (2011) 'Argentina: Macroeconomics, Re-primarization and the Environment', *Policy Matters*, 18, 48–71.

Cibils, A. & Allami, C. (2013) 'Financialization vs. Development Finance: The Case of the Post-Crisis Argentine Banking System', *Revue de la Régulation*, 13, 1–17.

Cibils, A. & Allami, C. (2017) 'Financiarización en la Periferia Latinoamericana: Deuda, *Commodities*, y Acumulación de Reservas', *Revista Estado y Políticas Públicas*, 5 (8), 81–101.

Cibils, A. & Pinazo, G. (2016) 'The Periphery in the Productive Globalization: A New Dependency?', in Levy-Orlik, Noemi & Ortiz, Etelberto, eds., *The Financialization Response to Economic Disequilibria: European and Latin American Experiences*, Edward Elgar, Cheltenham, 69–89.

Cooper, R. & Sachs, J. (1984) 'Borrowing Abroad: The Debtor's Perspective', *National Bureau of Economic Research*, Working Paper 1427.

Crotty, J. (2002) 'The Effects of Increased Market Competition and Changes in Financial Markets and the Structure of Nonfinancial Corporations in the Neoliberal Era', *University of Massachusetts*, Amherst: Political Economy Research Institute, Working Paper 44.

Cruz, M. (2006) '¿Pueden las reservas internacionales contribuir al crecimiento mexicano?' *Economía UNAM*, 3 (8), 115–124.

Demir, F. (2007) 'The Rise of Rentier Capitalism and the Financialisation of Real Sectors in Developing Countries', *Review of Radical Political Economics*, 39 (3), 351–359.

Dore, R. (2008) 'Financialization of the Global Economy', *Industrial and Corporate Change*, 17 (6), 1097–1112, [https://doi.org/10.1093/icc/dtn041].

Dos Santos, P. (2009) 'On the Content of Banking in Contemporary Capitalism', *Historical Materialism*, 17, 180–213.

Epstein, G. (2002) 'Financialisation, Rentier Interests, and Central Bank Policy', *Paper Prepared for Conference 'Financialisation and the World Economy*, Amherst: Political Economy Research Institute, University of Massachusetts, December 7–8, 2001.

Epstein, G. (2005) *Financialisation and the World Economy*, Edward Elgar, Cheltenham, UK.

Epstein, G. (2015) 'Financialization: There's Something Happening Here', *Political Economy Research Institute (PERI)*, Working Paper 394.

Erturk, I., Julie, F., Sukhdev, J., Leaver, A., & Karel, W. (2007) 'The Democratisation of Finance? Promises, Outcomes and Conditions', *Review of International Political Economy*, 14 (4), 553–575.

FAO. (2011) *La volatilidad de los precios y la seguridad alimentaria*. Informe del Grupo de alto nivel de expertos en seguridad alimentaria y nutrición del Comité de Seguridad Alimentaria Mundial, Roma.

Ferreres, O. (2005) *Dos siglos de economía argentina (1810–2004)*. Fundación Norte y Sur, Buenos Aires.

Foster, J. B. (2007) 'The Financialization of Capitalism', *Monthly Review*, 58 (11), 1–12.

Giarraca, N. & Miguel, T. (eds.) (2013) *Actividades extractivas en expansión: ¿reprimarización de la economía argentina?* Antropofagia, Buenos Aires, Argentina.

Gras, C. (2013) 'Agronegocios en el Cono Sur Actores sociales, desigualdades y entrelazamientos transregionales', *desiguALdades.net*, Working Paper Series 50.

Grigera, J. (2011) 'Desindustrialización, ¿agresión a la manufactura o reestructuración capitalista?', in Bonnet, A., ed., *El País Invisible: debates sobre la Argentina reciente*, Peña Lilo/Ediciones Continente, Buenos Aires, 81–102.

Hardie, I. (2011) 'How Much Can Governments Borrow? Financialization and Emerging Markets Government Borrowing Capacity', *Review of International Political Economy,* 18 (2), 141–167.

Krippner, G. (2005) 'The Financialisation of the American Economy', *Socio-Economic Review,* 3 (2), 173–208.

Lapavitsas, C. (2009a) 'Financialisation, or the Search for Profits in the Sphere of Circulation', *Ekonomiaz*, 72 (3), 98–117.

Lapavitsas, C. (2009b) 'Financialisation Embroils Developing Countries', *School of Oriental and African Studies*, Discussion Paper No. 14.

Lapavitsas, C. (2013) 'Financialization and Capitalist Accumulation: A Structural Account of the 2007–09 Crisis', in Kichiro Yagi et al., eds., *Crises in the Global Economy and the Future of Capitalism: Reviving Marxian Crisis Theory*, Routledge, Abingdon, 55–74.

Levy-Orlik, N. (2013a) 'Financialization and Economic Growth in Developing Countries: The Case of the Mexican Economy', *International Journal of Political Economy,* 42 (4), 108–127.

Levy Orlik, N. (2013b) *Dinero, estructuras financieras y financiarización: un debate teórico institucional*, Itaca, Ciudad de México.

Mader, P. (2013) 'Explaining and Quantifying the Extractive Success of Financial Systems: Microfinance and the Financialization of Poverty', *Economic Research-Ekonomska Istraživanja*, 26 (1), 13–28.

Martin, R. (2002) *Financialization of Daily Life*, Temple University Press, Philadelphia.

Massó, M. (2016) 'The Effects of Government Debt Market Financialization: The Case of Spain', *Competition & Change*, 20 (3), 166–186.

Mendoza, R. U. (2004) 'International Reserve-Holding in the Developing World: Self Insurance in a Crisis-Prone Era?' *Emerging Markets Review*, 5 (1), 61–82.

Murphy, S., Burch, D. & Clapp, J. (2012) *El lado oscuro del comercio mundial de cereales. El impacto de las cuatro grandes comercializadoras sobre la agricultura mundial*, Informes de investigación de Oxfam, Oxford.

Orhangazi, Ö. (2007) 'Financialisation and Capital Accumulation in the Non-Financial Corporate Sector: A Theoretical and Empirical Investigation of the US Economy 1973–2003', *University of Massachusetts*, Amherst: Political Economy Research Institute, Working Paper 149.

Painceira, J. P. (2009) 'Developing Countries in the Era of Financialization: From Deficit Accumulation to Reserve Accumulation', *Research on Money and Finance Discussion Paper No. 4*, London: School of Oriental and African Studies.

Palley, T. (2007) 'Financialisation: What It Is and Why It Matters', *The Levy Economics Institute of Bard College*, Working Paper No. 525.

Plihon, D. & Miotti, L. (2001) 'Libéralisation financière, spéculation et crises bancaires', *Revue d'économie internationale*, 85, 3–36.

Robles, M. J., Cuesta, S., Duryea, T., Enamorado, A. & Rodríguez, V. (2008) 'Rising Food Prices and Poverty in Latin America: Effects of the 2006–2008 Price Surge', *Inter-American Development Bank*, Washington, DC.

Rodrik, D. (2006) *The Social Cost of Foreign Exchange Reserves*, NBER Working Paper Series, no. 11952.

Salama, P. (2006) 'Deudas y dependencia financiera del Estado en América Latina', in Girón, A. (Coord.), ed., *Confrontaciones Monetarias: marxistas y post-keynesianos en América Latina*, CLACSO, Buenos Aires, 101–124.

Singh, C. (2006) 'Should India Use Foreign Exchange Reserves to Finance Infrastructure?' *Economic and Political Weekly*, 41, February 11, 517–525.

Soderberg, S. (2013) 'Universalising Financial Inclusion and the Securitisation of Development', *Third World Quarterly*, 34 (4), 593–612.

Stockhammer, E. (2004) 'Financialisation and the Slowdown of Accumulation', *Cambridge Journal of Economics*, 28 (5), 719–741.

Stockhammer, E. (2006) 'Shareholder Value-Orientation and the Investment-profit Puzzle', *Journal of Post Keynesian Economics*, 28 (2), 193–215.

Stockhammer, E. (2008) 'Stylized Facts on the Finance-dominated Accumulation Regime', *Competition and Change*, 12 (2), 189–207.

Tang, K. & Xiong, W. (2010) 'Index Investing and the Financialization of Commodities', *National Bureau of Economic Research*, Working Paper 16385.

Tonveronachi, M. (2006) 'The Role of Foreign Banks in Emerging Countries: The Case of Argentina 1993–2006', *Investigación Económica*, LXV (255), 15–60.

UNCTAD. (2011) *Price Formation in Financialized Commodity Markets: the Role of Information*, United Nations, New York and Geneva.

Van der Zwan, N. (2014) 'Making Sense of Financialization', *Socio-Economic Review*, 12 (1), 99–129.

9 A sectoral analysis of Mexico's external economic opening (1982–2016)

Abelardo Mariña and Sergio Cámara

The Mexican economy experienced an expansive long wave of capitalist accumulation from the second half of the 1930s until the beginning of the 1980s that until the end of the 1960s was characterised by high growth, low inflation and macroeconomic stability. The underlying causes were the favourable structural conditions of profitability and an institutional and normative framework that actively propelled productive capitalist accumulation and economic development. The take-off and progress of this expansive long wave was led by the model of industrialisation by substitution of imports (ISI), based on a *developmentalist* agenda of economic policies in which the domestic market was the engine of the accumulation process. The ensuing tendency of the rate of profit to fall took place in Mexico at the end of the 1960s and the beginning of the 1970s, along with international trends, and resulted in a structural crisis of profitability (1969–1981) that put an end to the expansive long wave.

The subsequent contractive long wave was characterised worldwide by the neo-liberal restructuring of the general conditions of capital valorisation, aimed at counteracting the fall in the general rate of profit and recovering its former level. This restructuring has implied three related main trends: precarisation of labour, globalisation and financialisation. The precarisation of labour was pursued to lower costs, the globalisation sought to broaden geographically and sectorally the scope of capitalist accumulation, and the financialisation reinforced the financial spaces as privileged means of capital valorisation. The historical context of this structural transformation has been the weakness of labour, the reinforcement of the power of transnational companies, the increase in importance of financial markets and institutions, and the renewed hegemony of the USA (Mariña & Cámara 2016:168–175).

In Mexico, the neo-liberal restructuring implied a change in the regime of capital accumulation from the domestic market-oriented ISI model to a manufacturing-export-led (MEL) model grounded in liberalisation policies and the external opening of the economy. These policies prevailed in Mexico given the support of local segments of the capitalist class to the agendas of the transnational corporations and the international economic institutions, particularly, after the political fraudulent victory in the 1988 presidential election of Salinas, who represented the most cosmopolitan, financialised and authoritarian local power group (ibid. 175–179). The new regime focussed on macroeconomic stabilisation through severe adjustment programmes that included a sharp reduction in real wages and restrictive fiscal and monetary policies. Active state intervention was replaced by the impulse of free market forces, particularly of international flows of the different forms of capital (mercantile, productive and financial), as the supposedly efficient mechanism of resource allocation to attain sustained development.

Despite the successive waves of liberalising reforms, the neo-liberal period has been characterised by significantly lower economic growth and higher inflation during the 1980s and 1990s, and a continuous devaluation of the Mexican peso. Foreign Direct Investment (FDI) inflows have not been enough to spur either productive investment, which has maintained relatively low levels in the last three and a half decades, or productivity growth, which has been feeble. The Mexican economy has shifted into a limited extensive model of growth based on the expansion of employment, which nevertheless has been insufficient to absorb the growth in the labour force, and on the acute reduction of real wages and the precarisation of formal and informal workers, thus seriously increasing inequality and deteriorating the living conditions of most of the Mexican population (Mariña & Cámara 2015:25–31; 2016).

The present chapter argues that the MEL productive restructuring of the Mexican economy has resulted in a new type of subordinate articulation to the world market framed within the neo-liberal patterns of the international division of labour. The external opening of the Mexican economy was subordinated to the global strategies of geographic relocation of transnational corporations, who have privileged Mexico to benefit from the relatively low labour costs and its proximity to the USA, the largest consumer market of the world.

The external opening reinforced the specialisation in labour-intensive manufacturing processes highly dependent on low wages for international competitiveness and on the global production chains, which fostered imports and disarticulated domestic productive chains. Consequently, the Mexican economy depends on the export strategies of foreign transnational manufacturing corporations, and on their imports of intermediate and fixed capital goods. The main outcome of this type of external dependency is a flawed insertion to the world market in which the incessant severe precarisation of labour becomes mandatory for maintaining the international competitiveness of the Mexican economy.[1] Correspondingly, competition by technical change and productivity growth has been secondary, revealing itself in an extremely weak process of productive investment.

Finally, the incapacity of the new regime of accumulation to reverse the trade deficit as a structural feature gives rise to the other main dimension of the neo-liberal subordinate articulation of the Mexican economy to the world market: its subordinate financialisation. The chapter corroborates previous arguments by analysing the evolution of the sectoral structure of the Mexican economy – agricultural, extractive, utilities, construction, manufacturing and service sectors – considering their specific articulations to the world market during the neo-liberal period.

The chapter is structured in six sections. After the introduction, the second section analyses the origins of the neo-liberal subordinate insertion of the Mexican economy into the new international division of labour. The third section examines the performance of the Mexican economy during neo-liberalism through the identification of the major economic sectors, the changing patterns of FDI inflows and foreign trade. The fourth section analyses the sectoral dynamics of productive investment and productivity growth and labour conditions to assess their relative impact as competitive factors. The fifth section shows the weakness, ineffectiveness and fragility of the Mexican MEL model. Finally, the sixth section puts forward the main conclusions.

Subordinate articulation to the world market

The Mexican ISI regime was characterised by an active state involvement in the economy through *developmentalist* industrial and trade policies that imposed quantitative restrictions on foreign trade, especially of consumer goods, and investment, by requiring a majority national ownership of firms operating in the country. The aim was to develop a national industrial structure specialised in manufacturing for the domestic market, which was seen as crucial to attain sustained economic growth and development. The process of import substitution went through successive stages.

The primary ISI stage, induced by the disruption of international trade as a result of the Great Depression and World War II, implied the substitution of imported non-durable goods and was fairly completed during the 1940s and 1950s. The substitution of durable consumer goods, the second stage of the ISI, unfolded during the 1960s. Transnational companies, mainly from the USA, had a crucial role in this process, both quantitatively and in terms of the type of technological and organisational characteristics of the consumer goods industries and their articulations with the world market. The imports of intermediate and capital goods were crucial in this stage. In later stages, the ISI would complete the more complex processes of substitution of intermediate and capital goods, industries would have the capacity to compete in the world market and the development strategy would turn into exports.

Although there was a reasonably complete substitution of consumer final goods and, to some extent, of intermediate inputs prior to the 1970 crisis, capital goods were substituted to a much lesser degree, and forward and backward linkages were insufficiently developed (Dussel 2000: Chapters 1 and 2). The truncation of the ISI was the result of its reliance on the transnational companies' strategies. The rising overvaluation of the Mexican peso during the fixed exchange regime (1954–1976) subsidised and, therefore, encouraged their imports of intermediate goods and scrap machinery from their parent companies. Additionally, the small but protected domestic market allowed for oligopolistic pricing. This arrangement generated very high profitability niches for the transnational corporations and their local partners, but also a structural manufacturing trade deficit that was financed with increasing difficulty by the trade surpluses in the primary and tourist sectors.

Consequently, the Mexican economy faced the external opening specialised in primary and manufacturing consumer along with intermediate goods produced for the domestic market in technologically and organisationally outdated processes.

The decline in the real manufacturing and minimum wages started since the late 1970s and rapidly deepened during 1982–1988; although it was not enough to boost the international competitiveness of most industries, it was certainly crucial, along with its geographical location, for the transnational corporations' restructuring strategies towards Mexico. Following their new global strategies of geographic relocation of assembly lines of production in low-wage countries, they moved their export-oriented plants to Mexico as a platform to the USA (Mariña & Cámara 2015:22–23; 2016:177).

The external opening was fast and abrupt, accomplished in three successive stages. The first stage of formal opening relates to the vulnerability resulting from the external debt crisis (1982–1987) and the consequent imposition of the neo-liberal agenda of corporations and international economic organisms: the International Monetary Fund and the World Bank. Transnational corporations widely utilised the tax-exemptions to the *maquila* export manufacturing segment under the Border Industrialization Program, established in 1965 and extended beyond the borders to all of the Mexican territory in 1985.[2] The elimination of quantitative restrictions to trade was complemented in 1986, with Mexico's entry to the General Agreement on Tariffs and Trade (GATT). The second stage of effective liberalisation (1988–1993) involved the drastic reduction of tariffs that led to the North American Free Trade Agreement (NAFTA). Finally, the implementation of NAFTA represents the third stage of subordinate integration to the USA (Mariña 2005:390–392). The rapid transformation of Mexico from a highly closed economy to one of the most open in the world evidences the indiscriminate nature of this process (Mariña 2009).

In this context, the external opening of the Mexican economy unfolded new patterns of specialisation and a subordinate articulation with the world market, particularly for the manufacturing sector. Two dimensions of this subordination ought to be highlighted. First, the Mexican economy became widely integrated into the global production chains of transnational companies, disarticulating domestic productive chains through their globalised import patterns of intermediate and fixed capital goods. Second, the international competitiveness of the local segments of the export industry heavily depends on extremely low, in international terms, labour costs, so as permissive labour, fiscal and environmental legislations and practices, making the precarisation of labour a structural necessity.

A sectoral analysis of the export-oriented economy

The neo-liberal restructuring of the Mexican economy entailed profound transformations of the economic structure since the external debt cyclical crisis in 1982.[3] The nature of these transformations can be related to the specificities of the external opening and its subordination to the globalising strategies of transnational companies. The present section analyses the aggregate and sectoral behaviour of several key economic indicators, summarised in Tables 9.1–9.3. The data are classified into four relevant neo-liberal sub-periods, plus a reference to the period 1970–1981, which comprises the end of ISI model. The 1982–1993 sub-period is characterised by the external debt crisis and the shaping of the neo-liberal era; the 1994–2000 sub-period relates to the boom of Mexican neo-liberalism; the 2001–2007 sub-period evidences the limits of the neo-liberal regime of accumulation in Mexico; and finally, the 2008–2016 sub-period is related to the global crisis of neo-liberalism.

The relocation of production plants of transnational companies to Mexico can be tracked by FDI inflows (Table 9.1). During 1982–1993, these

Table 9.1 Main economic indicators and goods and services trade, Mexico, 1970–2016

		1970–1981	*1982–1993*	*1994–2000*	*2001–2007*	*2008–2016*
Real GDP	*AAGR (%)*	6.8	1.6	3.6	2.0	2.0
Employees	*AAGR (%)*	4.1	1.2	2.4	1.2	1.2
Real GDP per employee	*AAGR (%)*	2.7	0.4	1.2	0.8	0.8
	AA (thous.)	271	315	342	368	386
Real compensation per employee	*AAGR (%)*	3.5	–2.3	–0.2	1.9	0.9
	AA (thous.)	123	97	97	113	123
Gross fixed capital formation	*% of GDP*	27.2	22.2	21.8	21.9	23.0
Foreign direct investment	*% of GDP*	0.6	1.1	2.4	3.1	2.6
	% of GCFC	2.2	4.9	10.9	13.3	10.9
Value of exports	*% of GDP*	8.7	14.6	25.9	26.8	33.4
Value of imports	*% of GDP*	10.1	16.4	26.7	28.4	35.0
Trade balance	*% of GDP*	–1.4	–1.8	–0.8	–1.7	–1.7

Source: System of National Accounts of Mexico, base years 2013, 2008, 1993, 1980 and 1970, Instituto Nacional de Estadística y Geografía (INEGI); Inversión Extranjera Directa, Secretaría de Economía; and World Development Indicators, World Bank. Data for Employees, Real GDP per employee and Real compensation per employee for the first period correspond to 1971–1981. AAGR = Average annual growth rate. AA = Annual average. Real figures correspond to 2013 prices.

inflows were around five times higher than during 1970–1981. With the implementation of NAFTA in 1994, the ratios of FDI/GDP ratio and FDI/Gross Fixed Capital Formation (GFCF) doubled in 1994–2000 and trebled in 2001–2007, though the growing trend was interrupted during 2008–2016. Manufacturing has been the main destination of FDI associated with the external opening and the unfolding of the export-led model, attracting over half of the total FDI in 1994–2016 (Table 9.2). Most of FDI in this sector corresponds to greenfield investment (new facilities). FDI accounted for almost one-third of the GFCF in 2003–2015, evidencing the relevance of foreign-owned transnational companies in the sector.

The sector of finance and insurance was the second destination, with 14% of total FDI in the same period, with a peak in 2001–2007. In this case, FDI is essentially brownfield investment (does not involve new facilities nor GFCF).[4] These FDI flows are related to the processes of privatisation and *foreignization* of commercial banks and other financial companies (Powell 2013: Chapter 7), and are explained by the high profitability of the financial spaces of valorisation as a consequence of the subordinate financialisation of the Mexican economy (see Section 5). Given that the banks do not finance productive investment (ibid.), their main sources of profitability, besides oligopoly services' fees and financial margins in consumer loans, are government bonds, having therefore a highly parasitic nature. The existence of a mostly foreign-owned private banking sector that does not contribute meaningfully to productive accumulation is a certain proof of the indiscriminate nature of the external opening of the Mexican economy.

The reception of FDI in other sectors has been less relevant, with Trade and Transportation, warehousing and information positioned in third and fourth places, respectively. Accommodation, food, arts, entertainment and recreation have shown a high FDI/GFCF ratio, mainly because of the presence of foreign hotel chains in the tourist industry. This ratio is also very high in Construction, especially from 2008 onwards, as a result of foreign involvement in public infrastructure projects. Finally, Mining and oil industry and Utilities have received increasing amounts of FDI, reflecting the privatisation of these strategic sectors, basically in 2008–2016.

The MEL model has implied a growing importance of foreign trade in the Mexican economy (Table 9.3). The total economy has increased its degree of openness (exports plus imports of goods and services to GDP) from 20% in 1981 to 81% in 2016. The degree of openness had a sharp increase with the implementation of NAFTA (1994–2000), stagnated during the 2000s, and had a milder increase during the neo-liberal global crisis (2008–2016). Manufacturing has been the leading export sector, increasing its share in the total value of exports throughout the neo-liberal period. While the manufacturing share of exports of goods averaged around 40% in the 1970s, and was as low as 23% in 1982, it reached an average of 63% in the first stage of liberalisation (1982–1993) and then increased to approximately 80% from 1994 onwards. During the neo-liberal period, Manufacturing changed from

Table 9.2 Main economic indicators by sector, Mexico, 1982–2016

			Agriculture, forestry, fishing and hunting	*Mining and oil industry*	*Utilities*	*Construction*	*Manufacturing*	*Trade*	*Transportation, warehousing and information*	*Finance and insurance*	*Real estate and rental and leasing*	*Education services and healthcare*	*Accommodation, food, arts, entertainment and recreation*	*Professional and business services*	*Government*
Real GDP	*AAGR (%)*	*1982–1993*	0.9	1.5	4.2	−0.4	1.8	0.5	1.7	4.4	4.0	2.4	1.4	2.2	1.5
		1994–2000	1.5	2.6	5.1	1.6	5.0	6.1	5.2	3.9	3.4	2.4	1.0	2.7	1.1
		2001–2007	2.5	0.7	6.5	2.3	0.7	2.8	3.4	7.2	3.3	1.6	0.0	2.2	−0.3
		2008–2016	1.6	−2.1	2.8	1.0	1.3	2.6	3.7	13.4	2.2	0.9	1.3	1.8	1.9
	Share (%)	*1982–1993*	4.1	11.1	1.0	9.2	17.0	14.4	6.4	1.1	9.8	7.9	3.7	8.5	6.4
		1994–2000	3.6	10.2	1.1	8.5	18.4	14.6	6.9	1.2	10.7	7.4	3.6	8.5	5.2
		2001–2007	3.4	9.7	1.3	7.8	17.8	16.6	7.7	1.6	11.2	7.0	3.0	8.5	4.4
		2008–2016	3.3	7.4	1.6	8.0	16.6	17.3	8.5	3.4	11.9	6.6	2.7	8.4	4.3
Employees	*AAGR (%)*	*1982–1993*	0.5	−1.0	2.7	1.8	0.3	1.8	1.9	1.0	4.8	2.9	3.1	0.2	1.9
		1994–2000	0.2	2.2	3.0	5.1	2.1	2.9	0.7	−1.5	9.2	−0.4	1.4	3.2	1.5
		2001–2007	1.8	2.0	4.2	2.8	−1.7	2.9	0.9	−1.1	3.8	1.4	−0.3	1.4	0.4
		2008–2016	1.6	2.9	0.4	−0.1	1.1	1.4	1.2	4.6	0.8	0.9	0.7	1.5	2.4
	Share (%)	*1982–1993*	8.5	1.1	0.4	8.0	21.5	11.1	7.5	1.6	0.6	10.4	5.0	19.5	6.9
		1994–2000	7.4	0.8	0.4	10.2	19.8	11.8	7.0	1.2	0.9	9.5	5.8	19.7	6.5
		2001–2007	7.1	0.8	0.5	11.2	17.8	13.0	6.7	0.9	1.2	9.2	5.1	20.6	6.0
		2008–2016	7.0	0.9	0.5	11.9	15.7	13.6	6.6	1.1	1.3	9.0	4.7	21.2	6.4
Real GDP per employee	*AAGR (%)*	*1982–1993*	0.4	2.6	1.5	−2.1	1.5	−1.3	−0.2	3.4	−0.7	−0.5	−1.7	2.0	−0.3
		1994–2000	1.3	0.4	2.0	−3.3	2.9	3.1	4.5	5.5	−5.3	2.9	−0.4	−0.5	−0.4
		2001–2007	0.7	−1.3	2.2	−0.5	2.5	−0.2	2.5	8.5	−0.4	0.2	0.3	0.8	−0.6
		2008–2016	0.0	−4.9	2.4	1.2	0.2	1.2	2.5	8.4	1.4	0.0	0.7	0.3	−0.4
	AA (thous.)	*1982–1993*	153	3,141	705	366	248	411	267	231	5,409	238	232	136	294
		1994–2000	167	4,514	819	290	317	422	342	350	4,018	267	214	148	277
		2001–2007	179	4,362	876	258	370	469	420	662	3,338	282	218	151	268
		2008–2016	182	3,086	1,130	258	408	490	497	1,168	3,547	287	224	154	262

(*Continued*)

			Agriculture, forestry, fishing and hunting	Mining and oil industry	Utilities	Construction	Manufacturing	Trade	Transportation, warehousing and information	Finance and insurance	Real estate and rental and leasing	Education services and healthcare	Accommodation, food, arts, entertainment and recreation	Professional and business services	Government
Real compensation per employee	*AAGR (%)*	*1982–1993*	−5.5	−2.1	−4.0	−4.9	−2.1	−2.9	−1.4	1.7	−3.3	−2.7	−2.2	−2.8	−0.6
		1994–2000	−3.6	3.1	−1.9	−1.3	−1.0	−2.8	−0.7	−3.1	−8.8	1.2	−1.4	0.5	−1.9
		2001–2007	0.8	−1.6	1.5	1.3	1.8	0.6	2.0	4.5	0.7	3.5	1.4	1.5	4.5
		2008–2016	0.8	−3.2	−0.9	0.2	0.5	0.6	0.2	0.5	−0.4	2.6	0.7	0.3	0.7
	AA (thous.)	*1982–1993*	49	179	213	99	112	108	127	311	155	133	65	69	163
		1994–2000	31	187	188	77	105	90	126	372	110	155	62	69	172
		2001–2007	31	226	208	85	121	93	141	428	84	205	68	76	216
		2008–2016	31	204	214	85	126	94	152	505	82	253	72	78	253
GFCF	*% of GDP*	*2003–2007*	17.8	30.5	29.3	3.7	24.2	18.9	12.2	2.5	58.0	3.2	8.6	3.1	49.3
		2008–2015	12.7	29.8	23.6	1.6	31.0	11.9	25.4	3.3	54.3	2.4	15.6	8.7	61.7
	Share (%)	*2003–2007*	2.7	10.3	2.6	1.4	18.8	14.0	4.6	0.3	33.2	0.9	1.2	1.3	8.7
		2008–2015	1.8	9.4	1.8	0.6	22.4	8.9	9.3	0.5	28.3	0.7	1.8	3.2	11.4
FDI	*% of GDP*	*1994–2000*	0.2	0.5	1.2	0.4	6.9	1.7	1.5	11.8	0.3	0.1	2.2	1.3	
		2001–2007	0.1	0.8	2.2	1.1	7.9	1.2	3.5	25.7	0.9	0.0	4.3	0.9	
		2008–2016	0.3	3.0	3.6	1.5	7.8	1.1	2.5	6.5	0.6	0.1	2.9	0.9	
	Share (%)	*1994–2000*	0.4	1.2	0.8	1.2	57.4	11.7	5.0	12.3	1.8	0.2	3.2	4.8	
		2001–2007	0.1	1.9	1.4	3.0	44.3	6.0	9.3	22.9	3.9	0.1	4.6	2.6	
		2008–2016	0.4	7.9	2.4	4.7	50.9	7.8	8.1	8.9	2.7	0.1	3.1	2.8	
	% of GFCF	*2003–2007*	0.5	3.2	5.2	33.9	35.3	5.3	22.1	635.9	2.0	1.4	59.2	31.2	
		2008–2015	2.6	10.0	12.8	88.5	24.2	10.4	9.4	194.7	1.2	2.6	19.4	11.0	

Source: System of National Accounts of Mexico, base years 2013, 2008, 1993 and 1980, INEGI; and Inversión Extranjera Directa, Secretaría de Economía. AAGR = Average annual growth rate. AA = Annual average. Real figures correspond to 2013 prices.

Table 9.3 Goods and services trade by sector, Mexico, 1982–2016

			Agriculture, forestry, fishing and hunting	*Mining and oil industry*	*Utilities*	*Manufacturing*	*Transportation, warehousing and information*	*Finance and insurance; real estate and rental and leasing*	*Accommodation, food, arts, entertainment and recreation*	*Rest of the services*
Value of exports	*% of GDP*	*1982–1993*	7.9	24.8	1.5	44.8	5.7	0.9	50.7	0.8
		1994–2000	16.3	32.2	0.3	105.2	5.2	1.3	43.6	1.1
		2001–2007	18.7	41.4	2.0	122.9	2.6	1.1	40.7	0.3
		2008–2016	29.3	49.2	1.9	162.4	1.3	1.6	49.7	0.1
	Share (%)	*1982–1993*	3.4	16.5	0.1	63.3	2.9	1.0	12.0	0.8
		1994–2000	2.8	8.0	0.0	80.2	1.6	0.8	5.8	0.7
		2001–2007	2.4	11.3	0.1	79.5	0.8	0.6	5.0	0.2
		2008–2016	2.9	10.0	0.1	81.8	0.3	0.7	4.1	0.0
Value of imports	*% of GDP*	*1982–1993*	9.4	1.1	1.7	64.4	3.7	2.2	44.4	1.1
		1994–2000	18.4	1.9	0.8	121.4	2.7	1.8	25.8	2.2
		2001–2007	20.7	2.4	0.2	149.0	2.5	2.6	26.9	1.4
		2008–2016	27.5	2.8	0.4	190.6	3.3	3.4	29.6	1.5
	Share (%)	*1982–1993*	3.6	0.6	0.1	81.0	2.4	1.9	9.4	0.8
		1994–2000	3.0	0.5	0.0	89.8	0.8	1.1	3.3	1.4
		2001–2007	2.5	0.6	0.0	90.7	0.7	1.4	3.1	0.9
		2008–2016	2.6	0.5	0.0	91.4	0.8	1.5	2.3	0.8
Trade balance	*% of GDP*	*1982–1993*	-1.6	23.7	0.1	-19.6	2.3	-1.2	6.3	-0.1
		1994–2000	-2.2	30.3	-0.5	-16.2	2.5	-0.5	17.8	-1.1
		2001–2007	-2.0	39.0	1.8	-26.1	0.1	-1.4	13.8	-1.1
		2008–2016	1.9	46.4	1.5	-28.2	-1.9	-1.8	20.0	-1.4
	Share (%)	*1982–1993*	5.5	-127.9	-0.1	224.3	-1.4	9.9	-12.0	1.2
		1994–2000	11.9	-244.4	0.9	399.0	-25.0	10.5	-76.5	23.6
		2001–2007	4.1	-169.8	-2.1	269.7	-0.3	13.2	-26.9	12.0
		2008–2016	-3.7	-188.8	-1.5	283.6	9.6	16.9	-32.8	16.6

Source: System of National Accounts of Mexico, base years 2013, 2008, 1993 and 1980, INEGI. Rest of the services include Education services and healthcare, Professional and business services, and Other services.

a sector producing to satisfy mainly the domestic market to an export sector (the value of exports to the gross value of production grew from 6.3% in 1970–1982 to approximately 50% in 2016).[5] The value of manufacturing exports and imports reached 338% of the sector's GDP during 2008–2016, reflecting a profound articulation with the global value chains, dominated by transnational corporations. The *maquila* strategy increased the import component of production and reduced the level of the domestic value added. This type of articulation is also expressed by the rapid increase in imports, outstripping exports, during the neo-liberal period. Beyond the over 90% share of manufacturing in the total value of imports, the trade deficit averaged around 27% of the sector's GDP in 2001–2016.

The rest of the sectors have had lesser relevance in Mexico's foreign trade. The weight of Mining and oil industry has fluctuated with the prices of commodities in the international markets, essentially oil. Nonetheless, there is a slight declining trend in exports during the neo-liberal period. However, the sector's surplus is still crucial to partially offset the manufacturing deficit. Another noteworthy sector in terms of foreign trade is Accommodation, food, arts, entertainment and recreation, which consolidated as the second surplus sector of the economy after Mining and oil industry; although its share in exports and imports decreases considerably in the neo-liberal period, its trade surplus has grown up to 20% of the sector's GDP in the last sub period, given the fast expansion of the tourist industry. The foreign trade of Agriculture, forestry, fishing and hunting has increased as a consequence of the external opening, but at a lesser rate, losing relative weight in the first three sub-periods and recovering slightly in the last one; this sector has had a negative contribution to the overall trade deficit, except in the last period in which it showed a small surplus. Utilities, Transportation, warehousing, and information, Finance and insurance, Real estate, and rental and leasing, and rest of services have had negligible contributions to the trade balance.

The transformations related to the external opening impacted the sectoral structure of the Mexican economy. The manufacturing sector sustained its relative weight in the economy during the first two sub-periods of neo-liberalism (1982–1993 and 1994–2000) as a result of the export boom (Table 9.2). Nevertheless, the increased competition in international trade from Asian economies, essentially after China's access to the World Trade Organization, slowed down the growth of the manufacturing sector, reducing its share in GDP during 2001–2016 and showing the limits of the new mode of articulation of Mexico to the world market.[6]

The service sector growth was slightly above average in the neo-liberal period before the global crisis, increasing its share in GDP between 1982–1993 and 2008–2016 by 5 percentage points. The service sector was characterised by having a two-tier growth with two clearly identifiable groups of subsectors. The winning sub-sectors were Trade, Transportation, warehousing and information, Finance and insurance, and Real estate and rental and leasing. Remarkably, the financial sector has been the fastest growing sector of the economy during the neo-liberal period, even during the 1994–2000 period and despite the 1994–1995 financial crisis, due to the sector's *foreignization* and the financialisation. The twenty-first century witnessed the explosion of this sector, especially during 2008–2016 in the aftermath of the Great Recession, coinciding with the deepening of the process of financialisation of the Mexican economy (see Section 5). The loser sub-sectors were Education services and healthcare, Accommodation, food, arts, entertainment and recreation, Professional and business services, and Government. In some of them, it has been the consequence of the diminished role of government in the economy. The case of Accommodation, food, arts, entertainment and recreation is striking, given the boost of the tourist industry shown in the positive trade balance.

In the neo-liberal period, Agriculture, forestry, fishing and hunting have grown below average, despite the US opening to the Mexican products, evidencing NAFTA negative net impact on that sector; even though the exports value soared, so did at a higher rhythm the value of imports. Therefore, these sectors lost nearly one-fifth of its weight in GDP between the first and the last neo-liberal sub-periods. Another sector with average growth below the average was Mining and the oil industry, which is noticeable given the elevated oil prices during the 2000s. The withdrawal of the public sector from productive investment, even in oil sector, prevented the Mexican economy from taking advantage of the favourable international terms of trade. Likewise, Construction was affected also negatively by the reduced role of the state, losing relative weight, with the exception of the last one. On the contrary, Utilities grew above average during the four neo-liberal sub-periods, almost doubling its GDP share, as a result of the open and backdoor privatisations.[7]

Competitive factors of the neo-liberal economy

This section evaluates the main competitive factors of the Mexican economy during the neo-liberal period at aggregate and sectoral levels. In the first part, investment rates and productivity growth are examined as indicators of competitive patterns based on dynamic advantages related to the incorporation of up-to-date technologies and innovation. In the second part, real wages and employment are examined as indicators of competitive schemes based on static advantages related to the flexibilising of the working day, the intensification of work and the decline in real wages.

The liberalisation policies implied a major turnaround in the driving forces of Mexico's economic growth. In contrast to the expansive long wave of the ISI period, based on mixed efforts of public and private investment, since the 1982 crisis the state was relegated by the private sector that ended up as the only engine of the process of capitalist accumulation. The sudden retreat of public investment as a consequence of the fiscal crisis of 1982–1987 and the collapse in private investment as a consequence of the profitability crisis implied a sharp decrease in total investment during 1982–1993 (GFCF/GDP shrunk by 5 percentage points in relation to that in 1970–1981, see Table 9.1). The partial recovery of the general rate of profit, along with the macroeconomic stabilisation policies and NAFTA enforcement, increased private investment, keeping public investment at very low levels, below the expansive long wave (Mariña & Cámara 2016:179–180).

One of the consequences of the feeble process of capital accumulation has been a weak growth of productivity. Measured by real GDP per employee, productivity was almost stagnant during the imposition and consolidation of neo-liberalism in 1982–1993. Its growth resumed after NAFTA (and the US boom between 1994 and 2000) and again slowed down in the twenty-first century (Table 9.1). The average annual growth of productivity in the neo-liberal period was 0.7%, which contrasts with the performance during the expansive long wave years (2.7% on average in 1971–1981).[8] The extreme weakness of investment and productivity growth in the Mexican economy, more severe even than in the global economy, is a result of the specific pattern of specialisation defined by the relocation strategies of the transnational companies.

From the previous analysis of FDI and trade flows, it can be seen that Manufacturing is highly dynamic in terms of investment, enjoying the largest sectoral share during 2003–2015 and investment rates above average (Table 9.2). The largest share of sectoral investment took place during 2003–2015 (Table 9.1).[9] Productivity growth was relatively strong during 2001–2007, but, despite the relatively high investment rate, it stagnated in 2008–2016. The rationale behind this apparent puzzle is the nature of the neo-liberal subordinate articulation of Mexico to the world market. Its specialisation in relatively low-technology processes has implied an investment biased towards the deployment of new structures with a relatively low participation of machinery and equipment and, consequently, of low productivity growth. Under the neo-liberal global scenario, the competitiveness of the Mexican manufacturing sector has not been based on productivity gains.

Finance and insurance is another highly dynamic sector in terms of FDI inflows and growth. Unlike Manufacturing, the growth of the financial sector is explained by a vigorous productivity growth during the neo-liberal period. In 1982–1993, GDP per employee in the sector was 27% lower than the economy's average, but, by 2008–2016, it turned three times higher, evidencing the improvement of the sector's efficiency. However, this growth is not supported by a sound process of capital accumulation in the sector, which has remained in rather low levels.[10] This performance indicates the capacity of surplus-value appropriation by the Mexican financial sector and clearly substantiates its extreme parasitic nature and its estrangement from the process of accumulation of productive capital.

The trade sector is among the rest of the sectors with a relatively high investment rate, compared to the USA.[11] In turn, Accommodation, food, arts, entertainment and recreation had similar average investment rates in both countries in the period 2003–2015. Notwithstanding, none of these sectors has had a virtuous performance of productivity growth. Quite the contrary, GDP per employee has decreased in the latter and had only a mild increase in Trade during the neo-liberal period. Again, the combination of high investment rates and productivity decline and/or stagnation must be explained by the bias towards the investment in structures with respect to equipment in a competitive environment dependent on low labour costs, a structural feature disseminated from the export sectors to the rest of the economy.

Most of the other sectors witnessed relatively low investment rates. This is particularly acute for Education services and healthcare, Construction, Agriculture, forestry, fishing and hunting, Professional and business services and, to a lesser extent, Mining and oil industry, Transportation, warehousing, and information, and Utilities. Except for the last two sectors, which had significant increases in productivity, the rest of the sectors performed accordingly, mimicking the overall weakness of investment and productivity growth.

As stated above, the discouragement of productive capital accumulation is associated with a competitive scheme based on static advantages related to the attainment and maintenance of low labour costs. This is reflected by the negative average annual growth rates of real wages, especially in 1982–1993 and 1994–2000 (Table 9.1). In 1988, the average real wage of the Mexican economy as a whole was 44% lower than its peak in 1981. The subsequent increases in real wages in 2001–2007 and 2008–2016 have been insufficient to recover their previous maximum levels. The average real wage was still, by 2016, 11% lower than that at its peak. The maintenance of low wages is a permanent necessity for the Mexican neo-liberal model of articulation to the world market, further evidenced by the continuous implementation of wage-restraint policies and anti-labour policies in general, especially through the government's fixation of the minimum wage.

Despite the boom in the manufacturing sector during the external opening, expressed in the elevated amounts of FDI investment received and the consequent relatively high sectoral investment rates, as well as in the export (and import) explosive growth, the negative performance of productivity is repeated and deepened in the case of wages (Table 9.2). The average real wage of the manufacturing sector decreased sharply during 1982–1993 and more slowly during the following sub-period (1994–2000, NAFTA early implementation), although was pushed down by the 1994–1995 crisis. During 1982–2000, it performed worse than the real wage of the overall economy. Its recovery lagged behind the rest of the economy in 2001–2016. In 2016, the manufacturing sector's wage was still 17% lower than at its peak in 1976. Consequently, the 16% positive differential of the average manufacturing wage in relation to the average wage of the economy during 1982–1993 by 2016 vanished.

Another negative feature of the competitive performance of the manufacturing sector is revealed in the dynamics of employment. Despite the export boom and GDP growth, employment grew at below par rates during the whole neo-liberal period, even decreasing steeply in 2001–2007. During the first three sub-periods, this is explained by relatively high rates of productivity growth that, in the neo-liberal context, is related to the increase in working hours and labour intensity rather than in a strong process of investment and technological change. Consequently, the manufacturing sector has lost approximately 7 percentage points of its employment share during the neo-liberal period 1982–2016. Clearly, manufacturing workers did not benefit from the export boom, given the perverse competitive scheme accompanying the external opening.

The maintenance of low real wage levels has been a shared feature in all sectors of the Mexican economy, with only some ephemeral and scattered exceptions in determined sub-periods in some sectors. Outstandingly, the service sectors that have performed better in terms of productivity growth, such as Finance and insurance, and Transportation, warehousing and information, did not experience sustained real wages increases.

The generalised faulty performance of real wages in all sectors confirms the broad dissemination of the static competitive advantages scheme to the overall Mexican economy. In terms of employment, the sectors that have significantly gained share are Construction, Trade and Professional services, while the sectors that have significantly lost shares are Agriculture, forestry, fishing and hunting, and Education services and healthcare. This behaviour relates to the dynamics of productivity; employment growth tends to be higher in sectors with a poor performance of productivity, and lower in sectors with better performance of productivity. In the case of Education services and healthcare, which are largely public services, it reflects the abandonment of the government's provision of these vital services, while real wages in the sector increased.

The export-model weakness, ineffectiveness and fragility

The MEL regime of capital accumulation, based on the neo-liberal subordinate articulation to the world market and, specifically, to the USA, has proven to be weak, ineffective and fragile. The weakness arises from the static competitive advantages dominant pattern, which derives into an extensive model of limited growth that, at the same time, is the consequence of the external dependency of the Mexican economy and reproduces such dependency. The ineffectiveness relates to the incapability to offset the structural trade deficit of the Mexican economy and to promote a meaningful economic development. Finally, the fragility relates to the subordinate financialisation and the consequent limited role of anti-cyclical policies.

As remarked in the previous section, the neo-liberal subordinate articulation to the world market grounded on a productive specialisation in low-technology, labour-intensive industries, with some limited exceptions, has endowed the Mexican economy with a deleterious competitive scheme based on static advantages. The main competitive tool of export sectors has been a sharp decline in real wages and the subsequent maintenance of low levels, as well as the prolongation of the working day and the intensification of work. The outcome has been the inhibition of productive investment as a means of competition and, therefore, of the potential virtuous dynamic competitive advantages related to technological change and innovation. This structural feature has been disseminated to the rest of the sectors of the economy.

Another consequence has been the consolidation of a regime of capital accumulation characterised by an extensive model of economic growth. During the neo-liberal period, the growth of employment has accounted for almost two-thirds of the economic growth, while the growth of productivity explains only one-third. This performance contrasts with the previous expansive long wave, when productivity accounted for more than half of economic growth.[12] Without any doubt, the ample industrial reserve army of the Mexican economy has reinforced this structural feature (Cámara 2018).

A second source of weakness of the export-led model of capital accumulation is the structural external dependency of the Mexican economy. On the one hand, the external opening has implied an increasing importance of foreign demand – especially from the USA; this situation has been reinforced by the stagnation of the domestic market as a consequence of the decline and stagnation of real wages and other types of workers' income. On the other hand, the subordination to the strategies of the transnational corporations has brought about a dependency on their global value chains; it has entailed an exhaustion of the limited domestic productive linkages developed during ISI and an even higher technological dependency on the imports of capital and intermediate goods.

Beyond its weakness, the external opening of the Mexican economy has been ineffective in two aspects. First, it has not been successful in reversing the structural trade deficit. Despite the export boom, the substantial trade surplus with the USA and the positive trade balance in oil and, to a lesser extent, in tourist services, the manufacturing deficit based on the non-*maquila* component amply offsets the overall balance (Table 9.3). Only, during 1985 and 1994–1995 steep devaluations, the balance of trade moved to a slightly positive territory, a situation reversed after the shocks were absorbed. Second, the external opening proved not to be a relevant source of economic development; beyond the meagre GDP growth, the deterioration of real wages, incomes and living conditions of most of the population is a manifestation of the excluding nature of the MEL model.

The structural trade deficit throughout this period has been a source of macroeconomic fragility. The trade deficit is not offset by the positive transfer balance as a result of remittances. In combination with the negative factorial services balance, it gives rise to a structural current account deficit, which needs to be financed by a positive capital account. Therefore, the Mexican export model is structurally dependent on foreign capital inflows, whose success relies on the assurance of profitability for the different kinds of investments, especially for the financial ones. This is the basis of the subordinate financialisation of the Mexican economy, an additional source of weakness and fragility of the export-oriented model (Mariña & Cámara 2018).

The financial investment profitability is attained through significant differentials of domestic real interest rates in foreign currency, essentially US dollars, in relation to the foreign real interest rates, especially of the USA. This differential requires an accurate combination of monetary, exchange and fiscal policies, which become subordinated to this aim. First, the monetary policy must be restrictive in nature, fixing elevated nominal interest rates and countering aggressively inflationary pressures. This policy is intended to provide a stable exchange rate, crucial to ensure foreign investment profitable convertibility. The contractive monetary policy reinforces the weakness of the Mexican economy and further inhibits productive investment. It also lessens the ability to respond to cyclical crisis, given its procyclical nature during contractions, a feature shared with fiscal policy (Correa et al. 2012; Levy 2014).

Generally, this monetary policy translates into an overvaluation of the exchange rate, which comes with an over accumulation of reserves beyond the requirements to react to short-term speculative attacks against the Mexican peso. Instead, the accumulation of reserves responds to the need to guarantee the convertibility of investments (public debt held by foreigners, foreign investment in capital markets, etc.) to foreign currency and avoid capital flights. The exchange rate policy is also very costly. First, the currency overvaluation hinders international competitiveness, imposes limits to wage increases and aggravates the trade deficit, creating a vicious cycle. Second, the increase in foreign reserves implies a further need to attract foreign capital. Third, the maintenance of reserves implies a financial and opportunity cost of a yearly 1.83% of the GDP, according to the estimations of Rozo and Maldonado (2015) for the 2008–2014 period.

Conclusions

The external opening that has characterised the Mexican economic neoliberal restructuring has entailed profound changes. These transformations emerge from the new forms of subordinate articulation of the Mexican economy to the globalised world market and the retreat of the state in the active promotion of economic development. The transnational companies took advantages of the low-cost structure, especially in wages, consolidated as a result of the restructuring processes to relocate their assembly production plants in Mexico as an export platform to the USA. Substantial FDI inflows were received by the manufacturing sector, which have underwent an export boom during the neo-liberal period, especially spurred by the implementation of NAFTA. Nonetheless, export growth came with an even faster import growth, given the dependency on the global value chains of the transnational companies and the limited competitiveness of local firms confronting consumer goods' imports.

The sectoral transformation of the Mexican economy has also reflected the specialisation in low-technology labour-intensive industries during the external opening, which expresses the relative dynamics of the manufacturing and service sectors, and the retreat of the state from the economy, which is expressed in the relative deceleration of Education services and healthcare, Construction, and Government, and the relative acceleration of the partially privatised utilities. The growth of Finance and insurance, which does not involve a banking sector financing productive investment, evidences the indiscriminate nature of the external opening, as well as the subordinate financialisation process, of the Mexican economy.

The external opening has propagated a perverse competitiveness pattern based on static competitive advantages, generated by the specific dynamics of the export sectors and disseminated to the rest of the economy. Productive investment and productivity growth have been inhibited as means of competition; instead, an extreme precarisation of labour based on the steep decline in real wages, the prolongation of the working day and the intensification of work has been pursued. The result has been a sluggish pace of economic growth, based on the extensive model of employment creation, which has not been enough to absorb the growing labour force. The dependency on foreign demand and on foreign capital inflows, given the inability of the export-oriented model to revert the structural trade deficit, also reveals the weakness and fragility of the Mexican economy. The failure of the external opening to provide the adequate foundations to promote economic welfare for most of Mexico's population raises the imperative to propose and develop an alternative agenda of economic development (Mariña & Cámara 2015:34–36).

Notes

1 In the pre-neo-liberal export pattern, international competitiveness depended much more on "natural" factors; the primary and tourist sectors represented almost two-thirds of the value of exports during 1970–1981 (System of National Accounts of Mexico, base year 1980, Instituto Nacional de Estadística y Geografía, INEGI).

2 This programme was established to compensate the termination of the Mexican Farm Labour (*Bracero*) Program in 1964 as an early attempt to develop a manufacturing export industry by fostering FDI and international trade (Douglas & Hansen 2003:1050–1055).

3 Although the 1976–1977 agreement with the International Monetary Fund initiated wage controls as an advancement of the neo-liberal restructuring, general deregulation and liberalization of international capital flows were averted as a result of the oil boom.

4 This explains that the sectorial FDI is almost three times the total GFCF during 2003–2015.
5 Data on foreign trade prior to 1982 come from Mariña (2005).
6 The USA, the main destination of Mexican manufacturing exports, has relatively specialised in corporate management and financial services. Therefore, the manufacturing sector has continuously contracted from 18.0% in 1982–1993 to 15.9% in 1994–2000, 13.2% in 2001–2007 and 12.1% in 2008–2016. The data on the USA in this paper come from the various sources of the *Bureau of Economic Analysis*.
7 This growth is even more conspicuous when it is considered that Utilities heavily reduced its GDP share in the USA during the neo-liberal period.
8 It also contrasts with the increase in productivity in the USA in the same period (1.6%).
9 Investment by sector data is only available in the *Mexican System of National Accounts* from 2003 onwards. The data for Mexico compare favourably to those for the USA, where the rate was of 19.1% in 2003–2007 and 21.4% in 2008–2015.
10 The sectoral rates of investment in Mexico sharply contrast with those of the USA: 15.4% in 2003–2007 and 13.4% in 2008–2015.
11 The investment rates in Mexico were 18.9% in 2003–2007 and 11.9% in 2008–2015 versus 9.7% and 7.9%, respectively, in the USA.
12 These data are also at odds with the same figures in the USA, where productivity growth accounts for almost 60% of economic growth.

References

Cámara-Izquierdo, S. (2018) 'Hegemonía y subordinación en los patrones neoliberales de cambio técnico en México y Estados Unidos', in G. Mendoza (ed.), *Title pending*. Mexico: Universidad Nacional Autónoma de México, forthcoming.

Correa-Vázquez, E., Vidal-Bonifaz, G., and Marshall, W. (2012) 'Financialization in Mexico. Trajectory and Limits', *Journal of Post Keynesian Economics*, 35(2), 255–275.

Douglas, L. and Hansen, T. (2003) 'Los Orígenes de la Industria Maquiladora en México', *Comercio Exterior*, 53(11), 1045–1056.

Dussel-Peters, E. (2000) *Polarizing Mexico. The impact of liberalization strategy*. Boulder and London: Lynne Rienner.

Levy-Orlik, N. (2014) 'La Política Monetaria y el Crecimiento Económico: la Tasa de Interés de Referencia del Banco de México', *Economía Informa*, 387, 21–42.

Mariña-Flores, A. (2005) 'La Reestructuración de la Industria Manufacturera Mexicana en el Marco del Tratado de Libre Comercio de América del Norte: Una Perspectiva de Largo Plazo', in J.L. Calva (coord.), *La economía mexicana bajo el TLCAN. Evaluación y alternativas*. Mexico: Universidad de Guadalajara/Universidad Nacional Autónoma de México, Vol. I, pp. 387–412.

Mariña-Flores, A. (2009) 'Cambios en la Articulación Comercial de América Latina con el Mercado Mundial a partir de 1973 en el Marco de la Crisis Estructural y de la Reestructuración Neoliberal', in J.A. Sánchez Daza (coord.), *Economía teórica y aplicada. México y el mundo*. México: Universidad Autónoma Metropolitana-Azcapotzalco/Eón.

Mariña-Flores, A. and Cámara-Izquierdo, S. (2015) 'Las especificidades de la crisis mundial en México. Una historia de integración subordinada a la globalización neoliberal', in J. Valenzuela, J.M. Ortega, S. Ortiz, and L.C. Hernández (coords.),

Crisis neoliberal y alternativas de izquierda en América Latina II. Mexico: Servicios Integrales para el Desarrollo de Proyectos Productivos del Campo y la Ciudad S.C., "El Barzón ANACC", pp. 15–38.

Mariña-Flores, A. and Cámara-Izquierdo, S. (2016) 'The structural causes of the severity of the world crisis in Mexico', in J. Santarcángelo, O. Justo, and P. Cooney (eds.), *Latin America after the financial crisis. Economic ramifications from heterodox perspectives*. Basingstoke: Palgrave MacMillan, pp. 165–191.

Mariña-Flores, A. and Cámara-Izquierdo, S. (2018) 'La Financiarización Subordinada en México desde una Óptica Macroeconómica', in N. Levy (ed.), *Financiarización y crisis de las estructuras productivas en países en desarrollo*. Mexico: Universidad Nacional Autónoma de México, pp. 103–128.

Powell, J. (2013) "Subordinate financialisation: A study of Mexico and its Nonfinancial Corporations", PhD dissertation, *School of Oriental and African Studies*, University of London, UK.

Rozo-Bernal, C. and Maldonado, N. (2015) 'Acarreo de Divisas y Costo de las Reservas Internacionales', *Documento de Trabajo No. 04*, Departamento de Producción Económica. Mexico: Universidad Autónoma Metropolitana-Xochimilco.

10 The natural resource curse and financial development of Mexico[1]

Alicia Puyana Mutis and Katya Pérez Guzmán

Decades of literature have explored the idiosyncratic challenges of export-led economic growth, especially in the case of relative wealth and the exports of commodities, which remains a central theme for Latin American countries. The economic, social and political effects of such international specialisation have been studied from different analytical perspectives by development economists, at least since the Great Depression and the end of World War II, using different versions of the unequal development, unequal exchange and the dependency schools. The theoretical issue that affects models such as Heckscher-Ohlin's, or the implications from Ricardo's and other relevant contributions, is as follows: Does free trade or export-led growth benefit all trading countries in the same manner?

Such concern has recently been analysed under the "natural resource curse" paradox, specifically regarding the Dutch Disease (DD), one of its macroeconomic manifestations affecting mainly developing countries, *the DD* where countries relatively rich in natural resources and specialised in their exports tend to have lower rates of economic growth and lower social development indicators. The existence of a curse, however, is still a matter of contention, as the literature is based mostly on results fusing averages in cross-country regressions. There has been less study dedicated to parcelling out how these postulated group averages vary for specific countries in Latin America, in distinct periods of time and with time lags.

The impacts of natural resource bonanzas, in terms of both prices and quantities (i.e. the discovery of a new oil field or new export commodity or mine), are studied under the neoclassical DD model. This model assumes full and efficient employment of the productive factors such as employment, total inter-sector mobility and the total elasticity of prices in both tradable and non-tradable sectors (Corden and Neary 1982). In these circumstances, these authors advise allowing the appreciation of the real exchange rate to permit the economy to adjust freely to new relative prices, even at the cost of harming the disadvantaged agriculture and manufacturing sectors.

Developing countries, including Latin America, diverge from the main assumptions of the neoclassical DD model, since these economies do not have well-functioning markets of production factors, goods and services, and capital and labour mobility is imperfect. In this context, for emerging economies, it made sense to prevent real exchange rate appreciation and to protect alternative sources of income and employment, with appropriate macroeconomic and sectoral policies. One example of these policies is investment in social and physical infrastructure in which developing countries tend to show important deficits. A second policy option is limiting oil production and exports to a level that will prevent the appreciation of the real exchange rate. Limiting oil production with this at criterion will avert the depletion of reserves and, by lowering oil exports revenue, the monetary and treasury authorities will not need to freeze revenue by saving abroad. A third policy option is to create a stabilisation fund to mitigate the impact of the instability of commodity prices.

Despite the extensive literature on the links between financial development and economic growth, further research is required to assess the relationship between financial development and the natural resource curse, or the DD.

The relationship between the financial sector and economic development seems to be straightforward and positive. For countries to grow investments to compensate capital depreciation and growth, finance is essential. Above this level, capital accumulation will guarantee both productivity and per capita GDP growth. Additionally, the quality of investments and their allocation does make a difference in the path of economic development. The quality of investments can counteract the effects of the DD through increasing productivity and non-resource sectors supply – both tradable and non-tradable sectors (Magud and Sosa 2010). Low and poor quality investments help to explain the causation of the resource curse, or why resource-rich countries tend to exhibit suboptimal growth rates, despite their relative wealth (Acemoglu et al. 2001).

As will be discussed in more detail below, along with facing the depletion of their own natural riches, resource-rich countries' productive investment is lower, so as human capital, and their institutional development is feeble, including financial institutions. Underdeveloped financial institutions tend to have weaker control over deposits, lending and investments, and therefore, low capacity to buffer the effects of high volatility of commodity prices and the appreciation of the real exchange rate (Gylfason and Zoega 2006). In fact, the underdeveloped financial system shows lower bank loan demand, lower level of long-term external finance and reduced finance for capital formation in productive sectors.

A key factor in the underperformance of investment is the double whammy produced by the boom and bust cycles of prices. An increase in prices, alongside with exchange rate revaluations, elevates present consumption preferences over future ones. Furthermore, savings and bank deposits shrink, government consumption expands, as well as international capital flows, all of which appreciates the real exchange rate. In the short term and perhaps medium terms, the economy expands, while tradable and non-resource productive sectors contract, or grow at a slower pace, generating economic structure differentiation. As the bonanza ends, financial flows reverse, economic growth shrinks and the government debt expansion stresses public finance (Beck and Poelhekke 2017; Manzano and Rigobon 2001). These effects tend to be stronger in economies that have fully liberalised its financial sector, like Mexico.

This chapter is divided into six sections, with this introduction as the first section. The second section reviews the relationship between the natural resource curse and financial development. In the third section, the Mexican economy and its financial system are analysed. The fourth section presents econometric analysis of the relation between natural resource wealth (in percentages of total wealth) and investments in natural resources, physical and human capital, as well as the relationship between the dependence of natural resources and financial development for Latin American countries. The fifth section presents econometric analysis, using fuel and ore exports in per cent of total merchandise exports as independent variables, to highlight resource specialisation and dependence, and includes additional financial development variables. The sixth section summarises the main conclusion of the chapter.

The natural resource curse and financial development

The up most goal of public policy should be to achieve sustained economic growth and social and political development. There seems to be consensus about the positive effects of investments in human capital and in science, as well as on long-term growth and reduced inequality. Classical economics considers natural resource abundance as the base for international specialisation and a driver of economic growth, providing that international specialisation reflects this abundance. In the middle of the twentieth century, economists formed in different academic schools questioned the classical specialisation principles. In order to develop, countries have to industrialise and change both their productive and exports structures.

Natural resource curse theories provide further challenges to this literature. Several explanations have been offered for why natural resource abundance can hinder long-term economic growth in developing economies. The main theory is the DD paradox; Corden and Neary (1982) argue that increases in export revenues are internalised through higher government and spending, intensive in non-tradable goods. Therefore, higher returns to capital in booming sectors lead to an upsurge in its demand for capital and labour, if the bonanza is to last over the long term. Corden and Neary (1982) suggest that the increase in public sector expenditure and in the booming sector induces the movement of factors of production, and leads to upturns in the wages and inputs prices in tradable non-booming sectors, even in the context of less than full employment.

The natural resource curse also implies macroeconomic instability and fiscal accounts dependence on revenues from commodity exports, which tend to intensify income concentration and reduce institutional quality (Mehlum, Moene, and Torvik 2006) that is associated with lower government savings and investments in education and other social services (Gylfason 2001). The causality of the natural resource curse is rather complex, and requires more detailed case studies to define necessary and sufficient factors, whose relative importance changes as the economy evolves.

Most importantly, the debate over financial development includes clarifying which configuration of the financial structure is best for different countries. Developing countries specialising in commodity exports frequently face three main challenges. First, the volatility of commodity prices and deterioration of the terms of trade unfold volatility in revenues. Second, there is problem in the managing of the increased amount of revenues from commodity exports in boom periods, and the ways to prepare for the subsequent busts. Third, changes in economic structure take place (including the premature reduction of manufacturing and agriculture as sources of GDP and employment), which has potential impact on the demand and supply of financial services.

Based on the Mexican economy, Puyana and Romero (2010) found that less developed economies opening to the international capital market negatively affect the profitability of investments and productivity growth. Prasad, Rajan and Subramanian (2007) and Gourinchas and Jeanne (2007) in this line of thought reject strong and positive relations between foreign capital and economic growth, confirming that countries that grow most are the least dependent on foreign capital. Large flows of external capital (investments, foreign aid or remittances) have the DD effects similar to commodity prices bonanzas. These flows of external resources tend to reduce domestic savings, to expand consumption inducing the fall of investment in other productive activities such as agriculture and manufactures and the deceleration of the economic activity (Botta et al. 2016; Magud and Sosa 2010; Nkuso 2004). Furthermore, the liberalisation of capital accounts induces capital outflows, as predicted by the Lucas's paradox, since capital tends to flow from capital-scarce countries to capital-rich developed economies, contradicting one of the central classical economic principles: that financial inflow seeks capital-scarce countries due to their higher interest rates. Additionally, these authors suggest that the protracted use of the exchange rate as price hinders productive investment and spurs the use of credit to finance consumption and housing. Therefore, imports tend to substitute domestic production.

The use of financial development to enhance economic growth in developing countries rich in natural resources is not clear cut as the studies cited below suggest. One view is that developing countries that follow export-led growth model, concentrated in commodity exports, tend to have lower levels of financial development, measured by private sector credits. In these economies, the capacity of the financial sector to mitigate the impacts of instability of commodity prices on economic growth could be reduced or even annulled.

Another group of studies confirm a negative relationship between natural resource abundance, dependence and financial development. Using cross-national panel comparisons, Kurronen (2015) examines the characteristics of the financial sector in economies rich in mineral resources that specialise in these exports. This study compares 128 countries, between 1995 and 2009, assuming that financial sector indicators reflect the productive structure of the economy, as suggested by Lin, Sun and Jiang (2009). If this were the case, countries with a productive structure heavily concentrated in mining would usually be dominated by large foreign-owned firms, which are not dependent on domestic credit. This study confirms both the negative correlation between a high concentration of minerals in total exports and the level of domestic bank credit to the private sector, and the positive correlation of the former with the size of the stock market (stock market capitalisation).

Kurronen (2017) expands on these results and finds new evidence with firm-level data, which suggest that resource firms use less credit and long-maturity debts, than non-resource firms do. Similarly, in resource-dependent economies, firms in other sectors have less debt than firms with similar characteristics in other countries. This author finds also that in mining and oil-exporting countries, oil price collapse affects adversely the financial strength of both resource and non-resource firms. In other countries, however, only the resource sector is harmed by the fall in oil price. Kurronen (2017) concludes that these alternative explanations confirm the negative impact of raw materials production and their exports on financial development, although several causal pathways need further explanation.

Hattendorff (2014), updated from 93 countries, between 1970 and 2007, in a cross-sectional panel analysis, explores how price volatility and the associated upsurges of real interest rates tend to reduce the size of the financial system in economies with exports concentrated in minerals and other commodities. These findings complement the Hausmann and Rigobon (2003) theoretical model of the "natural resource curse", where resource abundant countries tend to reduce their specialisation in resource-intensive exports to prevent the revaluation of the real exchange and interests' rates as well as the returns to capital. A pending issue in Kurronen (2017) is the question of reverse causality, and whether weaker financial development could also inversely lead a country to being more reliant on natural resource exports. To address this possibility, Hattendorff (2014) uses a set of instrumental geography-based variables for export concentration, which are highly correlated with resource abundance and dependence, confirming the unidirectional relation: export concentration has a negative effect on financial development, and not the other way around.

Saborowski (2011) proposes that financial sector development attenuates the appreciation of the real exchange rate induced by external capital flows, and considers financial development as an intervening variable that lessens the impact of real exchange appreciation on economic growth.

Moradbeigi, M. and Law, S.H. (2016) confirms the positive impact of a fully developed financial sector, which can channel oil revenues to more productive non-extractive activities.

Despite the increase of available research, the literature does not confirm or reject possible negative relationships between financial development and resource abundance in developing countries. The next sections carry out a detailed analysis of the Mexican economy and that of other Latin American countries, to contribute to the debate.

The financial limits of the Mexican export-led model

After more than three decades that the Mexican economic and political system underwent a process of economic liberalisation and structural reforms, which included the adherence of the General Agreement on Tariffs and Trade (GATT) and the signing of the North American Free Trade Agreement (NAFTA), Mexico experienced economic growth that was relatively low. In the neo-liberal period (1982–2017), the annual average growth rate was merely 2.3 %, and 2.5% for the NAFTA years (1995–2017), in which exports grew at 8% annually, a rate 3.5 times higher than GDP growth. Imports expanded faster than exports and the economy registered a permanent trade deficit. The contrasting rates of exports and GDP suggest that the link between these variables was severely dampen, and the imports income elasticity was intensified, which in 1982–2016 was 4.8 times higher than that in 1960–1982. Today, for each Mexican peso of GDP growth, imports increase by 38 centavos and to prevent further increases of current account deficit, the GDP cannot grow beyond 2.3%, the economic growth that took in the period 1982–2017.

Since the reforms were enacted, the Mexican economy has been hit by intense crises (1986, 1994 and 2008), suggesting that despite deep liberalisation and privatisation, monetary and fiscal austerity, and internal devaluation, economic stability is still far from guaranteed. Gross capital formation, labour and total factor productivity slowed down, and real minimum wages collapsed. Whereas employment has oscillated around 4.4%, occupation in the informal sector nears 60% (Puyana and Romero 2009).

Today, Mexico is a middle income, highly liberalised economy, but still a small economy, since it is a price taker in practically all its exports – including petroleum, in which Mexico is an important world exporter, but only accounts for the 2% of the international oil trade. Oil and mining contribute 8% of GDP and employment. Thus, the Mexican economy cannot be studied as an economy specialised or highly dependent on commodity exports, be it oil, minerals or agriculture products.

However, since government oil rent intake represented nearly 40% of total fiscal income from the late 1980s, Mexico's growth and investments depend on oil revenues, while government oil revenues average 5% of GDP in the 1990–2015 period (Puyana 2015). This allowed the Mexican government simultaneously collect income taxes at critically low levels and maintain a relatively high current expenditure, but with low levels of public investment. Such a policy mix has negative effects on capital formation, both as a percentage of GDP and in per worker terms. Low taxation and reduced public investment originate in the priorities of the Mexican monetary and fiscal authorities: macroeconomic stability and low taxation against economic growth and employment generation. Oil rent is a variable that Mexican authorities influence only by modifying the amount of oil produced and exported, the value-added tax on gasoline, or the oil rents extracted from PEMEX,[2] and increasing taxes to private companies.[3] Upon the reduction of oil rents, whether from falling world prices, reductions in the volume of production, or through sharing revenues with private investors, the government faces the dilemma of either reducing fiscal expenditure or increasing other taxes. So far, the option taken has been to maintain the high level of government intake from PEMEX, plunging the company farther into critical indebtedness.

Mexico has transformed from a country mostly specialised in commodities during the first half of the twentieth century to a major participant in the production of technologically sophisticated goods, such as automobiles and auto parts, machinery and equipment for the electrical and medical industries. Mexico has been inserted in each instance into global value chains with little or minimum value added, which allows for the characterisation of the Mexican growth model as an imports-intensive export model that replaces domestic by imported value added, which partly explains the increased income elasticity of imports. The driver of such development began with the structural reforms and the liberalisation of the economy in mid-1980s, which transformed the economic role of the state, put an end to the state-led industrialisation model and fully liberalised the economy. The implementation of NAFTA sealed this transformation, until 2018 when Donald Trump placed rejecting NAFTA as a high priority in his nationalistic agenda and imposed its renegotiation.

The exports of manufactured goods have increased almost continually since the country established the export-led growth model. In 2016, Mexico ranked fourth, seventh and tenth place in the world, respectively, in terms of exports of vehicles other than railway, machinery, and mechanical appliances and electrical machinery and equipment. The elevated imported content of these exports allows us to understand some features of the Mexican economy, including: first, the concentration of foreign direct investment in the less technologically intensive segments of the productive processes (Puyana 2017; Veintimilla 2016); second, the sustained growth of manufacturing exports, despite long periods of the appreciation of the Mexican Peso (Puyana 2015); and third, the contrast between exports of manufactures and low investments in the sector. In effect, in 2017, the stock of capital per worker is below 1982 (Puyana 2017).

The low rate of capital formation is a strange phenomenon, since Mexico has been an early and a rather radical reformer that liberalised the labour market, opened the capital account and privatised the banking system. The aim of these reforms was to stimulate private investment, both national and foreign. The low rate of capital formation is perhaps an effect of low public investment, which do not act as a catalyst for private investment, and the volatility of international oil prices and oil rents. With low investment opportunities, high intermediation costs and a low economic growth rate, Mexico is a country of high consumption, with a saving ratio of 23% of GDP. The high difference between the active and passive rates, together with low participation of bank credit in terms of GDP, also contributes to the weak trajectory of capital formation.

The structural changes that the Mexican economy has experienced since the mid-1980s allows for further analysis of the economic effects of oil and other commodity exports. As mentioned, today exports of manufactures amount concentrate 85% of total foreign sales, while in 1980, they represented 15 %. Yet during this 30-year time span, the participation of manufacturing in GDP has remained low, not surpassing the 18%. The sectoral share in employment declined to a mere 14% of total employment (Puyana and Romero 2009). By the same token, credit to investments in manufacturing and agriculture also declined. These tendencies are related to the oil exports and oil prices, the appreciation of the real exchange rate, and monetary expansion induced by public expenditure, as predicted by the DD model. In this way, Mexico shows signs that fiscal reliance on oil revenues created a set of incentives and policies that reduces finance for long-term investment, creating a negative relationship between natural resource wealth and financial development.

Natural wealth and financial development in Latin America

Similar stories are to be found in other Latin American countries, which since the end of the 1990s experienced important increases in commodity exports as a result of the expansion of commodities demand from Chinese and other countries. In the wake of this so-called "neo-extractivism", all countries showed similar symptoms as those displayed by Mexico (Puyana 2017).

The level of domestic credit to the private sector as percentage of GDP for Latin America and the Caribbean figures slightly above the Mexican figures. For the entire 1960–2016 period, the average in Mexico was 40%, while that of Latin America reached 48%. The gap has deepened since the 1980s to 41% and 58%, respectively. In 2016, Chile and Brazil registered the highest values of domestic credit to the private sector in terms of GDP, as 127% and 111% of GDP, respectively, as well as the highest Latin American averages since 1982 at 84% and 89%, respectively. Chile and Brazil fare similarly when compared with the group of middle-income faster growing developing economies, while Mexico ranks near to the group of middle-income developing countries with lower rates of economic expansion.

A similar pattern emerges in stock market capitalisation. The 1960–2016 averages of stock market capitalisation in terms of GDP for Brazil and Chile are 14% and 9%, respectively, which is higher than the rate for Mexico at 6%, and similar to those registered in 1982 among all middle-income countries worldwide. The average for Latin America (10%) is lower than the 41% registered among the world's middle-income countries in the same year.

These figures seem to confirm that the financial sector in countries rich in locally concentrated resources (point resources), like mines and oil fields, tend to show a shallower financial system, and weak deepening of financial services in economic and social activities, when compared to respective world averages. To explore this proposition, this section presents some econometric regressions between indicators of natural resource wealth and financial development. The two groups compared here are Latin American (LatAm)[4] countries with the highest proportion of wealth in point-source natural resources[5] and developed countries[6] (DC). Mexico is then compared separately to both set of countries. The financial variables presented in terms of GDP are domestic credit to the private sector, domestic money bank assets relative to deposits and central bank assets or deposits (as a percentage of total deposits), and stock market capitalisation.[7] The indicators related to the natural resource wealth are total rents[8] and total depletion of natural resource capital[9] in terms of GDP. The data are presented in year-time series and its ranges between 1970 and 2015, in averages.

The data presented in Table 10.1 show a possible inverse relationship between natural resources depletion and financial development. Specifically, the values of credit to the private sector, deposit money bank assets and stock market capitalisation are larger among DC than in the LatAm countries (Mexico excluded). Depletion is understood as the total extraction above a minimum sustainable level of natural capital stock. It is expressed as a negative value if rents obtained from extractive activities are not reinvested to maintain the life span of the resources. The higher depletion rates among Latin American countries show the negative impact of the specialisation of the region in exports of natural resource-based products which, if properly accounted for, should be imputed to DC or to importing countries that consume these goods.

Only Mexico's stock market capitalisation outperforms the Latin American average, with mixed results for the rest of the financial variables. Natural resource depletion in the LatAm block is three times higher than that for Mexico. In the case of the group of DC, the averages of the natural resource rents and depletion are 40% and 50% lower, respectively, to the values of Mexico. Further, stock market capitalisation among the DC group is eight times larger than the Mexican values. The econometric regressions are presented with lags for all the variables included in Table 10.2. For the Latin American block, measures of deposits and credits (with a lag) show a negative relationship with rents and the rate of depletion, while, among the DC,

Table 10.1 Credit, deposits, stock market, natural resource rents and natural resource depletion as percentage of GDP

	Latin America					*Mexico*					*Developed Countries*				
	Credit	*Deposits*	*Stock Market*	*Rents*	*Depletion*	*Credit*	*Deposits*	*Stock Market*	*Rents*	*Depletion*	*Credit*	*Deposits*	*Stock Market*	*Rents*	*Depletion*
1975	18.9	15.7	0.2	4.1	3.5	26.4	23.6	–	2.3	0.3	53.0	50.1	4.2	0.9	0.4
1985	23.8	20.1	0.4	4.3	3.5	11.0	19.3	1.1	8.5	3.8	55.0	55.0	10.4	1.6	0.9
1995	27.7	24.0	5.9	2.8	2.2	32.2	25.2	10.0	3.1	1.4	63.7	61.6	27.9	1.0	0.7
2005	28.5	28.8	4.0	6.6	5.1	15.0	20.2	5.8	5.7	4.7	69.2	62.6	77.2	2.0	1.3
2015	50.9	39.1	9.8	4.1	2.9	30.2	29.3	9.2	2.3	1.7	77.9	71.0	90.3	1.4	0.7

Source: World Bank. (2018). *Adjusted Net Savings*. Retrieved 20 March 2018, from World Bank Data Bank: http://databank.worldbank.org/data/reports.aspx?source=adjusted-net-savings&preview=on

Table 10.2 Latin America and developing countries: regressions and Johansen cointegration test

Endogenous Variable	*Intercept*	*Deposits*	*Credits*	*R^2 and $R^2_{adjusted}$*
Rents LatAm	1.344	0.084	0.037	$R^2 = 0.1871$
	(1.075)	(0.150)	(0.114)	$R^2_{adjusted} = 0.1493$
Depletion	1.686	0.081	-0.011	$R^2 = 0.088$
LatAm	(0.855)	(0.119)	(0.091)	$R^2_{adjusted} = 0.045$
Rents DevEc	-0.655	-0.026	0.057	$R^2 = 0.4519$
	(0.627)	(0.038)	(0.029)	$R^2_{adjusted} = 0.4265$
Depletion	-0.820	-0.001	0.027	$R^2 = 0.4740$
DevEc	(0.413)	(0.025)	(0.019)	$R^2_{adjusted} = 0.4495$

Johansen cointegration results (credit, deposits and rents) (credit, deposits and depletions)+Ho:r≤1; Ha:r>1*

*Trace value LatAm**	*Trace value LatAm+*	*Trace value DevEc**	*Trace value DevEc+*	*Critical value*
15.0921	14.9559	18.8271	14.8963	95%:18.17
				99%:23.46

no substantive change emerged. The negative relationship between current and lagged deposits with the rents and the extraction rate is maintained, although marginally stronger.

Contrary to the literature reviewed in previous sections, in Latin American, the lagged regressions show a positive relationship between domestic credit to the private sector and deposit money bank assets, with both natural resource rents and depletion. Running a simple regression, deposits and credits show a positive relationship with rents, but depletion shows a negative relationship with credit and a positive relationship with deposits. This relationship may represent the inflow of money lent by international banks after a primary export boom (Acosta 2013). For the DC group, deposits and credit are negatively or positively but non-significantly related to natural resource rents and depletion. Simple regressions show a negative relationship between rents and depletions with deposits, but positive with respect to credit.[10]

Lastly, to evaluate the long-term impact of natural resource rents on domestic credit to the private sector and deposit money bank assets[11] of the region, each yearly value across the time period was averaged. With these data, a Johansen cointegration test was performed to evaluate the relationships among the time series. For Latin America, the overall analysis shows strong evidence of cointegration. As Table 10.2 shows, the series are cointegrated at level 1, for the trace statistic and for the max statistic with two lags. For the Johansen cointegration test with credit, deposits and depletion, the three indicators are cointegrated at level 1 with two lags. Such cointegration is valid for the trace statistic and max statistic at a 5% critical value.

The DC group, presented in Table 10.2, shows evidence of level 1 cointegration for the trace statistic at both critical values using three lags, and for the max statistic at a 5% critical value. When we consider credit, deposits and natural resources depletion in terms of GDP, these indicators are cointegrated at level 1, with two lags. The trace statistic shows evidence of cointegration at a 5% critical value, but the max statistic shows no cointegration, nor does the trace statistic at a 1% critical value.

Specialisation in commodities and financial development in Latin American major fuel and mineral exporters

The results described in the last section points to a negative relationship between some financial indicators and natural resource wealth, measured by rents and depletion of all natural resources, for a statistically significant group of countries. However, the natural resource curse literature has been proposed as being most relevant for export specialisation in two types of commodities: fossil fuels such as oil and natural gas, and minerals. In this section, the econometric analysis is based on these indicators with data provided by the World Bank Development Indicators (see Table 4.3). Latin American major fuel and ore exporters are Venezuela, Mexico, Colombia, Ecuador, Bolivia and Peru. Argentina and Brazil are included in the group of fuel exports; Chile, Bolivia, Peru, Brazil and Mexico are in the group of ore exports.

Additional financial indicators are considered in these regressions to extend the findings beyond the widely used domestic credit to the private sector and stock market capitalisation measurements. Specifically, liquid liabilities are considered in terms of GDP, the ratio of overhead costs to total bank assets, net interest margins, stock market trade values and stock market turnover ratio. All variables are averaged for the period of study, and the log of the average is utilised in the regressions (see Table 10.3).

The regressions provide three main results. For the top fuel exporters, most regressions show a positive slope, which has different implications, as discussed next. In terms of liquid liabilities, the regression has a wider distance of the residuals from the tendency line, and therefore, the results are weaker. However, if a positive relationship were to be found in the more robust models of these countries, this would imply that the more a country relies on fuel exports, the larger the size of the financial intermediary's sector relative to the economy.

Two simple regressions using the deposit money bank assets and the domestic credit to the private sector indicators show a closer distance of the residuals to the tendency line, and a positive relationship. The first regression shows Bolivia as an important outlier, which makes the direction

Table 10.3 Equations for fuel and ore exports and financial variables as percentage of GDP

Dependent Variables	*Equations*
y = Liquid liabilities to GDP (%)	y = 0.0275(fuel) + 1.3805; R^2 = 0.0329, and y = −0.0082(ore) + 1.4508; R^2 = 0.0061
y = Deposit money bank assets to (deposit money + central) bank assets (%)	y = 0.0135(fuel) + 1.879; R^2 = 0.0073, and y = −0.0913(ore) + 1.9939; R^2 = 0.2001
y = Private credit by deposit money banks and other financial institutions to GDP	y = 0.023(fuel) + 1.3264; R^2 = 0.0132, and y = 0.0894(ore) + 1.3045; R^2 = 0.0526
y = Bank overhead costs to total assets (%)	y = 0.3333(fuel) + 0.2489; R^2 = 0.3052, and y = −0.088(ore) + 0.7723; R^2 = 0.1012
y = Net interest margin	y = 0.3212(fuel) + 0.3226; R^2 = 0.2315, and y = −0.1065(ore) + 0.9197; R^2 = 0.2829
y = Stock market capitalisation to GDP (%)	y = −0.5289(fuel) + 1.9048; R^2 = 0.7023, and y = 0.2337(ore) + 1.1313; R^2 = 0.0982
y = Stock market total value traded to GDP (%)	y = −0.7373(fuel) + 1.1026; R^2 = 0.2505, and y = −0.842 (ore) + 1.6616; R^2 = 0.1876
y = Stock market turnover ratio (%)	y = −0.2329 (fuel) + 1.2656; R^2 = 0.0214, and y = −1.3567 (ore) + 3.1116; R^2 = 0.5581

Note: The independent variable is named and calculated by the World Bank as fuel/ore exports as a percentage of total merchandise exports. For the sake of brevity, all throughout the text, the authors refer only to fuel/ore exports.

positive than it would otherwise be. The last section describes the reason behind this outlier. This potentially means that the higher the specialisation in oil exports, the larger the participation of intermediaries in financial activities. The second regression confirms the results of the last section, and contradicts the literature reviewed in the respective section: for the top Latin American fuel exporters, there is a positive relationship between fuel exports and domestic credit to the private sector.

The last two regressions, which utilise the measurements of bank overhead costs and the net interest margin, show a positive relationship. Both measurements indicate the level of efficiency of the financial intermediaries. A positive relationship means that additional fuel exports are related to higher inefficiencies in the financial sector. This positive relationship, however, was stronger for the overhead costs than for the net interest margin. In the latter model, the regression is influenced mostly by Venezuela, the country with the highest net interest margin and fuel export averages for the entire period.

The second set of regression tests the main hypothesis of this chapter, showing a negative slope of the regression tendency line using the three variables related to the stock market, which are stock market capitalisation, total value traded and stock market turnover ratio. The relationship has less dispersion of residuals away from the summary line, for the stock market capitalisation and total value traded, suggesting a strong and negative relationship. Venezuela is influential in the results for stock market capitalisation, having one of the lowest averages of this financial indicator, and the highest average for fuel exports.

Finally, most of the simple regressions between ore exports and financial indicators show negative relationships, going from low negative values in liquid liabilities to higher negative slopes for the stock market variables. The exceptions of these regressions include the measures of stock market capitalisation and domestic credit to the private sector, which show positive trends. The reason for this result was the influence of Chile, as the top ore exporter and the outperformer in terms of both of these indicators. Bolivia again was an important factor on the negative relationships.

Conclusions

This chapter discusses the impact of natural resource wealth and export specialisation on financial development. The main literature finds a possible negative relationship between both variables, based on cross-country analyses. Sound conclusions compel additional studies, complementary case studies and regional comparisons, and the inclusion of additional financial indicators for more nuanced contrasts, as presented here.

A brief study of Mexico is carried out, suggesting that, even though the country is not specialized in natural resource exports, it has followed by the book the recommendations emerging from the neoclassical Dutch Disease model by contracting public expenditure and allowing the exchange rate to appreciate. This study finds that Mexico shows lower levels of financial development, especially when compared to other Latin American countries.

Based on simple regressions and Johannsen cointegration models, this chapter also studies the relationships of natural resource wealth and depletion with three financial indicators, comparing Latin American countries and DC. One result is a lack of consistency in the direction of the regression curves. The DC are most advanced in terms of financial development, the Latin American region is less advanced and Mexico lies somewhere in the middle. The regressions are positive for some financial indicators, and negative for others, contradicting the main literature, which predicts positive relations across all of these measures. In a more focussed analysis of the effects of specialisation in export commodities of the major fuel and ore exporters of the region on the financial sector, we obtained similar results.

To conclude, we provide some explanations of these results and potential avenues for future research. How can such disparate results be understood, in order to choose a methodology and an analytical framework that best suit the problem at hand? The first obvious answer is the presence of confounding factors, or alternative causes, in the relationships proposed. A main suspect is naturally national income. Financial development is highly correlated with national income per capita, institutions and the rule of law, and less by geography and macroeconomic policies (Levine 1997, 2005). Because of this correlation, the regressions exhibit certain outliers, as in the cases of Bolivia (the country with the lowest income per capita level of the region) and Chile, the country with the highest level of per capita income.

A more sophisticated econometric model that accounts for all control variables that structure the causal relationship could provide one solution to this issue. However, the problem with this approach is that causality is not straightforward, especially as the variables to be included in the model are not clearly defined by the respective economic theories and, thus, result in "fragile" conclusions (Huang 2011:11). This is the reason why a debate around the causality of both financial development and the natural resource curse seems a never-ending discussion.

The simple regressions presented in this chapter are merely the beginning of understanding a much more complex problem, which requires more adequate methodologies of study such as (according to Huang 2011) a version of "extreme bounds analysis" to model uncertainty, or Bayesian methods. The authors of the present chapter suggest a deeper inquiry of all the possible causality paths involved, with system analysis methodologies, such as network analysis or system dynamics.

One of the aims of the present chapter is thus to establish the basic groundwork for delving deeper into the probable negative relationship between natural resource abundance, wealth or export specialisation, and financial development. One of the foremost steps in this direction is to establish the causal pathway. There are two different potential answers here. One is where measures of resource abundance directly impact measures of financial development, in a negative way. The other is where inadequate financial development is a necessary condition for leading natural resource abundance to less economic growth (as in the natural resource curse literature); with the resulting lower growth, there is even lower levels of financial development and a deeper resource curse, thus forming a negative causal loop.

Furthermore, natural resource abundance does not necessarily have to impact financial development directly, or vice versa. Two intervening variables have already been identified: macroeconomic policies and institutional quality (Huang 2011). Macroeconomic policy indicators, like inflation, have a role to play in both sides of the problem. On the one hand, high inflation relates to the lower performance of banks and equity markets. On the other hand, inflation can represent the path by which the natural resource curse translates into lower economic growth. Following this suggestion, a question emerges: if Mexico has focussed much of its macroeconomic policy on controlling inflation and gaining stability, why has its financial development fallen to levels below that of other countries with similar policies, such as Chile? This is a particularly important question, given that Mexico depends on oil revenues, as much as Chile relies on copper production and exports.

Lastly, another important variable, or characteristic, is the larger economic structure. The natural resource curse, through the DD, implies a specific shift from natural resource export-led economies away from manufacturing and agriculture, towards services and non-tradable goods. Such change in the economic structure can imply a related change in the demand of financial services, and thus have an effect on national financial development. Methodologies able to capture this structural change, such as network analysis of global trade, could be leveraged in this direction. This chapter opens more questions and offers answers, and thus, can serve as a reference for future research in such relevant topic of the challenges of financialisation in the Latin American export-led economies.

Notes

1 The authors thank Elizabeth Tellez-Leon for the support in the outline of this chapter; nevertheless, the content is the exclusive responsibility of the authors.
2 PEMEX is a nationally owned oil company, a public monopoly for all up- and downstream oil activities for most of the twentieth century, up until 2013.
3 The Energy Reform, enacted in 2013, allowed private investments in upstream oil activities in different types of contracts such as production sharing, association and risk sharing (for details, see Puyana 2015).
4 The countries included in this group are Argentina, Bolivia, Brazil, Chile, Colombia, Costa Rica, Ecuador, Peru, Uruguay and Venezuela.
5 Point-source natural resources is the name given to locally concentrated resources such as oil fields or mines. Agricultural land is called diffused natural resource.
6 The group of DC is integrated by Australia, Canada, Great Britain, France, Germany, Italy, Japan, South Korea, USA and Norway, selected by income from the lists of the G20 members.
7 Definitions of each financial indicator are found in the World Bank's *Financial Structure and Economic Development Database* (2008).
8 Total rents is the "Sum of oil rents, natural gas rents, coal rents (hard and soft), mineral rents, and forest rents", World Bank, 2018.
9 The World Bank defines depletion as forest rents times the excess of round wood harvest over the natural growth ratio of the value of the stock of energy resources to the remaining reserve lifetime (coal, crude oil and natural gas) + the ratio of the value of the stock of energy resources to the remaining reserve lifetime (tin, gold, leads, zinc, iron, cooper, nickel, silver, bauxite and phosphate) (World Bank, 2018).
10 Future research will examine the direction of credit flows to different economic activities to show if a larger proportion of credit is targeted at consumption and housing, and not to manufacturing and agriculture.
11 "Deposit money banks are resident depository corporations and quasi-corporations which have any liabilities in the form of deposits payable on demand, transferable by checks or otherwise usable for making payments" OECD Glossary of Statistic Terms, consulted in: http://stats.oecd.org/glossary/detail.asp?ID=592

References

Acemoglu, D., Johnson, S., and Robinson, J.A. (2001) 'The Colonial Origins of Comparative Development: An Empirical Investigation', *American Economic Review*, 91(5), 1369–1401.

Acosta, A. (2013) 'Extractivism and Neoextractivism: Two Sides of the Same Curse', *Beyond Development*, 61, 61–86.

Beck, T., Lundberg, M., and Majnoni, G. (2006) 'Financial Intermediary Development and Growth Volatility: Do Intermediaries Dampen or Magnify Shocks?' *Journal of International Money and Finance*, 25(7), 1146–1167.

Beck, T. and Poelhekke, S. (2017) 'Follow the money: Does the financial sector intermediate natural resource windfalls?' *Spatial Economics*, Tinbergen Institute, from https://research.vu.nl/en/publications/follow-the-money-does-the-financial-sector-intermediate-natural-r

Botta, A., Godin, A., and Missaglia, M. (2016). 'Finance, Foreign (direct) Investment and Dutch Disease: The Case of Colombia', *Economia Politica*, 33(2), 265–289.

Corden, W.M. and Neary, J.P. (1982) 'Booming Sector and De-industrialisation in a Small Open Economy', *The Economic Journal*, 92(368), 825–848.

Gourinchas, P. O., and Jeanne, O. (2013). 'Capital Flows to Developing Countries: The Allocation Puzzle', *Review of Economic Studies*, 80(4), 1484–1515.

Gylfason, T. (2001) 'Natural Resources, Education and Economic Development', *European Economic Review*, 45(4), 847–859.

Gylfason, T. and Zoega, G. (2006) 'Natural Resources and Economic Growth: The Role of Investment', *The World Economy*, 29(8), 1091–1115.

Hattendorff, C. (2014) 'Natural Resources, Export Concentration and Financial Development', *Working Paper*, Free University of Berlin, from www.diss.fu-erlin.de/docs/servlets/…/discpaper2014_34.pdf

Hausmann, R. and Rigobon, R. (2003) 'An Alternative Interpretation of the "Resource Curse": Theory and Policy Implications', *Working Paper* No. 942, National Bureau of Economic Research (NBER), Washington, DC.

Huang, Y. (2011) *Determinants of Financial Development*, Palgrave Macmillan, London.

Kurronen, S. (2015) 'Financial Sector in Resource-dependent Economies', *Emerging Markets Review*, 23, 208–229.

Kurronen, S. (2017) *Essays on Natural Resources and Finance*, Academic Dissertation presented to the Faculty of Social Sciences of the University of Helsinki.

Levine, R. (1997) 'Financial Development and Economic Growth: Views and Agenda', *Journal of Economic Literature*, 35(2), 688–726.

Levine, R. (2005) *Finance and Growth: Theory and Evidence*, in P. Aghion and S. Durlauf (eds.), *Handbook of Economic Growth*, 1, 865–934.

Lin, J.Y., Sun, X., and Jiang, Y. (2009) 'Toward a Theory of Optimal Financial Structure', *World Bank Policy Research*, *Working Paper* No. WPS 5038.

Magud, N. and Sosa, S. (2010) 'When and Why Worry About Real Exchange Rate Appreciation? The Missing Link between the Dutch disease and Growth', *IMF Working Paper* No. WP/10/271.

Manzano, O. and Rigobon, R. (2001) 'Resource Curse or Debt Overhang?' *Working Paper* No. 8390, National Bureau of Economic Research, Washington, DC.

Mehlum, H., Moene, K., and Torvik, R. (2006) 'Institutions and the Resource Curse', *The Economic Journal*, 116(508), 1–20.

Moradbeigi, M. and Law, S.H. (2016) 'Growth Volatility and Resource Curse: Does Financial Development Dampen the Oil Shocks?' *Resources Policy*, 48, 97–103.

Nkuso, M. (2004) 'Aid and the Dutch Disease in Low-Income Countries: Informed Diagnoses for Prudent Prognoses Prepared', *IMF Working Paper* No. WP/04 49.

Prasad, E. S., Rajan, R. G., and Subramanian, A. (2007). *Foreign capital and economic growth* (No. w13619). National Bureau of Economic Research.

Puyana, A. (2015) *La economía petrolera en un mercado politizado y global. México y Colombia.* FLACSO Mexico.

Puyana, A. (2017) 'Mexico, the Weak Link in Trump's Campaign Promises', *Real-World Economics Review*, (79), 142–157.

Puyana, A. and Romero, J. (2010) 'De qué Sufre la Economía Mexicana? Falta de Recursos u Oportunidades de Inversión?' *Economía Informa*, (363), 5–33.

Puyana, A., Romero, J.A.R.T., and Romero, J. (2009) *México: de la crisis de la deuda al estancamiento económico*, El Colegio de México, México.

Saborowski, C. (2011) 'Can Financial Development Cure the Dutch Disease?' *International Journal of Finance and Economics*, 16(3), 218–236.

Van der Ploeg, F. and Poelhekke, S. (2009) 'Volatility and the "natural resource curse"', *Oxford Economic Papers*, 61(4), 727–760.

Van der Ploeg, F. and Poelhekke, S. (2010) 'The Pungent Smell of "Red Herrings": Subsoil Assets, rents, Volatility and the Resource Curse', *Journal of Environmental Economics and Management*, 60(1), 44–55.

Veintimilla, V. (2016) *Instituciones de crédito y crecimiento económico: análisis de integración y causalidad para México. Evidencia empírica a nivel agregado y por sectores productivos. 1980–2014*, Tesis de doctorado en el TEC de Monterrey.

Part III

The growth of financial balance sheets

11 Financialisation in a small, open developing economy

The case of Chile[1]

Esteban Pérez Caldentey and Nicole Favreau Negront

The various definitions of financialisation highlight the prolonged decoupling between the real and financial sectors, and emphasise the predominance and growing role of the financial sector, as well as the financial motives, and financial institutions and agents over the functioning of the real economy (Palley 2014; Sawyer 2013; Hein 2012; Epstein 2006; Krippner 2005).

The divorce between finance and the real sector, among other factors, was facilitated by the emergence of extremely complex financial systems in terms of their institutional organisation, structure and instrument toolkit. These complex financial systems have also proven to be highly fragile. At the same time, the disconnection between the financial and real sectors provided a solid justification for financial deregulation (since the former was assumed to be driven by forces other than those underpinning the latter) strengthening, in this way, the process of financialisation.

The novelty of the current process of financialisation is not to be found in the phenomenon itself, but in the various dimensions in which it manifests, in both developed and developing economies, and in its wide generalisation of actors and economic transactions in the real and/or financial spheres of economic activity.[2]

Financialisation is reflected in the high rate of growth of the financial sector above that of the real sector; and in the prominent increase in the income share of the financial sector relative to total income. The improvement in the financial sector profitability has led businesses to direct their activities towards financial activities and also to take on higher levels of indebtedness.

Financialisation has important effects at the macroeconomic level. It promotes greater financial fragility since it is a source of instability and an obstacle to long-run economic growth. Moreover, financialisation has come with greater inequality of personal incomes and of the functional distribution of income, favouring profits over wages. The trend towards financialisation is not the result of market or financial imperfections related to intermediation. On the contrary, it is rather a direct consequence of the free movement of market forces.

This chapter discusses financialisation in Chile, a country which stands out for the successful application of free market principles to a small open developing economy. This chapter argues that the neo-liberal agenda pursued by different Chilean governments, since the middle of the 1970, contributed to generate a process of financialisation. This is visible, on the one hand, in the close association between economic performance and the price of metals. To the extent that the price of metals is determined in international financial markets (v.gr. copper), the evolution of the Chilean economy became dependent on a financial asset. On the other hand, the financial sector experienced one of the highest rates of growth in relation to other economic activity sectors, and achieved a significant share in total income and profits. In terms of its corporate structure, the financial sector is highly concentrated, with a high presence of foreign banks, based on financial conglomerates, which have expanded their activities beyond financial intermediation.

In addition, the expansion of the financial sector has been accompanied by a growing process of household indebtedness, and of the financial and non-financial sectors. In addition, lending to the real estate sector and consumers accounts for an increasing share of banks' portfolio at the expense of the productive sector. A detailed analysis of the non-financial corporate sector shows an increase in financial fragility.

This chapter is divided into six sections. Following the introduction, the second section describes the main policy measures of the neo-liberal policy agenda that Chile followed in the last four decades. The third section describes the Chilean production specialisation pattern, and it is argued that it is both a source of stability and instability. The section also establishes a link between finance, and the specialisation in natural resources to the functional and personal distribution of income. The fourth section discusses the importance and growth of the financial sector. The fifth section analyses the performance of the financial and non-financial corporate sectors. The sixth section presents the main conclusions of the chapter.

The context for financialisation: the neo-liberal agenda in Chile

For more than four decades, the economic development of Chile has been guided by a neo-liberal agenda, which privileged commercial and financial liberalisation and stability, altogether privileged macroeconomic equilibrium, over other policy objectives.

This agenda has been implemented through four channels: the promotion of privatisation and increased price flexibility over the productive sector and a wide range of social areas; the achievement of fiscal balance over the business cycle; the adoption of an independent monetary policy; and an increased external commercial and financial integration with the rest of the world. Within this framework, the role of government is considered subsidiary to the market; therefore, its interventions are limited to prove a minimal social safety net and for corrections to solve market imperfections.

In the past four decades, privatisation initiatives have expanded and they cover the main sectors of productive activity, such as agriculture, mining, manufacturing and services. In the particular case of mining, despite the fact that the Chilean constitution gives to the state the ownership of all mines, a system of concessions has developed that granted *de facto* control of most mining activity to the private sector. The private sector also operates and owns most of the telecommunication, financial, transport and maritime services. Social services such as health, education and pensions, where the government had historical presence, have also come under private hands.[3]

These privatisation efforts have been underpinned by a fiscal policy orientation to avoid the so-called "crowding-out effects", ensure adequate external risks to credit rating and provide a framework for the functioning of monetary policy. The fiscal rule that adjusts public spending in relation to the long-run behaviour of the economy has been a central piece to fulfil this goal. As for the monetary policy, it has the prerogative to keep price stability by dampening aggregate demand fluctuations around a long-term supply-determined trend. For the achievement of this objective, the monetary authority requires credibility and reputation that can only be achieved by granting the central bank a status of an independent and autonomous body, free from political influences and control.

Increased commercial and financial integration with the rest of the world entails the reduction and, eventually suppression of trade tariff and non-tariff barriers, financial liberalisation (including the liberalisation of interest rates) and opening up of the banking system to foreign ownership. It also meant the increased participation of Chile in trade and investment agreements,[4] in which Chile has 25 commercial agreements with more than 58 trade partners.

The application of these principles has had two central effects linked to financialisation. First, it fostered a pattern of production and export specialisation based on comparative advantages, generating a high dependence on natural resources (mining and agriculture), and more specifically on copper. Second, it strengthened the association between the Chilean economic performance and the ups and downs of international copper prices, determined mainly by international financial markets and financial speculation. The evolution of the copper prices and terms of trade also led to higher profit shares that widened inequality in the personal distribution of income (measured by the GINI index).

This model also fostered the growth of the financial sector and strengthened its influence over the rest of the economy. Finance turned out to be the most dynamic sectors and it accounts for higher shares of total income, wage bills and profits. In addition, the growth of the financial sector has created (non-regulated) financial conglomerates, whose activities expand beyond traditional banking operation, focussing on financial services.

Specialisation in natural resources

A source of stability and instability

Natural resources production and natural resource-based sectors represent an important contribution to economic activity. The decomposition of GDP by sectors of economic activity shows that natural resources and mining represented, in the 1980s, on average, 15% of GDP, increasing to 23% of GDP in the 1990s and 2000s, of which mining represented 10%, 18.8% and 19.3%, respectively.

The analysis of GDP on the expenditure side shows that natural resources explain a large part of the behaviour of exports and investment. Available data spanning from 1994 to 2017 show that natural resources and mining reached more than 75% and 50% of total exports of goods, respectively; and the formation of gross fixed capital formation is largely driven by mining activities.

Natural resource exploitation is also the main determinant of long-term financial flows. Foreign direct investment (FDI) in mining represents half of foreign investment; it contributes to expand the economic productive capacity and maintain the stability of the balance of payments, and it is a major source of liquidity.

Moreover, natural resources contribute to maintain fiscal stability. In comparison to other countries of Latin America with similar production structures, Chile's mining sector accounts for the biggest share of fiscal revenues. Data for 2016 and 2017 show that in Chile, mineral production generates roughly 15% of fiscal revenues (3% of GDP), which is above those of Peru, Bolivia or Colombia (7.4%, 3.2% and 1.3% of revenues, respectively; and 1.5%, 1.1% and 0.4% of GDP, respectively) (ECLAC 2016).

Also, copper revenues are used to maintain fiscal stability through the establishment of sovereign wealth funds. In 2006, Chile established two sovereign wealth funds, the Pension Reserve Fund (PRF) and the Economic Social Stabilization Fund (ESSF). The former serves as a buffer stock to cover any shortfall in the funding of future pensions, while the latter's function is to cover the fiscal gap in case of an unexpected decline in copper prices and revenues. In 2005, the government implemented a mining royalty to tax private mining activity to transfer the resources to an innovation fund.

At the same time that specialisation in mining is used to maintain macroeconomic stability, it is also a source of volatility and instability, since these commodities and its prices are, to a great extent, financially driven. Raw materials, such as metals, have taken on an increasing role as financial assets because its prices respond to changes in expectations on future demand rather than the actual supply and demand market conditions. Some manifestations of the growing role of these commodities as financial assets are their increasing activity in commodity future markets, including commodity derivatives, depicted by a co-movement among different commodity prices, between commodities and stock markets. In addition, these commodities have been used as collaterals for loans and credit.

Between 1995 and 2012, the number of outstanding contracts on commodity stock exchanges increased from US$36.6 to US$182 million for futures, and from US$373.6 millions to US$2.1 billion for options. Similarly, between 1998 and 2014, the volume of over-the-counter (OTC) commodity derivative contracts expanded from US$4.3 billion to US$2.2 trillion (notional amounts outstanding). Currently, commodity derivatives represent less than 0.3% of the total across all asset classes and exchange commodity futures and options represent roughly 14% of their total sum (FCA 2014).

The growing role of commodities as financial assets is also illustrated by the increased association (correlation) between the price and returns of financial assets such as equities (more traditional financial instruments) commodity-based financial instruments. The evidence based on monthly data for the periods 1991–2000, 2001–2007, 2010–2016 and 2010–2014 shows that the percentage of statistically significant cross-correlations (at 1%, 5% and 10% levels) between the different commodities indexes returns and volatilities (from agriculture, energy, industrial metals, livestock, precious metals and non-energy) including the Dow Jones AIG and Standard and Poor Commodity Indices (DJAIG, GSCI) and the stock indices of the Dow Jones Industrial Average (DJIA), Standard and Poor's 500 (S&P500) increases over time.[5] Specifically, for 1991–2000, the percentage of statistically significant correlations and volatilities reached 37.8% and 20%. For 2001–2007, they represented 55.6% and 28.9%; and for the last periods they expanded even more (75% and 66.7%, respectively).

Finally, another expression of commodities performing the role of financial assets is that they are used as collaterals in financial trades to raise liquidity, disconnecting spot and future prices (these practices have been widely used in commodities such as gold, copper and iron ore, and, to a lesser extent, in nickel, zinc, aluminium, soybean, palm oil and rubber). More illustrative examples have taken place in China in the context of significant positive differentials between domestic and foreign interest rates (Credit Suisse 2014a, 2014b; Goldman Sachs 2014; Morgan Stanley 2014; Tang & Zhu 2014).[6]

It can be argued that the performance of the Chilean economy is highly associated with the variation in copper prices and the terms of trade. According to data from the World Bank and the Central Bank of Chile (2018) between 1991 and 2017, the correlation coefficient between the rate of change of the price of copper (and the price of other metals) and the GDP growth rate is statistically significant. This result is mainly explained by the high degree of statistical association between both variables during commodity super cycle (2002–2008) with a coefficient of 0.67 for copper and 0.62 for other metals.[7]

Specialisation in mining and income distribution

The natural resource specialisation of Chile not only is a potential source of instability but also has negative effects on the functional distribution of income. This can be easily seen by decomposing the gross national disposable income (NI_t) into the gross domestic product (GDP_t), the net factor of payments to the rest of the world ($NPRW_t$), current transfers (CT_t) and the terms-of-trade effect (TTE_t), expressed as follows:

$$NI_t = GDP_t + NPRW_t + CT_c + TTE_t \tag{1}$$

The terms-of-trade effect equals the volume of goods and services exports (X_t) (or exports at constant prices) multiplied by the change in the trade price index:

$$TTE_t = X_t \frac{(P_x - P_m)}{P_m} = X_t \left(\frac{P_x}{P_m} - 1 \right) \tag{2}$$

where P_x, P_m = unit price indexes for exports and imports.

Substituting equation (2) in equation (1),

$$NI_t = GDP_t + NPRW_t + CT_c + X_t \left(\frac{P_x}{P_m} - 1 \right) \tag{3}$$

According to equation (3), while other factors remain equal, an improvement in the terms of trade $\left(\Delta \frac{P_x}{P_m} \right)$ translates into a rise in gross national disposable income (NI_t). On the basis of equation (3), it is possible to decompose the difference between gross national disposable income (NI_t) and gross domestic product (GDP_t) into net factor payments to the rest of the world ($NPRW_t$), current transfers (CT_t) and the terms-of-trade effect (TTE_t). In the case of Chile, according to central bank data, the terms-of-trade effect (TTE_t) is the main factor accounting for this difference.

Additionally, it is possible to decompose the gross national disposable income (IN_t) between the wage bill (wages and salaries) and profit (gross operating surplus), as is shown below:

$$IN_t = WN_t + B_t, \tag{4}$$

where,

WN_t = wage bill at time t; B_t = surplus at time t.

Putting together equations (3) and (4), the sum of the wage bill and profits can be expressed as a function of the domestic product (GDP), the terms-of-trade effect (TTE), net factor payments to the rest of the world ($NPRW_t$) and current transfers (CT_t)

$$WN_t + B_t = GDP_t + NPRW_t + CT_c + X_t \left(\frac{P_x}{P_m} - 1 \right) \tag{5}$$

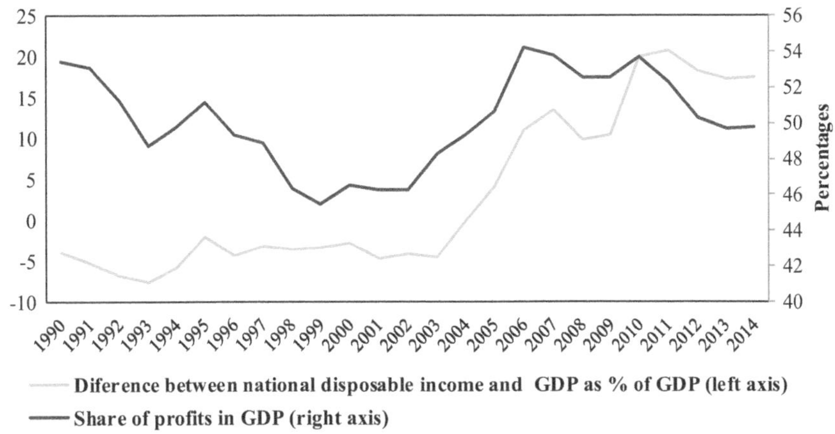

Figure 11.1 The evolution of national disposable income and the share of profits in terms of GDP.

Source: Authors' calculations based on National Accounts of Chile, Central Bank of Chile (2018).

According to equation (5), an improvement in the terms of trade $\left(\frac{P_x}{P_m}\right)$ can result in a higher wage and/or in higher profits. The evidence shows (Figure 11.1) that in the case of Chile, the improvement of terms of trade resulted in an increase in the share of profits (and as a counterpart of a decrease in the wage share). As shown in Figure 11.1, between 1990 and 2000, the profit share fell from 53% to 45%. However, from 2001 until 2011, coinciding with the commodity super cycle, the profit share increased continuously to return to the levels of the early 1990s (53% of GDP).

One of the most important implications of the change in the functional distribution of income towards profits is the increased inequality in personal income, which is even higher when capital gains are factored in. According to the World Bank, the GINI index values, excluding capital gains, reached 51.79 in 2005 and 50.84 in 2010. However, when capital gains are included, the values rise significantly (63 and 62 for the same years) (López et al. 2013).

The expansion and increasing importance of the financial sector

In the past three decades, the Chilean financial sector has witnessed significant growth in terms of volume, participants, instruments and products. This is the result of the commercial and financial liberalisation process, the privatisation in a wide number of activities, and the concentration of productive and financial ownership that has underpinned Chile's neoliberal agenda.

Between 1990 and 2015, the financial sector experienced one of the fastest growth rates of all economic sectors of economic activity (5%) above the average rate of growth of the economy as a whole (4.8%) and the mining sector (3.5%). In terms of assets as a percentage of GDP, the financial sector (including money bank deposits and of other financial institutions) expanded from 64% in 1984 to 67% in the late 1990s, surpassing the 100% threshold in 2010. In 2016, this ratio reached 117%. For the same year, if insurance and pensions funds are included in the computations, the financial sector assets represented 200% of GDP. Similarly, credit granted by money deposit banks and other financial institutions increased from 59% in 1984 to 99% in 2010 (Beck et al. 2016; WTO 2016; Superintendencia de Bancos e Instituciones Financieras 2016).

According to the distribution of functional income by sector of economic activities, the financial sector accounts for 19% of total income and profits. The manufacturing and mining sectors account for 11% and 16% of total income, and 11% and 25% of total profits, respectively.

The growing importance of the financial sector is also reflected in the remunerations paid to its employees relative to other sectors. A recent labour survey of the 17 sectors of Chilean economic activity, for 2012, shows that the financial sector pays the highest wages. The average wage in the financial sector reached $969,311 Chilean pesos, which is not only above the national average wage ($451,516 pesos), but also higher in terms of the average wage of the mining industry ($782,119 pesos). In line with this evidence, the distribution of income among the different economic sectors, between 2003 and 2015, shows that the share of financial sector wages relative to total wage income reached 17.3%, while that for other sectors such as agriculture, manufacturing and mining averaged 4.6%, 12.6% and 4%, respectively, in 2003, and 3.1%, 8.8% and 4.1%%, respectively, in 2015.

The growth of the financial sector is explained mainly through the performance of the banking system. The financial sector has diversified over time to include not only intermediation activities, but also insurance companies, capital markets and pension funds. However, in spite of the growing strength of these non-banking activities over time, the Chilean financial system is mainly bank based.[8]

The analysis of the banking system shows three major stylised facts. First, the banking system is highly concentrated. Currently, the banking system comprises 24 banks nationally established in Chile, of which 20 are privately owned and 1 is state-owned, and 4 are branches of foreign banks. Of these, four banks (Santander, Banco de Chile, Banco de Estado and Banco de Crédito e Inversiones (BCI)) account for over two-thirds of the total banking system assets (17%, 15.4%, 15% and 14.3% of total assets, respectively). This high level of concentration, in part, is a by-product of the mergers and acquisitions process that the Chilean financial industry experienced since the 1990s (Superintendencia e Instituciones Financieras de Chile 2016; Budnevich-Lefort 2010, July). Between 1990 and 2015, 21 mergers and acquisitions have taken place. All the major banks have been involved in these operations. In this period, Santander and the Bank of Chile participated in three (1995, 1996 and 2002) and two mergers (2001 and 2008), respectively. For their part, the Banco Bilbao Vizcaya Argentaria (BBVA), Corpbanca and Scotiabank participated in one merger (1995, 1999 and 2009).

Second, the banking system is highly integrated with the rest of the world with a high presence of foreign ownership. In addition to the branches of foreign banks, some of the major banking sector players including Santander, BBVA and Scotiabank (17%, 6.5% and 8% of total banking assets, respectively) are foreign owned.[9]

Third, the majority of banks, and in particular the most important banks, operate as a part of larger financial conglomerates. A financial conglomerate is defined as "any group of companies under common control or dominant influence, including any financial holding company, which conducts material financial activities in at least two of the regulated banking areas, securities, insurance (or pensions) (BIS 2012). Note that a financial conglomerate besides conducting activities in securities, insurance or pensions is also related in activities with the non-financial sector. Financial conglomerates participate in a range of diverse activities including, among others, agriculture, commerce, energy, manufacturing, mining, retail and telecommunications (OECD 2011). The government of Chile does not have an official definition of a financial conglomerate. However, it has a legal definition of economic groups, which is a broader concept and can be interpreted to encompass the notion of a financial conglomerate.

The Securities and Insurance Superintendencia (SVS) defines an economic group as follows:

> group of entities that display the kind of links in their ownership, administration, or credit liability that lead to a presumption that the economic and financial action of the members thereof is guided by the group's common interest or is subordinate thereto, or that there are common financial risks in the credits granted to them, or in the acquisition of securities issued by them.
>
> (Securities Market Law 18.045)
> (Superintendencia de Valores y Seguros 2016)

Available evidence by the SVS shows that the number of economic groups has increased significantly since the 1980s. The SVS recorded 12, 86, 92 and 140 economic groups in 1988, 2002, 2004 and 2016, respectively. The number of economic groups involved in financial activities has also increased; based on SVS data that economic groups provided, our own estimates show that between 2002 and 2016, the number of economic groups involved in financial activities (including banking services, insurance, stock market, administration of investment funds and real estate) increased from 23 to 46 (representing 27% and 33%), and currently there are 11 financial conglomerates. All of these are regulated by the Superintendencia of banks.

The existence of financial conglomerates has important implications in the way in which banks operate. By law, banks are not allowed to engage in activities not directly related to financial intermediation (LGB, Art. 69). However, since the majority of banks belong to financial conglomerates, the limitations on bank activities have a *de jure* rather a *de facto* effect. The OECD states:

> Banks...operate as part of larger conglomerates, where the bank itself is controlled by a holding company, which also controls a host of other group companies, which may include securities, firms, insurance companies and/or fund and pension managers. The bank itself can, however, own a brokerage company, which in turn cross-sells the products of the other group companies. In many cases, it appears that that the separation of the various activities is more of a formal than a functional nature.
> (OECD 2011, 21)

The majority of financial conglomerates participate mainly in insurance services and to a lesser extent in pension funds (Ahumada & Zambrano 2015).

The discussion of the financial sector and the non-financial corporate sector

The financial sector and its modus operandi

An analysis of the balance sheets and income statement of the Chilean banking system as a whole and at the individual level shows that bank's business model and strategy are not focussed on lending to the productive sector and even less so to small and medium enterprises (SMEs).

At the consolidated level, since 1990, lending to the business sector has represented approximately 43%–44% of banking total assets, and has remained relatively constant till present. The business loans in relation to total loans have declined over time. In 1990, they represented 71.7%, dropping by 10% in 2000. At the same time, consumption and real estate lending significantly increased. In 1990, they represented 28.3%, rising to 39%, in 2010, remaining thereafter at that level (Superintendencia de bancos e instituciones financieras de Chile 1990–2007, 2016).

The analysis also shows that bank's assets also depend on investment on financial instruments. At the consolidated level financial derivatives represent 5% of the value of all assets and 62% of all financial assets.

Table 11.1 Composition of loans, total income and profitability (1990–2015) in percentage

	1990	*2000*	*2005*	*2010*	*2015*
	Share of total loans				
Housing loans	22.4	25.3	28.8	26.1	26.4
Consumer loans	5.9	12	15.2	13	13.4
Business loans	71.7	62.7	56.1	60.9	60.2
	Share of total net income				
Housing loans	...	...	...	23.4	24.8
Consumer loans	...	...	...	30.1	27.8
Business loans	...	...	...	46.5	47.3
	Profitability				
Business	...	...	...	40	40
Non-commercial	...	...	...	60	60
Consumption	...	...	...	110	100

Source: On the basis of Superintendencia de Bancos de Chile. Reports for 1990–2007 and 2008–2015.

Note: Profitability was computed as the ratio of gross income received for business, non-business (consumer and housing) and consumer loans divided by total loans given to each of these sectors.

Moreover, the empirical evidence shows that housing and consumer lending is more profitable than lending to the business sector. The share of total net income from housing and consumption accounts for 52.6%, which is above the level registered by business loans.

Similarly, a rough estimation of loan profitability (as the ratio of gross loan income for the business and non-business (housing and consumption) sectors) shows that on average, banks are able to recover 40% and 60% of the loan the year in which they made the loan to business and non-business sectors. In the case of consumption, banks are able to recover the entire value of the loan the year in which they granted the loan (Table 11.1).

These results are consistent with the estimates of profitability indicators for selected financial conglomerates such as the rate of return over equity (ROE) and revenue minus expense before taxes and interest (EBIT). Both show an increase between the 1990s and the 2000s. Moreover, financial conglomerate profitability exceeds that of non-financial sector (13.8% versus 9.4% between 2000 and 2010; 11.9% versus 3.5% for 2015, respectively). The EBIT, which is often considered as a measure of profitability, five folded between 1990–1999 and 2000–2010, and three folded between 2000–2010 and 2015.

The consequences of financialisation

This financial model has not been conducive to social and economic development. The high levels of profitability consumers and housing loans have encouraged the increased indebtedness of households, while, at the same time, benefitting the construction and real estate rather than the productive sectors of economic activity. Most importantly, this financial model has fostered the financial exclusion of firms. Firms have also increased their leverage positions.

Available evidence on the income distribution, wages and profits among selected economic sectors (agriculture, manufacturing, mining and finance) shows that excluding the financial sector, the construction and real estate sector accounts for the largest share of total income, wages and profits (after the mining sector) (see Figure 11.2).

Between 2000 and 2015, household debt in relation to disposable income, increased from 35% to 63% (22% and 43% of GDP). Currently, 72.6% of households are in debt with financial institutions and, on average, 30% of household income is used to pay debt obligations (Central Bank of Chile 2010, 2015; Superintendencia de Bancos e Institutiones Financieras 2015). And, between 2008 and 2016, the non-financial corporate sector debt stock grew from 88.5% to 106.5% of GDP.

The non-financial corporate sector

The main indicators to assess the financial situation of the non-financial corporate sector are the state of liquidity (the quick ratio – QR), the solvency indicator (interest coverage ratio, debt-to-equity, short-term debt to total debt), the profitability indicator (rate of return over equity – $\left(ROE = \frac{Net\ Income}{Equity}\right)$ and the net profit margin (NPM), all of these computed for a sample of 598 corporations that report their results and

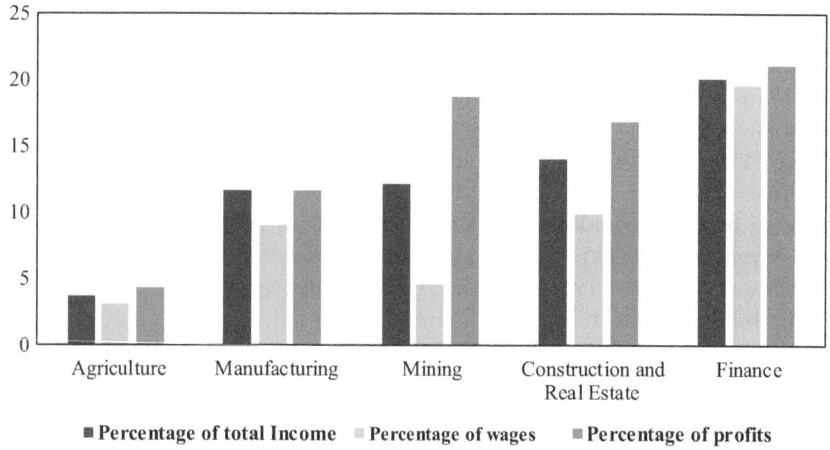

Figure 11.2 Selected sectors' share of income, wages and profits (2014) (in percentages of the total).

Source: Authors' calculations based on the basis of Central Bank of Chile (2018).

Note: Includes insurance services.

financial statements (period 2009–2016). The results are presented in three different ways for each year: (1) as a median value of all the firms; (2) as the percentage of firms that depending on the case, are either above or below the median value for the period 2010–2016[10]; and (3) as the percentage of firms that diverge for the threshold levels found in the literature.

The indicators of liquidity reflect the firm's ability to pay its short-term liabilities.[11] The QR, also known as the acid test ratio, considers the most liquid assets (assets minus inventories) that measure company's capacity to pay short-term obligations. It is traditionally considered that liquidity ratios equal to or greater than one mean that firms are able to meet their short-term obligations, while values of the liquidity ratio below one are an indicator of the opposite case. The solvency ratios such as the debt-to-equity ratio measure the ability of a company to cover its long-term obligations. Solvency ratios show the extent to which a firm depends on borrowing to finance its productive activity. Borrowing is compared to assets and equity.

There is no absolute threshold for the leverage ratios. These can vary widely depending on the phase of the business cycle, country size, development levels and the type of productive activity (leverage ratios tend to be higher for manufacturing and industry than services). The evidence in the case of Europe shows that leverage measured by the ratio of total assets to debt ratios reached 36.2% in 1999, peaked to 46.2% in 2009 (during the Global Financial Crisis) and decreased to 43% in 2011 (ECB 2012).[12] A more recent study that includes a set of 618 thousand firms operating in Italy, Spain, Portugal, Greece and Slovenia, for the period 2005–2014, finds that the leverage ratio (debt to financial assets) averages 0.48 (0.45 for the median) with a standard deviation of 0.3 (Gebauer et al. 2017). The study identifies thresholds for overleveraging at a debt-to-asset ratio of 80%–85%. Overleveraging refers to a situation where indebtedness has a statistically significant negative effect on investment (Pérez Caldentey, Favreau -Negront & Mendez 2018). The same methodology can be applied for a sample of 279 firms from Argentina, Brazil, Chile, Peru and Mexico, and a threshold level of 0.81 was achieved.

Another indicator considered in the interest coverage ratio (earnings before interest and tax divided by interest) indicates the facility of a company paying interest on its outstanding debt, and the extent to which a firm relies on short-term debt to pay its obligations.[13] As with the leverage ratio, there is no absolute threshold for the interest coverage ratio. Similarly, we think a useful benchmark is to determine whether the ratio is above or below one. Values below one may be an indication of weaker financial positions. For the ratio of short-to-total debt, we use 0.5 as the threshold. Finally, in the case of profitability, we did not use any specific criterion. We simply determined whether ROE and the NPM increased or decreased during the periods 2009–2010 and 2011–2016.

At the aggregate level, the evidence shows, with the exception of the ratio between short-term and total debt, a deterioration in the performance of the financial indicators. The QR stands on average at 1.15 and does not register changes in the period under consideration. However, the percentage of firms that are below this threshold and below the median QR has increased from 32.2% to 39.7%, and from 35.1% to 40.0%, respectively (Table 11.2).

Table 11.2 Chile: selected financial indicators for the non-financial corporate sector, 2010–2016

Financial Indicators	*2010*	*2011*	*2012*	*2013*	*2014*	*2015*	*2016*
Liquidity	*QR*						
Median	1.2	1.1	1.1	1.1	1.2	1.2	1.2
Percentage of firms with a QR less than one	32.2	39.9	41.3	45.9	39.5	39.7	39.7
Percentage of firms with a QR below the median value	35.1	39.3	40.9	41.4	41.6	39.6	40
Solvency	*Interest coverage ratio (ICR)*						
Median	4.8	3.8	3.2	3.4	3.5	3.1	3.3
Percentage of firms with a ICR less than one	22.2	23.9	23.7	20.6	21.8	21.9	20.4
Percentage of firms with a ICR below the median value	38.6	40.1	43.2	43.2	43.8	44.9	44
	Debt/equity (DP)						
Median	48.4	49.2	56.2	58.8	55.7	57.1	58
Percentage of firms with a DP less than 0.80	29.1	32.6	34.6	31.4	32.3	37.1	38
Percentage of firms with a DP below the median value	45.8	46.5	46.8	47.3	48.4	49	49.6
	Short-term debt relative to total debt (DCDL)						
Median	0.46	0.47	0.48	0.45	0.45	0.41	0.41
Percentage of firms with a DCDL less than 0.50	45.4	45.2	46.9	45.3	45	41	37.6
Percentage of firms with a DCDL below the median value	41.9	47-10	48.7	48.5	48.4	48.2	48.1
Profitability	*ROE*						
Median	11.1	9.5	8.9	8	7.3	6.6	7.5
Percentage of forms registering a fall in ROE			44.2			59	
Percentage of firms with a ROE below the median value	50	49.7	50	49.7	49.3	48.6	50
	NPM						
Median	9.4	7.2	5.8	6.6	6.5	6.2	7.4
Percentage of forms registering a fall in NPM			43.8			54.2	
Percentage of firms with a NPM below the median value	50			50.3	50	50	50

Source: On the basis of Bloomberg (2018).

The solvency indicators, with the exception of the short-term-to-total debt ratio, also reflect a worsening of the financial position of the corporate sector. The interest coverage ratio shows a decline, as well as an increase in the percentage of companies that is below the median (4.8% and 3.3%, and 38.6% and 44% for 2010 and 2016, respectively) (see Table 11.2).

Similarly, the data show an increase in the average leverage (48.4% and 58% for 2010 and 2016), and in the percentage of firms that is above the threshold of 0.80 and the median (29.1% and 38.0%, and 45.8% and 49.6% for the same years). In contrast to the behaviour of these indicators, the evidence shows a decline in the median of the short-term-to-total debt ratio and in the percentage of companies whose debt ratio of short term in relation to the total debt is below one (0.46 and 0.41, and 45.4% and 37.6% for 2010 and 2016, respectively).

In line with these findings, the average profitability (whether measured by ROE or NPM) decreases (11.1 and 7.5, and 9.4 and 7.4 for 2010 and 2016, respectively), and, at the same time, the percentage of companies which recorded a fall in profitability goes up (44. 2% and 59.0%, and 43.8% and 54.2% for the same years) (Table 11.2).

The sectors which have comparatively worse financial liquidity, solvency and profitability indicators are the food and beverages, trade, construction, telecommunications, water, gas and utilities, mining and energy, and wood. These sectors represent more than one quarter of the value of total assets and more than half of the expenditure on fixed capital and long-term investment, according to the data available on Bloomberg (2018).[14]

Conclusions

Chile is considered by orthodox (and non-orthodox) economists a successful case of free market application on small developing economies. From this standpoint, Chile exemplifies that the priorities of economic policy must focus on nominal stability and macroeconomic equilibrium, and that the adjustment of relative prices needs to be reinforced by governmental intervention, aiming to correct market failures and guarantee a basic social safety net that, altogether, generates the necessary conditions for sustainable long-run growth.

The greater financial depth and the capital market reforms allowed to develop debt markets, insurance and pension funds. At the same time, the process of liberalisation and financial integration have promoted the growth of trade, and increased external assets accumulation, which contributed to a more efficient resource allocation, strengthening the resistance to external shocks, thus reducing the volatility of income and production.

According to this interpretation, free market policies allowed income per capita to expand tenfold from US$1,380 in 1974 to US$13,540 in 2016, placing Chile in the group of high-income countries, and at the same time, poverty and indigence were significantly reduced. At the production level, Chile strengthened its specialisation in natural resources and market policies have been related to improved competitiveness in various subsectors of economic activity including in wine, fruit and forestry production.

Critics of this economic model correctly point that this process took place with a reduced productive diversification, shortcomings in research, technology and innovation, and slowdowns in productivity, and emphasise the strong and persistent inequality in personal income. However, they place these shortcomings only within the sphere of non-financial sector, which is a major shortcoming and an incomplete explanation of the current state of development of Chile.

In this chapter, it is argued that the development problems present within the non-financial sector are explained in part by the relationship and interaction between the financial and the rest of the economy. More specifically, as in other countries of the world, the financial sector acquired a greater preponderance and dominance over the real economy.

This process, called financialisation, in the case of Chile has an external and internal dimension. The external dimension goes far beyond the vagaries of short-term external financial flows. It includes the dominant effect that international financial markets have on commodities prices, and hence on the pattern of specialisation in production and exports, which have strengthened during financial booms (such as during the commodity super cycle). In short, the performance of the economy happens to rely on a financial asset that can lead to higher volatility and instability. This same phenomenon explains the patterns observed in the functional and personal distribution of income. Inequality in the case of Chile is explained, in part, by the relationship between finance and the productive structure.

At the domestic level, the financial sector weighs heavily in the economy due to the formation of financial conglomerates, whose activities have expanded beyond those financial intermediations, avoiding the regulations suited for a more traditional financial sector. Far from favouring production, the financial sector promotes household and non-financial corporate indebtedness. This may signal a gradual transition to a situation of greater financial fragility, which may have negative repercussions for investment and economic growth.

Notes

1 The opinions here expressed are the authors´ own and may not coincide with those of ECLAC. The authors are grateful for the research assistance provided by Cristóbal Budnevich.

2 Minsky (1982) argued that financial fragility occurred primarily in the financial sector, and to a lesser extent in the non-financial corporate sector. Households were not part of the progressive movement towards financial fragility.

Currently, the high indebtedness of the non-financial corporate sector and households both in developed countries and in some developing countries, including Latin America, is a reflection of the current process of financialisation. Financialisation has been traditionally studied mostly in the case of developed countries. Abeles et al. (2018) analyse the financialisation in the case of the developing countries, and more specifically, in Latin America.

3 The pension system was privatised in 1981.

4 Key to the external integration policy was the Law Decree 600 passed in 1974. It allows foreign investors to hold up to 100% of the equity of a firm in the vast majority of the productive sectors as well as to reinvest or repatriate profits. It also allows the right to bring capital into the country in goods and technology and the freedom to reinvest or repatriate profits.

5 Following Büyüksahin et al. (2010a), "the rate of return on the Ith investable index in period t is equal to $r_t^J = 100Log\left(\frac{P_t^j}{P_{t-1}^j}\right)$ where P_t^j is the value of the index I at time t. The volatility of an index in period t is $\left(r_t^j - \bar{X}\right)^2$, where $\bar{X}$ is the mean value of r_t^j over the sample period".

6 The most simple financing deal consists, in general terms, in a domestic company using a warrant of a commodity (a document issued by logistic companies, which represent the ownership of the underlying asset, in this case a commodity) to borrow a foreign exchange short-term loan. The warrant is then sold for cash in the domestic market and the proceeds are invested in asset yielding a higher rate of return than the interest to be paid on the foreign exchange loan (due to the significant positive local to foreign interest rate differential, i.e. the difference between a US letter of credit interest and a Chinese wealth management asset). The asset is then liquidated and the foreign loan is paid. Also, the available evidence indicates that the accumulation of inventories is carried out by the financial sector and more precisely by some of the former investment banks of the USA, including Goldman Sachs, JP Morgan, and Morgan Stanley. As noted by the United States Senate Permanent Subcommittee on Investigations in their report on Wall Street Bank involvement with Physical Commodities (November, 2014, p. 3): "Until recently, Morgan Stanley controlled over 55 million barrels of oil storage capacity, 100 oil tankers, and 6,000 miles of pipeline. JPMorgan built a copper inventory that peaked at $2.7 billion, and, at one point, included at least 213,000 metric tons of copper, comprising nearly 60% of the available physical copper on the world's premier copper trading exchange, the LME. In 2012, Goldman owned 1.5 million metric tons of aluminium worth $3 billion, approximately 25% of the entire US annual consumption. Goldman also owned warehouses, which, in 2014, controlled 85% of the LME aluminium storage business in the USA. Those large holdings illustrate the significant increase in participation and power of the financial holding companies active in physical commodity markets".

7 On the basis of World Bank and Central Bank of Chile (2018).

8 The stock market capitalisation as percentage of GDP, stock market total value traded as a percentage of GDP and stock market turnover ratio, which are the basic indicators to gauge the importance of the capital market, show increased strength over time. In 1990 and 2014, these indicators reached 34%, 5% and 7% and 90%, 12%, 12%, respectively. Insurance services and pension funds have followed a similar trend.

9 Superintendencia de Bancos e Instituciones Financieras de Chile (1990–2007, 2015).

10 We did not include 2009 since it is the year in which the Global Financial Crisis was felt in Latin America and Chile and its inclusion could distort the results.

11 Other liquidity indicators include the liquidity ratio and the cash ratio. The liquidity ratio measures the ability of a firm to cover its short-debt obligation with its current assets (i.e. those that can be converted into cash within a short time period). The cash ratio shortens further the period of time within which assets can be turned into cash by considering only cash and cash equivalents (e.g. marketable securities). In this sense, the cash ratio is an extreme version of a liquidity ratio, and can reflect the value of a firm under the worst scenario (bankruptcy).

12 Debt and assets exclude inter-company loans. Debt includes loans, securities and insurance technical reserves.

13 The interest coverage ratio can also be used as an indicator of liquidity risk.

14 Includes telecom fixed networks, health equipment and services, producers of oil and gas, technology equipment, materials and construction, retailers of food and pharmaceutical products, forestry and paper, general retailers, industrial metals and mining, industrial transport, investment in real estate and services, and support services.

References

Abeles, M., Pérez Caldentey, E., & Valdecantos, S. (eds.) (2018) *Estudios sobre la Financiarización en América Latina*, CEPAL, Santiago.

Ahumada, L. & Zambrano, M. (2015) 'Los Conglomerados Financieros en Chile. Diagnóstico, Comparación Internacional y Propuesta de Cambios Regulatorios', in Larraín, C. (ed.), *Basilea, la crisis financiera y la institucionalidad regulatoria en Chile*, 162–201, from www.abif.cl/wp-content/uploads/2015/05/libro-Reforma-financiera-baja-23042015.pdf

Banco Central de Chile (2010) 'Endeudamiento de los hogares en Chile: Análisis e implicancias para la estabilidad financiera', *Informe de Estabilidad Financiera*, Banco Central de Chile, from www.bcentral.cl/es/faces/estadisticas/EnCoyunturales/FinanHogares?_afrLoop=755095683941879and frWindowMode=0and _afrWindowId=10uak9a4yv_265#!%40%40%3F_afrWindowId%3D10uak9a4yv_265%26_afrLoop%3D755095683941879%26_afrWindowMode%3D0%26_adf.ctrl-state%3D10uak9a4yv_342

Banco Central de Chile (2015) 'Presentación principales resultados, EFH 2014', *Encuesta Financiera de Hogares 2014*, from www.bcentral.cl/es/faces/estadisticas/EnCoyunturales/FinanHogares?_afrLoop=756251295397321and_afrWindowMode=0and _afrWindowId=null#!%40%40%3F_afrWindowId%3Dnull%26_afrLoop%3D756251295397321%26_afrWindowMode%3D0%26_adf.ctrl-state%3D1y7g5hxj9_4

Banco Central de Chile (2018) Estadísticas económicas y cuentas nacionales.

Beck, T., Demirguc-Kunt, A., Levine, R., Cihak, M., & Feyen, E.H.B. (2016) *Financial Development and Structure Dataset*, June, from www.worldbank.org/en/publication/gfdr/data/financial-structure-database.

BIS (2012) Principles for the supervision of financial conglomerates. Basel Committee on Banking Supervision. https://www.bis.org/publ/joint29.pdf

Bloomberg. 2018. Bloomberg Data Services.

Budnevich Le-Fort, C. (2010) 'Fusiones Bancarias en Chile: Regulación y Experiencia Reciente', *Presentación ante la Junta Anual de Gobernadores de ASBA*, Madrid, www.cronologiabancaria.cl/sbifweb3/internet/archivos/DISCURSOS_9333.pdf

Büyüksahin, B., Haigh M.S., & Robe, M.A. (2010a) 'Commodities and Equities: Ever a 'Market of One'?', *Journal of Alternative Investments*, 12(3), 75–95.

CEPAL (2016) *Horizontes 2030*, CEPAL, Santiago.

Credit Suisse (2014a) 'Commodities Advantage: A Bit of Winter Chill', *Fixed Income Research*, 20 February.

Credit Suisse (2014b) 'Base Metals: Copper. Collateral Damage', *Fixed Income Research*, 21 February.

European Central Bank (ECB). 2012. "Corporate Indebtedness in the Euro Area." ECB Monthly Bulletin, February. Frankfurt am Main: European Central Bank.

Epstein, G. (ed.) (2006) 'Financialization and the World Economy', Edward Elgar, Northampton.

Financial Conduct Authority (FCA) (2014) *Commodity Markets Update*, February.

Gebauer, S., R. Setzer, and A. Westphal. 2017. "Corporate debt and investment: a firm level analysis for stressed euro area countries." ECB Working Paper Series No. 2101. Frankfurt am Main: European Central Bank.

Goldman Sachs (2014) Metal Detector. Days numbered for Chinese commodity financing deals, March 18.

Hein, E. (2012) The Macroeconomics of Finance-Dominated Capitalism – and its Crisis. Northampton: Edward Elgar.

Krippner, G. (2005) 'The Financialization of the American Economy', *Socio-Economic Review*, 3(2), 173–208.

López, R., Figueroa, E., & Gutiérrez, P. (2013) 'La 'Parte del León': Nuevas Estimaciones de la Participación de los Súper Ricos en el Ingreso de Chile', *Serie de Documentos de Trabajo*, SDT 379.

Minsky, H. (1982) *Can 'It' happen again. Essays on stability and finance*, M.E. Sharpe, New York.

Morgan Stanley (2014) 'The Commodity Manual. Collateral Damage in Copper and Iron Ore', *Morgan Stanley Research Global*, March 17.

OECD (2011) 'Chile Review of the Financial System', OECD Publishing, from www.oecd.org/finance/financial-markets/49497488.pdf

Palley, T. (2014) *Financialization: The economics of finance capital domination*. Palgrave Macmillan, New York.

Pérez Caldentey, E., Favreau Negront, N., & Mendez, L. (2018) Corporate Debt in Latin America and its Macroeconomic Implications, Levy Economics Institute. Working Paper 904, May.

Sawyer, M.C. (2013) 'What is Financialization?', *International Journal of Political Economy*, 42(4), 5–18.

Stephanou, C. (2015) 'Supervision of Financial Conglomerates: The Case of Chile', *World Bank Policy Research, Working Paper* No. 3553, from http://documents.worldbank.org/curated/en/820371468769916796/Supervision-of-financial-conglomerates-the-case-of-Chile

Superintendencia de Bancos e Instituciones Financieras Chile (2017) *Activos, Pasivos y Estado de Resultados del Sistema Bancario de Chile, Evolución 1990–2007*, from www.sbif.cl

Superintendencia de Bancos e Instituciones Financieras Chile, *Informe de Endeudamiento de los Clientes Bancarios 2015*, from www.sbif.cl/sbifweb3/internet/archivos/publicacion_10992.pdf

Superintendencia de Bancos e Instituciones Financieras Chile. Lista de Instituciones Fiscalizadas por SBIF 2016, from www.sbif.cl/sbifweb/servlet/ConozcaSBIF?indice=7.5.1.1 and idContenido=483

Superintendencia Valores y Seguros (2016) *Grupos Empresariales – Diciembre 2016*, from www.svs.cl/portal/principal/605/w3-article-23119.html

Tang, K. & Zhu, H. (2014) Commodities as Collateral, The Review of Financial Studies, Volume 29, Issue 8, 1 August 2016, 2110–2160.

World bank (2018) World Development Indicators. Washington D.C: World Bank.

12 Financialisation, growth and investment in Brazil

Luiz Fernando de Paula and Tiago R. Meyer

There is an extensive literature relating the process of financialisation with investment decisions. In general, there are two main channels in which financialisation negatively affects productive investment: (i) firms applying available domestic funds in financial assets when they offer larger short-term returns instead of productive investments and (ii) pressure exerted by the shareholders on the companies' managers in obtaining greater short-term returns and dividend payments. However, there are few studies related to financialisation and investment in Brazil, although some studies show that the Brazilian economy has characteristics of a financialised economy (Bruno et al. 2015).

During the last years, the Brazilian economy has been characterised by having a low rate of accumulation – approximately 15%–21.5% of GDP in the period 1995–2017. Its behaviour followed the economic cycle, either by increasing the growth of some components of demand (such as household consumption), or contributing to the economic slowdown as of 2014–2015. This abrupt reversal of the investment can be related somehow to the process of financialisation of the Brazilian economy, since firms may be adopting strategies based on the shareholder value orientation, in the meaning that they are accumulating fewer profits to reinvest in their real productive activities and obtaining more profitability derived from financial income. According to Miranda (2013), there are strong evidences that the Brazilian companies can be considered financialised, due to a type of governance closer to the Anglo-Saxon model that seeks short-term results and convergence to the maximisation of the shareholder value.

This chapter aims to analyse the relationship between financialisation and investment in Brazil since the implementation of the Real Plan, i.e. in the 1995–2017 period, a period marked by strong macroeconomic instability. In particular, the main questions that this work addresses are: (i) Has financialisation led to a greater distribution of profits and dividends to the detriment of investment in Brazil? (ii) Is there a crowding out process in which firms' financial revenues compete with returns related to productive investment?

This chapter is divided into five sections, including this introduction. The second section presents a brief review of the literature on the relationship between financialisation and investment. The third section analyses the macroeconomic context and characteristics of financialisation in Brazil in the period analysed here. The fourth section focusses on the relationship between financialisation and investment in Brazil in the 1995–2016 period, with the use of some accounting indicators built based on Economatica database.[1] Finally, in the fifth section, main conclusions are presented.

Relationship between financialisation and investment

The concept of financialisation[2] is broad, with no single formal definition, and is referred to financial activities. The more general concept of financialisation can be found in Epstein (2005:3), which defines the phenomenon as "increasing role of financial motives, financial markets, financial actors and financial institutions in the operation of the domestic and international economies". Stockhammer (2004) refers to the participation of "rentiers" in the income of non-financial companies and to the income obtained mainly through the payment of interest and dividends. Van Treek (2009) denotes financialisation as the growth of shareholder value, focussing on microeconomic aspects and their implications in the process of capital accumulation and economic growth. Liang (2010) puts forward the concept of global financialisation as the growth of power or influence of financial interests and institutions throughout the world. Krippner (2005) states that financialisation is a new pattern of accumulation in which financial channels are increasingly influenced by the determination of the profits of non-financial corporations to the detriment of traditional channels such as trade and commodity production. And, Braga's pioneering work (1985) relates financialisation to a systemic norm of wealth, since it produces a structural dynamic articulated according to the principles of the "financial logic" of capital reproduction.

French Regulationist School proposed the term of "financial-led capitalism", referring to a new regime of accumulation, which has spread throughout the world as a result of the adoption of neoliberal policies that encompass a set of policies related to financial liberalisation, labour market flexibility, shrinkage of developmental state, etc. (Boyer 2000). This new regime of accumulation developed in the light of the process of globalization (1970 and 1980) that imposed the "finance-led capitalism regime", which operated by the short-term financial gains, expanding the service sector expansion along with a process of deindustrialisation and job insecurity.

More importantly, the shareholder value approach provides a connection between financialisation and fixed capital investment. Specifically, the shareholder value becomes the norm of capitalism changes, spreading new policies and practices within firms that prioritise shareholder short-term maximisation that overlaps with other elements such as productive investment (Aglietta 2000).

There is a wide literature that seeks to establish the relationship between financialisation and fixed capital investment. These studies refer particularly to the United States of America (USA) and state that there has been a substantial expansion in financial investments of non-financial firms replacing fixed investments (or "crowding out"), and there has been an increase in firm's payments to financial markets. This trend can be related to the dominant corporate governance ideology, based on shareholder value orientation, whose main goal is "downsize and distribute" (Lazonick & O'Sullivan 2000), that focusses on short-term financial returns at the expense of fixed capital growth (Stockhammer 2004). Thus, by favouring the dividend payout, firms reduce retained earnings and contribute to decrease or to stagnate investments. In this perspective, non-financial companies are more related to assets grouping rather than capital accumulation ventures. Summing up, financialised firms are characterised by shifting from managerial priorities to short-term shareholders' interests.

According to Davis (2017a), the empirical literature on financialisation addresses a broad set of changes in the behaviour of non-financial firms, ranging from dividend payments growth, differentiating between income from fixed assets and financial activities, including financial derivatives earnings. A broad and recent review on the relationship between financialisation and investment suggests that there is robust and negative relationship between financialisation and fixed capital investment, although other studies are less conclusive, arguing that the investment rates of US firms also show a positive relationship between financial assets and investment (Davis 2017b), or that there is an unstated relationship between decline of accumulation rates and financialisation in the USA (Kliman & Williams 2014).

Orhangazi (2007) highlights two main channels, in which financialisation negatively affects productive investment. The first channel is related to the allocation of internal funds available for investments in financial assets when they offer larger short-term returns (besides being reversible unlike fixed assets). The second channel is related to the shareholder pressure exerted on firm's managers to obtain greater short-term returns and dividend payments, forcing them to prefer financial investment. Another incentive factor for short-term financial asset investment is modern firm management policy, in which managers have fixed salaries along with payments linked to the firms' performance, along with shareholders pursuing short-term yields, through imposing high stock prices and greater dividend payments. At the same time, the emergence of institutional investors, operating on a large scale and demanding high returns, pushed managers to increase dividend payments.

Thus, non-financial firm's managers were subjected to internal and external pressures to achieve short-term results and higher dividend payments. This movement creates two different constraints on real productive investment. First, assuming that domestic resource funds are cheaper or safer than external financing, financial payments reduce the available funds to finance investment through the fall of internal resources. Second, the time horizon of non-financial firm's managements is shortened, making more difficult to finance long-term investment projects, including research and development spending.

There are few studies analysing the relationship between financialisation and productive investment in Brazil. Miranda (2013) analyses, between 1995 and 2012, the impact of financialisation on the Brazilian economy and on non-financial public companies, and its effect on fragility, showing that an increase in shareholder wealth distribution had negative effects on gross fixed capital formation. Therefore, companies that increased short-term results over the long term converged to the Anglo-Saxon model of corporate governance. This shows that there is a dominance of rentier logic on the accumulation process of these companies, which can be considered financialised. It was also noted that the search for short-term results and convergence to the shareholder value maximisation increased the fragility of these companies and the economy, since the former increased the indebtedness in its capital structure without, necessarily, allocating these resources on productive activities. In this context, firms increased the dividend payout and share repurchase in order to raise the company's market value as well as the shareholder value. This policy was increasingly financed by financial activities and indebtedness, which increased the fragility of these companies and the instability of the economy.

Macroeconomic environment and characteristics of financialisation in Brazil

An overall analysis of the macroeconomic context[3]

Brazil, as other Latin American countries, implemented liberal reforms and economic openness during the 1990s based in the Washington Consensus (WC) .[4] The economic openness, in terms of import tax reduction, and the privatisation of state-owned firms (particularly in the steel sector) began during Collor de Melo's government (1991–1992). In Itamar Franco's government (1992–1994), price stabilisation was achieved (1994) with the implementation of the Real Plan and a stabilisation programme that used the exchange rate as a price anchor, and the de-indexation of the economy took place.[5]

In the 1990s, Brazil also liberalised its capital account. Since the first years of the 1990s, the acquisition of equities of domestic firms by foreign institutional investors was allowed through a special fund, and the special non-resident bank account was modified (CC5), operated by foreign financial institutions that, in practice, permitted both residents and non-residents to send abroad domestic monetary resources freely. The reintegration of Brazil, and other Latin American countries, to the international financial market was stimulated by the Brady Plan that renegotiated the external debt, both reducing interest payments and lengthening the terms of debt. In the 2000s were simplified the norms related to foreign exchange (FX) operations (Paula 2011, ch.4).

Summing up, the 1990 decade was marked by economic openness (trade and financial), state-owned firms privatisation and price stabilisation. But in this period, the international market also spread contagious effects from the Mexican, Asian and Russian crises, under a context of high external vulnerability. There were important structural changes in the Brazilian economy, namely economic openness, price stabilisation, external debt renegotiation and economic reinsertion of Brazil to the international financial market, etc., which altogether had a disappointing economic performance, that also need to be explained in the light of the 1992 and 2002 Brazilian crises, which reached a 2.5% average GDP growth of the 1990, very close to the 1980s (2.3%) and very low with 1950–1970 annual average growth (7.1%).[6]

The Real Plan (1994–1999) was successful in bringing inflation down fast, due to the combination of deindexation, exchange rate appreciation and a huge reduction in import taxes, as well as import tariff reduction in August 1994 (imports of more than 4,000 products had a 20% ceiling). In addition, "provisional measure"[7] that created the new currency, the "real", which initiated with a 1:1 parity to the US dollar (without knowing if the parity was fixed), allowed, in practice, the exchange rate to float until September 1994, and it was combined with a tight monetary policy, whose main effect was a quick increase in capital inflows and, consequently, a sharp appreciation of the exchange rate. In September 1994 was adopted a non-official band that pegged exchange rate between R$ 0.83 and R$ 0.86 and the Real exchange rate appreciated by 30% between July and December 1994. In order to reduce upward pressure on the exchange rate due to capital inflows, minimise sterilisation cost of these capital inflows and give some freedom degrees to the monetary policy (which operated on a semi-fixed exchange rate), the Ministry of Finance imposed a financial transaction tax (IOF – *Imposto sobre Operação Financeira*, in Portuguese) that ranged between 5% and 9% in the Foreign Funds on Securities (October 1994), increasing the minimum maturity requirements for capital inflows.

As referred above, the Real Plan brought inflation down fast due to the combination of exchange rate appreciation, high interest rates and a huge reduction in import taxes, which increased the Brazilian economic performance (GDP growth reached 5.3% in 1994) due to higher domestic consumption level. The tight monetary policy – including high real interest rates and higher reserves requirements on banking deposits, need to be understand due to the government's fear of a "consumer bubble", as the one occurred in the former stabilisation plan (the 1986 Cruzado Plan), and the need to attract capital inflows to generate capital account surpluses to cover the current account deficits.

The combination of demand expansion (in spite of the high interest rate), tight monetary policy and the overvalued exchange rate created immediate difficulties for Brazil's external sector. From 1995 to 1998, the trade balance accumulated a deficit of US$22.3 billion that combined with the deficit of service, and income investment (that rose from US$14.7 billion in 1994 to US$20 billion in 1996) caused a sharp increase in the current account deficit (increased from 0.2% to 2.4% in terms of GDP between 1994 and 1995, reaching 4.0% in 1998). In this context, high domestic interest rates vis-à-vis external interest rates were functional to attract short-term capital flows, but the Brazilian economy became highly fragile to short-term changes in the international situation, specifically to speculative attacks on the domestic currency (Paula & Alves 2000).

In 1999, after the crisis of the semi-fixed exchange rate regime that was the Real Plan main pillar, the government modified the economic policy structure, imposing a floating exchange rate regime and an inflation target system, which became the new anchor of prices. The new macroeconomic policy regime, under conditions of financial liberalisation enhancement, is inspired in "The New Consensus on Macroeconomics", whose main economic policy focus is price stabilisation.

In the first years of the 2000s, the Brazilian economy suffered from a number of international shocks (the US economic slowdown, and the Turkish and Argentine crises) and the 2002 confidence crisis in the light of the election of a leftist government, causing sudden stop in the foreign capitals, and consequently, a steady and abrupt exchange rate devaluation.

Lula da Silva's first government term (2003–2006), following a confidence crisis in 2002 with a massive speculative attack against the Brazilian currency, can be characterised by the continuity of the tripod of macroeconomic policies adopted after the 1999 currency crisis, which was the inflation targeting, on the basis of primary surplus targets and a (dirty) floating exchange rate regime. Under this framework, both fiscal and monetary policies continued to have an orthodox stance, featured by a wide primary surplus and the maintenance of a high real interest rate (albeit with a decreasing path), while the currency appreciated gradually.

In the beginning of 2003, the economy was favoured the benign international environment (commodities boom prices and high liquidity in the international financial market) that resulted in a high economic growth (4.7% on average between 2004 and 2008) free of external constraint. At the end of 2008, Brazilian economy was hit by the Global Financial Crisis (GFC), which caused immediate and deep impacts, but was relatively short, showing recovering signals by the middle of 2009, due to the combination of expansionary fiscal and monetary policies and policies oriented to mitigate the liquidity crisis in the banking sector.

Amid a positive external environment since 2004 (positive terms trade and growing capital flows), high interest rate stimulated speculative operations through portfolio investment and FX derivatives. These operations along with the current account surplus resulted in a significant currency appreciation. The interventions of the monetary authority in the FX market in 2005 did not curb the Real exchange rate appreciation, but increased FX reserves. The so-called "precautionary demand" for reserves contributed to the decrease in net public external debt and improved the country's external liquidity. Moreover, in this period, bank credit to the private sector recorded a significant growth, stimulating among other factors the payroll-deductibility of credit operations, which reduced bank risk and, consequently, the cost of loans to households.

The 2008 financial crisis effect impacted the economy through terms of trade and capital flows. Indeed, Lula da Silva's response to the GFC, although late, was an important shift from previous crisis episodes, where central government pursued procyclical policies, usually within the framework of the International Monetary Fund stabilisation programmes, hoping to steady financial investors humours, and unfolded a broad variety of countercyclical economic measures (Paula et al. 2015; Barbosa 2010) to, first, avoid the spread of the credit crunch, for which the *Banco Central do Brasil* (BCB, Central Bank of Brazil) adopted a series of liquidity-enhancing measures; second, the BCB intervened in the FX markets; third, the state-owned banks were encouraged to expand their credit operations to compensate for the private bank credits deceleration of credit supply and, fourth, the Ministry of Finance undertook fiscal measures to stimulate aggregate demand. This countercyclical reaction was possible, to a large extent, due to the policy space created by the shift towards a net creditor position in foreign currency of the Brazilian government; thereby the currency devaluation favoured public finance.

As a result of these countercyclical economic policies, after experiencing a recession in 2009 (GDP grew by – 0.2%), the Brazilian economy expanded by 7.6% in 2010; and more important international capital flows were restored. But the problems associated with periods of prosperity reappeared, including the tendency for the *real* to appreciate due to the new surge of capital inflows.

Since mid-2009, the Brazilian economy took place a new "twin boom" (commodities and capital inflows), based on a huge short-term capital inflow, boosted by the high differential between the internal and external interest rates. As the BCB resumed the exchange rate policy adopted before the crisis, Brazil's currency recorded a huge appreciation in 2009, followed by the imposition of capital flow regulations by the Ministry of Finance, which started with a tiny financial transaction tax on foreign portfolio investments (October 2009). Soon, these regulations were strengthened with the first measure targeting FX derivatives operations and administrative controls. Moreover, the BCB adopted macro prudential regulations to curb the domestic credit boom (Prates & Paula 2017).

During 2007–2010, the main macroeconomic results were the growth of GDP by an average of 4.5% per year, pushed up by higher investment spending, private consumption and exports. This was accomplished with an average annual inflation of 5.1%; while unemployment dropped from 9.3% to 6.7%. But the external sector position deteriorated significantly; the trade surplus dropped almost 27%, while the balance of payments' current account deficit reached more than 2% of GDP, since 2010.

In late 2010 and in 2011, the first year of Dilma Rouseff's term, the central government faced the dilemma of having a moderate economic growth and addressed inflationary pressures. In this context, immediately after Dilma Rouseff took office, the BCB increased the interest rate to avoid inflationary pressures caused by robust economic growth in 2010 and, at the same time, fiscal policy stance became more conservative (by the end of 2010, the interest rate and the primary fiscal surplus increased to 11.75% and 3.1% of GDP, respectively). Despite these changes in monetary and fiscal policies, in 2011, the Brazilian economy grew by 3.9%. In mid-2011 was introduced what the government labelled the "New Macroeconomic Matrix". This encompasses a set of countercyclical measures to boost growth in the context (while the euro was worsening) and increase the Brazilian industry competitiveness, damaged by years of currency appreciation and the greater competition in the external markets after the GFC.

The regulatory toolkit on spot and derivatives' FX markets was further broadened, as the previous measures had only mitigated the currency appreciation trend underlying the deterioration in competitiveness of Brazil's manufacturing sector in both external and domestic markets. It was completed by a gradual reduction in the SELIC interest rate,[8] that is the BCB's policy rate. Yet, as a precondition for these changes, fiscal policy was tightened in the first half of 2011. Due to the interaction of the new FX regulations, the monetary policy loosening and the global investor higher risk aversion, the Brazilian currency was depreciated as was intended.

In this occasion, unlike the post-subprime crisis, the economic measures failed to sustain economic activity and the Brazilian economy experienced a poor performance in 2012, since GDP increased only 1.9%.

In addition to the changes in interest and the exchange rate, the government launched a wide range of instruments that favoured the domestic manufacturing sector and seek to dampen inflationary pressures in face of the currency depreciation. In this context, a nominal freeze of public tariffs was imposed (energy and gasoline), and the state-owned banks reduce bank spreads and tax exemptions, without changing (in the first year) the overall fiscal policy stance (Mello & Rossi 2017; Paula & Pires 2017).

In April 2013, due to higher inflation rates, the BCB restarted to rise gradually and continuously the policy rate, and removed regulations on FX operations due to the Federal Reserve signalling that its quantitative easing policy would be stopped ("tapering"). At the same time, the Brazilian government further enlarged tax exemptions, and tried to intensify investment in infrastructure. Moreover, "Lava-jato"[9] operation was launched in the context of the oil prices decline and Petrobras reduction of its investments spending, which had a strong impact on overall investment (Mello & Rossi 2017).

Compared with the policies launched to neutralise the GFC contagion effect, the countercyclical fiscal policies were implemented during 2012–2014 (tax exemptions instead of public expenditures); it was extremely limited, with a small aggregate impact on production and employment (Paula et al. 2015). The same holds for public investment, which was significantly higher during 2006–2010.

At the end of Dilma Rousseff first government term, the main macroeconomic results were a drop GDP drop in growth rate from 3% in 2013 to 0.5% in 2014; and average annual inflation of 6.2%; and an accumulated current account deficit around USD 279.1 billion; and, surprisingly, the average unemployment rate dropped to 4.8% in 2014. Since the middle of 2014, the Brazilian economy reversed, affected by a set of factors where are included, the terms of trade deterioration (mainly because of the decline in commodities price), a hydric crisis took place and interest rate rose sharply, and since 2015, there was a fiscal adjustment and huge exchange rate devaluation. As a result, the average GDP growth in 2015–2016 was –3.6% p.a., while the unemployment rate came down (from 12.4% in December 2013 to 8.0% in February 2016).

In 2015, after Dilma Rousseff's re-election, the central government shifted its economic policy towards a more orthodox policy stance, becoming very important fiscal adjustments in the side of public expenditures, which was implemented to regain agents' confidence as a precondition for economic recovery. For this purpose, the Brazilian government committed itself to a primary fiscal surplus of 1.2% of GDP, along with a set of measures to reduce public expenditures (mainly the budget contingency), monitored prices were readjusted (energy and oil) and BCB further increased its policy rate from 10.92% to 14.14% p.a. from October 2014 to August 2015. Due to the 2015 strong devaluation, the BCB intervened in the FX market to reduce exchange rate volatility and offered exchange rate hedging to private agents, with the use of swap operations (Paula & Pires 2017). The efforts of fiscal adjustment failed as fiscal revenues dropped dramatically in 2015, and the Ministry of Finance had to revise its fiscal targets. In the light of the recession and increasing interest payments, the public nominal deficit increased even more in 2015. Net public debt over GDP, which had recorded its lowest level during the period under analysis in 2013 with 30.5%, again grew steeply (to 46% of GDP in 2016), while gross debt increased even more, from 51.5% to 69.6% over GDP in the same period.

At the beginning of 2016, Nelson Barbosa, the new Finance Minister, announced the strategy of fiscal consolidation which, among other things, was able to reverse the upward trend of public spending, which contradictorily compromised the capacity of the Brazilian State to implement public policies in the long term (Paula & Pires 2017). As for 2016, the spread of political crisis paralysed the government's actions, making impossible the adoption of any economic policy agenda until the impeachment of President Roussef in 2016.

From the start of President Roussef's impeachment in May 2017, Michel Temer began his tenure as president of Brazil, with Henrique Meirelles (former president of the BCB between 2003 and 2011) as the Finance Minister. In the new government, substantial changes in the economic policy took place, the economic tripod was reinforced, along with a conservative monetary policy (to rescue the BCB's credibility), a floating exchange rate was imposed with little BCB interference in FX market and public spending ceiling was imposed through "Constitutional Amendment number 95" (which set a maximum readjustment of public spending based on the headline consumer price index – in Portuguese "*Indice de Preços ao Consumidor*" - IPCA of the previous year), creating a straitjacket for countercyclical fiscal policies implementations. In addition, a set of neoliberal reforms were adopted, aimed at reducing the role of the State in the economy, which included labour reform (increased outsourcing of labour), limited BNDES's role in the long-termfinancing in the economy and a social security reform that was also proposed by the Temer government that later gave up of the project due to the lack of congressment's support.

Some characteristics of Brazil financialisation period

During the period of high inflation in Brazil (1981–1994), there was a strong financialisation process in the Brazilian economy, characterising a monetary regime that Bruno et al. (2015) labelled as a "financialisation regime led by inflationary gains", derived from the generalised indexation of contracts based on public indebtedness, very functional in high inflation environment. In this context, the rentier accumulation can occur due to "indexed money" (high liquidity financial assets that function as quasi-money). Indeed, the existence of "indexed money", short-term domestic-denominated financial assets, most of them indexed to the overnight rate of interest, managed the maintenance of savings in the domestic financial sector, avoiding the dollarisation of the economy but, at the same time, could unfold a process of hyperinflation in the light of a financial assets "flight risk" (Belluzzo & Almeida 1990).

The 1994 monetary stabilisation programme of the Real Plan led to a process of financialisation through interest-rate gains, replacing the previous monetary regime, that encompasses interest income and other financial gains from assets derived from public and private indebtedness, which operated at the same time as the process of financialisation through expansion of the consumer credit supply, expansion of private pension funds, insurance and new financial services. The "financialisation regime led by interest rate gains" differs from the "financialisation regime led by dividends gains" that dominate the financialisation of the US economy (see the second section), where the main source of agents' financial revenues does not stem from dividends, but from revenues derived from investments in public and private bonds, partly indexed to interest rates, which were maintained at very high levels.

Since the early 1990s, the financialisation process has been stimulated by the capital account liberalisation, which sets off speculation from both resident and non-resident. Indeed, Kaltenbrunner and Painceira (2017) argue that one of Brazil's financialisation features is what they label "subordinated financial integration" that links financialisation with cross-border capital flows and shapes a subordinated agent's relations with the financial markets due to carry-trade operations that explore interest rate differentials derived from very high Brazil domestic interest rates compared to developed economies (for instance, the US federal funds interest rates).

Under the "financialisation regime led by interest rate gains", until 2015, the government sought to reconcile the interests of rentist accumulation with redistributive social policies, favouring social segments, whose income derives from interest and other financial gains (Paula & Bruno 2017). Thus, financialisation was stimulated by two interrelated factors, which are an extremely high real interest rate and the permanence of an "overnight circuit" in the Brazilian economy, inherited from the period of high inflation, which was maintained high in the post-Real period, where the applications of economic agents are channelled, especially in times of high uncertainty. In fact, the real interest rate (discounted by the IPCA) was on average 5% p.a. during 2007 and 2016 (it peaked to an average p.a. of 12.5% between 2002 and 2006); on the other hand, short-term financial operations indexed to the SELIC rate (including Treasury Financial Bills, "Letras Financeiras do Tesouro" in Portuguese) and repo transactions ("compromissadas") increased from 35.4% of GDP in December 2006 to 40.7% of GDP in April 2015 (Salto & Ribeiro 2015). The increase and greater importance of financial wealth combining high liquidity with profitability, to which most of agents' applications (households, firms, financial institutions, pension funds, etc.) concentrate part of their financial resources, is one of the most important features of financialisation in Brazil.

As can be seen in Figure 12.1, since 1991, there has been a strong increase in the rate of financialisation, measured by the ratio of total financial assets to productive fixed capital stock, reaching a peak level in 2014 of more than 25%. At the same time, the growth rate of the stock of fixed capital shrank and remained on average at low levels, especially when compared to the 1970s, a decade marked by high economic growth. It should be highlighted that the increase in the rate of financialisation since the beginning of the 1990s followed the process of capital account liberalisation in Brazil, according to the analysis of Kaltenbrunner and Painceira (2017). Compared to the former decades, there is a sort of structural break in the series of the capital accumulation.

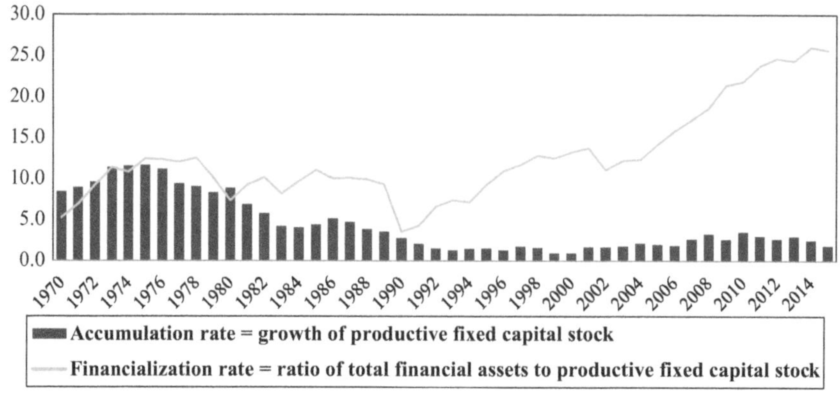

Figure 12.1 Finance-rentist accumulation versus fixed capital accumulation in percentage (1970–2015).

Source: Bruno and Caffé (2015) with data from IBGE – Brazilian Institute of Geography and Statistics, 2018.

In the period analysed in the next section (1994–2017), the investment rates expand between 2006 and 2013, but at a significantly lower level than in the former decades. In the next section, we analyse the relation between financialisation and investment in 1994–2017.

Financialisation and investment in Brazil

This section is divided into two parts: we start with the analysis of the overall investment in the period that range between 1994 and 2017, and in the sequence, we focus on the relationship between financialisation and investment of the Brazilian firms.

Brazil 1994–2017: an overview of investment

The Brazilian economy, since the 1994 Real Plan, has been highly volatile, with short economic cycles until 2002. From 2003, it presented a more solid trajectory of growth that was followed by a slowdown. The investment rate (investment-GDP ratio) played a central role in the economic performance of these periods, especially since 2006. In fact, during 2004 and 2013, the economic boom was led by household consumption that pulled investment spending, and during the cyclical reversal (since 2014), the deterioration of business expectations, in conjunction with other factors (deindustrialisation, currency overvaluation, increase in the economic agents' leverage and fall in firms' profitability) contributed to the economic slowdown.

Looking at the evolution of agents' expectations over the period analysed (Figure 12.2), which is measured by the confidence investment index (based on Fundacao Getulio Vargas (FGV) database), it can be anticipated that investment in both boom and downturn periods influences investment decisions and economic growth.

The investment rate shows four trends. First, between 1996 and 2000, the investment rate has a very volatile behaviour, and its trend is not defined through 2000 and 2006. In the subsequent period (2006–2013), the growth tendency of the investment rate reached a peak (21.5%), while in the third quarter of 2013, it shows a decreasing trend, reaching the lowest rate in the second quarter of 2017 (15.2%).

Among the movements of the investment rate, it should be highlighted that the strong downturn began at the end of 2013, after a robust growth cycle. As pointed out before, several factors may have contributed to the cyclical economic reversal and to the inversion of the investment trajectory, including the worsening of economic agent expectations. In fact, as illustrated in Figure 12.2, there is a process of worsening expectations since 2010 that intensified in 2013 that can be related to political factors ("*lava-jato*" operation and President Dilma Roussef's impeachment, among others) and a recessive cycle.

This drop in investment rate was also associated with deterioration of the firms' safety margins that resulted from the increased financial leverage during the economic boom period, which led to higher shares of the financial commitments over their profits. According to CEMEC (2016), the behaviour of firms' cash generation (EBITDA – earnings before interest, taxes, depreciation and amortisation) and financial expenses in the companies' net operating revenues shows opposite trends, with the former

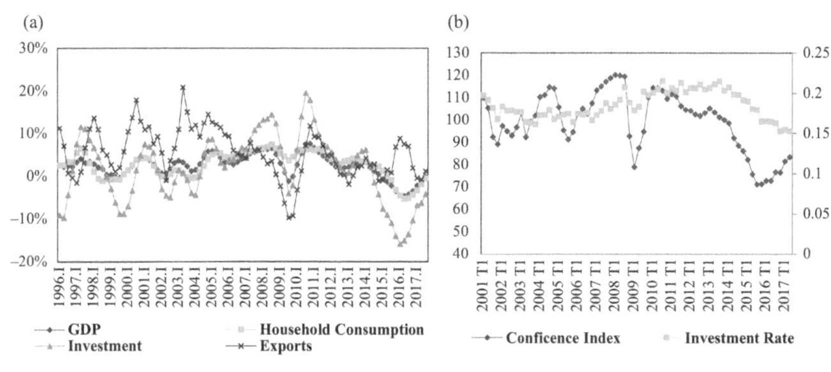

Figure 12.2 GDP Growth Rate evolution from the demand side* (left) and Investment Rate and Confidence Index of Investment** (right).

Source: IBGE 2018 and FGV 2018.

Note: (*) Accumulated rate of the last four quarters (compared to the same period in the previous year); (**) Investment Expectation Indexes – aggregation of respective indices of capital goods and construction material (industry), engineering services (services sector) and civil construction sector, with economic weights on the left axis and investment rate on the right axis.

showing an downward trend, while the latter has an upward trend.At the same time, there was a robust growth of the credit supply, especially by the federal state-owned National Development Bank (BNDES[10]) that was the main source of investment finance during the period, reaching the peak in 2013 and presenting a significant fall from 2014, as BNDES disbursement volume falls to the level of 2008. Therefore, there is a procyclical movement of supply of credit, with expansion during periods of economic growth, and contraction when the economic activity slows down, showing some evidence that the credit supply has an important influence on the behaviour of the private investment in the Brazilian economy.

The slowdown of the operational performance of Brazilian firms can be directly related to economic recession scenarios, mainly due to demand factors, and can also be related to higher financial costs, because of the higher interest rate and the 2015 currency devaluation, which led to higher shares that companies' foreign currency debts between 2015 and 2016 (CEMEC 2016).

The company's performance turned worse due to different factors already pointed out, which, in turn, also had negative effects in investments decisions. Historically, self-financing, or retained earnings, has been the major source of private investment finance in Brazil, in addition to BNDES loans. Therefore, the business profitability deterioration can have affected the investment through two different channels, first, by the deterioration of entrepreneurs' expectations and, second, by the reduction of firms' own resources to carry out the planned investments.

Since 2014, the fall of firms' profitability was partly related to the fall in aggregate demand, causing companies to have smaller ability to pass on cost to prices. The increase in domestic interest rates meant that financial expenses grew faster than operating costs, contributing to the decline in the net profitability of companies. In addition to the increase in indebtedness, the impact of the exchange devaluation on the external debt of the companies also affected net profit margins, albeit heterogeneously among the sectors.

As highlighted by IEDI (2016), the fall in profitability was an important component in the process of economic downturn. This process was exacerbated by the worsening in the economic environment that combined retraction of domestic demand and low level of capacity utilisation rate with dynamism still insufficient of the external market, making hard the recovery of productive investment. In addition, the study shows that companies have made less and less long-term investments, especially in fixed assets, and have sought to maintain an appreciable volume of financial investments and cash on hand.

Financialisation and investment of the Brazilian firms

As seen in the second section, financialisation according to the shareholder value approach, can affect fixed capital investment through two channels.

In periods of greater uncertainty, companies tend to choose to invest more in financial assets and less in fixed assets, leading to a trade-off between both assets, given the difference in assets' reversibility and maturity. The other channel is related to companies' management change to a pattern related to shareholder wealth maximisation.

In the Brazilian case, under a macroeconomic environment characterised by high interest rates and a very volatile exchange rate, non-financial companies had incentives to allocate their resources to financial assets, especially in periods of high uncertainty and high interest rates.

In order to analyse the evolution of the share of financial assets in companies' investment portfolio, Figure 12.3 shows the evolution of the share of financial revenues in the companies' operating income. Between 1995 and 2016, this ratio varied between 4% (1995) and 13% (2016), showing a significant growth, but still presenting low levels. The main contributions of the financial revenues in the company's performance occurred in years of high uncertainty and high interest rates, particularly in 1998, 2002 and 2015–2016.

In addition, to prove the progress of the financialisation process, it is necessary to evaluate a broader set of indicators, such as the share of financial income and operating revenues over the total assets of non-financial companies listed on the stock exchange market in 1995–2016 period. The variables show divergent trends, and the turnover of the operational assets (operating revenues/total assets) has a downward trend since 2005, while the ratio financial revenue over total assets shows an oscillatory and upward trend in 2005–2015, which can depict the financialisation trend of the Brazilian companies.

However, it should be highlighted that the share of financial revenues over total assets is still very low, compared to the share of operating revenues, although one could expect that in most cases, operating revenues should be the main source of earnings of a productive firm.

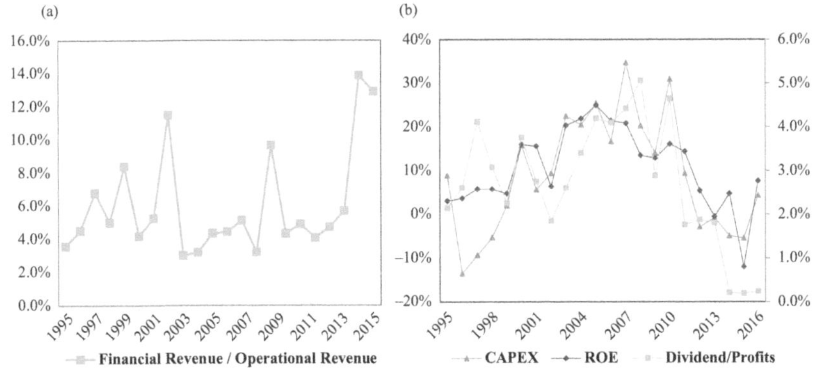

Figure 12.3 Financial revenues and operating revenues over total assets (right) and growth rate of expenditures with capital goods (CAPEX), distributed dividends over gross profit and return on equities (ROE) (left).

Source: Authors' elaboration with data from Economática (2018).

Figure 12.3 also shows the evolution of the growth rate of investment expenditures ("capital expenditures" -CAPEX), ROE and the ratio of "distributed dividends over gross profit". The data show some similarity in the movement of the three variables, which contradicts the financialisation hypothesis; mainly a greater distribution of dividends can have a negative impact on investment. Still, the investment expenditures seem to respond to the changes in profitability, while dividend payouts follow this latter variable.

In this way, according to the indicators used, it cannot be concluded categorically that a financialisation process is taking place in the Brazilian firms through the shareholder value channel since dividend payments are not been distributed at the expenses of investments. Furthermore, there is some trend showing a greater importance of financial revenues (with exception of 2003 and 2004), but still has a small share in the firms' return, with greater importance to periods of interest rate peaks and exchange rate volatility that corresponds to periods of greater macroeconomic instability. In other words, firms seem to extract some advantages of periods of instability by the channel of interest gains.

Conclusions

Brazil's monetary regime is characterised by some authors as a regime of "financialisation led by interest rate gains" because of the existence of an overnight circuit in Brazil combined with high real interest rates. In this chapter, we analysed the relationship between financialisation and investment in Brazil after 1994, and according to the literature on financialisation, there are two main channels in which financialisation can negatively affect productive investment: by directing available domestic funds towards investments in financial assets when they offer larger short-term returns; and by the pressure exerted by shareholders on companies' managers to obtain greater short-term returns and dividend payments.

We first showed that since 1990, the reduction in the accumulation rate was followed by a gradual and sharp increase in the financialisation rate, hence there is some evidence that financialisation is underway in Brazil after the process of capital account liberalisation. However, once the accounting indicators of the big set of Brazilian firms, although financial revenues have some importance in the firms' return, were analysed, there is no clear evidence that dividend payments have been done at the expenses of the productive investments, at the least in the period analysed in this work.

So, it can be concluded that firms' financialisation is still an ongoing process in Brazil but not consolidated yet. But what does explain the high level of financialisation ratio in Brazil? The existence of vast amount of financial wealth combining high liquidity and high yield, in which a great part of the economic agents (households, firms, financial institutions, pension funds, etc.) allocates a big share of their financial resources, is one of the most important features of financialisation in Brazil.

Notes

1 We have used accounting data from all listed companies during the period of the survey.
2 For a comprehensive review, see van der Zuan (2014).
3 The section is based on Paula (2011, chapter 3), Paula et al. (2015), Ferrari-Filho and Paula (2015), Paula and Pires (2017) and Prates et al. (2018).
4 The Washington Consensus related the stimulation of economic growth with liberalising reforms, notably macroeconomic discipline, trade openness and market-friendly microeconomic policies. The capital account liberalisation was not included in the original WC, added to the multilateral institutions proposal of the World Bank (Williamson 2000).
5 The Brazilian inflation was an inertial phenomenon. Prices were adjusted on a daily basis and the contracts were adjusted by former inflation (a mechanism known as "correção monetária"). The Real Plan, in March 1994, introduced the Real Unit of Value (Unidade Real de Valor in Portuguese – URV), as the new standard of monetary value, while the cruzeiro real (CZR) continues to be used as a legal tender. The URV, an average index of three representative inflation indexes in Brazil, was designed to be a unit of account linked to the US dollar, aimed to stimulate the economic system and find a sustainable price standard, and also aimed to recover the notion of a stable unit of account in the economy. In July 1994, the Real Plan converted the URV into a legal tender, creating a new currency – the "real", see Ferrari-Filho and Paula (2003).
6 Data provided in this section are obtained from Brazil Government data bank (IPEADATA) and Central Bank of Brazil website.
7 The provisional measure ("*medida provisória*" in Portuguese) is a legal act in Brazil through which the President of Brazil can enact laws without approval by the National Congress; it has to fulfil two requirements to be used: urgency and relevance of the matter to be regulated.
8 The *Sistema Especial de Liquidação e Custodia* – SELIC (Special Clearance and Escrow System) is the Central Bank of Brazil's system for performing open market operations in execution of monetary policy. The SELIC rate is the Bank's overnight rate.
9 In March 2014 was launched the "*Lava-jato*" operation (Car Wash), with the Federal Police of Brazil and the Court to deal with corruption allegation in the state-controlled oil company Petrobras.
10 The Brazilian Development Bank (BNDES) is a federal state-owned bank and the main financing agent for development in Brazil. It plays a fundamental role in stimulating the expansion of industry and infrastructure in the country.

References

Aglietta, M. (2000) 'Shareholder Value and Corporate Governance: Some Tricky Questions', *Economy and Society*, 29(1), 146–159.

Barbosa, N. (2010) 'Latin America: Counter-Cyclical Policy in Brazil: 2008–09', *Journal of Globalization and Development*, 1(1), 1–12.

Belluzzo, L.G. & Almeida, J.S.G. (1990) 'Crise e Reforma Monetária no Brasil', *São Paulo em Perspectiva*, 4(1), 63–75.

Boyer, R. (2000) 'Is a Finance-Led Growth Regime a Viable Alternative to Fordism? A Preliminary Analysis', *Economy and Society*, 29(1), 111–145.

Braga, J.C. (1985) 'Temporalidade da Riqueza: Teoria da Dinâmica e Financeirização do Capitalismo', Doctorate thesis, IE/UNICAMP, Campinas.

Bruno, M. & Caffé, R. (2015) 'Indicadores Macroeconômicos de Financeirização: Metodologia de Construção e Aplicação ao Caso do Brasil', in Bruno, M. (ed.), *População, Espaço e Sustentabilidade Contribuições para o desenvolvimento do Brasil*, 35–61, IBGE, Rio de Janeiro.

CEMEC (2016) 'Endividamento das Empresas Brasileiras: Metade das Empresas não Gera Caixa para Cobrir Despesas Financeiras em 2015/2016', *Nota CEMEC*, 06, IBMEC, August.

Davis, L.E. (2017a) 'Financialisation and Investment: A Survey of the Empirical Literature', *Journal of Economic Surveys*, 31(5), 1332–1358.

Davis, L.E. (2017b) 'Financialisation and the Nonfinancial Corporation: An Investigation of the Firm-Level Investment Behavior in the US', *Metroeconomica*, http://onlinelibrary.wiley.com/doi/10.1111/meca.12179/full

Economática (2018) http://www.economatica.com, [access in 01/03/2018].

Epstein, G. (ed.) (2005) *Financialisation and the world economy*, Edward Elgar, Cheltenham.

Ferrari Filho, F. & de Paula, L.F. (2003) 'The Legacy of the Real Plan and an Alternative Agenda for the Brazilian Economy', *Investigación Económica*, LXII (244), 57–92.

Ferrari Filho, F. & de Paula, L.F. (2015) 'A Critical Analysis of the Macroeconomic Policies in Brazil from Lula da Silva to Dilma Rousseff', *Brazilian Keynesian Review*, 1(2), 218–227.

FGV–Fundação Getúlio Vargas (2018), from http://portalibre.fgv.br/main.jsp?lumChannelId=402880811D8E34B9011D92BA032B198D, [access in 05/01/2018].

IBGE (2018) Brazilian Institute of Geography and Statistics (2018), from https://www.ibge.gov.br/estatisticas-novoportal/economicas/contas-nacionais.html, [access in 05/01/2018].

IEDI (2016) 'Sem lucro, sem investimento', *Carta IEDI* No. 738, Instituto de Estudos para o Desenvolvimento Industrial (IEDI).

Kaltenbrunner, A. & Painceira, J.P. (2017) 'Subordinated Financial Integration and Financialisation in Emerging Capitalist Economies: The Brazilian Experience', *New Political Economy*, doi:10.1080/13563467.2017.1349089

Kliman, A. & Williams, S. (2014) "Why 'Financialisation' Hasn't Depressed US Productive Investment", *Cambridge Journal of Economics*, 39(1), 67–92.

Krippner, G. (2005) 'The Financialisation of the American Economy', *Socio-Economic Review*, 3(2), 17–208.

Lazonick, W. & O'Sullivan, M. (2000) 'Maximizing Shareholder Value: A New Ideology for Corporate Governance', *Economy and Society*, 29(1), 13–35.

Liang, Y. (2010) 'Interdependency, Decoupling and Dependency: Asian Economic Development in the Age of Global Financialisation', *International Journal of Political Economy*, 39(1), 28–53.

Mello, G. & Rossi, P. (2017) 'Do industrialismo à austeridade: a política macro dos governos Dilma', *Texto para Discussão*, 309, IE/UNICAMP, July.

Miranda, B. (2013) 'Impactos da financeirização sobre a fragilidade micro e macroeconômica: um estudo para a economia brasileira entre os anos de 1995–2012', Doctorate thesis, CEDEPLAR/UFMG, Belo Horizonte.

de Paula, L.F. (2011) *Financial liberalization and economic performance: Brazil at the crossroads*, Routledge, London.

de Paula L.F. & Alves Jr, A.J. (2000) 'External Financial Fragility and the 1998–1999 Brazilian Currency Crisis', *Journal of Post Keynesian Economics*, 22(4), 589–617.

de Paula, L.F. & Bruno, M. (2017) 'Financeirização, Coalização de Interesses e Taxa de Juros no Brasil", *Revista Princípios*, 151, November.

de Paula, L.F., Modenesi, A., & Pires, M.C. (2015) 'The Tale of the Contagion of Two Crises and Policy Responses in Brazil: A Case of (Keynesian) Policy Coordination', *Journal of Post Keynesian Economics*, 37(3), 408–435.

Paula, L.F. & Pires, M. (2017) 'Crise e perspectivas para a economia brasileira', *Estudos Avançados*, 31(98), 125–144.

Prates, D.M. & de Paula, L.F (2017) 'Capital Account Regulation in Brazil: An Assessment of the 2009–2013 Period', *Brazilian Journal of Political Economy*, 37(1), 108–129.

Prates, D.M., Fritz, B., & de Paula, L.F. (2018) 'Varieties of Developmentalism: A Critical Assessment of the PT Governments', *Latin American Perspectives*, forthcoming.

Orhangazi, O. (2007) 'Financialisation and Capital Accumulation in the Non-financial Corporate Sector: A Theoretical and Empirical Investigation of the U.S. Economy: 1973–2003', *Working Paper PERI*, No.149.

Salto, F. & Ribeiro, L. (2015) 'Operação Compromissada, Gosto de Subdesenvolvimento', *Valor Econômico*, 08/05/2015.

Stockhammer, E. (2004) 'Financialisation and the Slowdown of Accumulation', *Cambridge Journal of Economics*, 28(5), 719–741.

Van Treeck, T. (2009) 'The Political Economy Debate on "Financialisation" – A Macroeconomic Perspective', *Review of International Political Economy*, 16, 907–944.

Van der Zuan, N. (2014) 'Making Sense of Financialisation', *Socio-Economic Review*, 12, 99–129.

Williamson, J. (2000) 'What Should the Word Bank Think about the Washington Consensus?', *The World Bank Research Observer*, 15(2), 251–264.

13 Financial structure and big corporations in scenarios of increasing indebtedness in Mexico

Gabriel Gómez Ochoa

The economic development model implemented in Mexico 30 years ago has depended on manufactured exports to drive growth. This has involved the entry of large multinational companies to exploit the country's comparative advantages, as well as the establishment of large domestic corporations with close foreign ties through foreign trade, partnerships, investments and a range of financial transactions.

Overall, these domestic corporations have benefited greatly from the model, and have expanded to become a focus of economic activity, including exports, investment outside Mexico and, of course, financing. The global economic situation today is typified by low interest rates and high liquidity, and the corporations have attracted an extraordinary amount of foreign finance, which has meant an unprecedented availability of funds.

Non-financial companies domiciled in Mexico, and in Latin America as a whole (CEPAL 2017, Vtyurina et al. 2017), have experienced a rapid increase in indebtedness in the years since the global financial crisis. Domestic financing began to increase in 2005, while foreign financing began to do so in 2009. According to the Debt Securities Statistics database of the Bank for International Settlements, the debt of non-financial corporations in international markets grew from 17,737 billion dollars in 2008 to 144,356 billion in 2016, equivalent to an annual average rate of growth of 30%, in other words half of the total amount for Latin America and the Caribbean (289 billion dollars).

The growth of private debt of non-financial enterprises is a global phenomenon (Alter & Elekdag 2016, Financial Stability Board 2015), but in Mexico, it has been of such magnitude that in recent years, it has doubled in proportion to domestic product. However, this indebtedness has not been reflected in real variables such as capital formation or production in the Mexican economy, although the financing structure of many domestic corporations has changed.

Very high debt levels, mainly held in foreign currencies, and a stagnant world economy could encumber firms and corporations that are not able to increase their flows of cash and foreign exchange. Overall, company debt can also have an impact on macroeconomic performance and financial stability, and even on public finances (Feyen et al. 2016). In other words, instead of boosting economic growth, the extent and concentration of debt can become yet another hindrance to growth.

The analysis of corporate financial structure took as its starting point the theoretical framework developed by Modigliani and Miller (1958). Several approaches have emerged from this analysis, giving rise to more realistic explanations of the significance of the sources of financing and their implications. In addition to debt-related tax issues, and the problems arising from asymmetric information, the analysis suggests that specific characteristics should be accounted for, such as size, years in business, the sector, as well as the type of product or service offered, which all play an important role in financing decisions. Some features of the institutional and financial environment are relevant, such as the level of development of financial markets, the types of relationships between companies and investors, and the implementation of creditors' and shareholders' rights.[1]

Nevertheless, the widespread indebtedness of the large non-financial corporations in Mexico suggests that the global monetary circumstances, which have provided the opportunity to gain access to relatively cheap financing, have been more influential than any of the other factors affecting the structure of financing. This might have led to many of these companies becoming highly leveraged, without this being reflected in their investments, income and profitability.

Financial statements in the Economática database were reviewed to analyse the characteristics and effects of indebtedness of large private non-financial corporations established in Mexico, to try to find out how their process of indebtedness had affected their financial structure since 2006, and how this is related to company performance, specifically in terms of turnover, profitability and assets make-up.

The sample of companies is very diverse in terms of size, foreign links, classification of activity and the type of goods or services produced. It includes 42 mainly manufacturing-oriented corporations of which 16 are makers of goods for end user consumption, particularly foodstuffs, drinks and tobacco. The remainder are producers of equipment and inputs, including six producers of construction materials and four makers of chemical products. There are also 23 services companies, including ten telecommunications and seven non-basic service companies such as hotels, restaurants and leisure companies. Finally, the set includes 15 construction companies, 11 commercial firms, 5 transport companies and 4 mining companies.

All are, or were, participants in domestic capital markets, either because their shares were quoted on the stock exchange or because they issued debt instruments, which is why the information about them is public. Most of the companies have domestic capital, with organisational ties to large foreign companies, which, in turn, are multinationals.[2]

This chapter has five sections. After this introduction, the second section aims to describe the process of private company indebtedness in Mexico since 2006. This involve a review of aggregate figures, drawing distinctions between the sources of financing. The third section offers an overview of the indebtedness of large companies, also from 2006, identifying some of the characteristics of the set and revealing the changes in the overall structure of financing during the period under analysis. The fourth section gives a brief presentation of the relationship between capital structure and profitability indicators of the sample analysed, while the section that follows classifies companies by their principal source of financing and identifies the performance of each group with variables such as company size, income, profitability, investment and industry. The last section provides a brief summary of the main conclusions.

The growing indebtedness of private companies in Mexico

Global policies promoting cheap money and increased liquidity worldwide have in effect also brought about the increased indebtedness of private companies in Mexico. Nevertheless, it should be explained that the growing tendency to channel formal financial resources from all possible sources began in 2005–2006. Previously, there had been several years of stagnation when the banking sector was being cleaned up in the aftermath of the economic and financial crisis that began in December 1994 with the devaluation of the peso, and which gave rise to the so-called "tequila effect".

This trend accelerated after 2010, and by 2016, the accumulated volume of financing in place was three times the 2005 level. Although the starting point was low, the real average annual increase in funds channelled to private companies was 10.9% over the period 2006–2016. This pace of growth, added to the sluggish growth in production, means that the funds available to companies in proportion to GDP increased from 13% in 2009 to 29% in 2016.[3]

The increase in financing for the stated period has been unequal in terms of the sources. Credit from domestic private banks, which makes up the largest proportion, grew at a modest rate with a yearly average of 4.2% between 2006 and 2015, but, in 2016 alone, the increase was 12.8%.

The state-owned development bank sector increased its lending to companies in the period analysed by a yearly average of 17%, but given its insignificant starting point, it barely reached the equivalent of 1.8% of domestic product in 2016. This barely exceeds the figure for non-bank financial intermediaries (NBFI), which reached 1.5% in the same year.[4] The debt market, the other formal source of finance for companies in Mexico, also increased the extent of its lending, notably after 2008 when its average annual rate was 14%, reaching 4.1% of GDP in 2016.

Foreign financing sources have ostensibly contributed to the growth of funds raised by companies domiciled in Mexico. As a whole, foreign credit and debt issues in international markets increased significantly between 2004 and 2008, followed by stagnation for two years, and then growing by a yearly average of 15% between 2011 and 2016 (measured in 2010 Mexican pesos), which implies a doubling of the total, reaching the equivalent of 11.1% of domestic product.

In reality, the growth of foreign credit was modest, as levels remained low from 2008 to 2012, but there was a clear recovery in the following years, which made it possible to exceed the previous peak level in 2008. In 2016, the volume of this credit was equivalent to 3.4% of GDP, and was 25% higher than public development banks and non-bank intermediaries put together.

The truly extraordinary growth has been in the issued of debt abroad, particularly after 2010, when a rising trend began, which ended up quadrupling between 2010 and 2016, reaching the equivalent of 7.7% of GDP. It is very clearly the second largest source of funding for companies, only behind private banking in Mexico with 10.1% of GDP.

Unlike the domestic debt market,[5] foreign issuances are exclusively long term and repayment dates of less than one year represent barely 5% of the total. In addition, 94.3% of this amount is at a fixed rate. There was a slight reduction of dollars as the currency of issue in favour of euros. In 2016, two-thirds were in dollars, with approximately 20% in euros and 10% in Mexican pesos, an average figure for the last ten years.

To emphasise the unprecedented level of foreign debt certificate issues by companies domiciled in Mexico, as well as their volume in relation to Latin America, it is useful to note that according to Bank of International Settlements (BIS) data (see Note 3), at the close of 2016 Mexican companies accounted for half of all this type of debt on the subcontinent, with a total of 148 billion dollars, more than double that of Chile and Brazil put together, which are the next countries with 41 and 34 billion dollars, respectively.

Naturally, given the limited involvement of the financial sector in economic activity, the majority of financing is focussed on large companies, which are the best clients for private banking, domestic and foreign investors, and even for other sources of financing.[6]

In this sense, if we assume that both foreign financing (credit and debt securities) and domestic market debt issues are received by large companies, it can therefore be deduced from the data on the distribution of credit by company size published by the National Banking and Securities Commission (CNBV. Comisión Nacional Bancaria y de Valores)[7] that large companies received more than 75% of all financing, equivalent to 21.8% of GDP, while the remaining 25% went to all other companies (6.9% of GDP).

Suppliers are also a source of financing outside the formal financial sector, which is more important in some cases than even bank credit or debt issues. All the large companies are financed by this means to some extent, but in certain sectors it is fundamental. In spite of the fact that only information on companies registered with the Mexican Stock Exchange is available, the extent of supplier financing was greater than development banks and NBFI until 2015.

The last decade, notable for the international financial crisis and the rather unsuccessful efforts to escape it, has seen a growing degree of indebtedness among companies domiciled in Mexico accompanied by unequal access to financing. This has involved important changes to the manner in which such companies are financed, in other words to their capital structure.

The debt issued in Mexico and abroad has become more important for financing business than domestic and foreign credit (Figure 13.1).

The volume of international liquidity combined with low rates of interest in the major financial centres has been a decisive factor in the evolution of finance, and therefore of the structure of business financing. As well as the difference in rates, the process of international bank deleveraging and the need for better performance by institutional investors has led to international banking focussing more on sovereign debt and institutional investors on the acquisition of corporate debt (Deutsche Bank 2013, FMI 2015).

This led large companies to acquire funds abroad instead of in the domestic capital market.[8] In fact, since 2014, the volume of funds available to large companies through debt issues abroad exceeded financing from private banking by 10.3%. The gap widened in 2016 to 13.8%.[9]

Risks associated with foreign indebtedness have of course increased: the depreciation of the peso has increased the level of leveraging and servicing of the debt, and added to the stagnation of economic activity, it places companies with insufficient foreign currency income from exports or subsidiary profits in a difficult position.

The circumstances that have favoured indebtedness abroad are currently changing. As the USA gradually "normalises" its monetary policy, Europe and Japan give assurances that they will stay the same as long as necessary

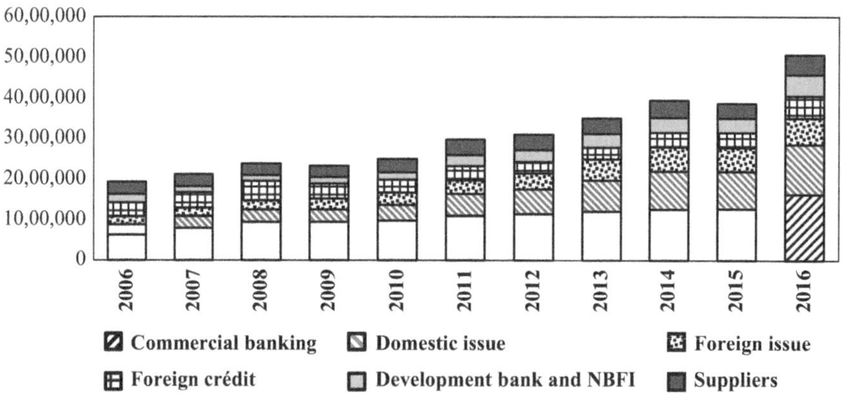

Figure 13.1 Financing of large companies by source of funding 2006–2016 (millions of pesos, Dec. 2010 values).

Source: CNBV, Base de Datos del Ahorro Financiero y Financiamiento en México, disponible en www.gob.mx/cnbv/articulos/reporte-de-ahorro-financiero-y-financiamiento-en-mexico-a-marzo-de-2017?idiom=es.

(Draghi 2017, Kuroda 2017). It is possible that many companies with foreign debts will find it difficult to continue securing funding and will return to domestic capital markets (Sobrun & Turner 2015).[10]

As a result, it is important to understand changes in the capital structure of companies domiciled in Mexico, so that a relationship can be established with such companies performance.

Some features of indebtedness in large companies

Global financial and monetary conditions, together with the need to expand Mexico's financial system, given its scarce participation in the allocation of financing, have led to substantial changes in both the financial structure of large non-financial companies domiciled in Mexico and the sums involved.

A sample of 100 large companies registered with the Mexican Stock Exchange was examined in order to understand the changes prompted by growing indebtedness. This set of companies accounts for 50% of the total indebtedness (credit and debt issue) recorded by the CNBV in Mexico at the close of 2016.[11] Also, because of the type of companies involved, they account for 75.8% of the total current issue of debt securities, although only 32.7% of the total credit for private companies.

First of all, growing indebtedness driven by the issue of debt securities has altered the level of leveraging, since the total assets of the sample grew faster than shareholder's equity from 2006 to 2016. Thus, a majority of the assets were financed by liabilities rather than by the companies' own funds. In 2006, corporate capital made up 48% of total assets, falling to 39% ten years later.

Another measure of leveraging is financial debt.[12] In 2006, it was equivalent to 53.8% of shareholder's equity, while in 2015, it reached 94.4%, falling to 88% the following year. Taken as a whole, the sample of large companies today depends more on financing than on its own funds, since in 2014, capital was just below 50% of financial resources. This change manifests itself in various ways, depending on the type of debt acquired by each company.

As indicated above, the issue of debt abroad or in the domestic market was the most dynamic source for channelling funds to large companies, while credit grew at a slower pace, clearly altering the respective proportions.

Figure 13.2 indicates first that capital ceased to be the main source of funds for large companies, taking the sample as a whole. Second, domestic and foreign debt issue replaced credit as the principal form of financial borrowing. Third, suppliers have maintained a constant level of importance as a source of financing for large companies.

It must also be noted that long-term borrowing was more common than short-term borrowing for the two types of debt. For credit, long-term borrowing accounts for 65% of the total for the whole period, with a few variations. Long-term debt securities became more preponderant, accounting for 84% of the sample in 2006 and reaching 94% of the total in 2016.

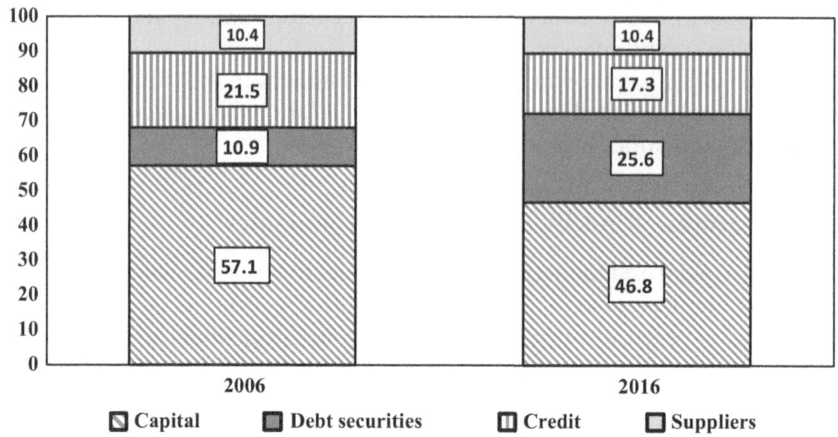

Figure 13.2 Structure of financing (%).
Source: Economatica, 2017, accessed August 8, 2017.

The conclusions of the analysis indicate that changes in the financial structure of large companies are related to a series of trends. First, to a pronounced reduction in the ratio of profits to shareholder's equity (ROE) from 18.4% in 2006 to 9.75% in 2016. Second, to a drop in the profit-to-total assets (ROA) ratio from 8.8% in the first year of the study to 3.8% in the final year. Third, to a continued fall in the ratio of sales income to total assets for the same period from 76.2% to 63.6%. Fourth, to a less pronounced fall in the ratio of operating results (Earnings Before Interest and Taxes, EBIT) to shareholder's equity. Fifth, to stability of the ratio of volume of sales income to fixed assets (property, plant and equipment). Finally, there was a reduction in the ratio of fixed assets to non-current or long-term assets, at the same time as an increase in the ratio of intangible assets to fixed assets.

If these results, associated with a change in the structure of financing, remain unchanged or worsen, this could give rise to a serious threat to the set of companies, since the combination of an increase in liabilities and lower income and profits could lead to non-payment of debt, a reduction in the scale of operations, and in the worst case to bankruptcy. As these are large conglomerates, the simultaneous deterioration of several companies could become another hindrance to economic growth and development.[13]

Nevertheless, these results are only an indication of aggregate trends since they are taken from a set of 100 companies with very different characteristics. Although they offer a panorama that helps to guide analysis, they only permit a few general conclusions. Segmenting the sample of companies by their principal source of financing, while noting which of the aforementioned trends change or stay the same could therefore reveal some interesting specific information.

Changes to the structure of financing, income and profitability

Although the diversity of the companies included in the research makes it difficult to formulate general and conclusive findings, it has the advantage of showing the dominant corporate structure in the country, allowing a number of trends to be deduced. In this light, the sample gives an idea of the level of concentration. One company alone, América Movil, accounted for 18.3% of total assets. It also accounted for 24% of total financing, 38% of the issue of long-term bonds and 50% of short-term bonds.

The ten largest companies had 58% of the assets, controlling 64.4% of financing (67% of short-term and 51% of long-term). Apart from the largest of these, they are not the most profitable among the sample of companies, but not one had a net loss during the whole period. Nor are they the most leveraged. Only two made heavy use of credit and one of debt issue. Although they are large, two did not use debt securities to finance themselves and one of these two is the only one of the ten largest companies to make substantial use of supplier financing.

Although the aggregate figures indicate that debt grew more than capital, in other words there was an increase in leveraging, many companies saw a reduction in leveraging. Thus, of the 100 companies reviewed, 39 reduced their leveraging in 2016 in comparison with the first year of the study. There were various scales of reduction, from less than 1 percentage point up to 30 points, with a mean of 10.7 and a standard deviation (SD) of 9.2. The majority (61) increased their leveraging, from 1 percentage point up to 40 (mean 17.0, SD 11).

One indicator of the limited development of the domestic debt market is that 38 companies in the sample reported that they did not use this source of funding during the period. This included two of the largest firms in the sample. The ten which used domestic and/or foreign debt, financed 46% financed 46% of their assets via this means with a SD of 12.3, and these are among the most highly leveraged.

Seventeen companies accrued net losses over the period as a whole, with a very wide variation, from the equivalent of 0.4% of their capital to up to 50%. There is no obvious relationship with any aspect of their financial structure. It is noteworthy that just one of these companies made intensive use of credit as a source of financing.

Segmentation of the sample

The sample was divided into three categories in accordance with the principal source of financing: capital, debt issue and credit. Each set includes a different number of companies due to the selection criteria, which are set out below.

Financing through capital. It would appear logical for the majority of companies to reduce moral hazard problems by financing themselves essentially by their own resources. In other words, on average during the period, two-thirds (67 companies) used 50% or more capital as a source of finance (with a mean of 69.4%, SD 12.0).

Taking this into account, it was decided to analyse the 61 companies whose indebtedness increased, and then to class these according to their principal source of financing in relative terms.

Capital intensive are those companies which are above average for the sample, which accounts for 34 companies with the following characteristics:

- twenty-one never supplemented their finances by issuing debt;
- thirteen issued debt, but only five used it for between 5% and 16% of their total financing, and none more than this;
- all 34 used credit, half used it for between 15% and 29%, none more than this;
- nine resorted to suppliers as a source of financing, with only one company among those making heavy use of supplier financing;
- all except one are relatively smaller companies in the sample. As a whole (without the largest), they only represent 14.7% of the assets, less than 0.5% each;
- only four companies had net losses throughout the whole period, three of these to a minor extent (between 1.5% and 2.2% in relation to their capital);
- the rest had positive but variable results with an average ROE[14] of 9.1% (SD 5.3); only two companies were among the most profitable during the whole period;
- regarding operations, sales income fell as a proportion of total assets in 18 cases. The average fall was slightly less than half; however, in 16 cases this proportion increased, by 50% on average;
- throughout the period, 23 companies reduced the proportion of fixed assets (plant, machinery and equipment) in relation to total assets, therefore only 11 increased their investment in fixed assets. This implies that the majority of companies financed by their own resources increased their investment in other assets (investment in other companies, intangibles and commercial loans);
- according to the sample, this set consists mainly of manufacturers and service providers, followed by construction, therefore it is not possible to tell whether capital financing was more heavily used by a particular sector.

In summary, the results are very varied and on occasion contradictory. Nevertheless, it is possible to say that capital-intensive industries tend to supplement their finances with credit more than debt issue. Few had losses, although they are not very profitable; there was no clear relationship with the behaviour of their income and they are among those displaying a tendency to reduce their fixed assets. This is a relatively low risk subset, but the number of companies with reduced income is a concern.

Financing by means of debt issue. The selection of this set was based on those whose principal source of finance was the debt securities market (short and long terms), including those with a higher proportion of capital, but without exceeding 50% of total financing. Only 12 companies fell into this set.

Companies with heavy debt security financing had the following characteristics:

- two of these had slightly more capital financing, but all had more than 30% of their funds in debt securities. The average for the 12 was 43.7% (SD 12.3);
- half were among the most highly leveraged of the whole survey, hence they also used a relatively high proportion of credit to finance their operations;
- six used 10% or more supplier credit in their total financing;
- since the largest was in this set, together these 12 companies accounted for 27% of total assets, but if the largest is excluded they only account for 8.8%, or 0.81% each on average;
- they accounted for practically half of the funds from debt issue, including short and long term;
- this small set includes, on the one hand, six of the companies with net losses (two with the largest losses), and on the other hand, five of the most profitable (paradoxically, the two most profitable);
- in seven of these companies, sales income fell by, on average, 30 percentage points in proportion to total assets between 2006 and 2016, while in the others income increased by 46%;
- in terms of the type of financial assets, in seven cases there was a reduction in the proportion of fixed to total assets. This reduction was 25% on average between 2006 and 2016, while in the remaining five it increased by 27%. The proportion of fixed assets to long-term assets follows the same trend;
- it is noteworthy that 7 of the 12 companies are service based, 3 are in the manufacturing sector, while there were no commercial companies in this set.

The relationships are more ambiguous in this set than in the previous, but an obvious point must be made on the narrowness of the debt market as a means of finance for national companies. It is a very concentrated market accessed by just a few companies. Logically, there is a relationship between debt issue and leveraging, particularly because this type of company also makes use of credit.

There is a notable absence of any relationship with profitability in this set, since it includes the companies with the highest profits, as well as the highest losses, which once again muddies the picture since half saw increased sales, while the other half saw a drop. It is a set in which there are several companies with high risks from the fall in operational income and accumulated losses.

Intensive credit users. This set of 15 companies uses credit as the principal means of financing, and they were selected using the same method as the debt security users. Their main features are:

six of the companies did not use debt to supplement their financing, and only four had a greater use of capital than credit;

only three of these are within the most highly leveraged bracket, two principally supplemented their funds through suppliers and the other made use of debt securities;

this set accounts for 17% of the assets of the sample and includes the second largest company. If this is excluded the proportion drops to 9.7%, meaning an average of 0.69% per company;

so far as profitability is concerned, there are four companies in this set which experienced net losses during the period, which were between 8% and 15% of shareholder's equity. The remainder experience modest gains, except for two whose ROE is among the highest of the sample;

as a proportion of total assets, sales income fell in 11 out of 15 companies in the set. In 2016 the drop was on average around 45 percentage points over the 2006 level. The four with a higher rate only attained 17% on average;

nine companies reduced their fixed assets as a percentage of their total assets; on average this reduction was 40 percentage points. However, in the remaining six this proportion increased by 73%. Both of the above were in the full period from 2006 to 2016;

eight were from the manufacturing sector, three from construction, but none from services.

In summary, companies which use credit as a source of financing do not supplement it with debt or from suppliers; therefore, they are restricted to their own funds and credit. They generally obtain positive but modest results. There is an accentuated tendency to reduced sales income in proportion to investment and there is no clearly identified trend where investment in fixed assets is concerned. As in the other two categories, there must be a concern over the number of companies whose income has fallen, since this jeopardises payment of debts, especially bank debts.

The most heavily financed by suppliers. There is a set of ten companies whose primary or secondary source of financing is from suppliers, but it is the principal source in only two cases. The characteristics of this set are:

financial contributions to each company range between 20% and 60%, with a mean of 33% (SD 11.3);

the issue of debt was the primary source in just one case, in two it was in credit while the primary source for the remaining seven was their own resources. Thus, the first three are also among the most highly leveraged;

it is the only set clearly identified with a sector: six of these are commercial companies, and of the remainder, two are in manufacturing, one in air transport and the other is a house builder;

three experienced net losses, five had modest profits while two had high gains;

six companies reported a fall in sales as a percentage of assets with an average fall of 20% per company. Companies with increased sales saw a 10% rise on average;

eight reduced their fixed assets in proportion to their long-term assets, which points to an increase in assets such as investments in other companies, intangibles and commercial loans to third parties.

In summary, supplier funding is essential for companies in the commercial sector. Companies principally financed by capital also use it as a supplement. Since there are losses as well as gains there is no clear relationship with profitability. There is also a certain tendency towards a drop in sales income in relation to total investment, as well as the acquisition of long-term assets other than fixed assets.

Conclusions

The current development model has meant that in the present situation, large companies operating in Mexico have increased their indebtedness to an extraordinary extent. The extent, pace and structure of indebtedness of private companies in recent years is unprecedented. In less than ten years, its percentage has doubled in relation to GDP, even though it remains one of the lowest rates in the world.

International monetary and financial conditions have stimulated the extended availability of funding for companies; nevertheless, these conditions are changing and there is no certainty how longer it will continue. When the world's key central banks cease to operate flexible monetary policies, access to funding will become difficult, especially to the foreign financing which has seen the most growth.

The growing flow of resources to companies has led to a very significant change in the structure of their liabilities. Private banking based in Mexico has seen a notable reduction in its share in favour of foreign financing, particularly financing from bond issues. Another important change is the growing issue of debt in the domestic market, which was insignificant until a few years ago, but is now equivalent to nearly 4% of GDP. These changes have led to company finance in Mexico developing a dependence on debt issue as the mechanism of choice, with a preference for foreign sources.

The analysis of 100 companies domiciled in Mexico has reinforced the idea that indebtedness grew more than corporate own funds; therefore, there was an overall increase in the degree of leveraging. This fact coincides with a general fall in profitability, in income in proportion to assets, as well as in fixed asset investments.

On the one hand, these trends threaten healthy corporate development because it would seem that companies are taking on excessive risk, and on the other hand, they threaten the recovery of the domestic economy because if such a significant set of companies shows discouraging figures, there is no reason why it should be very different for the rest of the economy.

Additionally, in the midst of global economic uncertainty and stagnation, foreign currency debt implies high debt repayment risks, especially abroad.

Analysis by firm demonstrates that the trends are real, but inconsistent, since many companies display opposite tendencies. There is no evidence of clear patterns in the structure of financing or in sectoral trends of profitability and investment. Nevertheless, this does not obviate the large risks from growing indebtedness.

Indeed, it is cause for concern that of the 61 companies that did increase their debt, more than half (36) experienced falling operating profits in proportion to their assets, while 13 had net losses during the period. Considering that these are large conglomerates, which have complex commercial, financial and property networks in Mexico and abroad, it is logical that in the event of further deterioration to their financial situation, there might be negative systemic impacts on the Mexican economy.

Thus, global economic conditions do not appear more favourable in the short and medium terms. The global economy follows no clear course. There are indications of both recovery and uncertainty (FMI 2017).

If the world economy recovers, it is possible that a number of companies will be able to recoup income, but they will certainly have problems with financing because economic recovery brings with it the normalisation of monetary policies, in other words higher interest rates and decreased liquidity. On the other hand, if uncertainty prevails and stagnation continues, indebted companies may encounter demand problems, the exchange rate risk will remain and there will be difficulties generating sufficient cash flows to repay the debt, particularly foreign exchange, which could further compromise their financial viability and that of their creditors, suppliers and partners. Recovery and stagnation both entail their own risks due to the increase and concentration of financing in such a short time.

Notes

1 Summaries of recent approaches to indebtedness and company valuation in the present context can be checked in Jarmuzek and Rozenova (2017) and Financial Stability Board (2015).

2 Only corporations with financial figures for their Mexican operations have been included, therefore large foreign multinational companies have been excluded, such as automotive or electronic industry assemblers, which are heavyweights in the domestic economy.

3 Although the financing of private companies has doubled in a relatively short period in relation to domestic product, the figure – 29% – is much lower than the average for emerging economies, and even more so for that of developed countries. This rate is even among the lowest rates in Latin America. The

figures for all countries reporting information can be checked at BIS Statistics Explorer: http://stats.bis.org/statx/toc/LBS.html

4 Private sector companies include private individuals with business activities. NBFI include non-bank financial companies, multipurpose financial institutions, lessors, factoring companies, general warehouses, credit unions, microfinance companies, cooperative savings societies and Financiera Rural (the state-owned rural development financier).

5 In the domestic debt market, approximately 92% of debt securities issued by private companies are for more than one year; however, in mid-2017, approximately 29% of debt was for repayment in less than 364 days. See Bank of Mexico: www.banxico.org.mx/SieInternet/consultarDirectorioInternetAction.do?sector=7&accion=consultarCuadro&idCuadro=CF301&locale=es

6 Even development bank funds and development funds channelled to companies by second-tier private banks are focussed on large companies, since the final decision on the allocation of funds is partly theirs. For more information, see Table R9 of the Full-Service Banking Statistics in the National Banking and Securities Commission (CNBV) information portfolios: "Cartera actividad empresarial: saldo por tamaño de empresa con apoyo de Fondos y Banca de Desarrollo. Portafolio total" [Commercial activity portfolio: balance by company size with the support of Development Banking and Funds. Total Portfolio].

7 The information can be seen under the R0 table. "Cartera actividad empresarial: número de créditos, acreditados y saldo por tamaño de empresa. Portafolio total" [Commercial activity portfolio: number of credits, recipients and balance by company size. Total Portfolio], also from the CNBV. It is worth remembering that the allocation of second-tier funds channelled by the development bank and private bank development funds appears in this latter's financial statements; therefore, the assumption set out at the top of the paragraph is more realistic.

8 There has been a large gap between foreign and domestic interest rates throughout the period of the research and, in recent months, it has further widened. For example, the average difference in Mexican monetary policy rates vis-à-vis the Eurozone, the USA and Russia in the period 2010–2016 has been 4 percentage points. With the increase in the Mexican rate in September 2017, the gap widened to seven points.

9 Even though it is not a focus of this research, it is worth giving some idea of the exchange rate risk, as foreign currency credit from private banks to large companies in Mexico at the end of 2016 reached 32% of the total. This was of course at interest rates lower than credit in Mexican pesos. The information can be seen at table R2 of the information portfolios of the CNBV. "Cartera actividad empresarial: tasas de interés, plazos y saldo por tamaño de empresa. Portafolio Total" [Commercial activity portfolio: interest rates, terms and balances by company size. Total Portfolio].

10 It is evident that the excessive indebtedness of the large private companies is not just a risk affecting them individually, rather it places the economy as a whole at risk by various channels. The analysis of this phenomenon lies outside the scope of this research. The Financial Stability Board (2015) and Jarmuzek and Rozenova (2017) provide a reminder of these risks.

11 The CNBV periodically publishes its database of Financial Savings and Financing in Mexico. Figures up to the first quarter of 2017 can be viewed at: www.gob.mx/cnbv/articulos/reporte-de-ahorro-financiero-y-financiamiento-en-mexico-a-marzo-de-2017?idiom=es

12 This term includes financial liabilities with a cost attached: credits, debt securities and various creditors. It does not include other financial liabilities or other credits without costs attached.

13 The lack of information for analysis is another very important risk. The Bank of Mexico (2014: 51) states: "There is no public information on companies in general which have issued debt abroad, which would be necessary for a precise analysis of the risks that have been assumed, but information is available on the companies quoted in the Mexican Stock Exchange". It also makes it clear that the majority of foreign corporate bond placements are made privately, in compliance with Rule 144A and Regulation S of the United States Securities and Exchange Commission, which make it possible not to register foreign securities.

14 For the return on equity (ROE) calculation in this section alone, the profits for the whole period were added and were divided first between the average shareholder's equity for the period, and afterwards by the number of years. This is the most precise method for the purposes of this section.

References

Alter, A. and Elekdag, S. (2016) 'Emerging Market Corporate Leverage and Global Financial Conditions', *IMF Working Paper*, 16/243.

Bank for International Settlements (2017) *BIS Statistics Explorer*, viewed 13 September 2017, from http://stats.bis.org/statx/toc/LBS.html.

Estadísticas, Mercados Financieros (2017) from www.banxico.org.mx/sistema-financiero/estadisticas/mercados-financieros--tipo-ca.html.

Bank of México (2014) *Reporte sobre el Sistema Financiero 2014*, from www.banxico.org.mx/publicaciones-y-discursos/publicaciones/informes-periodicos/reporte-sf/%7BD65B2A12-08BF-ED51-33B6-9AECB09DED2E%7D.pdf.

CEPAL (2017) *Capital Flows to Latin America and the Caribbean: Recent Developments*, ECLAC, U.N. www.cepal.org/en/publications/42059-capital-flows-latin-america-and-caribbean-recent-developments

CNBV (2017) *Portafolio de Información*, from www.cnbv.gob.mx/Paginas/PortafolioDeInformacion.aspx.

Deutsche Bank Research (2013) 'Corporate Bond Issuance in Europe', EU Global Monitor Finance, January.

Draghi, M. (2017) 'Introductory Statement, President of the European Central Bank', *ECB Press Conference*, Frankfurt am Main, 26 October.

Economatica (2017) General data accessed in August.

Feyen, E., Ghosh, S., Kibuuka, K. and Farazi, S. (2016) 'Global Liquidity and External Bond Issuance in Emerging Markets and Developing Economies', *Policy Research Working Paper*; No. WPS 7363, World Bank Group, Washington, DC.

Financial Stability Board (2015) 'Corporate Funding Structures and Incentives', *Final Report*, August.

FMI (2015) '¿Debería preocuparnos el apalancamiento empresarial de los mercados emergentes?', *Informe sobre la Estabilidad Financiera Mundial*, viewed 1 October 2017, from www.imf.org/~/media/Websites/IMF/imported...issues/.../2015/.../_sums.ashx.

FMI (2017) *Global Financial Stability Report: Is Growth at Risk?*, October, Washington, DC.

INEGI *Banco de Información Económica*, from www.inegi.org.mx/sistemas/bie/.

Jarmuzek, M. and Rozenova, R. (2017) 'Excessive Private Sector Leverage and Its Drivers: Evidence from Advanced Economies', *IMF Working Paper*, WP/17/72.

Kuroda, H. (2017) *Quantitative and Qualitative Monetary Easing and Economic Theory*, Governor of the Bank of Japan, Speech at the University of Zurich in Switzerland, November 13.

Modigliani, F. and Miller, M. H. (1958) 'The Cost of Capital, Corporation Finance and the Theory of Investment', *American Economic Review*, 48 (3), 261–297.

Sobrun, J. and Turner. P. (2015) 'Bond Markets and Monetary Policy Dilemmas for the Emerging Markets', *BIS Working Papers*, No 508, August.

Vtyurina, S., Robles, A. and Sutton, B. (2017) 'A License to Issue (Anywhere): Patterns and Drivers of Corporate Bonds in Latin America', *IMF Working Paper*, WP/17/157, July.

14 Financial capital flows and FOREX activities in Mexico

Finance or speculation?

Noemi Levy

The Mexican peso (MXN) has been the highest traded currency of developing economies, ranking first in Latin America, even though the Mexican economy's performance has been rather weak in relation to the regional average and with respect to other emerging economies, especially throughout the era of financialisation.

In this chapter, we want to understand why Mexico's currency reached this position and how it has affected the financial and productive systems' stability. The working hypothesis here is that Mexico's insertion into the international market was deep and broad because it coupled its productive and financial structures with the North American region (specifically to the USA), thus laying the groundwork for its currency's internationalisation. However, this was not enough to stabilise the Mexican financial system, since the volume of foreign exchange (FOREX) transactions involving MXN was extremely high and Mexico's Central Bank could not handle them.

The outstanding features of Mexico's economy compared to those of other emerging countries are its commercial openness and the dominance of foreign capital in most of its productive and financial sectors, with almost limitless access to international units of account (US dollars) through foreign investment and Mexican FOREX transactions involving the MXN. However, it has still not attained financial stability.

In this context, although FOREX involving the peso provide high volumes of liquidity to the Mexican government and corporations operating domestically, this has not strengthened Mexico's capital market. These FOREX trades take place on the margins of the Mexican economy, through cross-border transactions led by non-reporting institutions to diversify their balance sheets and are so huge that they neutralise the Mexican Central Bank's ability to stabilise the exchange rate. Therefore, foreign institutions' moods and extra-economic events become important determinants of capital flows and liquidity for the Mexican economy and, in general, for emerging economies.

Based on this, it is argued that two contradictory forces operated in the Mexican economy during the financialisation era. On the one hand, the

Mexican unit of account has internationalised to manage its economic openness through Mexican private monetary debt convertibility, which accesses the US dollar, without developing domestic capital markets; and, on the other hand, countercyclical policies and regulations to stabilise the financial system have been neutralised.

This chapter is organised into five sections. Following this introduction, the second section discusses payment settlements in the post-Bretton-Woods-System financial market and their impact on emerging economies. The third section analyses Mexico's financial openness and its insertion into the international economy. The fourth section reviews MXN-FOREX, highlighting their impact on financial stability, and the fifth section states the main conclusions.

Financial rearrangements in the gold demonetisation era

The end of dollar-gold convertibility (1971) led to mayor institutional changes in the financial system that modified the perception of money in the economy, giving way to the creation of an international monetary system driven by private debt. Money emerged as a contract pure and simple, totally divorced from commodities, revealing its basic essence: a sign value that only represents value; and, more importantly, therefore, private monetary deposits can cancel debt, eliminating any possibility of central government control of money supply. Thereby, money is issued on demand, and finance is clearly separated from savings, which is a result of investment.

These institutional settings led to the full recognition that money is structurally endogenous, a theoretical stance forcefully put forward by the circuitists (Graziani 2003; Lavoie 2003; Moore 1989; Rochon 1999),[1] creating a consensus that central banks are unable to control money supply and reaffirming that high-powered money is not required to settle debts (Graziani 2003).

The spread of private-monetary-debt dominance to the international financial market had various consequences, notably the divorce of finance from savings (Avdjiev, McCauley & Song 2015; Borio & Disyatat 2015), trade surplus being displaced by foreign investment flows (direct and portfolio investment) as a means of accessing international money and emerging currencies' private bank debt becoming highly convertible in the international market, modifying developing economies' access to international reserves.

In this new international scenario, the "pure credit theory of money" was replaced by the "monetary theory of credit", in which money is no longer viewed in terms of credit transactions, and the clearing system governs financial markets, cancelling claims and debts and carrying forward the differences (Schumpeter 1954:717).

In the international system, bank deposits became the leading means of payment and acquired the ability to destroy debts; credit creation internationalised and was led by private agents on demand, changing the dominant causality from credits to deposits. In addition, production and trade went beyond national boundaries, which means that production was driven by global supply chains. A major characteristic of this production arrangement is that demand detached from supply (Bellofiore et al. 2011). Under these circumstances, finance is defined as "incurring liabilities and acquiring assets of different countries",[2] breaking free from the "triple coincidence in international finance" (see Avdjiev et al. 2015).

In addition, debts expanded more rapidly than production and banks' balance sheets (and those of financial and non-financial corporations) inflated and became highly dependent on liquidity provisions, whether solvent or not.[3] Illiquidity was prevented by matching payment commitments with income or claims or assets, opening a wide field for hedging activities to prevent illiquidity.

In this context, hedging mechanisms attained utmost importance in the global financial system, dominated by flexible or semi-flexible exchange rates, coupled with flexible interest rates, transferring financial risks to private agents (Eatwell & Taylor 2000). More specifically, hedging mechanisms assumed the task of preventing financial losses (or reducing risks), which, however, could also unleash speculative activity by betting what prices would prevail in the future or taking advantage of price trends in financial markets.

Historically, hedging activity acquired importance at the beginning of the twentieth century, when the gold bullion standard weakened, and after the demise of the Bretton Woods System that demonetised gold and reintroduced flexible exchange rates. In this context, hedging mechanisms spread to prevent financial risk; however, they are not free from speculation and instability; thus, "not all these hedges are speculation" (Toporowski 2017). This argument challenges Keynes's assumptions of capital market operation in his *General Theory* (Chapter XII 1936) and moves closer to Minsky's financial instability hypothesis (1975, 1986).

In this context, commercial banks are important mechanisms for accessing international liquidity to settle debts. This takes place through commercial banks holding reserve currency in the form of commercial bank deposits in international units of reserve; commercial banks' willingness to innovate against reserve currencies, which means international bank's willingness and ability to convert other assets, bonds and other currencies into the international unit of reserve currency; willingness of commercial banks of reserve currency unit (US dollars) to extend credit; and countries that issue international reserve currencies, developing current account deficits to supply reserves to the rest of the world (Toporowski 2017).

Liquidity access in the various forms described above is especially relevant for small and developing countries that do not issue international reserve units. Also, finance in their local currency is limited; consequently, they are highly dependent on international finance.

Emerging countries' position in the international financial system continued to be highly dependent on external finance even though some countries' local currencies became internationalised. Under this new system, one currency, US dollar, is dominant and maintains "exorbitant privileges" *vis-à-vis* current account disequilibria (De Cecco 2012:2).[4]

Therefore, the hegemon continues to extract surplus from non-hegemonic countries, sparking disagreements over the mechanism whereby this takes place. In terms of Latin America, in the twentieth century, two views were put forward. The ECLAC (Economic Commission for Latin America and the Caribbean) hypothesis of "unequal terms of trade" (1949) and the *dependentistas* view (Marini 1968) that followed Luxemburg's arguments (1913), coining the term "underdevelopment", from which it follows that these economies are unable to achieve development due to surplus extraction.

Today's discussion has moved to the "monetary hierarchy" argument (de Paula et al. 2017; Harvey 2009; Kaltenbrunner & Panceira 2017; among others), based on the idea that international money hierarchies exacerbate uneven development. This extends the Latin American dependency theory argument, based on the concept of "underdevelopment", which claims that these economies are unable to close their economic gap with developed countries; the difference here is that surplus extraction takes places through the financial sector. Kaltenbrunner and Panceira summarise this argument as follows:

> The asymmetric and subordinated international integration, which constrains national strategies of development and self-determination, has traditionally been analysed in the context *of trade relations and foreign direct investment (at the core of which stood the ability to develop autonomous processes of technological innovation* [author's emphasis] ... However, these 'real' economic relations have been complemented, if not outpaced, by the growth in international financial markets and ECEs' [emerging capitalist economies'] integration into them ... Just as their integration through product markets, these surging financial relations have been characterised by dependency, subordination, and hierarchies.
>
> (Kaltenbrunner & Panceira 2017:4)

In the same vein, it is argued that the international financial market is a two-tier system, in which reserve and non-reserve currencies operate; and, as mentioned above, the US dollar is the international unit of account but, instead of bank notes, liquidity relies on "commercial bank credits backed by bank loans to firms and governments"; and in which "most of the debts in US dollars are in smaller, poorer countries, because larger, richer countries can finance more of their needs with internal debt rather than borrowing from abroad" (Toporowski 2017:124).

Therefore, international markets provide finance to financial and non-financial corporations and central agencies, which can expand production and accumulation, but they are also used to "refinance" debt. Therefore, this process takes place by converting liabilities of one currency into others, lengthening the liability term structure that, altogether, reduces financing costs and provides long-term liquidity to the financial system. These operations can alleviate external liquidity constraints, but are not exempt from speculative activities and financial instability; from this, it is concluded that "not all international credit operations are 'speculation'. But not all refinancing is without crisis" (Toporowski 2017).

In this context, emerging economies highly dependent on international credits based on US dollars are subject to international institutions' moods, and this creates financial instability. Therefore, the immediate outcome of emerging economies' liquidity expansion beyond domestic production boundaries can lead to financial instability. This discussion is developed in the next section.

The financialisation of the Mexican economy and its insertion into the world economy

The emerging economies were financialised by opening the external account in the context of fading domestic borders for the productive, commercial and financial sectors; this was the basis for the free movement of financial flows and began with the breakdown of the Bretton Woods System. In this section, I will discuss the characteristics of the economic opening through the Mexican economy's external account.

Financial variables became dominant in developing countries, particularly in Latin America, based on an export-driven accumulation model. In my opinion, this has failed because of the structural deficit in the current account, which has been a structural element in the region's economies.[5]

In the 1980s in particular, in light of the foreign debt crisis, Mexico started off on the path to a profound trade opening, not always reciprocated by its foreign counterparts (the USA). In that same decade, exports became more dynamic, combined with economic paralysis, a foreign trade surplus and a lower current account deficit. All this was followed by a financial and productive opening in 1990 and 1993, respectively (see Table 14.1).

One particular trait of Mexico's export-driven production model is stagnant gross fixed capital formation amidst accelerated export growth specialised in manufactured goods, combined with primary goods (oil). This created the first paradox of the organisation of Mexico's production in the neoliberal era, which combines the production and export of manufactured goods, including goods with cutting-edge technology, with low gross fixed capital formation. The result is a production model organised on the basis of *maquiladora* plants, which import and assemble duty-free components for export. This prevents industry from acting as a pole of attraction for the rest of the economy, thus reproducing the dependency of manufacturing of the import-substitution period (Fajnzylber 1987/1989).

This contradiction explains the Mexican economy's huge trade opening (the ratio of exports plus imports to GDP) that expanded rapidly over the last four decades, and by over 50% and 60% in the twenty-first century (see Table 14.1). Thus, the dynamic sector of the economy, manufacturing exports, is accompanied by a growing number of imports, which validates Arvadiej, McCauley & Song (2015) and Borio & Distayat hypothesis (2015) that production has spread over several countries and regions through global production chains, dominated by pyramid-shaped structures driven by the developed countries due to the concentration of technological advances and their domination of know-how (De Cecco 2012).

A second important aspect that changed production was remittances sent by workers from outside Mexico, mainly the United States, which became a driver of consumption. Transfers, on the income side of the current account under remittances between 2000–2009 and 2010–2016, came to approximately 2% of GDP and 8% and 7% of exports, respectively (see Table 13.1). This implies that the size of the domestic market came to depend on the income of workers outside Mexico.

The third element is that the rent paid to non-resident agents, annotated under outflow in the current account,[6] represents profits, both reinvested and remitted, and interest that does not come back into the country. On average, in the 1990s and so far in the twenty-first century, this item has represented approximately 3% of GDP per year (see Table 14.1) in a context of low national and foreign interest rates. This is an indicator of the growing participation of foreign capital in profits produced in Mexico, which are transferred to the rest of the world, invigorating production elsewhere.

A fourth difference is the growing, steady influx of foreign capital into the Mexican financial system. In the 1980s, total liabilities were greater than current account deficit financing needs; and they increased even more in the first and second decades of the twenty-first century, after slight reductions in the 1990s, explained by the 1994 Mexican crisis (see Table 14.1).

The growing influx of capital to Mexico's financial system indicates a relative autonomy of financial flows *vis-à-vis* the Mexican economy's productive activity, which nevertheless did not become fully independent. Specifically, after the 1994 financial crisis, in light of the North American Free Trade Agreement (NAFTA), the volume of liabilities in the form of foreign direct investment (FDI) grew rapidly.[7] This can be explained by the entry of large foreign corporations into the Mexican economy via mergers with large domestic companies and acquisitions by foreign capital.[8] This led to a huge centralisation of capital (Bellofiore et al. 2011), with strong horizontal linkages to the rest of the world, accompanied by an international concentration of capital (global production chains) that weakened internal linkages and introduced a profound foreign penetration of production.

Table 14.1 Mexico's insertion to the world economy, average in relation to GDP, in percentage

	1980/89	*1990/99*	*2000/99*	*2010/16*
Exports + Imports	32.9	42.7	54.1	64.3
Exports – Imports	2.9	-1.6	-1.7	-1.4
Current Account +/-	1.0	-3.3	-1.3	-1.5
Gross fixed investment	20.2	18.2	21.2	21.8
Income (current account)	20.0	22.5	29.0	34.3
Exports	17.9	20.5	26.2	31.5
Transferences	0.9	1.1	2.1	2.0
Outflows (current account)	21.1	25.8	30.3	35.8
Imports	15.0	22.2	27.9	32.8
Rents	6.1	3.6	2.4	3.0
Financial account	*1980/89*	*1990/99*	*2000/99*	*2010/16*
Liabilities	3.7	5.0	3.5	6.4
FDI	1.4	1.9	2.9	2.6
FPI	0.0	2.1	0.5	3.7
Other investment	2.4	0.9	0.1	0.2
Assets	-0.1	-0.2	-0.1	-0.1
FDI	0.0	0.0	-0.5	-1.0
FPI	-0.2	-0.5	-0.5	-0.2
FPI liability composition		**2.1**	**0.5**	**3.7**
Public sector		0.7	0.0	2.8
Bonds & notes issued in international market		0.6	-0.3	1.0
Money market instruments		0.0	0.3	1.8
Private sector		1.4	0.0	0.9
Bonds & notes issued in international markets		0.5	0.0	0.7
Money market instruments		0.9	0.1	0.2

Source: Author's own calculation based on Banco de Mexico, Payment Balance, MBP5 data. Data of access: 01/08/2017.

Foreign portfolio investment (FPI) is another important item that figures strongly on the liability side of the current account during the financialisation period. It is made up of short-term, non-loan, very volatile financial flows, attracted by instruments issued essentially by the public sector and to a lesser extent by the private sector. On average, the ratio of FPI to GDP was very high in the early 1990s (see Table 14.1). This can be explained by the entry of capital prior to Mexico's 1994 financial crisis as a result of the opening of the Mexican Stock Market (BMV – Bolsa Mexicana de Valores). A second period of strong FPI expansion came after the 2008 Global Financial Crisis (GFC) in the context that the dropping yields of the US financial market. The public sector was the biggest bond issuer, and private bond issues rose sharply after the GFC (see Table 14.1). This can be explained by the liberalisation of the Mexican money market in 1990 and, later, by the intense government activity in financial markets to renegotiate the foreign debt and stabilise Mexico's currency.

One additional piece of information is that the typical financialisation activity in developed countries, done through bond transactions, in Mexico became a source of diversifying portfolios, averaging 1.7% of GDP (1% in the public sector and 0.7% in the private sector) between 2010 and 2016. This is explained by the expansion of *translatina* corporations (multinationals based on capital from Latin American countries) and other multinationals in Mexico.

Based on this, there is no doubt that the financial market internationalised in the context of a profound transnationalisation of production and trade opening. This required growing liquidity in international units of value (US dollars), acquired through international debt instruments, mainly short-term financial investment, subject to great instability (Harvey 2009).

FOREX transactions and their impact on financial stability

The Mexican economy's financial opening was accompanied by another very specific factor, the internationalisation of the MXN. The net-net calculation, which eliminates double counting between dealers who carry out transborder and local transactions, makes global observation of transactions in each currency possible. The liquidity from daily average MXN-FOREX related transactions increased 13 times between 2001 and 2013, and, although they decreased in 2016, they were nine times higher than 2001 (see Table 14.2). The expansion of FOREX in MXN was faster than that of FOREX as a whole. So, we are witnessing explosive growth of FOREX transactions in MXN on the international market (see Table 14.2). Despite the low ratio of MXN-FOREX to total FOREX – in the year with the greatest turnover of MXN-FOREX, they barely reached 2.5% of the total (see Table 14.2) – in 2013, MXN-FOREX reached the eighth position worldwide (higher than all the other emerging economies), and, in 2016, 11th place, surpassed by China, which led the emerging countries. So, a first element is that Mexico's currency became an international asset that strongly increased the convertibility of monetary liabilities denominated in pesos on the world market.

The magnitude of the explosion of MXN-FOREX compared to productive sector variables indicates that these transactions are relatively unlinked to the behaviour of "real" variables. Specifically, the MXN-FOREX ratio to GDP increased eight-fold between 2001 and 2013, and six-fold between 2001 and 2016. The ratio of MXN-FOREX to the trade opening quadrupled between 2001 and 2013 and almost sextupled between 2001 and 2016. The ratio of MXN-FOREX liquidity to total liabilities (quantified in the external financial account) quadrupled between 2001 and 2013 and almost sextupled between 2001 and 2016 (for all of the above, see Table 14.2).

Table 14.2 Tendencies and composition of World and MXN FOREX transactions

	Tendencies and composition of World and MXN FOREX transactions					
	2001	*2004*	*2007*	*2010*	*2013*	*2016*
Expansion 2001=1						
MXN FOREX	1.0	2.0	3.9	5.0	13.4	9.6
Total FOREX	1.0	1.6	2.7	3.2	4.3	4.1
MXN/FOREX total (%)	0.8	1.1	1.2	1.3	2.5	1.9
	Global market exchange liquidity and productive indicators					
FOREX MXN/GDP	5.1	9.6	13.7	17.3	39.2	33.9
FOREX MXN/ X+M	10.3	17.7	24.0	28.4	60.8	43.3
FOREX MXN/ Liabilities	113.7	262.1	272.2	222.6	483.9	635.6
	MXN FOREX transactions by locations (%)					
Local transactions	42.7	35.4	39.6	31.2	40.2	33.3
Cross Border	57.3	64.6	60.4	68.8	59.8	66.7
	MXN FOREX by instruments (%)					
Spot	50.1	56.2	37.4	36.3	42.0	44.6
Forward	6.7	8.4	11.7	10.8	10.2	12.3
FOREX Swaps	43.3	35.3	50.9	47.5	42.8	36.8
Monetary Swaps	0.0	0.0	0.0	0.7	0.6	0.2
Options and others	0.0	0.0	0.0	4.6	4.5	6.0
	MXN FOREX by institutional counterparties (%)					
w/ reporting dealers	59.7	65.7	34.6	40.7	33.3	34.1
with other financial institutions	32.4	26.7	52.5	44.6	60.0	58.3
w/ non-financial customers	7.9	7.5	12.9	15.0	6.7	7.5
	Distributional location of emerging countries FOREX (net-gross base), %					
China	0.0	0.0	0.2	0.4	0.7	1.1
India	0.2	0.3	0.9	0.5	0.5	0.5
Korea	0.6	0.8	0.8	0.9	0.7	0.6
Mexico	0.5	0.6	0.4	0.3	0.5	0.3
Brazil	0.3	0.1	0.1	0.3	0.3	0.3
Chile	0.1	0.1	0.1	0.1	0.2	0.1

Source: Author's calculations based on BIS, 2001, 2004, 2007, 2010, 2013 and 2016.

A more detailed analysis of the location of the FOREX transactions, their composition and the institutions involved shows that the opening has been very rapid, susceptible to great instability. In terms of location, regardless of the nationality and residence of the agents involved, FOREX in pesos is dominated by transborder transactions, that is, they are mainly carried out with agents outside Mexico (see Table 14.2). At the same time, looking at them by kind of instrument, between 2001 and 2016, FOREX swaps predominate, followed by spot transactions. This follows the world trend, dominated by currencies that operate as international units of value.

If this is combined with institutional counterparts, we find that the "Other Financial Institutions" had the greatest participation, particularly since 2007. And these institutions seek to diversify their portfolios (Rime & Schrimps 2013), which makes their de-stabilising effect on the local financial system even clearer.

Between 2013 and 2016, non-reporting banks dominated the category of "Other Financial Institutions", representing almost half the transactions of this group, followed by institutional investors, hedge funds and proprietary trading firms (PTF), which represent between one-third and one-fourth of these transactions. In last place, we find the public sector of institutional investors (development banks). As to be expected, the non-reporting banks concentrate their operations in FOREX swaps, as does the public sector. Private institutional investors and hedge funds concentrate on cash transactions. Therefore, the institutional counterparts that use transactions involving MXN seeking to diversify their portfolios and make financial profits through exchange rate operations destabilise operations in the local market and lead the exchange and interest rates to react to the perceptions of financial institutions not located in Mexico. Their main reason for operating in these currencies is to diversify their balance sheets and financial earnings.

One final piece of information that indicates the instability generated by the liquidity of the FOREX market is the small size of Mexico's financial centre. An accounting of the currency exchange operations from the local perspective (discounting the duplications between local dealers, measured on a net-gross basis) shows that the financial centres in Latin America, and specifically in Mexico, are smaller than those of the emerging economies of Asia. In 2001, Mexico and Korea had financial centres of similar size, but that changed over the following years. The magnitude of FOREX operations in Mexico has stagnated, while in the other economies, it has increased, particularly in China, followed by South Korea and India. However, Mexico's was the largest financial centre in the region.

The almost unlimited access to international liquidity generated by the internationalisation of Mexico's currency was not enough to stabilise the financial system. One example of this was the movement of the nominal exchange rate, overvalued in the 2002–2004, 2005–2007 and 2011–2013 periods (see Table 14.3). The peso devaluated in 2008–2010 and 2014–2016 due, respectively, to the GFC and US attempts to normalise its monetary policy. Mexico's interest rate continued to follow US rates, measured by objective rates in both countries. At the same time, the margin between CETES (Certificados de la Tesorería) and Treasury Bonds also widened, reaching 55 and 66 points in 2011–2013 and 2014–2016, respectively (see Table 14.3).

Table 14.3 Interest rates, exchange rates and international reserves

	1990–98	*1999–01*	*2002–04*	*2005–07*	*2008–10*	*2011–13*	*2014–16*
	Nominal exchange rates						
Average	5.2	9.5	10.6	10.9	12.4	12.8	15.9
Standard deviation	2.6	0.1	0.8	2.6	1.2	0.4	2.7
	Real exchange rate						
Average	14.0	12.1	12.3	12.3	13.1	12.7	14.7
Standard Deviation	1.9	0.6	0.5	0.1	0.7	0.7	1.5
	Interest rates margins						
Target rate Mexico					6.0	4.4	3.4
Target rate USA					0.3	0.3	0.3
US TB, 3 months*	5.0	4.8	1.4	4.2	0.6	0.1	0.0
CETES 90 days **	18.8	8.2	4.8	3.7	4.7	3.7	3.1
	Asset and international reserves, billions of dollars						
NIA***		44.9	64.2	87.2	95.2	180.2	178.1
NIR ***		40.9	61.5	78.0	85.4	176.5	176.5
NIAf ****		19.3	19.4	23.0	8.0	58.2	9.5

Source: Author's calculations based on Banco de Mexico data and Board of Governors of the Federal Reserve System, Selected Interest Rates (Daily), H15 www.federalreserve.gov/releases/h15/data.htm and (CF16I19:P199) – Information on Banco de Mexico´s International Assets and (CF101) – Money Market Representative Interest Rates. Accessed 12/04/2016.

Notes: US Treasury Bonds, ** Treasury Certificates, CETEs*: average between 2014 and 2015. NIA: Net International Assets, in stocks. NIR: Net International Reserves, in stocks. NIAf: Net International Assets, in flows. Billions of dollars is thousands of millions. ***Accumulated data in the period. **** Last observation of the year.

The impact on the balance of international assets and international reserves increased significantly, doubling between 1990–2001 and 2005–2007, dropping during the 2008–2010 crisis, and repeating that performance from 2014 to 2016. The cumulative flows of net international assets are more sensitive to international shifts. In the period of the GFC, they dropped to almost one-third, ratcheting up almost seven-fold in 2011–2013 due to the huge drop in US interest rates, and falling again between 2014 and 2016.

Conclusions

The institutional changes made in the 1970s drastically transformed the financial system, creating a structurally endogenous international market driven by private money. This was part of the globalisation of the economic system that internationalised production, finance and trade and made financial capital relatively autonomous *vis-à-vis* production.

One important consequence of these changes was the increased international liquidity and new ways for productive factors to move around. On the international level, investment flows displaced loans, liquidity increased *vis-à-vis* production and balance sheets expanded.

This was accompanied by centralisation of capital through FDI, which broadened out the domination of big international consortia. The resultant increasing influence of FPI is characterised by being short-term, and therefore, highly unstable.

The internationalisation of production, financing and trade changed the system of payments and modified access to liquidity in international units of value. This particularly affected emerging countries, because they issue limited credits in their own currencies. With this new institutional arrangement, international liquidity moved into dollar-denominated debt, which did not imply issuing more dollars. The currency of developed economies and some emerging economies became convertible to dollars, generating a huge volume of transactions subject to financial innovations and substantial trade in financial instruments in the FOREX market.

Amidst this process, Mexico is one of the most enigmatic of the emerging countries because, not only did it go through one of the biggest economic openings of the developing countries, but it also inserted itself into the North American region through a trade deal (NAFTA). The agreement integrated Mexico's dynamic productive sector into the international consortia, generally dominated by US capital, and adjusted the country's financial system to the US system, allowing it to be dominated by foreign capital. All this together made the Mexican currency "credible", also making it the most tradable of the emerging economies.

The peculiarity of FOREX transactions involving MXN is that they circulate on the "margins" of Mexico's economy without developing local financial centres. In this context, short-term international currency liquidity became more available to agents operating in Mexico; however, it was very unstable.

The volume of the peso-denominated FOREX transactions was very high, making it impossible for the Banco de México to influence the exchange rate and forcing it to increase the margin between the two interest rates. So, exchange and interest rates were influenced by transactions by medium-sized non-reporting financial institutions (which do not report to central banks), whose main objective is to diversify portfolios and increase financial earnings, depending on events outside of Mexico.

Therefore, the decisions made by institutions that trade in Mexican currency on international markets are not linked to what happens in Mexico, but they affect the most sensitive prices of economic growth and capital formation (i.e. fix investment spending).

Notes

1 German-Austrian monetary theory put forward the concept of money endogeneity, around which consensus was reached until the first half of the twentieth century (Chick 2005).

2 Avdjiev et al. write,

> Take the concrete instance of a US branch of a global European bank that borrows dollars from a US money market fund, and then lends dollars to an Asian firm through its Hong Kong branch. The bank may be headquartered in London, Paris or Frankfurt, but the liabilities on its balance sheet are in New York and the assets on its balance sheet are in Hong SAR. No obvious mapping relates this bank's balance sheet to a GDP area or to GDP components within the GDP area.
>
> (Avdjiev et al. 2015:5–6)

3 In Toporowski's words,

> Banks may be solvent (in the sense that the value of their assets equals the value of their liabilities) but still become illiquid, if so much of their assets are tied up in illiquid assets (loans or real estate) that they do not have sufficient liquid assets to pay out withdrawals and maturing claims (deposits borrowed, or loans and bonds in their liabilities).
>
> (Toporowski 2017:6)

4 Exorbitant privileges occur if the hegemon

> can pre-empt the world output, structurally coming first in the pecking order, with everybody else dividing among themselves what is left, the issuer of the world currency can run deficits as big as it finds fit to, and the rest of the world will just have to run as big a surplus, its resources being pre-empted by the center country.
>
> (De Cecco 2012:4)

5 The current account deficit has been a structural characteristic in Latin America since the primary export model, dominant from the beginning of the last century until the interwar period, the era of import-substitution industrialisation (1940–1981), the neoliberal period (1980–2017) and even the pre-capitalist period (Kregel 2002).

6 Remittances derived from profits are another specific characteristic of the region's countries, discussed extensively in the 1960s. See Caputo and Pizarro (1970).

7 The Foreign Investment Law of 1993 allowed foreign capital to invest in almost every sector of production, except energy and oil, two areas that also opened up after the 2013 structural reforms.

8 The FDI is not directly linked to gross fixed capital formation. According to the new regulations, it is only classified as such if it surpasses 10% of a corporation's total assets.

References

Avdjiev, R., McCauley, and Song, H., (2015) 'Banking free if the triple coincidence in international finance', *BIS Working papers No. 534*.

Bellofiore, R., Garibaldo, F., and Halevi, J. (2011) 'The Global Crisis and the Crisis of European Neomercantilism', *Socialist Register* (47), 121–140.

BIS. (2001) Triennial Central Bank Survey, Foreign exchange and derivatives market activity in 2001. *Statistical Annex* Tables, March 2002.

BIS. (2004) Triennial Central Bank Survey Foreign exchange and derivatives market activity in 2004; *Statistical Annex Tables*, March 2005.

BIS. (2007) Triennial Central Bank Survey Foreign exchange and derivatives market activity in 2007; *Statistical Annex Tables*, March 2008.

BIS. (2010) Triennial Central Bank Survey. Report on global foreign exchange market activity in 2011.

BIS. (2013) Triennial Central Bank Survey, Global foreign exchange market turnover. *Tables revised*, published in February 2014.

BIS. (2016) Triennial Central Bank Survey, Global foreign exchange market turnover. *Tables revised*, published in September 1st, 2016.

Borio, C. and Disyatat, P. (2015) 'Capital flows and the current account: Taking financing (more) seriously', *BIS Working Papers No. 525*.

Caputo, O. and Pizarro, R. (1970) *Desarrollismo y capital extranjero. Las nuevas formas del imperialismo en Chile*, Ediciones de la Universidad Técnica del Estado, Santiago.

Cepal. (1949) 'Estudio Económico de América Latina', in Bielschovski (coord), *Cincuenta Años de Pensamiento en la Cepal. Textos Seleccionados* (1998), Volume I, Fondo de Cultura Económica-Cepal, Santiago.

Chick, V. (2005) 'Lost and found: some history of endogenous money in the twentieth century' in G. Fontana and R. Realfonzo (eds.), *The Monetary Theory of Production, tradition and Perspective*, Palgrave, Macmillan, London, 56–66.

De Cecco, M. (2012) 'Global Imbalances: Past, Present, and Future', *Contributions to Political Economy*, 31(1), 29–50.

de Paula, L.F., Fritz, B., and Prates, D.M. (2017) 'Keynes at the Periphery: Currency Hierarchy and Challenges for Economic Policy in Emerging Economies', *Journal of Post Keynesian Economics*, May 23, 1–20.

Eatwell, J. and Taylor, L. (2000) *Global finance at risk. The case for international regulation*, The New Press, Nueva York, 1–258.

Fajnzylber, F. (1987/1998) 'La industrialización de América Latina: de la "caja negra" al "casillero vacío"', in Bielschovski (coord.), *Cincuenta Años de Pensamiento en la Cepal. Textos Seleccionados*, Volumen II, Fondo de Cultura Económica-Cepal, Santiago.

Graziani, A. (2003) *The Monetary Theory of Production*, Cambridge University Press, Cambridge, 1–176.

Harvey, J. (2009) *Currencies, Capital flows and Crises, a Post-Keynesian Analysis of Exchange Rates*, Routledge, Canada.

Kaltenbrunner A. and Panceira. J-P. (2017) 'Subordinated financial Integration and Financialisation in Emerging Capitalist Economies: The Brazilian Experience' in New Political Economy, from doi:10.1080/13563467.2017.1349089

Keynes J.M. (1936/1986), Teoría General de la Ocupación, el Interés y el Dinero, FCE.

Kregel. J. (2002) 'Do we need alternative Financial Strategies for Development in Latin America?' *Paper presented Cuarto Seminario de Economía Financiera "Cooperación e instituciones y asimetrías financieras en América latina"*.

Lavoie, M. (2003) 'A primer on endogenous credit-money', in L.P. Rochon and S. Rossi (eds.), *Modern Theories of Money*, Edward Elgar, Cheltenham, 506–543.

Luxemburg, R. (1913) *The Accumulation of Capital*, Routledge and Kegan Paul LTD, London.

Marini, R.M. (1968) 'Subdesarrollo y Revolución en América Latina', *Tricontinental*, November.

Kato, L. and Huerta, G. (2015) 'Financiamiento, acumulación y concentración de capital en grandes empresas mexicanas', in N. Levy, C. Domínguez, and C. Salazar. (coords.), *Crecimiento Económico. Deudas y Distribución del Ingreso: Nuevos y Crecientes Desequilibrios*, Facultad de Economía and Instituto de Investigaciones Económicas, UNAM.

Minsky, H. (1975) *Las razones de Keynes*, Fondo de Cultura Económica.

Minsky, H.P. (1986) *Stabilizing an Unstable Economy*, Twenty Century Fund, U.S.A.

Moore. (1989) 'On the Endogeneity of Money Once More', *Journal of Keynesian Economics*, Spring 11(3), 479–487.

Rime, D. and Schrimps, A. (2013) 'The anatomy of the global FX market through the lens of the 2013 Triennial Survey BIS', *Quarterly Review*, December, 27–43.

Rochon L.P. (1999) *Credit, Money and Production. An Alternative Post-Keynesian Approach*, ch. 5, Edward Elgar, Cheltenham UK, North Hampton, MA. USA.

Schumpeter J. (1954) *History of Economic Analysis*. Allen and Unwin, London.

Toporowski J. (2017) Lectures for the Department of Economics, University of Bergamo, March-April.

15 Exchange rate policy restrictions on a high-volatility environment

The Mexican currency

Nora Ampudia Márquez and Luis Raúl Rodríguez Reyes

Since the mid-1980s, Mexico's economic development model has been outward-oriented. The volume of international trade represents 70% of gross domestic product (GDP),[1] and approximately 80% of imports are intermediate goods. These two facts taken together make inflation very sensitive to exchange rate volatility, particularly since late 1994, when Mexico established a free-floating exchange rate regime. If we add to this the neglect of the domestic market and huge dependence on external savings, we can understand why the accommodative monetary policy of the developed countries' central banks have forced the Banco de México (BdeM) to consistently intervene in the exchange market to prevent the inflationary impact of a peso depreciation and to raise the reference rate to contain capital flight.[2]

Throughout 2017, BdeM has been forced to make public statements and justify its continual interventions in the foreign exchange (FOREX) market, arguing that they are due to the need to create order in the market to prevent the depreciation of the peso turning into an exchange-rate pass-through (ERPT), which, in turn, would create secondary effects. And, the BdeM specifies that there is no exchange rate target (Carstens 2017).

This is part of a global phenomenon characterised by excess liquidity in international financial markets and a process of integration, globalisation and financial liberalisation that has created growing instability. The result seems to be an exchange rate war, a struggle for competitiveness via prices, and the need to place goods in the foreign market due to domestic markets' poor performance.

The objective in this chapter is to demonstrate the increasing ineffectiveness of Mexico's exchange rate policy with a global, financialised currency in light of an export-driven accumulation model strongly impacted by exchange rate volatility. The chapter is divided into five sections including this introduction. The second section analyses Mexico's exchange-rate policy since the inauguration of the free-floating regime and the establishment of different forms of intervention into the FOREX market. It will also discuss the restrictions that international financial instability has imposed on Mexico's economic model. The third section analyses the accelerated globalisation of the peso in the context of financialisation. The fourth section discusses the role of structural changes in the international currency market regarding Mexico's peso. And the fifth section establishes possible alternatives for Mexico's exchange rate policy and lays out our conclusions.

External shocks and exchange rate policy in Mexico (1994–2017)

The analysis of exchange rate policy in the period of the free-floating exchange rate system has been divided into three stages: the first ranges from the beginning of the banking-financial crisis and the transition to the floating exchange rate system beginning on 22 December 1994, until 14 September 2008, when Lehman Brothers went bankrupt. The second stage is from September 2008 to September 2014, when Janet Yellen announced the possibility of beginning to normalise US monetary policy, sparking marked exchange rate volatility in Mexico. This second stage includes the application of an unconventional monetary policy by the Federal Reserve Board (the FED, the US central bank) called quantitative easing (QE), which reduced the reference rate to around zero and caused a sharp monetary expansion in three stages with a strong impact on the carry trade.[3] The third stage goes from October 2014 to 2017 and is characterised by the fall in international raw material (oil) prices and the victory of Donald Trump, whose campaign promises and aggressive recommendations have caused a great deal of uncertainty and marked dollar/peso volatility.

Over these three periods, Mexico's economy was subject to strong external shocks that created great uncertainty and exchange rate volatility, putting monetary policy in a straitjacket and reducing the margin for fiscal policy freedom.[4] However, this volatility accentuated as the Mexican peso became a global currency and went through financialisation, as we will analyse in the third section of this chapter.

With the 1994 banking and financial crisis and given the depletion of international reserves, the BdeM was forced to leave the currency market and move towards a floating exchange rate system, establishing two basic objectives: first, to not intervene in free operations of the FOREX market, and second, to foster its development, deepening and liquidity by creating new financial instruments and welcoming new participants (Sidaoui 2005). To avoid exchange rate volatility, the bank deepened the peso derivatives and FOREX market and developed different instruments for direct and indirect intervention (Werner & Milo 1988). Among the former were temporary access to liquidity, the isolation of Mexican oil operations and those of other federal government institutions that receive dollars and are obliged to sell them to the BdeM, as well as discretional sales of dollars in the currency market. With regard to the latter, it developed US dollar call options.[5] Dollar auctions were carried out in four ways: direct auctions with and without a minimum price, extra auctions and complementary auctions. Plus, auctions of exchange rate hedges were added.

In addition, it maintained a positive margin *vis-à-vis* the US interest rate, raising the target rate, and negotiated a flexible line of credit with the International Monetary Fund (IMF) to discourage speculative attacks against the peso.

In the early stages of the system, the BdeM established facilities for loans to commercial banks to avert and retain the execution of its external liabilities, through loans in dollars given to the Fund for Insured Deposits (Fondo Bancario de Protección al Ahorro – FOBAPROA), which, in turn, assigned the funds to the banks requesting assistance (Sidaoui 2005).

In the first stage (1996–2001), a mechanism for accumulating international reserves (MARI, for its initials in Spanish) was established to replace international reserves and create confidence, a more stable exchange rate, and less country risk. This was accompanied by a programme of dollar auctions to mitigate the effects of external shocks. Although the amount was not very significant, the mechanism did impact the willingness of speculators to act due to the daily auction announcements. In this period, the peso had not yet become globalised, and therefore, this type of intervention was effective since it operated in a local market.

From May 2003 to mid-2008, another mechanism was established to reduce the rate of accumulation of international reserves (MRARI, for its initials in Spanish), with the aim of reducing the cost of their accumulation. This mechanism also used dollar auctions. Initially, the interventions were small, US$200 million a day, and the sale was not always awarded to anyone, since its main objective was to discourage speculation. Financial reforms were also carried out and new institutions created to give the FOREX market liquidity, depth and stability. Outstanding among the measures created were the Mexican Derivatives Market (MEXDER), the opening of an options market and the authorisation for MEXDER to allow foreigners to participate, all implemented in 1998.

The second stage began with the spread of the subprime crisis in September 2008 and the restructuring of monetary policy through increases in the target rate to avoid capital flight. The target rose five times in one year, going from 7% to 7.75%. It later moved down to reactivate the economy, also taking advantage of the fact that the FED had decreased its own and that the peso was appreciating given the constant entry of portfolio capital.[6]

Between April and October 2009, a swap line was created with the FED to auction credits in dollars to credit institutions in Mexico. In that period, the target rate dropped six times, from 7.7% to 4.5% between February and July 2009. From October 2008 to April 2010, daily dollar auctions resumed and five extra auctions were held for a total of US$11 billion in October. From March to June 2009, an additional auction mechanism was implemented that operated together with the daily mechanism.

Given international markets' great volatility, the MARI was reactivated through auctions of options to sell between February 2010 and November 2011, followed by the reactivation of dollar auctions to create order in the FOREX market from November 2011 to April 2013. In that year, the BdeM reduced the target rate three times, lowering it from 4% to 3.5% to spark greater economic dynamism.

The third stage, beginning in September 2014 and lasting until 2017, was the most volatile. In that period, dollar auctions began again from December 2014 to January 2016, and the MRARI was reactivated between March and November 2015 to complement the auctions. That same month of November, the complementary auctions began again and the bank announced the possibility of making a discretional intervention. In February, it raised the target rate to 3.25% to try to reverse capital flows, even though the FED had not changed its target interest rate, and in 2016, it raised the target rate five times, going from 3.75% to 5.75%.

Throughout this period, two mechanisms coexisted: the regular and the supplementary auctions, which were all suspended in January 2017. In February, the bank raised the target rate again to 6.25% and, on February 27, given the market's lack of reaction since it is basically foreign, the BdeM designed a new mechanism: auctions of exchange rate hedges with a US$20-billion ceiling for credit institutions authorised to operate with derivatives. By November 2017, 18 auctions had been held on five different dates, with total awards of US$3.5 billion; and, from March to June, the target rate rose three times, going from 6.5% to 7%. Thus, in no more than 17 months, the target rate went from 3% to 7%, raising the price of credit options and slowing the economic growth process with a high inflationary pass-through: annual inflation jumped from 2.6% to 6.6% between June 2016 and November 2017.

Disregarding the two first years of the flexible exchange rate regime when volatility was extreme, the first stage showed a noticeable reduction in volatility, and the BdeM considered the exchange rate policy a success because it was effective in absorbing external shocks without affecting inflation. However, beginning in 2008, and particularly during the great financial crisis, volatility continually increased, intensifying in the second stage and broadening in the third stage (see Figure 15.1).

The increased volatility was the product of unconventional, accommodative monetary policies between 2008 and 2015 due to the huge liquidity injected by the main central banks (approximately US$10 trillion) (Rozo 2016, 38).

In addition, the reduction of reference rates to nearly zero was an incentive for carry trade speculation that generated large influxes of capital to the emerging economies, among them, Mexico. From late 2008 to 2017, Mexico received US$324.565 billion in foreign portfolio investment, peaking in 2012, with 2.0% of the world total, and dropping in 2016 to 1.5%.

FED and European Central Bank (ECB) desynchronised and diametrically opposed accommodative policies also had an impact. They caused intense

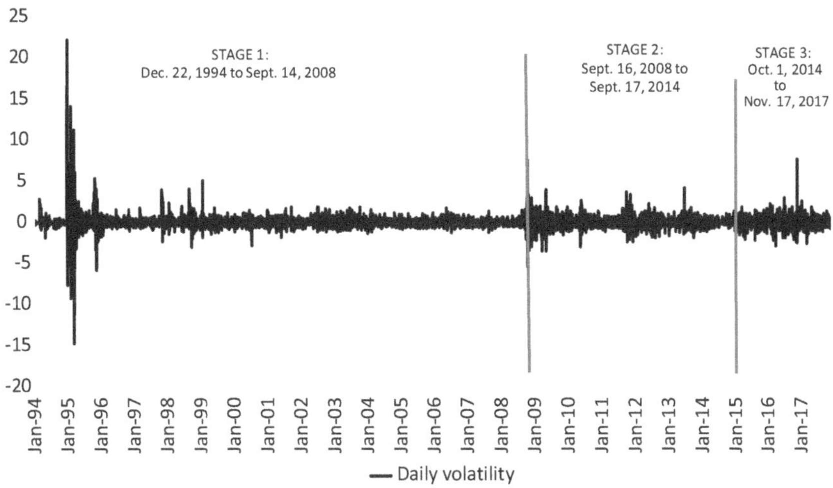

Figure 15.1 Dollar/peso volatility (daily percentage variation).

Source: Authors' calculations based on data from Banco de México, Historic Exchange Rate Series. www.banxico.org.mx/SieInternet/consultarDirectorioInternetAction.do?accion=consultarCuadro&idCuadro=CF102&sector=6&locale=es.

movement of transborder investment seeking higher yields and greater security, both of which they found in Mexico with higher interest rates, stable public finances, low inflation, and deep, liquid financial markets.

Globalisation and financialisation of the peso: exchange rate policy to the limit (2014–2017)

The financialisation of currencies is the result of a series of intimately linked phenomena, including exploding liquidity in international markets, the fall of the average world growth rate and of productive investment, increased concentration of income and wealth, and low levels of domestic consumption worldwide.

As part of this process, surplus liquidity was channelled towards financial markets, seeking its revaluation through portfolio investments, through a continual exchange of currencies that imprinted the exchange market with its own dynamic, turning it into an instrument that offered great opportunities for speculation. The result was a disconnection between international trade flows of goods and services and exchange transactions, turning the exchange rate into "a financial asset highly suited to speculative activities" (Rozo 2016, 20). In this context, monetary policy loses the autonomy to impose order in the FOREX market and retain capital.

The concept of globalisation of a currency is much broader than that of its internationalisation since it relates the use of currencies in transborder transactions with the relative weight worldwide of different factors. Outstanding among these are national GDP, the volume of international trade, the volume as a receiver and issuer of foreign investment, the volume of the debt, derivatives, and FOREX markets, plus the degree of development and depth of the financial market (Thimann 2009). According to Thimann, in 2009, the Mexican peso ranked first among the emerging economies as a global currency.

The financialisation and globalisation of the Mexican peso resulted from the joint effect of fiscal discipline, the trade opening and the structural reforms of Mexico's financial sector in the last decade of the twentieth century. All of these led to a period of macroeconomic stability that had not been experienced since the era of *desarrollo estabilizador* (stabilising development).[7]

In the first years of the twenty-first century, Mexico was characterised by a relatively low, controlled fiscal deficit, an inflation-targeting monetary policy and a free-floating exchange rate regime; all of this provided national and international investors with certainty. According to Cota (2015), Mexico managed to make its currency one of the three emerging country currencies that was traded 24 hours a day, five days a week. However, the levels of dollar/peso transactions did not correspond to the relative size of the Mexican economy or its trade and mainly took place outside of Mexico (McCauley & Scatigna 2011). This implies the existence of speculation and the search for risk hedging coverage that coincides with the figures Levy-Orlik and Domínguez report (2017). They show that trade in the Mexican peso increases more rapidly than the volume of total transactions in the international money market in crisis periods.

The current sophistication of international money markets rests on the proliferation of financial derivative use. These are based on a mixture of currencies, which are used for speculation and produce distortions in relative prices because they augment the movement of the benchmark currency. In addition, the use of Mexico's currency as a hedge against the fall in international basic raw material prices creates new economic policy challenges.

Financial capital flows are not passive, nor are they accommodative, but they are procyclical, and international trade plays a secondary role in determining currency prices. This is because exchange rate transactions are directly linked to capital, since the financial sector operates under a different logic from that of the real economy, and economic agents' expectations are what drive the financial assets market (Harvey 2009). This is what is happening to the Mexican peso. For that reason, volatility has increased in the third stage, linked more to expectations about the probable effects of phenomena than to their fundamentals.

According to Eichengreen (2017), currencies become a vehicle for transborder investment, guided by financial transactions and used basically as a hedge to take advantage of arbitrage opportunities. The issue is that the Mexican government prepared the way for this by creating a deep, liquid

Table 15.1 Floating exchange rate system

	Stage 1: 22 Dec. 1994 to 14 Sept. 2008	*Stage 2: 16 Sept. 2008 to 17 Sept. 2014*	*Stage 3: 1 Oct. 2014 to 17 Nov. 2017*
Average exchange rate	9.58	12.92	17.28
Mean exchange rate	9.76	12.96	17.34
Lowest value of the dollar	4.74	10.59	13.38
Highest value of the dollar	11.63	15.37	21.91
# Data	3456	1520	644
Standard deviation	1.46	0.63	2.09
Variance	2.14	0.40	4.35
Average volatility: daily percentage change	0.033	0.018	0.049

Source: Developed by the authors using Banco de México data. www.banxico.org.mx/SieInternet/consultarDirectorioInternetAction.do?accion=consultarCuadro&idCuadro=CF102&sector=6&locale=es

secondary market and establishing conditions to continually operate with financial assets, liberalise the capital account and impose a flexible exchange rate.

In the three periods analysed, the exchange rate is the most volatile in Stage 3 (see Table 15.1), which is even more volatile than in the initial stage, when the BdeM abandoned the FOREX market and deactivated the currency band. This is due to the fact that starting in 2014, external shocks have a greater impact because they directly affect the country's economic dynamic since they are the result of the combination of a series of factors: the fall in commodities prices, particularly that of oil;[8] announcements and decisions about normalisation of US monetary policy and the negative discourse of first candidate and later President Trump about Mexico;[9] the difficult renegotiations of the North American Free Trade Agreement,[10] begun in August 2017, together with a promise of a fiscal reform that would reduce corporate taxes; and, finally, the recession in the US industrial sector, with which Mexico is strongly integrated in productive chains.[11]

On the whole, these phenomena fed the strong volatility of international capital flows and sparked sharp depreciations of the peso against the dollar.[12] The periods of exchange rate volatility broadened and brought into question BdeM commitment to fighting inflation and the floating exchange rate system.

Most of the dollar/peso transactions take place outside Mexico; in 2016, only 17.9% took place inside the country,[13] and the other 82%, on the international market. Ten years earlier, in 2007, the figures were 40% and 60%, respectively (Banco de México 2016; McCauley & Scatigna 2011).

The globalisation of the peso has been very swift: in 1998, it represented 0.4% of all world FOREX transactions; in 2013, it came to 2.6% and in 2016, 2.2%. If we consider the participation of the dollar, whose respective values are 86.8%, 87% and 86.6%, we can see that Mexico's figures have only relative weight among the ten main global currencies. In the world derivative market, we went from 0.83% in 2001 to 2.53% in 2013, and 1.92% in 2016.

Today, international capital flows have a new dynamic and structure, increasing the interdependence and reflexivity of the prices of different financial assets and accentuating volatility of exchange rates worldwide. Financial markets and their products are very sophisticated, and using financial robots to determine the precise moment to carry out transactions magnifies price jumps not only of financial assets, but also of currencies in a recursive movement that magnifies exchange rate variations. This forces countries with flexible exchange rate systems like Mexico to look for techniques for indirect intervention in the FOREX market, while others impose fiscal, administrative and legal restrictions on capital flows.

The role of structural changes in the Mexican peso's international market

In the process of establishing the flexible exchange rate in Mexico, monetary authorities operated using the theory of disappearing intermediate regimes, which states that in an atmosphere in which international capital is increasingly interconnected, only extreme exchange rate systems are sustainable. This theory posits that hard-pegs, such as a monetary union or a currency board and controlled flotation or pure flotation free exchange rate regimes, are the most sustainable in the face of speculative attacks (Martínez Trigueros 2005).

The exchange rate regime picked was the *de jure* flotation regime (Romero 2005), which is flotation managed through central bank interventions. This change in exchange rate policy produced new behaviour in economic agents, who began to perceive the shocks in the exchange rate as transitory due to the BdeM's credible commitment to stabilising inflation. This can be observed since 2001, through the separation of inflationary prospects and exchange rate depreciation (Capistrán, Ibarra-Ramírez, & Ramos-Francia 2011). As a result, the floating exchange rate system has been maintained, while the exchange rate's inflationary pass-through on prices was reduced (Capistrán, Ibarra-Ramírez & Ramos-Francia 2011; Martínez Trigueros 2005).

The new set-up also allowed economic agents to better estimate their risks due to exchange rate exposition. In addition, the Mexican economy's fundamentals in terms of indebtedness and public spending and the monetary policy's credibility generated relative macroeconomic stability during the first and second stages when it was faced with high volatility internationally. However, when the Mexican peso became a global currency,[14] this reduced the exchange rate and monetary policy's effectiveness with regard to the inflationary pass-through, particularly from 2016 to 2017, when the peso reached greater relative value and lost *vis-à-vis* the US dollar.

In September 2014, then FED President Janet Yellen (2014) for the first time mentioned the possibility of normalising monetary policy. This implied a new scenario that increased the possibilities of raising the reference rate in the near future. Given this, economic agents anticipated the interest rate hikes, and capital flows to Mexico reversed: between November 2014 and September 2016, approximately US$48 billion invested by foreigners in government bonds were pulled out (Instituto Belisario Domínguez 2016). This strengthened the dollar against the Mexican peso, and between November 2015 and February 2016, the dollar appreciated 42% and the BdeM increased its reference rate by 50 base points.

This outflow of capital was not the first or the last the authorities would face. However, it was different in one important way: for the first time, the Mexican peso acted as a global currency, with more than 80% of transactions occurring abroad and in operations involving financial derivatives using the peso as a hedge against losses in value of other emerging currencies and commodities (Cota 2015; Levy-Orlik & Domínguez 2017).

This diminished the effect of the dollar auctions on the exchange rate, making it difficult for local, focalised BdeM measures such as dollar auctions and the sale of exchange rate hedges to be effective ways of decreasing speculation.

As mentioned above, the BdeM response in this third stage was to raise the reference rate ten times between December 2015 and June 2017. This was an attempt to maintain an attractive differential with the US yields and thus diminish the velocity of speculative investment outflows. The result was a negative impact on Mexico's already not-very-dynamic economy.

However, this monetary policy was incapable of containing the rapid depreciation of the peso, and the BdeM could do little to reduce exchange rate volatility without disrupting the economy. One proof of its lack of control over volatility was the variation in the exchange rate once the US presidential election was over.

When the Republican Party won the election, two issues immediately arose: the anti-free-trade platform on which it had been elected and that led to the beginnings of a trilateral renegotiation of NAFTA in 2017, and the prospect of a fiscal reform that would reduce corporate taxes. This prompted the dollar/peso exchange rate to rise to historic heights in January 2017, when it reached 21.91 pesos per dollar. However, when the US legislative agenda got bogged down and financial market players began to realise how complicated it would be to negotiate the changes in the US Congress, the exchange rate returned to under 18 pesos per dollar. Nevertheless, when US fiscal reform issues became relevant again and differences began to emerge in the final rounds of NAFTA renegotiations, the exchange rate rose rapidly.

It is important to point out that despite the growth of Mexico's domestic and foreign debt as a proportion of GDP in the last ten years, the macroeconomic fundamentals have remained healthy enough to ensure that Mexico maintains its credit rating as designated by the main rating agencies. However, this has not prevented volatility, which has also been impacted by the generalised use of financial derivatives for trading in the Mexican peso. It should be pointed out here that the very first exchange rate futures deals took place in 1970, but the peso derivatives market was not fully developed until the MEXDER was created in 1998 and the CME agreement was reached in 2011 (Levy-Orlik & Domínguez 2017).

This is backed up by the information reported in the Bank for International Settlement (BIS) tri-annual surveys that according to Levy-Orlik and Domínguez (2017), between 1998 and 2016, 46% of daily trade in the Mexican peso was done through FOREX swaps, 35% in spot transactions, 12% in forwards and 6.8% in other derivatives.

The use of financial derivatives, which are based on the parity of the peso with another currency, is generalised even in the operations inside Mexico. The tri-annual BIS survey for 2016 reported that seven out of every ten transactions involving the peso, carried out by 17 financial institutions, took place using financial derivatives, mainly swaps, of which 91% matured in under seven days (Banco de México 2016).

The use of financial derivatives allows investors and speculators to bet against the peso, shorting without a cover, which is also called a "naked short". That is, they can sell pesos and purchase dollars through a derivative without needing to back up the operation with a loan or hedge.

In addition, depending on the kind of strategies used, this type of operation makes it possible to leverage with little risk of loss, making it the ideal instrument for financial speculation. The importance of these operations is that the existence of the naked short in liquid financial markets means that at moments of high volatility, the exchange rate moves in a single way (Payne 2012).

Another phenomenon that should be pointed out is the use of the peso to protect risks to commodities and other emerging currencies. As mentioned above, the peso is one of the most liquid currencies globally speaking and the second-most-traded emerging currency in the world. This, together with the absence of barriers to the entry and exit from the market and the fact that it is available 24 hours a day, five days a week, turns it into the favourite currency in the face of a fall in commodity prices, as well as the proxy hedge for emerging countries' risk in general, particularly Latin American countries (Cota 2015).[15]

Upper and Valli (2016) present evidence that despite the fact that the emerging market economies represent half the world economy, if measured in purchasing power parity, the derivatives based on their currencies are heavily underdeveloped with regard to their potential. This is because they are less financially developed, less integrated into the global economy and have low per capita income, while liquid currencies like the Mexican peso and the South African rand also stand out because of the complexity of the financial derivatives that they trade in.

Alternative exchange rate policies

A final issue this chapter must take up is the analysis of the main alternatives the BdeM, together with the country's economic authorities, has to increase the effectiveness of exchange rate policy and combat the transfer of exchange rate shocks to pricing processes. According to what has been explained above, the FOREX market has changed structurally with regard to other episodes of exchange rate volatility in the past. This makes changing excessive exchange rate volatility in this new scenario a greater challenge. Even the IMF has justified the need for protection policies for the exchange rate, which it calls capital flow management measures (CFM) (Rozo 2016: 76, 85). In this regard, some international examples have been used to this end that the BdeM could explore.

The first example of these interventions is banning naked short sales that were used as a temporary measure in financial stock markets during the 2008 crisis and observed during the Greek 2011–2013 crisis (Payne 2012).

Another alternative is the control of capital used by Brazil as a shield against international volatility; this took the form of taxes on carry trade flows, which are activated and deactivated according to the international economic cycle. Brazil has recently levied a tax on the value of financial derivatives (Chamon & García 2016).

Mexico could use these policies to reduce extreme exchange rate volatility. However, at least two factors must be considered here. First, the BdeM would face a geographical, jurisdictional problem in implementing this type of measures because most of the trade in the Mexican peso occurs outside the country; and to be able to implement an effective speculation-control measure, it would have to be done in close coordination with the international monetary authorities.

Second, and even more importantly, imposing capital controls would imply that Mexico would be changing its exchange rate regime and would implicitly be establishing an exchange rate target regime, sending contradictory signals to those established over the last 25 years.

The BdeM would have three alternatives. The first is to continue with a monetary policy with inflation targets and to support the discourse with movements of the reference rate in line with that objective, maintaining the credibility achieved in the market. The second is to seek better communication and international coordination in order to diminish the volatility of the currencies of emerging countries. And the third would be to continue offering derivatives on the market through leveraged exchange rate hedges, which would increase the potential for its interventions to maintain order in the market.

Conclusions

The floating exchange rate regime, with free entry and exit of capital flows, and the financial and fiscal reform turned the Mexican peso into a global currency, whose volume of operations is inconsistent with the Mexican economy's volume of international trade or relative importance. However, it does profoundly affect the domestic economy due to its heavy dependence on foreign trade due to the export-driven growth model.

This model is coming under heavy fire, given the impact of exchange rate volatility on inflation and the reduction it imposes on the manoeuvring room for monetary and fiscal policy. To this must be added that an important part of trade in the peso in international markets is speculative and has the aim of hedging against risks related to emerging markets.

The globalisation of the economy, together with the generalised use of financial derivatives in international currency markets and the facilities the Mexican peso offers by being available 24 hours a day, five days a week, creates a volatility of the peso that is greater and fundamentally different from that which the country faced in other historic periods. In the past, the causes were imbalances in the public budget, the current account or the capital account. Today, maintaining healthy fiscal accounts, an open economy and healthy economic fundamentals does not guarantee a stable currency.

The actions of the BdeM have lost effectiveness in moderating the volatility of the exchange rate; the target rate has been increased at the cost of slowing down the economy; and a strong inflationary pass-through has presented itself again, with a heavy impact on the dynamism of the economy.

The BdeM cannot place its trust in the use of traditional stabilisation tools since dollar/peso transactions occur in the international market; and the size of that market is such that even if it were local, the average weight of the central bank's interventions would have no significant impact.

Any alternative or stabilisation requires either international cooperation through BdeM coordination with international monetary authorities or a return to schemes of capital control. A third way forward is to continue with the regime of inflation expectations as a basis for establishing a monetary policy and acting in consequence through the reference rate, intervening through leveraged exchange rate hedges. However, the latter has proven to be insufficient in moments of high volatility created by the recent changes in US monetary policy, and brings into question one of the banners held the highest in the last 25 years in Mexico: the decrease in the exchange rate pass-through.

Notes

1 Figures from the second quarter of 2017.

2 In Mexico, the exchange-rate pass-through (ERPT) has decreased since 1994 as a result of different factors, outstanding among which are the following: 1) a new vision of how to manage public finances called New Public Management, complemented by eliminating fiscal domination, explicitly setting the goal of sustainable public finances, privatising public companies and reducing the size of the state; 2) making the BdeM independent and establishing an inflation-target strategy; 3) opening the economy and liberalising the current and capital accounts; 4) using control of wage hikes as an inflationary anchor and

a mechanism to attract foreign investment; and 5) the growing interdependence and globalisation of the economy, which fosters the development of global value chains that reduce production costs.

3 Carry trade is a strategy that consists of borrowing funds in a currency from a country that has a low interest rate (funding currency) to be invested in financial assets from another country with higher interest rates (investing currency).

4 In 2015 and 2016, three public spending cuts were made in the amount of Mex$560 billion, or approximately 3% the value of GDP. This was the result of plummeting international oil prices in 2015 and the volatility generated in international markets (Albarrán 2016).

5 This strategy was used during the 1996–2003 stage of recomposition and accumulation of international reserves; from 2010 to 2012, it consisted of placing dollar sale options through monthly auctions. With this instrument, the BdeM was forced to purchase dollars against pesos from the option holder.

6 From January 2009 to 2014, the peso appreciated, going from 14.94 to 11.62 dollar/peso, that is, by 22.1% (Rozo 2016).

7 "Desarrollo estabilizador" was a period (1958–1970) in which Mexico achieved high economic growth and low inflation and maintained a fixed exchange rate.

8 Although oil exports represent no more than 5% of the total and public finances have reduced their dependence on oil income to less than 20%, international investors continue to think that we depend heavily on oil. In fact, in 2015 and 2016, a strong correlation existed between the exchange rate and the international price of oil, and this was heavily influenced by net speculation in the Chicago Market (Siller 2016).

9 Regarding the construction of a wall, the repatriation of immigrants, obstacles to sending remittances and the repatriation of US companies. Remittances are the country's second source of foreign currency: from 2007 to 2016, they came to an annual average of US$23.733 billion.

10 Mexico is heavily dependent on the USA: more than 80% of our exports go there; 60% of foreign direct investment comes from there; and 90% of our tourists are US Americans.

11 Different studies show a strong correlation between the US industrial cycle and Mexico's manufacturing cycle; the greatest volume of trade is intra-firm; and strong intra-company and intra-sectoral value chains have developed between the two countries (Delajara 2012; Torres & Vela 2002).

12 Between January 2014 and January 2017, the peso depreciated 67% against the dollar, and at the high point of the 2008 crisis (from September 2008 to March 2009), it dropped 45%.

13 A daily average of US$1.9 billion were dollar/peso transactions in 2016.

14 The events leading up to the globalisation of the peso were an aggressive financial reform in 1998 that liberalised active and passive interest rates; the 1989 Brady Plan; the implementation in 1982 of exchange rate hedges called TESOBONOS; the re-privatisation of the banks between 1991 and 1992; the beginning of warrants being used in the Mexican Stock Market (BMV) in 1992 and their listing on the Luxemburg and London Stock Exchanges between 1992 and 1994; the initiation of operations with options on Telmex ADRs on the Chicago Board Options Exchange; Mexico's entry into the OECD in May 1994; the BdeM becoming independent in 1994; the transition toward an inflation target strategy; the authorisation of operations with US-denominated derivatives and deposits in local currency with foreign financial institutions at the Chicago Mercantile Exchange (CME); the creation of the Derivate Market, named MEXDER in 1998; the creation of an options market and dollar/peso futures operations; the establishment of inflation targets in 2001; the authorisation for banks to make forward foreign currency transactions; and, finally, the adoption of a reference rate or target rate in 2007 (Ramos-Francia & Torres 2005).

15 Mexico shares the characteristic of being tradable 24 hours a day, five days a week, with the Turkish lira and the South African rand, but both of these are less liquid than the Mexican peso (Cota 2015).

References

Albarrán, E. (2016) 'Recortes al gasto por más de 500 mil millones de pesos', *El Economista*, 26 June, viewed 20 November 2017, www.eleconomista.com.mx/economia/Recortes-al-gasto-por-mas-de-500000-millones-de-pesos-20160626-0103.html

Banco de México (2016) *Press release: Bank for International Settlements (BIS) Triennial Bank Survey of foreign exchange and derivatives market activity in April.*

Capistrán, C., Ibarra-Ramírez, R., and Ramos-Francia, M. (2011) *El Traspaso de Movimientos del Tipo de Cambio a los Precios: Un Análisis para la Economía Mexicana, Banco de México*, Working Papers No. 2011–12, 1–25.

Carstens, A. (2017) *Challenges for Monetary Policy Implementation in Mexico*, viewed 7 August, from: www.banxico.org.mx/publicaciones-y-discursos/discursos-y-presentaciones/presentaciones/%7B4ECFE4D1-C850-418A-130C-F8205B600E22%7D.pdf

Chamon, M., and García, M. (2016) 'Capital Controls in Brazil: Effective?' *Journal of International Money and Finance*, 61, 163–187.

Cota, I. (2015) 'Why Traders Love to Short the Mexican Peso', viewed 30 April 2017, from: www.bloomberg.com/news/articles/2015-07-26/to-hedge-just-about-anything-traders-are-shorting-mexico-s-peso.

Delajara, M. (2012) *Sincronización entre los Ciclos Económicos de México y Estados Unidos*, viewed from: www.banxico.org.mx/publicaciones-y-discursos/publicaciones/documentos-de-investigacion/banxico/%7BD80698DA-6F2E-B6D3-CE33-F51309ABD113%7D.pdf

Eichengreen, B., Mehl, A., and Chitu, L. (2017) *How global currencies work: past, present, and future*, Princeton University Press, Princeton.

Harvey, J. (2009) *Currencies, capital flows and crises: a post Keynesian analysis of exchange rate determination*, Routledge, Kansas.

Instituto Belisario Domínguez. (2016) 'Análisis de la Reciente Volatilidad del Tipo de Cambio', *Análisis de Coyuntura*, 6, 1–13.

Levy-Orlik, N., and Dominguez, C. (2017) 'The Internationalisation of the Mexican Peso and the Increased Financial Instability', *Paper presented on Foreign Exchange Swaps and the Money Markets*, University of London, SOAS, 24 February 2017.

Martinez Trigueros, L. (2005) 'La política cambiaria y monetaria en México: lecciones de una década de flotación cambiaria', *Información Comercial Española-Monthly Edition*, 821, 11–29.

McCauley, R., and Scatigna, M. (2011) 'Foreign Exchange Trading in Emerging Currencies: More Financial, more Offshore', *BIS Quarterly Review*, March, 67–75.

'Migraciones y remesas: sucesos recientes y perspectivas', El Financiero, viewed 4 October 2017, from: www.elfinanciero.com.mx/economia/mexico-recibira-este-ano-remesas-record-pese-a-efecto-trump-bm.html.

Payne, J. (2012) 'The Regulation of Short Selling and Its Reform in Europe', *European Business Organization Law Review*, 13(3), 413–440.

Ramos-Francia, M., and Torres, A. (2005) *Reducción de la Inflación a través de un Esquema de Objetivos de Inflación: la Experiencia Mexicana*, viewed from: www.banxico.org.mx/publicaciones-y-discursos/publicaciones/documentos-de-investigacion/banxico/%7B21884449-3E92-3F92-AED6-C4E273D-87FE8%7D.pdf

Romero, I. (2005) 'El Tipo de Cambio en la Economía Mexicana, 1949–2002', *Comercio Exterior*, 55(3), 216–224.

Rozo, C. (2016) *Capital especulativo y blindaje financiero en México*, Universidad Autónoma Metropolitana, Centro de Estudios Sociales y Opinión Pública, Mexico.

Sidaoui, J. (2005) *Central banking intervention under a floating exchange rate regime: ten years of Mexican experience*, viewed from: www.bis.org/publ/bppdf/bispap24r.pdf

Siller, G. (2016) 'La correlación entre el tipo de cambio y los precios del petróleo', *El Financiero*, viewed 10 March, from: www.elfinanciero.com.mx/monterrey/la-correlacion-entre-el-tipo-de-cambio-y-los-precios-del-petroleo.html

Thimann, C. (2009) *Global Roles of Currencies*, viewed from: www.ecb.europa.eu/pub/pdf/scpwps/ecbwp1031.pdf

Torres, A., and Vela, O. (2002) *Integración Comercial y Sincronización entre los Ciclos Económicos de México y los Estados Unidos*, viewed from: www.banxico.org.mx/publicaciones-y-discursos/publicaciones/documentos-de-investigacion/banxico/%7BD79AB388-16FC-BD5E-F9E5-B4D20560374E%7D.pdf

Upper, C., and Valli, M. (2016) '¿Mercados de derivados emergentes?' *Informe Trimestral del BPI*, 1–16.

Werner, A., and Milo, A. (1988) *Acumulación de reservas internacionales a través de la venta de opciones: el caso de México*, viewed from: www.banxico.org.mx/publicaciones-y-discursos/publicaciones/documentos-de-investigacion/banxico/%7B4C478DC1-EEEF-DD3D-3DCB-E1F4AC927262%7D.pdf

Yellen, J. (2014) *Transcript of the Chair Yellen's Press Conference September 17, 2014*, Federal Open Market Committee, Board of Governors of the Federal Reserve, 1–22.

Index